Interdisciplinarity and Social Justice

SUNY Series, Praxis: Theory in Action

Nancy A. Naples, editor

Interdisciplinarity and Social Justice
Revisioning Academic Accountability

Edited by
Joe Parker
Ranu Samantrai
and
Mary Romero

Published by State University of New York Press, Albany

For information, contact State University of New York Press, Albany, NY
www.sunypress.edu

Production by Robert Puchalik
Marketing by Michael Campochiaro

Library of Congress Cataloging-in-Publication Data

Interdisciplinarity and social justice : revisioning academic
    accountability / edited by Joe Parker, Ranu Samantrai, and Mary Romero.
        p. cm.
    Includes bibliographical references and index.
    ISBN 978-1-4384-3135-2 (hbk. : alk. paper)
    ISBN 978-1-4384-3136-9 (pbk. : alk. paper)
    1. Interdisciplinary approach in education. 2. Social justice. I. Parker, Joe, 1956–
II. Samantrai, Ranu. III. Romero, Mary.

    LB2361.I47 2010
    375'.001—dc22   2009033547

10 9 8 7 6 5 4 3 2 1

Contents

II. Critiques of Interdisciplinary Fields

III. Interdisciplinary Claims to Social Justice

Acknowledgments

The editors would like to thank Lako Tongun, Michael Ballagh, and Susan Phillips for helping organize the conference, Interdisciplinarity and Social Justice, on February 11–12, 2005, at Pitzer College, where several of the papers included here were first presented. Funding for that conference came from the Printed Word funds and an anonymous donor at Pitzer College, and an additional Research and Awards grant from Pitzer College supported publication costs.

Appreciation is due to Anish Kapoor, who kindly gave his permission to reproduce the illustrations of "Marsyas" (2002) in Lisa Lowe's essay. Lindon Barrett's essay includes excerpts from "Mercantilism, U.S. Federalism, and the Market Within Reason" published in *Accelerating Possession: Global Futures of Property and Personhood*, ed. Bill Maurer and Gabriele Schwab (Columbia University Press, 2006), 99–131. Portions of Ellen Messer-Davidow's essay were previously published as "Why Democracy Will Be Hard To Do" in *Social Text*, vol. 24 (Spring 2006): 1–35, Duke University Press. Mary Romero's contribution is reprinted from *Contemporary Justice Review*, 11.1 (Mar. 2008): 23–37. A fuller version of Robyn Wiegman's essay appeared in *Boundary 2*, vol. 26, no. 3 (1999): 115–50, Duke University Press.

Comments from an anonymous peer reviewer were helpful in developing the volume, as was the work of Larin McLaughlin, our SUNY Press editor. We thank Daniella Gutierrez and Rebekah Sinclair for compiling our index.

We also thank Winston James and Leila Neti for helping bring Lindon Barrett's essay to publication. The passing of Lindon Barrett at such a young age was a tragic and unfortunate event for interdisciplinary studies and for us all.

The editorial process has weathered surgeries, adoptions, multiple moves, computer crashes, and other events. We owe a debt of gratitude to our families for their support and to our colleagues for their patience and perseverance. Ranu Samantrai would like to dedicate her work on the volume to her brother, Rajeev Samantrai, who would have been its first and most enthusiastic reader.

Chapter One

Interdisciplinarity and Social Justice

An Introduction

Joe Parker and Ranu Samantrai

Introduction

Many interdisciplinary fields exemplify the political ambivalence that characterizes the U.S. academy: ostensibly a critique of that institution's role in reinforcing inequalities, their very existence indicates a belief that the academy may also be an equalizing force in society. Supporters of the ethnic studies, cultural studies, and women's studies programs founded in the late 1960s, for instance, carried their battles from political movements into universities in the faith that changing the production of knowledge would transform social relations, broaden access for the disenfranchised, and thereby change the agents and the consequences of knowledge production. The pattern of scholars and activists joining forces to open fields of research and teaching continued in subsequent decades with the emergence of environmental studies, film and media studies, and gay and lesbian or queer studies. Recent additions—including critical race studies, disability studies, transgender studies, critical legal studies and justice studies, diaspora studies, border studies, and postcolonial studies—take as their epistemological foundation the inherently political nature of all knowledge production, a principle shared by the essays of the present volume.

Through trenchant critiques of disciplinary predecessors, interdisciplinary fields often have defined themselves in contrast with established disciplines. Their attempts to query the conditions and consequences of knowledge production have prompted changes that reach into traditional

1

disciplines and extend beyond the academy to movements for social justice (Bender). For instance, because the staffing needs of innovative programs and evolving disciplines have set in motion institutional changes necessary to accommodate new types of scholars, hitherto disenfranchised groups have gained greater access to sites of knowledge production (Boxer; Feierman; Stanton and Stewart; Messer-Davidow). From literature to sociology and into the physical sciences, scholars are engaging the difficult task of unraveling how assumptions about race, gender, class, colonization, and sexual orientation are embedded in the structure of interdisciplinary as well as disciplinary practices that, in turn, intervene to recreate the world in the image of those assumptions (Shiva; Deloria).

In addition to predictable resistance from practitioners of traditional disciplines, interdisciplinary fields have encountered some institutional, intellectual, and political criticisms from other quarters as well. Even as they have become established features of the academic landscape, they have struggled to maintain their affiliations with social movements (Boxer; Loo, and Mar; Messer-Davidow) and are now frequently subject to criticism from within those movements. Present variations of interdisciplinarity turn a critical eye to the political nature of truth production and to those who claim to be its producers. Their proponents acknowledge that interdisciplinary practices are not innocent of political and epistemological complicity with multiple structures of oppression.[1] Moreover, the shift from Enlightenment assumptions and epistemology to postmodern practices has prompted an evaluation of the political and ethical implications of social movements that remain organized around such putatively fixed universals as identity or liberation.

Interdisciplinary fields are no longer provocative newcomers to the U.S. academy. Although their proliferation in some ways is a measure of their success within the academy, the success of their attempts to hold the academy accountable for its claims of promoting the general welfare and contributing to a just society remains an open question. *Interdisciplinarity and Social Justice* takes this moment in their history to review the effects of interdisciplinary fields on our intellectual and political landscape, to evaluate their ability to deliver their promised social effects, and to consider their future.

Interdisciplinarity: A Contested History

Several influential publications on interdisciplinarity render considerations of politics and social justice secondary or obscure them altogether. Two such books were published early in the formative 1970s following international seminars organized by the Organization for Economic Cooperation and Development (OECD): *Interdisciplinarity: Problems of Teaching and Research in Universities* (Michaud et al.) and *Interdisciplinarity and Higher Education* (Kocklemans). Two additional influential volumes by Julie Thompson Klein followed in the 1990s (*Interdisciplinarity*; *Crossing Boundaries*). Taking such fields as social psychology and biochemistry as prototypical, Klein defines interdisciplinarity as the attempt to synthesize existing disciplinary concepts with the goal of achieving a unity of knowledge for a nonspecialized general education (*Interdisciplinarity* 12). This apolitical, holistic approach to interdisciplinarity, which we would term multidisciplinarity, is found across the board in the academy from the humanities (Fish) to science research centers (Weingart) to professional associations (Newell).[2] But Klein's history largely disregards the social and intellectual challenges to academic orthodoxy and the politics that were the breeding ground for interdisciplinary programs.[3] Absent that context, Klein advocates an interdisciplinarity that rejects narrow specialization in favor of an integrative blend of disciplines on the grounds that social needs are best served by the latter's general education approach (*Interdisciplinarity* 15, 27, 38).

Area studies and development studies offer early examples of an interdisciplinarity that assumes the neutrality of disciplinary truth claims and seeks their integration. But since area studies (including American studies) emerged in the U.S. academy during the early years of the Cold War, any neutrality they claim is belied by their reliance on the category of the nation-state (Brantlinger 27; Shumway) that, in turn, naturalizes colonial territorial boundaries (Chow, "Politics and Pedagogy" 133–34; Kaplan and Grewal 70–72). The divisions suggested by Asian studies and American studies parse difference into manageable and essentialized areas domesticates a global network of contradictory power relations, whereas development studies spin evidence of inequity and injustice into tales of inevitable progress (Sbert; Rafael; Pletsch; Esteva; Escobar).

But against the neutrality of disciplinary knowledge stands an array of scholarship that uncovers the messy history of disciplinary norms linked to social inequalities and entangled in lengthy, highly politicized struggles about authoritative claims to truth (Moran 8; Steinmetz, *Politics*; Messer-Davidow, Shumway, and Sylvan). Hans Flexner and others note that the emergence of modern notions of disciplinarity in European academies in the nineteenth century coincided with the industrial revolution, agrarian changes, and "the general 'scientification' of knowledge" (Flexner 105–06 ctd.; Klein, *Interdisciplinarity* 21; Moran 5–14). As a consequence, modern education shifted toward specialized teaching based on research configured by the modern disciplines, which in turn was driven by industrial demand for emergent technologies and appropriately trained employees. Lorraine Daston has argued that the traditional European emphasis on liberal humanism as the basis for educational authority was replaced between the 1810s and 1840s in Germany by the research seminar that linked specialized training to emerging professions such as philologist or laboratory scientist, university teacher or industrial chemist (71–72, 77–78). Rather than the philosopher's skillful thought unifying the knowledge practices of advanced education, in the newly configured German university, critical thought was supplanted by the form and values of the seminar itself: diligence, punctuality, performance of written and oral work on schedule, careful attention to minute detail, devotion to technique, and a cult of thoroughness, responsibility, and exactitude (78, 82). The spread of what has come to be known as the German model of the research university throughout Europe and its colonies combined with the attendant proliferation of specialized disciplines and their seminar format for advanced study to produce the modern, seemingly worldwide university.

Joe Moran notes the expanding impact of the physical sciences in the nineteenth century, when they became the measure for all other knowledge and the template for the new fields now known as the social sciences (Moran 5–7; Haskell; Shumway and Messer-Davidow). Following Michel Foucault (*Clinic*), Michel de Certeau (1984), and Terry Eagleton, James Clifford has argued that from the seventeenth century onward, the natural sciences defined themselves in opposition to the humanities by contrasting their aim of transparent signification with an emphasis on rhetoric (in rhetoric or literature), pressing their claims to facticity against the status of fiction, myth (in literature), or superstition (religion), and practicing objectivity in contrast with subjectivity (Clifford 5). Thus the natural sciences pressed even the humanities to adopt the criteria of evidence and argumentation modeled on modern reason, as exemplified by mathematics in the physical sciences (Moran 7). Indeed, Moran argues that the move towards interdisciplinary study in the humanities challenges precisely the preeminence of science as the predominant model for disciplinary truth claims. Such histories suggest the importance of examining the complicity of the modern research university with the industrialization of modern society, the enclosure of agrarian lands, the emergence of market economies and the modern professions, and attendant questions of exploitation, inequality, and injustice (Flexner; Althusser; Bourdieu).

In Michel Foucault's widely influential account (*Discipline*; "Subject and Power"), the French Enlightenment provides the backdrop for the formation of modern discipline understood as both bodily discipline and docility and disciplined knowledge forms. Vincent Leitch summarizes a permeation of the social by discipline so detailed and thorough as to produce the modern disciplinary society:

> [From] the 1760s to the 1960s—the modern era—societies became increasingly regulated by norms directed at the "docile body" and disseminated through a network of cooperating "disciplinary institutions," including the judicial, military, educational, work-shop, psychiatric, welfare, religions, and prison establishments, all of which entities enforce norms and correct delinquencies. . . . In casting the school as a "disciplinary institution," Foucault has in mind specifically the use of dozens of so-called disciplines, that is, microtechniques of registration, organization, observation, corrections, and control [such as] examinations, case studies, records, partitions and cells, enclosures, rankings, objectifications, monitoring systems, assessments, hierarchies, norms, tables (such as timetables), and individualizations. The disciplines, invented by the Enlightenment, facilitate the submission of bodies and the extraction from them of useful forces. These small everyday physical mechanisms operate beneath our established egalitarian law as ideals, producing a counter law that subordinates and limits reciprocities [. . . .] Universities and colleges deploy the micro disciplines to train and discipline the students in prepa-rations not only for jobs and professional disciplines, but for disciplinary societies. (168)

This configuration of educational institutions also accounts for the multiplication of the specialist societies and journals that still remain pow-erful regulatory and enforcement mechanisms in the Eurocentric academy. Foucault's account has been central to much interdisciplinary work that names the trouble with established disciplines in the Eurocentric univer-sity (Brown; Messer-Davidow, Shumway, and Sylvan; Shumway; Said; R. Young).

The competing histories of the justice effects of the modern disciplin-ary university reviewed here suggest numerous ways to understand the relationship between interdisciplinarity and social justice. The narratives of Flexner, Daston, and Moran indicate that the modern, disciplinary academy limits the audience of academic writing to other specialists in the academy, industry, and government, even as it supplies that audience with evaluative criteria such as originality, viability, and the regulative mechanisms of the research seminar (Daston 79). Against that backdrop, interdisciplinarity may be understood as returning critique to the center of the educational enterprise while changing the social groups that benefit from the educational enterprise. The Foucauldian account also implies that interdisciplinarity can be an intervention into a modern microphysics of power to prepare students not for disciplinary society but for practices that ground social relations outside those defined by the professions and by measures of capitalist productivity.

Justice Through New Objects of Knowledge and New Methods

Within education, interest in social justice increased dramatically in the 1960s and early 1970s as students and faculty on campuses worldwide learned from anticolonial liberation struggles in the global south and linked their language, tactics, and goals to change primary, secondary, and postsecondary education (Ali and Watkins; Katsiaficas; Committee; Editorial Staff; Omatsu). For instance, in their early years, ethnic studies in the United States resulted from broad, cross-racial coalitions demanding third-world liberation for students domestically and overseas (Caute; Naison; Acree; Whitson and Kyles; Wang). As Steven Feierman has shown in an analysis of the discipline of history, decolonization in the global south combined with multiple liberation and civil rights movements in the global north to provoke a major shift in the academy, evidenced by increasing racial, gender, sexual preference, and national diversity of scholars at work in academic institutions and consequent major shifts in historiography. Greater interest in social justice is also seen in a general crisis of epistemology, signaled by dramatically decreased satisfaction with knowledge protocols and with the social effects of academic work (Boxer; Carson; Deloria; Eagleton; Feierman 84–86; Foucault, *Archaeology*; Guha and Spivak; Miller; Said; Steinmetz, "Decolonizing"; Chakravorty, this volume), or what Levinas has termed "ontological imperialism" (qtd. Feierman 167–68). From the crisis in the credibility of educational institutions emerged a number of interdisciplinary fields that refused disciplinary claims to political neutrality and objectivity, preferring instead to direct their research and teaching openly toward the aims of social justice.[4]

Through a complex process of negotiated agreements with university leaders and, in the case of public institutions, with state officials (J. Cohen), the fields of study that emerged were generally named in terms of discrete social groups contextualized, as in the case of environmental studies, both as particular objects of knowledge and as agents of change. In the United States, these included fields—such as Black Studies, Chicano studies, and Asian American studies—that rejected disciplines dominated by white faculty and the erasure of non-white objects of knowledge; early women's studies programs that emphasized the study of women as a corrective both to their erasure from the humanities and to the pervasive sexism of the academy and the society (Boxer; Messer-Davidow); and Native American studies that rejected imperialism in the academy. These were accompanied in England by an attention to socioeconomic class that brought the concerns of the working class to the center in the academy (Hall; Williams, *Revolution* 57–70). And comparable changes were occurring around the globe as students and faculty engaged in social struggles turned their attention to transforming the academy in Tokyo, Mexico City, Lagos, Rio de Janeiro, Cairo, and across western and eastern Europe (Zolov; Ali and Watkins; Caute). The extraordinarily high level of interest in engaging the politics of knowledge production is indicated, for example, by the exponential rise in the number of women's studies courses in the United States: from about seventeen in the academic year 1969–1970, to about seventy-three in the following year, to nearly seven hundred in 1971–1972. In the ensuing decades, some eighty campus-based research centers, autonomous professional associations, and thousands of feminist presses, book series, journals, and newsletters have been established (Messer-Davidow 83–85).

Joined under the umbrella of interdisciplinarity, disparate emergent methods and pedagogies shared a rejection of the commonplace belief in the neutrality of academic knowledge.[5] Participants explored research topics, pedagogies and methods in the hope of countering inequalities naturalized by the truth claims of the academy: racial and gender inequities given the alibi by the biological and social sciences, global economic disparities defended by much of history and economics—the list is very long. One common strategy involved invading the fields once claimed by the natural and social sciences while working to redefine the terms, methods, and politics of knowledge. For example, the interest in class issues in Black Studies, women's studies, postcolonial studies, and film studies, as well as in literature and philosophy, may be read as an attempt to contest the claim to ownership of the economic by the field of economics, as we see in the work of Lindon Barrett, Alex Juhasz, and Patrick Brantlinger in the present volume. The emphasis on broadening the notion of the political to include the personal, the body, and the quotidian in feminism, literature, and ethnic studies may also be seen as an attack on claims to monopolize the political by those in the field of political science or on claims to know the body by biologists, as seen here in essays by Mary Romero, Robert DeChaine, and Joe Parker. Questions about environmental impacts and limits may be seen as a struggle for ownership of the natural world between those in environmental studies and chemists, biologists, and engineers. Frequently, interrogations of the modern academy came about from questions regarding the content of scholarship, for instance as a consequence of demands to know about topics that had been erased or demeaned by seemingly neutral methods, canons, and protocols—for example, African American authors in literary studies, working-class members in histories, or the effects on women of drugs that scientists tested only on men. Indeed, one way to understand the emergence of interdisciplinary fields is as a struggle over ownership of objects of knowledge with high-stakes implications for social relations.

The logic of linking interdisciplinarity to social justice through naming new objects of knowledge obtains as more recent arrivals—queer studies, diaspora studies, media studies, critical legal studies, critical race studies, and postcolonial studies—gain footholds in the academy. A similar logic is pursued by fields—disability studies, transgender studies, critical whiteness studies, and critical masculinity studies—waiting often impatiently in the wings for their turn on the stage of academic legitimacy. The continuing proliferation of interdisciplinary fields, along with their ongoing promiscuous relations with each other and with the disciplines, suggests that the disciplinary form of the modern academy has failed to contain the challenge to its own status as a neutral, objective institution with only neutral or positive social effects. The larger threat to justice targeted by these newly emerging fields is the same as that identified by the more established interdisciplinary fields: the definitive tendency of the dominant to appropriate the emergent under the limits of justice in modern societies (Williams, *Marxism* 121–27; Spivak, *Death* 1–3, 10–11 and n. 15, 106).

Many scholars working in interdisciplinary fields conceptualize justice primarily in the tradition of the European Enlightenment as retribution for crimes or damages and as fairness of distribution. Inequality is taken as a sign of the failure of modern institutions to render real such modern ideals;

research and teaching, then, seek to promote greater equality by critiquing social and legal practices and by training young people to increase the pace of social change (e.g., Montoya-Lewis, Messer-Davidow, and Soldatenko in this volume). In this widely practiced approach, justice means a fair, universal application of public policies and legal standards to all members of society, with the goal of an equal distribution of resources. But some fields have divided because of debates about the most politically efficacious methods and epistemes, pedagogies and theories for achieving this version of justice. There are those in women's studies (Messer-Davidow 129–213) and cultural studies (Bennett; Appadurai; Milner; Brantlinger in this volume), among other fields, who hold that the move to interdisciplinarity has been a political failure (Loo; Miller; Soldatenko in this volume). Others, such as the feminist Wendy Brown, resort to urging the abolition of their own interdisciplinary fields, so discouraged are they by the continuing complicity of those fields with modern conceptions of politics, power, the individual, and other such foundational terms (Brown; Wiegman, "Introduction" and "Progress" 131–22 and 140 n. 28). Still others have refused to join the academy or have left it entirely in order to pursue the work of social justice in venues they believe to be less compromised by institutional forces and regulations.[6]

Changing conceptions of justice, power, and knowledge have rebounded in fields founded on putatively coherent objects of knowledge that each requires its own autonomous area of inquiry. Amy Robinson, for instance, argues that analogies between race and sexuality consolidate each as an autonomous sphere. The resulting segregation of the two leads to the presumption of "the normative whiteness of the gay subject," a problematic development from an antiracist position (qtd. Joseph 274). Similar analogies between feminist studies and lesbian and gay studiessuggesting that the two fields are discrete domains have been critiqued by Judith Butler who, using intersectionality, contends that sexual difference is central to understanding sexual orientation ("Against Proper"; ctd. Joseph 274). Rey Chow has argued against the foundational terms of area studies and comparative literature as haunted by essentializing and conservative notions of culture, history, territory, and language in their reinscriptions of the nation-state and the first world as universal norms (*Writing Diaspora* 16–17, 128–29). Such arguments suggest that for the purposes of social justice, the most appropriate objects of study are located at the intersections of fields separated by the linguistic-cum-disciplinary pressures of regulatory regimes. Yet there is no obvious or explicitly designated institutional basis for such work; we will return to this point when considering the next steps for interdisciplinarity.

Motivating these criticisms are the disciplinary pressures, both within the academy and in social movements, to constitute coherent, readily recognizable objects as grounds for social movements and fields of study. Despite the best efforts of those working in interdisciplinary fields, the disciplines are still largely effective at defining the terms and limits of coherence and visibility, and thereby of academic legitimacy and credibility (Bowman, "Alarming"; Messer-Davidow). As Wendy Brown and others have argued, however, the politically conservative character of the very objects of knowledge that shape both fields of study and social movements require caution, critique, and constructive responses that make explicit the costs of allowing foundational concepts to determine the politics and ethics of interdisciplinary work (Brown; Wiegman, "Introduction" 3 and "Object Lessons," 356–58, 378–85; Stryker 14). Such seemingly neutral terms as "women," "nation," "society," "culture," "political," "liberation," and "resistance" consolidate assumptions that render both academic study and social movements complicit with problematic modern institutions, histories of domination, and erasures of subordinated groups. Bringing these defining objects of knowledge to crisis allows those in interdisciplinary fields to "sustain the interrogation of the object" of knowledge and the politically troubled complicities and assumptions that sustain and regulate them (Wiegman, "Introduction" 3).

Once the motivation of interdisciplinary work, modern notions of justice are now scrutinized and found wanting by some. For those who advocate critical self-examination from within interdisciplinary fields, the principal task now is to interrogate the limits of our understanding of justice and, perhaps paradoxically, to render visible the injustices of simultaneously silenced and normalized coercions and violences effected through the often subtle enforcement mechanisms of disciplinary society. That aim requires a constant refusal of certainty so that, in the view of Gayatri Spivak, objects of knowledge are rendered intelligible even as the knowing subject remains critical of every success at rendering something intelligible ("Power/Knowledge" 28). Based on a recognition of the highly politicized history of language in limiting the politics and ethics of practice, Spivak follows Foucault in researching the ways that the subject subjects itself to certain power/knowledge relations through the ability to know ("Power/Knowledge" 28, 34, 39). Such scholarship, which Judith Butler identifies as "the desubjugation of the subject within the politics of truth," places the limits of intelligibility at the heart of work toward social justice, with the latter conceived as spaces and relations that refuse norms that install modern social hierarchies and the violences on which they depend ("Doing Justice" 622, 35). By marking each act of naming as overdetermined by the troubled modern history of language and intelligibility, interdisciplinarity can open up a plurality of ethics, so that ethical knowledge practices may, in the words of André Glucksmann, "make appear the dissymetries, the disequilebriums, the aporias, the impossibilities, which are precisely the objects of all commitment" (qtd. Spivak, "Power/Knowledge" 40). Inquiry is brought to productive crisis when the intelligibility of the object of knowledge is taken as its central question. Against the limits of modern knowledge, we can respond by tracking those limits as an index of the ethics and politics of the knowledge practices we perform (McClintock; Radway; Spivak, "Subaltern Studies"; Sullivan 37–56; Brown).

An interdisciplinarity located at this juncture can seek to account for and resist disciplinary domestication in ways retain concern for ethics and social justice. As in papers by Barrett, Wiegman, Parker, Chakravorty, and others in the present volume, the practice of interdisciplinarity can take the social construction of knowledge as a political project focused on issues of justice. Likewise, Paul Bowman has argued for interdisciplinary practices that are "alterdisciplinary" in their thoroughgoing attention to the complicity of disciplines with social hegemonies. According to Bowman, rather than present knowledge as definitive, correct, and sacred, as the disciplines tend to do, interdisciplinarity "open[s] up the fissure or wound which is the university's very constitutive incompletion ... an injury ... also an *in-jury*, in the sense of being tied to the injurious, the un-just" ("Alterdisciplinarity" 67). Simon O'Sullivan argues for a reconception of interdisciplinarity using the concept of the rhizome developed by Giles Deleuze and Felix Guattari. To oppose the disciplinary effect of fixing knowledge, to which cultural studies has been subject, O'Sullivan argues that the purpose of scholarship is "not to *understand* the world ... but rather to create the world differently ... which involves less an object of study, even less does it involve a reading, an interpretation of objects.... Instead it involves a *pragmatics* ... to reorder our 'selves' and our world" (82, 84). Cultural studies "does not name a discipline but rather a *function* ... a deterritorialisation from other disciplines, from academia, and inevitably from itself" (88). Here interdisciplinarity turns against the limits of its own defining object of knowledge, rendering its own practices subject to critique in order to resist the disciplinary stabilization of meanings and fields and the consequent normalization of social hierarchies and their violences.

Justice Through the Turn Toward Difference

As activists and academics critique their own epistemologies, some have also become unwilling to allow their scholarship to be determined by the practices of modern social movements. Drawing eclectically from multiple sources to rethink truth claims and knowledge protocols, they have reshaped the politics and ethics of the object of knowledge as well. The approaches we now consider are characterized by this cautious, even suspicious stance toward the linkage of interdisciplinary scholarship and political action.

One of the earliest and most influential such gestures has come to be known as the theory of intersectionality, first articulated by the Combahee River Collective in the mid-1970s: "[W]e are actively committed to struggling against racial, sexual, heterosexual, and class oppression and see as our particular task the development of integrated analysis and practice based upon the fact that the major systems of oppression are interlocking" (13). By naming identities located at the intersection of multiple, linked oppressions, the Collective made visible the erasures effected by the narrow scope both of academic inquiry and of social movements. Their critique encompassed traditional disciplines as well as new interdisciplinary fields and extended from the white-dominated feminist and male-dominated black liberation movements to the black feminists of the National Black Feminist Organization (NBFO) founded in 1973. Similar positions on intersectionality are found in publications from the late 1970s and early 1980s, including the important 1981 anthology of the writings of women of color, *This Bridge Called My Back: Writings by Radical Women of Color*, edited by Cherríe Moraga and Gloria Anzaldúa.

Intersectionality has led to numerous fundamental changes in social movements and in the epistemological practice of disciplinary and also interdisciplinary work. In particular, it has prompted a shift from identity to difference in gender and race studies, together with criticism of essentialist and universalist conceptions of such foundational categories as gender, race, sexuality, and nation. Intersectionality has also secured the function of theory as a critique not only of epistemology and the academy but also of power relations within social movements.[7] In so doing, it has shifted analyses of power away from an emphasis on the universal and toward theories of justice that attend to difference and heterogeneity. The far-reaching impact of this reorientation is evident in the work in critical legal studies and philosophy (Willett; Cornell, Rosenfeld, Carlson) and by feminist philosophers and social critics, such as Iris Marion Young and Nancy Fraser, who advocate the modification of traditional principles of redistributive justice to recognize the justice claims both of identitarian groups and of group heterogeneity. In a less modernist vein, Jean François Lyotard has argued for the centrality of heterogeneity, difference, and incommensurability in our thinking about justice. Rather than the totalizations of universal principles (*Postmodern* 66), he emphasizes working at the limits of the protocols and prescriptions of justice (*Just* 100), for instance, by questioning the homogenizing categories of race, class, gender, sexual orientation, and citizenship that ground many modern movements for social justice. The proliferating postmodern reconsiderations of justice (Mouffe; Nancy, *Creation*; Badiou; Derrida, "Legal Force"; Cornell, Rosenfeld, Carlson; Ziarek) are themselves examples of interdisciplinary interventions into what was once the territory of disciplines (philosophy, law) and of social movements.

Other interdisciplinary reconsiderations of epistemology resulting from an emphasis on difference and its concomitant rejection of essential and universal categories have built on dissatisfaction with modern objectivity as the prototypical convention for legitimating truth claims, with varying results. Among feminists, for example, Emma Perez and Joan Scott reject outright the possibility of objective knowledge (Perez; Scott 1–27), in contrast with others who argue for revisions of objectivity (Harding; Haraway; Moya and Hames-Garcia). The wide-ranging consequences of the move to epistemological uncertainty are evident in challenges to essentialism and naturalized conceptions of the body in race-, gender-, sexuality-, and disability-based fields, as for example in critical race theory (Delgado, "Introduction" xv). From the perspective of this analytic stance, hostility to theory appears as a reluctance to relinquish access to an unmediated and objective knowledge of transparent reality. It may also be an unintentional and contradictory refusal to mark the hierarchies, hegemonies and economies of value that render disciplinary (and institutionalized forms of interdisciplinary) knowledge "exclusive, and always in some measure violent, unethical, and biased" (Bowman, "Alarming" 70).

Suspicion of the European Enlightenment promise of transparent knowledge has had a significant impact both on long-established fields such as feminist/women's studies, cultural studies, and critical legal studies, and on more recent arrivals such as postcolonial studies, queer studies, and disability studies. That change might be characterized as an increased vitality resulting from renewed discussions about goals and methods, epistemologies and politics. To be sure, gains in vitality and relevance have been accompanied by a loss of unity and homogeneity, as practitioners

critique the inability of their own interdisciplinary fields to break with
the foundational categories of modern epistemology. Moreover, critiques
of disciplinary knowledge protocols have generated a number of new
interdisciplinary fields that, by seeking institutional acceptance without
compromising their stance of dissent, attempt to carry the impact of epistemological uncertainty into the very heart of the academy. Some—such
as postcolonial studies (Spivak, *Post-Colonial*; Said; R. Young), subaltern
studies (Guha and Spivak; Chaturvedi), queer studies (Corber and Valocchi; Kirsch; Warner), and critical race theory (Delgado, "Introduction" xv;
Unger)—are associated with already well-respected social justice movements.
Others name objects of knowledge comparable with those of women's
studies or ethnic studies in that they attend to social groups that have been
erased, ignored, or demeaned by the modern academy, such as transgender
studies (Stryker and Whittle), diaspora studies (Gilroy; Tololyan), border
studies (Rosaldo; Anzaldúa), and disability studies (Davis). Several fields
investigate social norms naturalized under modernity; critical whiteness
studies (Rasmussen; López; Dyer; Naison) and critical masculinity studies
(Sedgwick; Halberstam; Gardner; Berger) exemplify this critical tendency.
Yet others emphasize newly influential technologies and industries that have
not received prominent attention from the academic disciplines of the late
nineteenth and early twentieth centuries; included in this list are cinema
studies, film studies, and media studies.

These approaches to interdisciplinarity draw on protocols and objects
of knowledge that are not possible within the terms of the modern disciplines. Roland Barthes is often quoted as arguing that interdisciplinary work
creates new objects of knowledge and even a new language to produce an
"unease in classification" (qtd. Moran 16) important not only for academics
but also for the foundational workings of meaning itself:

> Interdisciplinary work, so much discussed these days, is not about
> confronting already constituted disciplines (none of which, in fact,
> is willing to let itself go). To do something interdisciplinary it's
> not enough to choose a "subject" (a theme) and gather around
> it two or three sciences. Interdisciplinarity consists in creating a
> new object that belongs to no one. (Barthes, qtd. Clifford 1)

Others are inspired by Foucault's examples of instances when scholarship has introduced "a new object, calling for new conceptual tools, and for
fresh theoretical foundations . . . a true monster, so much so that [modern
knowledge] could not even properly speak of [it] . . . [unlike someone]

committing no more than a disciplined error" (*Archaeology* 224). Such claims on behalf of interdisciplinarity exceed reformist demands by some interdisciplinarians for increased attention to already established, disciplined objects of knowledge. Instead, their ambitious scope suggests that the desire to peg knowing to ethics and justice may be prompting an epistemic break as interdisciplinarians debate the most appropriate knowledge protocols and logics for achieving their aims (Bono, Dean, and Ziarek; Castronovo; Nancy, "Answering"; Gasché).

Another Justice: New Protocols and Logics

By drawing on knowledges and logics violently attacked or overlooked in the aporias of modern knowledge protocols, some practitioners of interdisciplinarity have argued for constituting knowledge of that which is effaced and occluded. Included in such knowledge are the violent, frequently deadly effects of social practices, effects that contradict claims to progress and mythologies of equality (Anzaldúa 5–12; Devi 98, 118; Foucault, *Discipline* 265–67, 302–03; White 135). The current of interdisciplinarity examined in this section questions modern epistemologies by exposing their imbrication with overt and direct violence. It also provides persuasive critiques of the more subtle, internalized, destructive effects resulting in what we have so far named inadequately as docility (Anzaldúa 20, 22, 59; Devi 109–10, 118, 127, 142; Foucault, *Discipline* 11–12, 16, 274–75; White 136, 41).

In lieu of modern knowledge protocols, Robyn Wiegman (among others) supports a feminist interdisciplinary politics that seeks to render legible the ways that troubled identity categories themselves reproduce exclusions and violent silencing (Wiegman, "Progress of Gender" 107, 127–33). She points out that relying on politically troubled institutional terms of legibility or on exclusionary claims to commensurability between the names of interdisciplinary fields and their object domains have failed to achieve idealized relations of justice (Wiegman, "Introduction" 11, 140 n. 27). Just as identitarian logic and realist referents place under erasure such objects of knowledge as female masculinities, gay and lesbian studies, intersexualities, sexual minority cultures, and transgender identities and communities. So, too, the violent policing by the Euro-American medical tradition of normative gender boundaries—in their sanctioning, for example, of surgical interventions following intersex births—erases the very possibility of intersexed subjectivities and communities. Wiegman asks us to recognize the failure of categorical completeness as a critical achievement in order that "the very issue of knowledge formation ... [might] be rigorously and consistently thought in the field domain of Women's Studies or gender studies." (Wiegman, "Progress" 129) Such work does not escape the violence and "exclusion, contradiction, and incommensurability" but takes the problems which accompany any object-centered work and place them at the center of the work of the field. For Wiegman resignifying interdisciplinary fields in this way makes it possible to reject a realism that carries out exclusionary violence to instead investigate the social justice implications of failures of identity, while exploring the constructive intellectual and social ends to which such incoherence may be put (Wiegman, "Progress" 129, 130-32, 140 n. 28). Similarly, from within disability studies, transgender studies, and queer studies come charges that, instead of positioning people with disabilities and lesbian, gay, bisexual, and transgender (LGBT) people as subjects with agency, "numerous professional and academic disciplines ... concentrate upon the management, repair, and maintenance of physical and cognitive incapacity" (Mitchell and Snyder 1, qtd. McRuer, "Good" 97). By challenging not only modern laboratory science but also social welfare policy and medical practices, activists and scholars in these fields show that they have much to contribute to social movements that seek to restore agency to groups that modern limits of visibility would rather objectify than empower, rather modify or medicate than celebrate and legitimate. In a similar fashion, Laura Donaldson has argued convincingly against the epistemic violence of the erasure in some postcolonial work of indigenous issues and the persistent "woman question," rendering invisible the ways subalterns achieve subject status (Donaldson and Kwok 5; Donaldson 45, 51-54). On this important final point regarding subject status, there is some congruence in queer, disability, postcolonial, feminist, and subaltern studies to suggest that, insofar as it resists the normative foundations of the modern subject, interdisciplinarity may assist efforts by members of marginal groups to claim subject status and political agency.

Eve Sedgwick, Susan Jeffords, and Judith Butler reject the necessity of universal, essential, and coherent identities as preconditional foundations for social order or for putatively neutral knowledges (Sullivan 38; 43–46; Sedgwick *Epistemology* 8; Butler "Proper Objects"). This approach explores naturalized norms as part of contested and contradictory fields of power, so that interdisciplinarity becomes a type of anti-identitarian "queer" that seeks to liberate both knowledges and bodies from effective subjection. Rather than represent queer as an identity extension to gay and lesbian (C. Cohen 438–39, 459–60; Sullivan 43–56), this notion of the queer functions as a cipher for the more destabilizing methods and aims of interdisciplinarity. In that function, it is analogous to "crip" in relation to disability studies (McRuer, *Crip Theory*) and, to a lesser extent, gender studies in relation to women's studies and postcolonial studies in relation to third world studies.

In rejecting stabilized knowledge practices founded on the fixity of the disciplinary (and interdisciplinary) object of knowledge, some interdisciplinary work has turned toward new criteria for determining not only the character of knowledge but also attendant conceptions of justice. Like Wiegman and Butler, Spivak regards the knowing subject as itself an effect produced by conjunctures within a network of structures, forces, and disciplines, rather than as the autonomous individual will pursued by early subaltern studies of historiography (Spivak, "Subaltern Studies" 213–14). If that autonomous subject is amenable to and reinforced by disciplinary investigation, then Spivak proposes interdisciplinarity as "an institutional calculus for recoding or instrumentalizing undecidability" (Spivak, *Death* 49). Spivak's emphasis on undecidability reaches to the social hierarchies and unequal relations between self and other inscribed in language itself (*Death* 52). Her rejection of the fixity and determinism carried out by language reconstitutes not only the limits and politics of the object of knowledge, but also of the collectivities with which writing and reading subjects align themselves. This indeterminacy strategy thereby aims to allow readers and knowers to "open entry into responsibility with the subaltern other" (Spivak, *Death* 69).[8]

Such critical reflections on the conditions of knowledge lead to reconsiderations of the concept of justice with implications that reach far beyond the academy. A number of interdisciplinary activist-academics shift their very construal of justice by appropriating the language of fields as far-flung as medicine or law for newly politicized ends, for instance, by naming their goals as healing or reconciliation. The repair work (Spelman) in question may involve healing the alienation that divides subject from object and that arranges subjects in social hierarchies or as the centralized and the marginalized (O'Sullivan 86; Taussig). For Anzaldúa, interdisciplinary work carries out a healing of the bleeding *herida abierta* or open wound that is the borderlands/la frontera, and of the splitting of self from other that makes possible hatred, violence, and exploitation (Anzaldúa, Preface [n.p.], 3, 86, 202–03). According to Anzaldua, those who are healed practice interdisciplinarity according to a logic that appears crazy or nonsensical to those still under the spell of the disciplines (Anzaldúa 19, 197), but they become intermediaries comfortably at work in the ambiguities and contradictions at the crossroads where differences meet (Anzaldúa 80).

And sometimes justice takes unrecognizable forms. For example, Spivak argues that the most appropriate politics and ethics for interdisciplinary work take the form of earning the trust of the subaltern (Spivak, "Power/Knowledge"), apparent in moments of great intimacy and even love (Spivak, "French Feminisms Revisited" 166–71; Spivak, "The Politics of Translation" 180–83). As one of Mahsweta Devi's characters remarks, despairing at the ineffectiveness of the nation-state and at the inability of journalistic knowledge and mass-media news even to recognize the violent effects of injustice and colonization, "To build it [real exchange] you must love beyond reason for a long time" (Devi 195–96). Healing, reconciliation, love—such aims sidestep the contractual logic of modern justice, in search of, as David Carrol writes, another "justice that . . . does not put an end to disputes and differences, that is continually in search of its rules and laws rather than presupposing and simply applying them to each case" (Carroll 75, qtd. Ziarek 85).

The prominence of epistemology and theory within interdisciplinary scholarship has perhaps been the most controversial factor for those who seek to emphasize the academy's obligations to foster the practice of justice. Criticisms and counter-critiques are plentiful between those, often self-named realists, who rely on objectivist or materialist measures of injustice and those who have cast off from the stable shores of realism to question its normalization, its politics and ethics, and ultimately, its utility for the ends of social justice variously conceived. One of the difficulties of these debates is that the various approaches use different methods for measuring political effectiveness: Whereas some emphasize economic redistribution or policy changes, others draw attention to redefining the limits and terms of the political, and still others promote practices that make legible forms of injustice that are rendered invisible by the knowledge protocols of modern epistemes. Certainly the debates are indicators of the contested character of academic politics. Yet they also mark interdisciplinarity as a place where competing academic protocols, standards, and logics, together with the goals and values of social justice movements, are made explicit in order to be debated, interrogated, and reshaped.

Overview of Essays

The present volume is an attempt to present a range of carefully considered responses from social justice perspectives to one or more visions for interdisciplinarity. Each essay explicitly or implicitly responds to critiques of established disciplines, while also engaging activist and scholarly literature that is critical of aspects of interdisciplinary academic work.

Essays in the first section attend to the social justice issues at stake in critiques of the disciplines. Lisa Lowe contends that the social sciences have been brought to an epistemic crisis not through the interventions of poststructuralist theory but rather through their own failure to grasp the full implications of globalization. She notes that social scientists have long used metaphors to explain the relations between cultures, social systems, nations, and economies that characterize globalization, thereby questioning presumptions of socioeconomic stability while failing to capture widening economic inequalities and proliferating forms of difference. By exposing the social justice implications of the literary character of social science, Lowe displaces the hierarchy of the scientific over the literary and turns the totalizing claims of modern social science against their own truths.

Mary Romero deploys critical race theory to link the field of sociology with the history of racism in the United States and shows how the preoccupation with meritocracy, mobility, and assimilation normalizes whiteness and middle-class standards that mask privilege and sociostructural disadvantages. Using as her case study the actions of the Chandler, Arizona, police and immigration officials that inscribe citizenship on the body and systematically degrade communities of color, she uncovers the failure of sociologists of immigration to learn not only from critical race theory but also from another subfield, the sociology of race. Romero's use of an interdisciplinary method brings issues of civil rights and human rights to the forefront of research and positions them as catalytic for bringing together communities of color as allies across differences in citizenship status.

Raquel Montoya-Lewis links epistemological and socioeconomic issues with a comparative analysis of Native American tribal courtroom procedures to demonstrate how forms of justice unavailable in the U.S. courtroom may be achieved. By telling localized stories of tribal courts in which she has presided as judge through the prism of critical legal studies, Montoya-Lewis rejects generalizations that would assimilate specificity to the national legal hegemony. At the same time, she illustrates the interventions of hegemonic legal structures, such as "the law of white spaces," in which her stories occurred.

Mrinalini Chakravorty reads the undisciplined play of juxtaposed historical, literary, and political registers by the Anglophone Arab woman writer and journalist Ahdaf Soueif as providing a Pan-Arab yet heterogeneous catalyst for Middle Eastern struggles against Western imperialism. Chakravorty demonstrates how moments of careful transfer and translation within and between disciplinary knowledges and dominant and marginalized cultures produce alternative discourses for recognizing the claims of the dispossessed. This brings to crisis the legitimacy of the Western modernizing project that, although entrenched in the institutional authority of governments, nations, and universities, all the while bolsters its power through the capture of markets and by its logic of commodification. By identifying her tactical opposition to habits of scholarship and journalism that produce the Middle East as a particular kind of sublime commodity in the West, Chakravorty presents Soueif as crisscrossing the bounds of fiction and history, legitimacy and marginality, and legibility and illegibility to confront urgent questions of violence, torture, and rights.

The volume's second section examines the nature of claims to social justice in interdisciplinary fields. Patrick Brantlinger anchors cultural studies in the study of value as a counter discourse to the claim of capitalist economics as the modern "science of value." Proposing that ethical considerations should be central to all academic fields, he holds that postmodern theories fail to provide meaningful opposition to capitalist globalization and to recent U.S. economic policies. In so doing, he makes explicit some of the stakes in counterattacks from the left against the postmodernist rejection of class as a foundational concept. Alex Juhasz works back and forth between personal narrative and a Marxist analysis of praxis in cinema and media studies to argue for a revived emphasis on social change in interdisciplinary fields. By focusing on histories both personal and transnational of the emergence in the academy of cinema studies, queer studies, and women's studies, Juhasz recovers a leftist tradition of activism linking academic and cultural production with social justice.

Joe Parker takes up the question of refusals of the domestication of both disciplinary and interdisciplinary academic work by critically examining the writing, teaching, and other embodied practices of Michel Foucault, Joan Wallach Scott, and Gayatri Chakravorty Spivak. Parker finds promising avenues for dedisciplining academic work in the reconstitution of the power effects of knowledge through building horizontal solidarities disrupted by the modern power/knowledge regime, in the exploration of ways the body may resist docility, and in work against the grain of the modern general distributional economy of bodies (prisoners, women factory workers, the subaltern).

In the final paper of this section, Mike Soldatenko documents how the internal colonialism model influential in the early years of Chicano studies became an important template for activist leftist research, only to fall prey to the internal colonialism of interdisciplinary fields, including Chicano studies itself. Interdisciplinarity promised an epistemological revolution within the academy and a departure from the problematic heritage of traditional disciplines in the social sciences and the humanities. Yet it failed to recognize how its own inevitable disciplinary practices ultimately would work to manage Chicano studies as part of the hidden curriculum.

The final section reminds practitioners of interdisciplinarity that there are numerous pitfalls in attempts to render social justice central to academic and social movement practices. Robyn Wiegman suggests that the turn to the particular, the embodied, and the local has not been a successful strategy for those who would interrogate whiteness. Based on a reading of canonical works in critical whiteness studies and of *Forrest Gump*'s appropriation of racialized U.S. history, Wiegman outlines how particularity is not the opposite of the universal. Instead, it is the site that affords white power its historical and political elasticity, the site for the emergence of histories and inequalities of racial asymmetries and oppressions. By illuminating how antiracist whiteness is constructed through analogies with the injury and minoritization of racialized minorities in ways that reinscribe the unified, masculinist humanist subject, Wiegman suggests that particularism in itself is insufficient for anti-racism.

Lindon Barrett argues that African American Studies privileges the starkest symptomatic drives of the insistent, mass violence by which Western modernity reiterates itself. Documenting that violence through an analysis of the historical role of race in modern Western commodity fetishism, he carefully critiques the ways in which the rationalizing of "the oppression of people of color" reiterates modern Western subjectivity. Barrett draws on Slavoj Žižek to constitute a more unruly African American Studies in which desire and the subject may become recalcitrant to being mapped by the administrative and intellectual taxonomies of the academy and yet still constitute communities of social justice.

Robert DeChaine works between border studies and communication studies to critique the turn towards borderlessness in postmodern figurations, taking for his central case study the medical humanitarian group *Médecins Sans Frontières* (Doctors Without Borders) and the *sans frontiérism* (without borders) movement its has spawned. Critical of that organization's universalist assumption of a human that preexists the political, DeChaine follows political geographers and others in arguing for the presence of the political in all constitutions of spatial relations. Fostered by postmodern scholarship, *sans frontiérism*'s affect-charged challenge to difference can also be read as a mode of discipline that, in the name of humanity, insists that all space be available to the homogenizing reach of culturally specific norms.

Leila Neti's comparison of black internationalism in the first half of the twentieth century with contemporary interdisciplinary academic movements suggests the need for academics to accommodate diverse sites of knowledge production within a coherent analytic structure that creates contact points while also allowing for necessary spaces of difference. Neti's analysis attends to the risk of working with stable categories of discipline and nation even while attempting to displace the power dynamics of center and periphery that they install. By contrasting W. E. B. Du Bois's vision for global solidarity with the cosmopolitanism of Kwame Anthony Appiah, Bruce Robbins, and others, she argues that examinations of violence, power, and race must avoid normalizing universalisms in favor of productive solidarities. Neti looks to African American involvement in global anticolonial causes as offering a possible resolution to the debate about universalism and particularism that perplexes social justice movements. That model of dialogue within difference, she suggests, might also serve interdisciplinary endeavors as they attempt to create viable points of contact across epistemological borders.

The successful conservative counteroffensive on the advances made by progressive social movements inside and outside the academy comes under scrutiny by Messer-Davidow. She takes as her main case study the retrenchments in accessibility to higher education for racial minorities, single parents, and low- to middle-income students that have weakened egalitarian claims to social justice. Arguing that some research must be written for deployment in public and policy-making arenas, Messer-Davidow demands accountability to social justice concerns from academics, and demonstrates that real-world problems are complicated cross-sector phenomena that must be understood through an interdisciplinary or multidisciplinary approach.

Miranda Joseph's account of one attempt to defend interdisciplinary programs in a time of shrinking university budgets is a cautionary tale of the increasing commodification of scholarship. Even fields such as cultural studies, founded on the critique of commodification, find themselves in danger of being domesticated as interdisciplinarity becomes a rubric for collaboration across the nonprofit/for-profit border, in a manner that renders cross-sector collaboration little more than a business model. Meanwhile, accounting mechanisms used to measure the performance and hence the value of academic programs cannot accommodate the questioning of epistemological foundations that does not translate easily into "real world" (which too often means revenue producing) applications. Nevertheless, Joseph maintains that because scholars do not have the luxury of believing themselves distanced from the market, we must attempt to shape the terms on which our work is counted and translated.

In an afterword inspired by the essays, Ranu Samantrai reflects on the indeterminate relation between scholarship and activism. Using as her example one of the many recent controversies about cultural expressions that exacerbate tensions between majority and minority constituencies, she notes that scholarship and activism each fails to provide the certainty needed by each other: scholarship cannot stabilize the truth on which activism relies, and activism is not able to orient scholarship on a clear course between incommensurate claims for justice. Instead of seeking their unification, she suggests that their common hope of a just society is served best when each functions as a challenge to the other, in a collaboration grounded in mutual provocation.

Taken together, the papers of *Interdisciplinarity and Social Justice* render visible the violences, exclusions, power differentials, and occluded objects of knowledge that disciplinary and many interdisciplinary knowledge practices refuse to acknowledge. As the crisis of legitimacy for the modern academy continues apace, its claim to neutrality and the objectivity of Enlightenment-derived forms of science seems decreasingly convincing amidst the ongoing proliferation and promiscuity of interdisciplinary knowledge practices. The demand for accountability to the changing epistemological landscape, whether aimed at disciplines or at interdisciplinary fields, works against the domestication of knowledge that inevitably accompanies institutional success. For interdisciplinary methods that continue to rely on objectivity, that demand may come from critics of modern epistemes who caution against the risk of installing universalisms that subtly reinforce unequal power relations. Or, for interdisciplinary practices that develop new protocols for logic and epistemology, new constitutions of social relations, and new conceptions of justice, the demand may come from critics who point out a certain failure to engage with pragmatic and even urgent needs in what some see as the "real." Each of the papers in this volume asks that moves toward interdisciplinarity in the academy and in social movements be accountable to that once-stable, now less-easily-assumed, less-readily-knowable, and perhaps ever-elusive criterion of social justice. How will we respond?

Notes

1. We have in mind such indictments of the disciplines as the argument that the schemas for racial and gender hierarchies that confirmed the lesser civilizational status of non-Europeans, women, and the working class came from the human sciences. But for arguments against the claim that disciplines are complicit in inegalitarian social relations, see, among many others, Anderson and Valente.

2. One measure of the debate about the necessarily compromised politics of the process of achieving "success" in the academy (departmental status with tenure lines, journals, professional associations, and so forth) is the proliferation of terms naming the phenomena of interdisciplinarity. Some object to "interdisciplinary" because it suggests innovation limited to interaction between already established disciplines; indeed, we prefer "multidisciplinary" as the more accurate name for that phenomenon. Some opt for "transdisciplinary," "postdisciplinary," or even "antidisciplinary" to reject the implication that fields such as cultural studies or women's studies have become little more than one more domesticated academic endeavor among already accepted disciplines. We prefer to reserve "interdisciplinary" for those fields producing new forms of knowledge that move both education and social movements towards greater social justice. For further discussion of the terms, see Bowman, Moran, Newell, and Thompson-Klein, among others.

3. Although Klein notes the sudden increases in funding for such in the 1960s and 1970s, she is unable to explain their causes or to explain the skyrocketing interest in extradisciplinary research (*Interdisciplinarity* 35–37). Her reading of the critiques of the modern academy by ethnic studies and feminist critics reduces those critiques to calls for pluralism without responding to the significant criticisms of educational institutions that they formulated (95).

4. Although signs of success of progressive student movements, such changes were also intended, in the words of the Organisation for Economic Co-operation and Development (OECD), to "de-fuse the student rebellion" (Michaud et al. 12).

5. As Soldatenko argues in the present volume, the precise link between the rejection of disciplinary knowledge practices and claims of interdisciplinarity was not always carefully articulated, but the link was widely argued and led to important institutional changes in the academy.

6. To our regret, the perspectives of this important group are missing from the current collection.

7. We are aware of the objection that the reliance on theory indicates the persistence of androcentrism, class elitism, and Eurocentrism or white supremacy, because much of what counts as theory draws on the philosophical writings of economically privileged white males of Europe and many of its practitioners are well educated, economically privileged whites, or economically privileged members of other racial groups (hooks, "Cultural Studies" 128–33; "Postmodern Blackness";

Cook-Lynn 124–25; Smith 14, 28–40). Such objections often overlook the well-known ways in which theory has been used to attack racism (Delgado; Donaldson; Dyer; Gilroy), androcentrism (Boxer; Berger, Wallis, and Watson; Fraser), class elitism (Marx; Spivak, "Subaltern"), and Eurocentrism itself (Cixous and Clément 70–71; Derrida, "White" 213; R. Young). These critiques also often assume that theory can be distinguished clearly from activism or practice, assumptions that Marx and many others who combined theory and practice would reject. The prominence of theory in interdisciplinary scholarship may also be understood within a Eurocentric history of the academy as a return to the central role of critique in knowledge protocols and social justice work. If philosophy provided the synthesizing, critical frame for the European and classical models of knowledge and education, if only for male social elites, theory would seem to be a likely replacement candidate for those who wish to see knowledge production and social practice held accountable by some synthesizing critique (Zavarzadeh; Wiegman, "Progress of Gender" 120–21, 108, 127; Spivak, *Critique*; Ransom). Moreover, much theory in interdisciplinary fields takes as its explicit objective the imperative to reach well beyond its modern European limits in order to reconstitute, on multiple fronts, the limits of critique.

    8. Similar practices of indeterminacy have been influential in critical legal studies (Derrida, "Force of Law"; Dalton; Cornell, Rosenfeld, Carlson), and in numerous other interdisciplinary fields.

Works Cited

Acree, Eric. "Spotlight on the Africana Library." Ithaca, 2004. Web site. IRIS News and Notes. Cornell University Library. 8 Nov. 2007 <http://www.library.cornell.edu/iris/archives/notes2/notes_042004.html>.

Ali, Tariq and Susan Watkins. *1968: Marching in the Streets*. New York: Free Press, 1998.

Althusser, Louis. "Ideology and Ideological State Apparatuses." *Lenin and Philosophy, and Other Essays*. Trans. Ben Brewster. New York: Monthly Review Press, 1972. 127–86.

Anderson, Amanda, and Joseph Valente, eds. *Disciplinarity at the Fin De Siècle*. Princeton: Princeton UP, 2002.

Anzaldúa, Gloria. *Borderlands/La Frontera: The New Mestiza*. San Francisco: Spinsters/Aunt Lute, 1987.

Appadurai, Arjun. "Diversity and Disciplinarity as Cultural Artifacts." *Disciplinarity and Dissent in Cultural Studies*. Ed. Cary Nelson and Dilip Parameshwar Gaonkar. New York: Routledge, 1996. 23–36.

Badiou, Alain. "Truths and Justice." *Metapolitics*. Trans. Jason Barker. New York: Verso, 2006 (1998).

Bennett, Tony. "Cultural Studies: A Reluctant Discipline." *Cultural Studies* 12.4 (1998): 528–45.

Berger, Maurice, Brian Wallis, and Simon Watson, eds. *Constructing Masculinity*. New York: Routledge, 1995.

Bono, James J., Tim Dean, and Ewa Plonowska Ziarek. "Introduction: Future, Heternomy, Invention." *A Time for the Humanities: Futurity and the Limits of Autonomy*. Ed. James J. Bono, Tim Dean, and Ewa Plonowska Ziarek. New York: Fordham UP, 2008. 1–14.

Bourdieu, Pierre. *Homo Academicus*. Stanford: Stanford UP, 1988.

Bowman, Paul. " 'Alarming and Calming, Sacred and Accursed'—the Proper Impropriety of Interdisciplinarity." *Cultural Studies, Interdisciplinarity and Translation*. Ed. Stefan Herbrechter. New York: Rodopi, 2002. 55–71.

———. "Alterdisciplinarity." *Culture, Theory & Critique*. 49.1 (2008): 93–110.

Boxer, Marilyn J. *When Women Ask the Questions: Creating Women's Studies in America*. Baltimore: Johns Hopkins UP, 1998.

Brantlinger, Patrick. *Crusoe's Footprints: Cultural Studies in Britain and America*. New York: Routledge, 1990.

Brown, Wendy. "The Impossibility of Women's Studies." *differences: A journal of Feminist Cultural Studies* 9.3 (1997): 79–101.

Butler, Judith. "Against Proper Objects." *differences: A journal of Feminist Cultural Studies* 6.2–3 (1994): 1–26.

———. "Doing Justice to Someone." *GLQ: A Journal of Gay and Lesbian Studies* 7.4 (2001): 621–36.

Carroll, David. "Rephrasing the Political with Kant and Lyotard: From Aesthetic to Political Judgement." *Diacritics* 14.3 (1984): 74–88.

Carson, Rachel. *Silent Spring*. Boston: Houghton Mifflin, 1962.

Castronovo, Russ. "Within the Veil of Interdisciplinary Knowledge? Jefferson, Du Bois, and the Negation of Politics." *New Literary History*. 31.4 (2000): 781–804.

Caute, David. *The Year of the Barricades: A Journey through 1968*. New York: Harper & Row, 1988.

Certeau, Michel de. *The Practice of Everyday Life*. Trans. Steven Rendall. Berkeley: U of California P, 1984.

Chaturvedi, Vinayak, ed. *Mapping Subaltern Studies and the Postcolonial*. New York: Verso, 2000.

Chow, Rey. "The Politics and Pedagogy of Asian Literatures in American Universities." *Writing Diaspora: Tactics of Intervention in Contemporary Cultural Studies*. Bloomington: Indiana UP, 1993. 120–43.

———. *Writing Diaspora: Tactics of Intervention in Contemporary Cultural Studies*. Bloomington: Indiana UP, 1993.

Cixous, Hélène, and Catherine Clément. *The Newly Born Woman*. Trans. Betsy Wing. Manchester: Manchester UP, 1986.

Clifford, James. "Introduction: Partial Truths." *Writing Culture: The Poetics and Politics of Ethnography: A School of American Research Advanced Seminar.* Ed. James Clifford and George E. Marcus. Berkeley: U of California P, 1986. 1–26.

Cohen, Cathy J. "Punks, Bulldaggers, and Welfare Queens: The Radical Potential of Queer Politics." *GLQ: A Journal of Gay and Lesbian Studies* 3 (1997): 437–65.

Cohen, Julie A. "Reforming the University: Student Protests and the Demand for a 'Relevant' Curriculum." *Student Protest: The Sixties and After.* Ed. Gerard DeGroot. New York: Longman, 1998. 153–68.

Combahee River Collective. "A Black Feminist Statement." *All The Women Are White, All the Blacks Are Men, but Some of Us Are Brave: Black Women's Studies.* Ed. Patricia Bell Scott, Gloria T. Hull, and Barbara Smith. New York: The Feminist Press at the City University of New York, 1982. 13–22.

Committee, Columbia Strike Coordinating. "Six Demands." New York City, 1968. Web site. n.a. 9 Nov. 2007 <http://www-personal.umd.umich.edu/~ppennock/doc-Columbia.htm>.

Cook-Lynn, Elizabeth. "American Indian Intellectualism and the New Indian Story." *Natives and Academics: Researching and Writing About American Indians.* Ed. Devon Mihesuah. Lincoln: U of Nebraska P, 1998. 111–38.

Corber, Robert, and Stephen Valocchi, eds. *Queer Studies: An Interdisciplinary Reader.* Malden: Blackwell, 2003.

Cornell, Drucilla, Michel Rosenfeld, and David Gray Carlson. *Deconstruction and the Possibility of Justice.* New York: Routledge, 1992.

Dalton, Clare. "An Essay in the Deconstruction of Contract Doctrine." *Yale Law Journal* 94 (1985): 997–1114.

Daston, Lorraine. "The Academies and the Unity of Knowledge: The Disciplining of the Disciplines." *differences: A journal of Feminist Cultural Studies* 10.2 (1998): 67–86.

Davis, Lennard, ed. *The Disability Studies Reader.* 2nd ed. New York: Routledge, 2006.

Deleuze, Gilles, and Felix Guattari. *A Thousand Plateaus: Capitalism and Schizophrenia.* Trans. Brian Massumi. Vol. 2. London: Athlone Press, 1988.

Delgado, Richard, ed. *Critical Race Theory.* Philadelphia: Temple UP, 1995.

———. "Introduction." *Critical Race Theory.* Ed. Richard Delgado. Philadelphia: Temple UP, 1995. xiii–xvi.

Deloria, Vine, Jr. "Ethnoscience and Indian Realities." *Spirit and Reason: The Vine Deloria, Jr., Reader.* Golden, CO: Fulcrum Publishing, 1999 (1992). 63–71.

Derrida, Jacques. "Force of Law: The 'Mystical Foundation of Authority.' " Trans. Mary Quantance. *Cardoza Law Review* 11.5–6 (1990): 921–1045.

————. "White Mythology." In *Margins—of Philosophy*. Trans. Alan Bass. Chicago: U of Chicago P, 1982. 207–71.

Devi, Mahasweta. *Imaginary Maps: Three Stories*. Trans. and Intro. Gayatri Chakravorty Spivak. New York: Routledge, 1995.

Donaldson, Laura E. "The Breasts of Columbus: A Political Anatomy of Postcolonialism and Feminist Religious Discourse." *Postcolonialism, Feminism, and Religious Discourse*. Ed. Laura E. Donaldson and Kwok Pui-lan. New York: Routledge, 2002. 41–61.

Donaldson, Laura E., and Kwok Pui-lan. "Introduction." *Postcolonialism, Feminism, and Religious Discourse*. Ed. Laura E. and Kwok Pui-lan Donaldson. New York: Routledge, 2002. 1–38.

Dyer, Richard. *White*. New York: Routledge, 1997.

Eagleton, Terry. *Literary Theory: An Introduction*. Minneapolis: U of Minnesota P, 1983.

Editorial Staff, Asian American Political Alliance. "Asian Studies: The Concept of Asian Studies." *Roots: An Asian American Reader*. Asian American Political Alliance, 1.6 (Oct. 1969). Ed. Amy Tachiki, Eddie Wong, Franklin Odo, with Buck Wong. Los Angeles: UCLA Asian American Studies Center, 1971 (1969). 264–65.

Escobar, Arturo. *Encountering Development: The Making and Unmaking of the Third World*. Princeton Studies in Culture/Power/History. Princeton: Princeton UP, 1995.

Esteva, Gustavo. "Development." *The Development Dictionary*. Ed. Wolfgang Sachs: Zed Books, 1992. 6–25.

Feierman, Steven. "African Histories and the Dissolution of World History." *Africa and the Disciplines: The Contributions of Research in Africa to the Social Sciences and the Humanities*. Ed. Robert Bates, V. Y. Mudimbe, and Jean O'Barr. Chicago: U of Chicago P, 1993. 167–212.

Fish, Stanley. *Professional Correctness: Literary Studies and Political Change*. Cambridge: Harvard UP, 1995.

Flexner, Hans. "The Curriculum, the Disciplines, and Interdisciplinarity in Higher Education." *Interdisciplinarity and Higher Education*. Ed. Joseph J. Kocklemans. University Park: Pennsylvania State UP, 1979.

Foucault, Michel. *The Archaeology of Knowledge and the Discouse on Language*. Trans. A. M. Sheridan Smith. New York: Pantheon Books, 1972.

————. *The Birth of the Clinic: An Archaeology of Medical Perception*. Presses Universitaire de France, 1963. Trans. A. M. Sheridan Smith. New York: Vintage, 1973.

————. *Discipline and Punish: The Birth of the Prison*. Trans. Alan Sheridan. New York: Vintage Books, 1979.

————. "The Subject and Power." *Michel Foucault: Beyond Structuralism and Hermeneutics*. Ed. Hubert L. and Paul Rabinow Dreyfus. Chicago: U of Chicago P, 1983.

Fraser, Nancy. *Justice Interruptus: Critical Reflections on the "Postsocialist" Condition*. New York: Routledge, 1997.

Gardner, Judith Kegan, ed. *Masculinity Studies and Feminist Theory: New Directions*. New York: Columbia UP, 2002.

Gasché, Rodolphe. "European Memories: Jan Patočka and Jacques Derrida on Responsibility." *Derrida and the Time of the Political*. Ed. Pheng Cheah and Suzanne Guerlac. Duke UP, 2009. 136–157.

Gilroy, Paul. *The Black Atlantic: Modernity and Double Consciousness*. Cambridge: Harvard UP, 1993.

Guha, Ranajit, and Gayatri Chakravorty Spivak, eds. *Selected Subaltern Studies*. New York: Oxford UP, 1988.

Halberstam, Judith. *Female Masculinity*. Durham: Duke UP, 1998.

Hall, Stuart. "The Emergence of Cultural Studies and the Crisis of the Humanities." *October* 53 (1990): 11–90.

Haney López, Ian. *White by Law: The Legal Construction of Race*. New York: New York UP, 1996.

Haraway, Donna Jeanne. "Situated Knowledges: The Science Question in Feminism and the Privilege of Partial Perspective." *Simians, Cyborgs, and Women: The Reinvention of Nature*. New York: Routledge, 1991. 183–201.

Harding, Sandra G. "Introduction: Eurocentric Scientific Illiteracy—a Challenge for the World Community." *The "Racial" Economy of Science*. Ed. Sandra Harding. Bloomington: Indiana UP, 1993. 1–22.

Haskell, Thomas. *The Emergence of the Professional Social Sciences*. Urbana: U of Illinois P, 1977.

hooks, bell. "Culture to Culture: Ethnography and Cultural Studies as Critical Intervention." *Yearning: Race, Gender, and Cultural Politics*. Boston: South End Press, 1990. 123–33.

———. "Postmodern Blackness." *Yearning: Race, Gender, and Cultural Politics*. Boston: South End Press, 1990. 23–32.

Jeffords, Susan. *The Remasculinization of America: Gender and the Vietnam War*. Bloomington: Indiana UP, 1989.

Joseph, Miranda. "Analogy and Complicity: Women's Studies, Lesbian/Gay Studies, and Capitalism." *Women's Studies on Its Own*. Ed. Robyn Wiegman. Durham: Duke UP, 2002. 267–92.

Kaplan, Caren and Inderpal Grewal. "Transnational Practices and Interdisciplinary Feminist Scholarship: Refiguring Women's and Gender Studies." *Women's Studies on Its Own*. Ed. Robyn Wiegman. Durham: Duke University, 2002. 66–81.

Katsiaficas, George. *The Imagination of the New Left: A Global Analysis of 1968*. Boston: South End Press, 1987.

Kirsch, Max. *Queer Theory and Social Change*. New York: Routledge, 2000.

Klein, Julie Thompson. *Crossing Boundaries: Knowledge, Disciplinarities, and Interdisciplinarities*. Charlottesville: UP of Virginia, 1996.

————. *Interdisciplinarity: History, Theory, and Practice*. Detroit: Wayne State UP, 1990.

Kocklemans, Joseph J., ed. *Interdisciplinarity and Higher Education*. University Park: Pennsylvania State UP, 1979.

Leitch, Vincent. "Postmodern Interdisciplinarity." *Theory Matters*. New York: Routledge, 2003. 165–71.

Loo, Chalsa, and Don Mar. "Research and Asian Americans: Social Change or Empty Prize?" *Amerasia Journal* 12.2 (1985–86): 85–93.

Lyotard, Jean-François. *Just Gaming*. Minneapolis: U Minnesota P, 1985.

————. *The Postmodern Condition: A Report on Knowledge*. Minneapolis: U of Minnesota P, 1984.

Marx, Karl. "Manifesto of the Communist Party." *The Marx-Engles Reader*. Ed. Robert C. Tucker. 2nd ed. New York: W. W. Norton and Company, 1978 (1972). 473–500.

McClintock, Anne. "The Angel of Progress: Pitfalls of the Term 'Post-Colonialism.' " *Colonial Discourse and Post-Colonial Theory: A Reader*. Ed. Patrick Williams and Laura Chrisman. New York: Columbia UP, 1994. 291–304.

McRuer, Robert. "As Good as It Gets: Queer Theory and Critical Disability." *GLQ: A Journal of Gay and Lesbian Studies Special Issue: Desiring Disability: Queer Theory Meets Disability Studies* 9.1–2 (2003): 79–106.

————. *Crip Theory: Cultural Signs of Queerness and Disability*. New York: New York UP, 2006.

Messer-Davidow, Ellen. *Disciplining Feminism: From Social Activism to Academic Discourse*. Durham: Duke UP, 2002.

Messer-Davidow, Ellen, David Shumway, and David Sylvan, eds. *Knowledges: Historical and Critical Studies in Disciplinarity*. Charlottesville: U of Virginia P, 1993.

Michaud, Guy, Léo Apostel, Guy Berger, and Asa Briggs, eds. *Interdisciplinarity: Problems of Teaching and Research in Universities*. Paris: Organization for Economic Co-operation and Development Publications, 1972.

Miller, Maurice Lim. "Whom Should Academic Researchers Serve?" *Amerasia Journal* 12.2 (1985–86): 95–99.

Milner, A. "Can Cultural Studies Be Disciplined? Or Should It Be Punished?" *Continuum* 13.2 (1999): 271–81.

Mitchell, David T., and Sharon L. Snyder. "Introduction: Disability Studies and the Double Bind of Representation." *The Body and Physical Difference: Discourses of Disability*. Ed. David T. Mitchell and Sharon L. Snyder. Ann Arbor: U of Michigan P, 1997. 1–33.

Moraga, Cherrie, and Gloria Anzaldúa, eds. *This Bridge Called My Back: Writings by Radical Women of Color*. New York: Kitchen Table, Women of Color Press, 1983.

Moran, Joe. *Interdisciplinarity (The New Critical Idiom)*. New York: Routledge, 2002.

Mouffe, Chantal. "Which Ethics for Democracy?" *The Turn to Ethics*. Ed. Marjorie Garber, Beatrice Hanssen, and Rebecca L. Walkowitz. New York: Routledge, 2000. 85–94.

Moya, Paula M. L., and Michael Roy Hames-Garcia. *Reclaiming Identity: Realist Theory and the Predicament of Postmodernism*. Berkeley: U of California P, 2000.

Naison, Mark. *White Boy: A Memoir*. Philadelphia: Temple UP, 2002.

Nancy, Jean-Luc. "Answering for Sense." *A Time for the Humanities: Futurity and the Limits of Autonomy*. Ed. James J. Bono, Tim Dean, and Ewa Plonowska Ziarek. New York: Fordham UP, 2008. 84–93.

———. *The Creation of the World or Globalization*. Trans. and Intro. François Raffoul and David Pettigrew. Albany: SUNY P, 2007.

Newell, William H., ed. *Interdisciplinarity: Essays from the Literature*. New York: College Entrance Examination Board, 1998.

O'Sullivan, Simon. "Cultural Studies as Rhizome—Rhizomes in Cultural Studies." *Cultural Studies, Interdisciplinarity, and Translation*. Ed. Stefan Herbrechter. New York: Rodopi, 2002.

Omatsu, Glenn. "The 'Four Prisons' and the Movements of Liberation: Asian American Activism from the 1960s to the 1990s." *The State of Asian America: Activism and Resistance in the 1990s*. Ed. Karin Aguilar-San Juan. Boston: South End Press, 1994. 19–70.

Perez, Emma. *The Decolonial Imaginary: Writing Chicanas into History*. Bloomington: U of Indiana P, 1999.

Pletsch, Carl E. "The Three Worlds, or the Division of Social Scientific Labor, Circa 1950–1975." *Comparative Study of Society and History* 23 (1981): 565–90.

Radway, Janice. " 'What's in a Name?' Presidential Address to the American Studies Association, 20 November, 1998." *American Quarterly* 51.1 (1999): 1–32.

Rafael, Vincente L. "Cultures of Area Studies in the United States." *Social Text* 12.41 (1994): 91–111.

Ransom, John. "Introduction: Rethinking 'Critique.' " *Foucault's Discipline: The Politics of Subjectivity*. Durham: Duke UP, 1997. 1–9.

Rasmussen, Birgit Brander. *The Making and Unmaking of Whiteness*. Durham: Duke UP, 2001.

Robinson, Amy. "The Ethics of Analogy: Critical Discourse on Race and Sexuality." Stanford Humanities Center: Unpublished lecture, 1997.

Rosaldo, Renato. *Culture and Truth: The Remaking of Social Analysis*. Boston: Beacon Press, 1989.

Said, Edward W. *Orientalism*. New York: Vintage Books, 1979.

Sbert, José. "Progress." *The Development Dictionary*. Ed. Wolfgang Sachs: Zed Books, 1992. 192–205.

Scott, Joan Wallach. *Gender and the Politics of History*. 1988. New York: Columbia UP, 1999.

Sedgwick, Eve Kosofsky. *Between Men: English Literature and Male Homosocial Desire*. New York: Columbia UP, 1985.

———. *Epistemology of the Closet*. Berkeley: University of California Press, 1990.

Shiva, Vandana. *Monocultures of the Mind: Perspectives on Biodiversity and Biotechnology*. Atlantic Highlands: Zed Books, 1993.

Shumway, David R. *Creating American Civilization: A Genealogy of American Literature as an Academic Discipline*. Minneapolis: U of Minnesota P, 1994.

Shumway, David R., and Ellen Messer-Davidow. "Disciplinarity: An Introduction." *Poetics Today* 12.2 (1991): 201–25.

Smith, Linda Tuhiwai. *Decolonizing Methodologies*. New York: Zed Books, 1999.

Spelman, Elizabeth V. *Repair: The Impulse to Restore in a Fragile World*. Boston: Beacon, 2002.

Spivak, Gayatri Chakravorty. *A Critique of Postcolonial Reason: Toward a History of the Vanishing Present*. Cambridge: Harvard UP, 1999.

———. *Death of a Discipline*. Wellek Library Lectures in Critical Theory. New York: Columbia UP, 2003.

———. "French Feminisms Revisited." *Outside in the Teaching Machine*. New York: Routledge, 1993. 141–71.

———. "More on Power/Knowledge." *Outside in the Teaching Machine*. New York: Routledge, 1993. 25–52.

———. "The Politics of Translation." *Outside in the Teaching Machine*. New York: Routledge, 1993. 17–32.

———. *The Post-Colonial Critic: Interviews, Strategies, Dialogues*. Ed. Sarah Harasym. New York: Routledge, 1990.

———. "Subaltern Studies: Deconstructing Historiography." *The Spivak Reader: Selected Works of Gayatri Chakravorty Spivak*. Ed. Donna Landry and Gerald M. MacLean. New York: Routledge, 1996. 334.

Stanton, Donna C., and Abigail J. Stewart, eds. *Feminisms in the Academy*. Ann Arbor: U of Michigan P, 1995.

Steinmetz, George. "Decolonizing German Theory: An Introduction." *Postcolonial Studies* 9.1 (2006): 3–13.

Steinmetz, George, ed. *The Politics of Method in the Human Sciences: Positivism and Its Epistemological Others*. Durham: Duke UP, 2005.

Stryker, Susan. "(De)Subjugated Knowledges: An Introduction to Transgender Studies." *The Transgender Studies Reader*. Ed. Susan and Stephen Whittle Stryker. New York: Routledge, 2006. 1–17.

Stryker, Susan, and Stephen Whittle, eds. *The Transgender Studies Reader*. New York: Routledge, 2006.

Sullivan, Nikki. *A Critical Introduction to Queer Theory*. New York: New York UP, 2003.

Taussig, Michael T. *Shamanism, Colonialism, and the Wild Man: A Study in Terror and Healing*. Chicago: U of Chicago P, 1991.

Tololyan, Kachig. "The Nation State and Its Others: In Lieu of a Preface." *diaspora* 1.1 (1991): 3–7.

Unger, Roberto Mangabeira. *The Critical Legal Studies Movement.* Cambridge: Harvard UP, 1986.

Wang, Ling-chi. "Chronology of Ethnic Studies at U.C. Berkeley." Berkeley, 1997. Web site. Department of Ethnic Studies, U.C. Berkeley. 9 Nov. 2007 <http://ethnicstudies.berkeley.edu/chronology/>.

Warner, Michael, ed. *Fear of a Queer Planet: Queer Politics and Social Theory.* Minneapolis: U of Minnesota P, 1993.

Weingart, Peter, and Nico Stehr. *Practising Interdisciplinarity.* Toronto: U of Toronto P, 2000.

White, Patrick. "Sex Education; or, How the Blind Became Heterosexual." *GLQ: A Journal of Gay and Lesbian Studies Special Issue: Desiring Disability: Queer Theory Meets Disability Studies* 9.1–2 (2003): 133–47.

Whitson, Helene, and Wesley Kyles. "On Strike! Shut It Down!" San Francisco, 1999. Web site. J. Paul Leonard Library, San Francisco State University. 9 Nov. 2007 <http://www.library.sfsu.edu/exhibits/strike/case3-text.html>.

Wiegman, Robyn. "Introduction." *Women's Studies on Its Own.* Ed. Robyn Wiegman. Durham: Duke UP, 2002. 1–44.

———. "Object Lessons: Men, Masculinity, and the Sign of Women," *Signs* 26.2 (2001): 355–88.

———. "The Progress of Gender: Whither 'Women'?" *Women's Studies on Its Own.* Ed. Robyn Wiegman. Durham: Duke UP, 2002. 106–40.

Willett, Cynthia. *The Soul of Justice: Social Bonds and Racial Hubris.* Ithaca: Cornell UP, 2001.

Williams, Raymond. *The Long Revolution.* London: Chatto & Windus, 1961.

———. *Marxism and Literature.* Oxford: Oxford UP, 1977.

Young, Iris Marion. *Justice and the Politics of Difference.* Princeton: Princeton UP, 1990.

Young, Robert. *White Mythologies: Writing History and the West.* New York: Routledge, 2004 (1990).

Zavarzadeh, Mas'ud, and Donald Morton. *Theory as Resistance: Politics and Culture after (Post)Structuralism.* Critical Perspectives. Ed. Douglas Kellner. New York: The Guilford Press, 1994.

Ziarek, Ewa Płonowska. *An Ethics of Dissensus: Postmodernity, Feminism, and the Politics of Radical Democracy.* Stanford: Stanford UP, 2001.

Zolov, Eric. "Protest and Counterculture in the 1968 Student Movement in Mexico." *Student Protest: The Sixties and After.* Ed. Gerard DeGroot. New York: Longman, 1998. 70–84.

Section I

Critiques of Disciplinarity

Chapter Two

Metaphors of Globalization

Lisa Lowe

A second class of words in which comparisons are made. The pond
after rain, a lily.
    Watershed and water level. Coinciding glint of scales and scrap-
ers. Conjectural poles.

—Myung-mi Kim, "Exordium"

On a trip to London in the winter of 2003, I viewed Anish Kapoor's
sculpture "Marsyas" at the Tate Modern Museum. Kapoor's astonishing
piece occupied the entire length of the enormous 150-meter-long and 35-
meter-high Turbine Hall that had once housed the gigantic turbines of
the nineteenth-century Bankside Power Station. Because of its impressive
size, made of three steel rings joined together by a single span of dark red
PVC membrane, and occupying the entire length of the enormous hall, it
was impossible to view "Marsyas" in its totality from any single position;
it was necessary to walk its length, passing underneath it, over it, and
around it. Viewing the sculpture from a number of perspectives, it evoked,
all at once, *both* the vast hulls and masts of the seventeenth-century ships
that had brought African slaves and then Asian indentured workers to
the colonized Americas, *and* the twenty-first-century telecommunications
technologies whose reaches permit the worker in the metropolis to call
her mother back in the village. The ensemble of fabric and steel textures
evoked both a premodern sense of nature and the late modern devices of
industry. Furthermore, the dramatic contrasts of the physical presence of
the massive red sculpture and the negative space of the cavernous hall in

which it was built thematized the violent material contrasts of the last three centuries: the promises that progress, development, and expansion would bring increasing freedom and prosperity, contradicted by the terrors of genocide, poverty, and war.

I open my discussion with this work because it not only captures the scale, movement, uncertainty, and contradictions that are indices of what we have termed for some decades "globalization," but it also thematizes *the problem of representation itself* with respect to our late modern present. That is, we would hardly expect artists to represent the contemporary global condition through realist notions of verisimilitude. Rather, the sculpture by Kapoor, a Bombay-born son of a Hindu father and Iraqi mother and émigré to Britain, uncannily evoked the "structure of feeling" of a globalization simultaneously riven and interconnected (Lowe, "Immigrant Literatures"; Raymond Williams), Raymond Williams having elaborated the concept of a "structure of feeling" as "a record of the felt sense of the quality of life at a particular time and place . . . social experiences *in solution*, not yet *precipitated*." The sculpture as viewed from both above and below and the

impossibility of occupying more than a single perspective at any given time mediated in a striking manner not merely the *multiperspectival*, but the *geohistorical* condition of globalization (Taylor). By *geohistorical*, we mean that globalization is not merely a contemporary stage, but rather the longer, extended set of diverse processes that have linked multiple spaces through logics at once political, economic, and cultural. Neither evenly integrating nor rendering homogeneous all parts of the world, these processes have varied in time and location and taken place quite differently in unlike parts of the world. Each space, perspective, and temporality brought together through global processes has a presence in making and transforming our contemporary world condition. Globalization encompasses captive enslaved Africans, Asian "coolies," early northeastern American garment workers, women assembling VCRs in Baja California *maquiladoras,* indigenous shrimping practices in Colombia, and the latest biomedical technologies for genetic engineering. It includes the Nigerian village, the Los Angeles suburbs, and the global cities of New York, London, Tokyo, or São Paolo. In this sense, globalization cannot be represented iconically or totalized through a single developmental narrative; it is unevenly grasped, and its representations are necessarily partial, built on the absence of an apprehensible whole. There is no single history of who or what is global, but rather it requires a more complicated set of representations that not only mediates its "structure of feeling" but also inaugurates a critical genealogy of the representational traditions that have constituted, however inadequately, the manners of knowing its diverse conditions.

If Kapoor's sculpture explicitly thematizes that representing globalization is an *aesthetic* problem, I am suggesting that representing globalization constitutes implicitly an *epistemological* problem of what can be known as well. Observing that the empirical social sciences within the U.S. university have resorted to *metaphors* to describe globalization, I distinguish this referential use of metaphor from the aesthetic practices of metaphor in culture and observe that cultural works often include a diversity of critical hermeneutics for reading globalization's conditions of both possibility and impossibility.[1] In the last twenty-five years, the scholarly disciplines of sociology, political science, economics, history, and geography, among others, have sought to define "globalization," describing a condition of unprecedented global exchange, interpenetration, conflict, and connection, characterized by movements of goods, peoples, and money. Yet mere global connection is hardly a recent phenomenon; in the ancient world, there were empires, conquests, slavery, trade, diasporas; European colonial expansion began in the sixteenth century, reaching its heights in the nineteenth century. Hence, with their representations of *globalization*, late-twentieth-century social scientists desired to name a specific shift: the way in which, since World War II and decolonization, there has been a transformation of nation-states into an international network of linked political economies, and within the last three decades, an acceleration in the scale, mode, volume, and degree of exchanges and interdependency. Scholars have sought to translate the unknowability of postmodern globalization into the terms of what modernity has known. Sociologists note that the worldwide reach of capitalism has exacerbated the cleavages and contradictions between traditional forms of human society and instrumental rational bureaucracies that Weber had already observed of the late nineteenth century (Wallerstein, *Modern World-System*; Sklair; Sassen). Economists measure increased gross domestic product, a consequence of processes like mixed production and flexible accumulation that, since the 1970s, have permitted very mobile capital to lay hold of specific forms of sometimes quite immobile labor, markets and materials in locations like export processing zones in Asia or Latin America, or immigrant enclaves in industrialized Europe or North America (Greider; Gray). In other instances, economists put forward data on consumption, employment, real wages, or imports and exports, however much this data cannot represent or measure the social costs of globalization, the destruction or depletion of community, environment or resources over time (Rodrik). Political scientists study governments, parties, and interactions of levels of state, as well as international law, diplomacy, and international organizations, and develop scientific models for understanding international political systems. In each of these, political scientists are guided by liberal political theory and its classic story of freedom acquired through the joining of like-minded individuals into a political society or state in order to protect their individual liberties (MacPherson); hence, liberal forms of government and state become an *ideal type* for measuring societies as they enter the international fold (Keohane and Nye). Historians excavate the past through the study of archives and form coherent narratives from linked sequences and patterns in events. Whereas nineteenth-century historians represented the progress of the modern era by documenting the development of the nation from its earlier, unenlightened past, global processes of the second half of the twentieth century have demanded of historians new forms of study that reach beyond the nation-state, seeking to represent relationships between cultures, regions, and economies that formed the conditions from which the modern world emerged (Chakrabarty). Since the late 1980s, anthropologists, who once employed the ideal type of Western industrialized society to study "traditional" non-Western cultures, have discussed the discrepancy of knowledges between modern and nonmodern cultures (Clifford; Clifford and Marcus; Asad). Cultural anthropology now references modernization as a history of asymmetrical power and has developed new ethnographic methods for studying the cultures that have emerged from the history of encounter.[2]

If the vast, shifting processes and conditions of globalization are in excess of the efforts to represent them, then perhaps all descriptions or explanations of globalization are either fragmentary, partial, or rhetorically displaced; that is, they are metaphors for globalization itself. Aristotle defined *metaphor* as "giving the thing a name that belongs to something else; the transference being either from genus to species, or from species to genus, or from species to species, or on grounds of analogy" (Preminger 490). The modern rhetorician Kenneth Burke discussed *metaphor*, and its variants, *metonymy, synechdoche, catachresis,* and so forth, as devices for seeing something in terms of something else: It brings out the thisness of a that, or the thatness of a this. It involves the "carrying over" of a term from one realm to another, a displacement that necessarily involves varying degrees of incongruity or lack of equivalence; the metaphor depends on an implicit acknowledgment that two realms compared are never identical (Burke 504). The "frisson" of the metaphor is that sensation in which similarity and difference coincide, or the sensation of the coincidence of both similarity and its "excess." Traditionally, metaphor has been represented as a trope of transference in which an unknown, or an imperfectly known, is described in terms of a known. Metaphors can also convey spatial orientations, like near-far or center-periphery. The linguist George Lakoff employs the term *ontological metaphors* to convey those instances when the experiences of those far away are rendered as if they were immediate, as if we experience their experiences ourselves (Lakoff and Johnson). Current electronic media and visual culture are, of course, replete with these metaphorical experiences. I use *metaphor*, then, not only as a versatile figure that attempts to translate globalization's unknown into the mundane terms of the known, but also as a figure that states the irreducibility of what it attempts to represent. The *metaphoricity* of globalization is the rhetorical proliferation of figures that attest to the desire to render what is not yet fathomed as objectively known. If the U.S. social sciences have been dramatically challenged to revise their paradigms in light of the processes and conditions of late-twentieth- to early-twenty-first-century globalization, in what sense is metaphoricity the sign of this revision? To renew the argument made quite persuasively by Hayden White some years ago about the poetics of nineteenth-century historical narratives: We commit a serious error if we understand metaphor to be the exclusive province of literary, cultural, or aesthetic language, a presumption that was at the heart of the nineteenth-century separation of science and art, and the consequent division of humanistic and scientific knowledges (White). Histories have forms, styles for "telling" the past, and conventions through which they successively reproduce what White called "the explanatory effect." Revising the narrative frameworks for understanding American slavery, Walter Johnson has termed this sometime violent process the "historical politics of time-making" (152). Modern history often portrays a single, secular human experience developed over time, putatively shared by all. Historians may aspire to realism and to represent events "as they actually happened," but they perform poetic, stylistic, and rhetorical acts to do so, and the manner in which they resort to such literary conventions changes over time in relation to the forces and imperatives of their moment. So it is not simply that late-twentieth-century social science descriptions of globalization must be understood as rhetorical and figurative, but also that the social sciences resort to metaphor precisely for the purpose of addressing "globalization," that is, exactly at the point at which the conditions they seek to explain exceed the modernist empirical social science paradigm.

Modern sociology emerged in the late nineteenth century as the scientific study of human social behavior and the structure of societies. Durkheim's pioneering use of empirical evidence and statistical material in the study of society, and Weber's methodology of historical comparative study based on the analytic construct of an *ideal type,* were fundamental to twentieth-century sociology and influenced other social sciences, like political science and economics (Durkheim; Giddens; Lemert). Weber's well-known thesis was that social behavior had come to be dominated more and more by goal-oriented rationality and instrumentality and less and less by traditional values or emotions, a tendency he named the "iron cage" of industrial society.[3] For the larger part of the twentieth century, social scientific paradigms relied on this unit of industrial society bounded within one nation and presumed what Akhil Gupta and James Ferguson have called the "isomorphism" of place, culture, language, and state. In this sense, the Weberian paradigm of comparison advanced an implicit *narrative* emplotting a development of societies from premodern to modern, investing a positive value in the trajectory of modernization. The *modern* became not merely the "ideal type" to be measured against, but the universal apex of development to be attained and achieved. In the first half of the twentieth century, social sciences not only privileged Western modernity, but also produced evidence that non-Western or nonmodern societies needed industrial development and social modernization. With the founding of area studies in U.S. universities during World War II and in its vast expansion and institutionalization in the postwar period of Soviet–U.S. confrontation, social science methodologies were adopted for the study of "areas" of keen interest to the United States, such as East Asia, Southeast Asia, South Asia, the Middle East, and Latin America (Breckenridge and van der Veer; Cumings; Miyoshi and Harootunian; Rafael).

Modernization studies epitomized the Western-centered developmentalism that cast societies in these non-Western "areas" as culturally different "latecomers." In the work of Marion Levy or Talcott Parsons, for example, the Asiatic or "oriental" was cast as successful "latecomer" to Western modernity, as opposed to the African or Muslim "deviance." Sociologists of religion like Robert Bellah (*Beyond Belief; Religion and Progress*) differentiated between the "this-worldly asceticism" of Protestant Christianity in the industrial West and the less modern, "world-rejecting" belief systems of non-Christian societies, going so far as to argue that the social and economic development in China and Japan was due to a "Protestant ethic analogy in Asia." Despite the many critiques of orientalist knowledge productions by Edward Said, Rey Chow, Talal Asad, and others, the contemporary "clash of civilizations" thesis revitalizes precisely this historical demonizing of Islam as an irrational "culture of violence" antagonized by the pressures of modernization. Contemporary comparative sociologists of religion (Juergensmeyer) frequently recur to this model of cultural difference, casting Islam as a resurgent religious fundamentalism in critical protest to the current materialism of globalization. Modernization approaches in area studies in effect created a global hierarchy of societies in which "non-modern" and "less modern" spaces were distinguished as *racially* different. "The *racial* [was] articulated as the category distinguishing modern technological and cultural conditions from those which are spatially adjacent to but temporally distant from modernity," Denise da Silva has observed.

This modernization model was firmly established in the U.S. sociological study of race and ethnicity as well. As Henry Yu and Roderick Ferguson have asserted, Chicago School sociologists in the early and mid-twentieth century studied "orientals" as *ethnic* groups who could become an assimilable "model minority," in relation to Negro *racial* difference constructed as irremediably, or "pathologically," deviant. Insofar as increased international immigration in the late twentieth century has rendered the U.S. national discussion of race and ethnicity more global and diversified, we might also say that a pluralistic discourse of "difference" continues to work through a *governmentality* that assimilates immigrant newcomers who resemble the normative *ideal type* and "racializes" those whose "cultural differences" seem too "different"—whether the alleged cultural difference inheres in a lack of literacy or education or a suspected threat to national security.

In the 1990s, the Gulbenkian Foundation commissioned a study (Mudimbe et al.) in which sociologists argued that changed geopolitical conditions in the post–World War II period both issued from and contributed to the radical altering of the social sciences, naming three developments after 1945 that profoundly affected the structure of the social sciences put into place in the preceding hundred years. The first was the change in world political structure, including the emergent economic strength of the United States after World War II within a world politically defined by the so-called Cold War between the United States and USSR and the decolonization movements and historical reassertion of non-European peoples in the world.

The second development was the largest expansion of the world's productive capacity and population it had ever known, between 1945 and 1970, involving a scalar expansion in nearly all spheres of human activity. The third was the quantitative and geographic spread of the university system, leading to a multiplication, however unevenly realized, across the developed and developing worlds, of the numbers of professional social scientists. Each of these three new global social realities, the commission argued, posed a problem for the social sciences, how they had been institutionalized, and how they explained "society."

As the social sciences attempt to keep pace with the shift, and to account for the history of relationships between cultures, regions, and economies that formed the conditions for the contemporary period, new ethnographies perform reciprocal or comparative studies of the people, places, and discoveries that had been "forgotten" in former accounts. If modern sociology before postwar globalization described society as rational, bureaucratic, separated into public and private spheres of activity, and bound within a single social world in one nation, then the global interdependencies and connections between and among regions and activities previously conceived as separate have challenged the sociological paradigm. For a sociology that tacitly assumed that human beings live in one national, rationally integrated social world at a time, cross-border relations, subcultures, transnational multilingual communities, and religious syncretism were all seen as idiosyncratic or problematic (Calhoun). Yet with contemporary globalization, the social sciences are increasingly pressured to make these the very phenomena through which the social must be understood. Not only is the notion of the individual moving in a linear fashion through a single, stable social totality eclipsed within the world of globalization, in which travel, transnational production, and international media make the world global and multiple, but many people may have always lived in multiple spaces and among differences of nation, language, religion, gender, race, and class (Lowe, "Utopia"). Faced with the challenges of describing explain these historical and contemporary phenomena, the social sciences have turned to metaphors.

Metaphoricity, then, names a tropological, but ultimately epistemological, dilemma of representing postmodern globalization; the rhetorical surplus expresses the still very "modern" desire to master what will not be mastered, to rationalize as comprehensible the incomprehensible. Among the range of social scientific discourses in which globalization is most commonly explained, we find metaphors of various kinds of accelerated motion: from the *migration* of workers, refugees, or cosmopolitans to the *circulation* of goods, products, and commodities; to the rapid electronic *transfers* of capital and commerce; from the *contagion* of diseases, from SARS to AIDS, to the telecommunication *flows* of images, information, and ideas; from the *spread* of world religions, from evangelical Christianity to fundamentalist Islam; from the *flexibility* of capital and post-Fordist mixed techniques that permits increases in both production and accumulation to the *flux* of shifts in national, regional, and international sovereignty, alliance, interdependence, and coalition. To convey, for example, the unprecedented migrations of laborers required for the global economy, social scientists employ metaphors that reference fluids in the human body, traffic on streets, routes of highways, speed of jet travel, the rootlessness of the nomad, and so forth. Yet, more frequently, the figurative strategies characterizing globalization are *metonymic* and *synechdochic*; that is, they employ variants of *metaphor* in which the ensemble is reduced to one idiom, or the part used to symbolize the whole.

Sociologists, for example, have invoked AIDS as a metaphor for globalization. Roland Robertson identified six phases of globalization—from early global exploration through European dominance to the Cold War—and invoked the figure of the AIDS epidemic to represent the sixth phase. For Robertson, the advent of AIDS represented not merely the rise of actual diseases and pandemics, but it also symbolized a "new" phase of risk and peril at a global level that included the revival of ethnic divisions and wars, the influences of global media, and the rise of militant fundamentalisms; AIDS was Robertson's metaphor for the insecurity of a world in which the older certainties associated with European modernity had been displaced. AIDS figured a range of "globalization panics," from global environmental dangers to fear about financial volatility. When AIDS was first identified in the United States in 1981, about four hundred thousand people were identified with the disease; during the next ten years, more than 10 million people became infected with the HIV virus; research now documents that more than 33 million people worldwide are living with HIV and AIDS (Smith and Naím). In a sense, AIDS began as a metaphor that represented the confounding of medical science by a disease that penetrated bodies and defied national boundaries; yet as medical treatment became available in the United States and wealthier nations, the understanding of AIDS as a catastrophic third-world epidemic has swiftly become a metaphor for the range of dangers associated with globalization (Patton, Irwin). It singles out one aspect of a greater, undetermined set of processes, in which disease is meant to stand in for the entirety of the larger complex of risks and effects of global contacts; like SARS or avian flu, it is a metaphor for a foreign contagion of deleterious, unforeseen effects of globalization, whose reach is as yet beyond the apprehension or control of rationalizing science.

The movement of immigrants, in particular, transnational Chinese, has been another common metaphor of globalization. The essays collected in Aihwa Ong and Donald Nonini's *Ungrounded Empires: The Cultural Politics of Modern Chinese Transnationalism*, for example, study the "some 25 million Chinese outside of China, the bulk of whom are concentrated around the fast-growing Pacific Rim . . . well-placed to play a key role in realizing the potential and promise of globalization" (4). Drawing from a wealth of ethnographic research conducted in sites throughout the Asia Pacific, the editors and essayists contended that it is impossible to understand globalization without examining transnational movement and settlement as part of the strategies of accumulation by Chinese under capitalism. They began their analysis with a discussion of the limitations of the Cold War–era Parsonian social scientific explanation of Chinese culture that emphasized "norms" and values" of "Chinese culture," from entrepreneurial spirit to loyalty to native place, to studies of family firm behavior. They connected this "culture and personality" bias to later business school discourses from the 1980s that sought to explain the "East Asian economic success" through likewise culturalist explanations of neo-Confucianism discipline. *Ungrounded Empires* discussed a range of Chinese transnationals in Taiwan, Hong Kong, Singapore, and Malaysia; the Chinese "astronauts" and "parachutists" (who vault to other countries while their families "stay in place"), who study in the United Kingdom or the United States obtaining educational "capital," or who work as mobile industrialists, financiers, or manufacturers throughout Asia. Ong and Nonini argue that "Chinese transnationalism" emerged in the 1970s, alongside the regimes of flexible accumulation and mixed production and its new modes of social organization, as Chinese adapted to new configurations of the production and distribution of goods and services, moving and connecting intraculturally across the diaspora. In light of the reorganization of labor processes and practices, including subcontracting and outsourcing, Ong and Nonini argue that "the distinctive transnational strategies of diaspora Chinese have converged even more closely with the circuits of accumulation within flexible capitalism across the Asia Pacific" (19–20). In the discussions of globalization in the last three decades, transnational Chinese immigration figured not only as a metaphor for the economic modernization of China, Taiwan, Singapore, and Hong

Kong, where Chinese are the largest cultural or ethnic group, but "Chinese transnationalism" also became *the* privileged metaphor for a range of trends associated with the larger area of East, South, and Southeast Asia, of the "Pacific Rim" or the "Asia Pacific" as a general political economic region (Connery; Dirlik; Gourevitch). The metaphor not only left Asia undifferentiated, but it also obscured the role of U.S. and multinational capital invested in the development of specific industries, on the one hand, and the ramifications of this rapid development in different countries—from Malaysia to the Philippines to South Korea—in terms of their local labor, environment, and technology bases, on the other.

In 2004 and 2005, economists began to issue ominous warnings about China's economic growth and the U.S. trade imbalance with China, and since the "success" of the 2008 Beijing Olympics, the current figure of a "Chinese takeover" has now eclipsed that of the transnational Chinese migrant as the *sign* of globalization. Thomas Friedman's *The World is Flat*, for example, employed the metaphor of a *flat world* to capture the sense that the playing field of competition between China and the United States has evened. But whereas the *flat world* metaphor may convey the U.S. anxiety about China's productivity, it obscures, of course, the *unflat* inequality that continues to exist between the industrialized G-8 and Latin America and Africa. Friedman uses the metaphor to caution U.S. policy makers and economists that they have not realized the dramatic erosion of the U.S. science and technology base relative to the social and political support for education and training in China and India. Although many countries—ranging from those in Western Europe and Canada to China and India—provide for social welfare (education, health care provisions), Friedman argues that the U.S. withdrawal from this commitment disadvantages U.S. industries. He makes the neoliberal recommendation that market-friendly attention to social welfare will advance U.S. ability to compete in a "flat world." When, in 2004, *Business Week* reported a massive shift in economic power created by "the China Price" and heralded that the U.S. trade deficit with China would likely soon pass $150 billion, the "Chinese takeover" became the newest metaphor for globalization.

We might reflect that in the 1990s, just a decade earlier, the pervasive circulation of U.S. commodities, like Coca-Cola or McDonald's, was the metaphor of choice for globalization: from George Ritzer's claim that contemporary society is afflicted by "McDonaldization," the spread of American consumerism that reduces all tastes and experiences to a single pattern, to Benjamin Barber's argument that characterized globalization in terms of an exacerbated struggle between religious revivalism and the accelerated profit-driven market, for which "McWorld" was the moniker. McDonald's was the metaphor for cultural homogenization, the mass production that converts everything into equivalent units for consumption and the global reach of commercial saturation by media conglomerates, like Sony, Nike, and Microsoft, that have eroded the distinction and autonomy of "traditional" cultures, both Western and non-Western. Also, the "fast food" of McDonald's stood for what David Harvey famously termed the "space-time compression" of globalization, the sense in which new technologies have created an apparent shrinking or elimination of distances and a general reduction of time spent. Because jets travel approximately fifty times faster than a sailing ship, it was said that the world of the 1960s was about one-fiftieth the size of the world in the sixteenth century. Telecommunications media and the Internet link localities around the world and make it possible to maintain social relationships of direct interaction across any distance. Yet the distribution of such media has always been notoriously uneven, and access to it differs enormously across separate localities; middle-class U.S. Americans or northern Europeans may watch one of numerous televisions in their single-family homes, yet members of a Mexican village may have to walk fifteen miles to a small nearby town to receive the weekly news broadcast on a television in a central bar or restaurant. Metaphors that previously implied global uniformity and homogeneity dramatically underestimated the ways in which global processes widen historical disparities and proliferate new forms of difference. Today's metaphors of globalization more often emphasize the deepening of cleavages between rich and poor and the multiplicity of worlds linked by unpredictable processes: whether natural disasters like tsunamis and hurricanes or environmental disasters like global warming, whether the hazards of linked financial markets in which a regional stock market crash affects the global economy or acts of "terrorism" and the terrifying condition that the overextended military ambitions of one nation, the United States, could bring the entire world into war.

Social scientists who do conceptualize globalization as deepening the cleavages between rich and poor perceive a worldwide struggle between those who seek more equitable, sustainable development for the global poor and the private economic interests of transnational corporations. They study global social movements and transnational advocacy networks that have addressed issues like medical aid for the world's poor, human rights violations, or women's rights (Keck and Sikkink). A group like Greenpeace, once a small group of activists protesting the nuclear bomb tests in Alaska in the 1960s, is now a massive transnational organization that can call on millions of supporters to carry out highly publicized actions and has played a significant role in creating a global ecological sensibility and a cultural awareness of environmental destruction threatening human extinction (Wapner). Global environmentalism has become a global social movement in the face of degradation from acid rain, air pollution, tropical deforestation, and the thinning of the ozone layer, but it is also a metaphor—the figure of *global warming*, in particular—that captures both the peril of apocalyptic destruction and the promise of collective means for imagining survival (Pellow; Oreskes). If the world at the end of the nineteenth century was one in which some spaces of nature remained still untouched, our present historical moment is one in which resources have reached depletion, have been utterly used and spent. Wastefulness has proliferated new toxins, new diseases, and new hazards to fear, and there appears to be nothing left to extract, waste, or spoil. Insofar as the depletion and pollution of our physical world has resulted in climate change, global warming itself has also become a metaphor alluding to the varieties of limits and possibilities of this moment of globalization: overextended military ambitions that have given rise to desperate, bloody opposition; excessive luxury for the few creates the desperate poverty and destitution of the many. Global warming is at once a metaphor for catastrophic degradation of the environment and for the understanding that greed and self-interest are entirely inadequate for the creation of a global ethic that might adequately address or adjudicate the means for collective human survival.

Finally, since September 2001, the U.S. war on terror has been the most frequently invoked *metaphor* for globalization, calculated to figure and condense wide-ranging anxieties about national security and survival within an incomprehensibly complex world order, conjuring a lethal enemy whose threatening presence has justified the revival of U.S. militarism and nationalism reminiscent of its policies and practices of the Cold War period. After the attack on the World Trade Center, the "Bush Doctrine" proclaimed the right of the United States to wage preemptive war on "terrorists" or "rogue states." The metaphor of the *war on terror* references two "schools" of political science that address international relations: the "neorealist" school that believes states are the major actors in world affairs, that international anarchy is the principle force shaping states, that states in anarchy are predisposed toward conflict and perpetual struggles for security and power; and the "neoliberal" school that understands international relations in terms of "complex interdependence" among nations, and multiple channels and institutions of cooperation and collaboration (Baldwin; Keohane; Keohane and Nye). Neoliberals envision a global society that functions alongside individual states by means of regional treaties or hemispheric economic trade agreements; key are institutions such as the United Nations and increasing numbers of international nongovernmental organizations (NGOs) addressing issues from environmental protection to human rights to nuclear deterrence. This latter "institutionalist" approach had come to represent the mainstream analysis in the political science of international relations in the two decades after the Cold War (Kahler and Walter). Yet after September 2001, the United States under the George W. Bush administration pursued a foreign policy that must be termed not simply "neorealist" but as "neoconservative," taking up a course that rejected international diplomacy and justified military force as a rational instrument of power, harkening back to understandings of "national security" from the political realist approach of the Cold War period. Neoconservatives argued that, unlike Europe, the United States should not have reduced its military power after the Cold War and that the aggressive unilateral stance in Iraq was necessary for the U.S. recuperation of its global stature (Kagan and Kagan).

The Bush administration stated its prerogative to use preemptive force by pointing to the "terrorist" threat of September 11 and declaring a state of exception in which international institutions like the United Nations, regional economic alliances, and multilateral diplomacy were inadequate to achieve global cooperation. This state of exception rationalized the use of force and suspension of civil rights to maintain domestic order and was used to justify the invasions of Afghanistan and Iraq. The global unilateralism of the U.S. invasion of Iraq broke with the "international regime—the principles, norms, and governing arrangements of interstate interdependence—that had been in effect for at least three decades. Moreover, the representation of the war in Iraq as a *necessary war* drew on the concept of just war defined by circumstances in which a state has been attacked or invaded, when there has been a violation of international laws. Yet the representation of *necessary war* in Iraq not only fabricated a connection between the September 11 events and Saddam Hussein, but it also masked the ongoing conditions within which dominant states subjugate internal populations, stateless populations, without any formal declarations of war. What is called "terrorism" is often the uprising of defenseless, subjugated people fighting against state-sanctioned violence; they are named "terrorists" not only to delegitimize their actions and to justify "war" against them, but also to gain popular support for the exercise of state and military violence as a means for dominating regions, populations, and resources. Thus, the processes and conditions of globalization in the last two decades have challenged the certainty and efficacy of a nineteenth-century notion of the modern nation-state that informed the *ideal type* in sociology, political science, economics, history, and geography. Insofar as the modern concepts of state, society, sovereignty, production, history, territory, and culture persist, they are gradually and increasingly eclipsed by the simultaneous emergence of altogether new conditions. The social scientific turn to metaphors to describe our present global conditions precisely registers this paradox. Above all of the modernist legacies, it is perhaps the concept of a future guaranteed by social progress that still persists within our present context; it continues to abstractly organize many of the social and political activities of our contemporary world. We uphold the promise of modern progress within conditions that raise the gravest questions about its eternal or universal validity. The presumption of a future guaranteed by progress is troubled everywhere by the realization that for the last half-century, we have lived in a world that survived the use of nuclear weapons, and that we cannot know if and how a world with such destructive capability can continue to survive. Maintaining its survival will not come about through a refortification of nationalism and the nation-state or through concepts of diplomacy or militarism from a former era now incommensurate with our own. Unanswerable questions, like that of imagining a future within the global conditions of the last decades, have pressed the empirical social sciences to its epistemological limits.

The ethical and epistemological difficulty of globalization is thus registered by the rhetorical excess that becomes apparent when empiricism reaches a threshold and the social sciences turn to metaphors to figure globalization. The purpose of observing this turn is not to discredit metaphorical language as "less true," but to make some distinctions between the uses of metaphor in the different contexts of the social sciences and culture and to suggest that these distinct projects entail quite different definitions of "culture" and understandings of "culture's" place on the horizon of meaning. Although we traditionally associate metaphor with aesthetic culture, the social scientific recourse to metaphor actually often indicates an underestimation of "culture." Although social scientists commonly declare that "culture" is an important barometer of globalization, their analyses have tended to subordinate culture as a passive effect of political economic processes, whether relegating culture to the waning sphere of "tradition" within modernization or in conceiving of culture as commodified entertainments through claims that globalization has either homogenized or hybridized culture. In either case, "culture" is conceived as secondary and ephemeral to, rather than constitutive of, the social, and it is largely understood to be a static repertoire of symbols that merely reflects the social structure. To the contrary, we can appreciate that the cultural mediations of globalization are much more than inert effects or symptoms of an a priori social structure or political economy and may provide us with more profound diagnoses and prescriptions of our condition. Arjun Appadurai has elegantly persuaded us that the migrations and interdependencies of globalization have created new cultural maps, giving rise to new social identities, overlapping affinities and worldviews, and Ulf Hannerz has argued that global cultural processes are far more complex than earlier ideas about cultural flows from center to margin and that they exceed the simplifications of global homogenization or corruption of the periphery. In mediating the "structure of feeling" of this global epoch, works of literature, journalism, film and visual culture, music, monuments, or electronic digital culture not only represent the most dominant social trends, but they also express residual traditions and emergent ideas as well. Moreover, *culture* includes not only forms of expressive culture, but also the variety of practices that range from the conduct of households to the inhabiting of public space, to attitudes and presumptions about belonging to township or community, homeland or world. Material and situated, cultural practices of representation enunciate and organize subjectivity, affect, memory, and imagination within the social; through cultural practices, the social is understood and interpreted, and ultimately, it is through the representational media of culture that social change is newly conceptualized and desired.[4] Culture provides languages and spaces for critically interpreting what can be known about the history of global processes and their effects and innovates those languages and spaces for imagining the transformation and reorganization of that world.

If the social sciences employ metaphors as a detour or supplement to empirical explanation, the use of metaphor in literary, aesthetic, or cultural works operates rather differently because of the poetics of *figures* within the denser operations of narrative *allegory*. *Allegory* shares with *metaphor* reference to another level of meaning, but *allegory* has a narrative basis that alludes to one or several simultaneous structures of events or ideas. Not strictly a genre, but rather a formal principle employed since antiquity, modern *allegory* may allude to narratives in which meaning has been traditionally figured and presents an hermeneutic to instruct us how to read after the failure of those narrative meanings.

I want to close with a consideration of Alejandro Gonzáles Iñárritu's recent film *Babel*, which I hope might permit me to be more specific about metaphors in cultural texts and social scientific explanation. *Metaphors* may naturalize themselves as fixed, unchanging truth, or they may offer alternative forms that present themselves as precisely not total or mastering, whose circumscribed incompletion or impasse is not a failure but an illumination of the conditions within which a truth may be posited and contested. Some metaphors mask the nonequivalence between the figure and what it represents, contributing to misrecognition and the naturalization of the social relations under globalization; others implicate us in the incommensurability and generate alternative analyses and critiques of the social order presented as naturalized. *Babel*, I would suggest, goes beyond the referential use of metaphor within an empirically given totality to present a tale that is an *allegory* of globalization, implicating the viewer in an *hermeneutic* for reading those processes. Like Kapoor's sculpture with which I began, it thematizes the problem of representation itself with respect to the comprehension of the geohistorical conditions of globalization. As its title suggests, the film alludes to the biblical story of mankind's hubris in building the Tower of Babel, after which man was divided into languages, confounded and scattered across the world. The allusion to the biblical Babel suggests that the contemporary project of global universality through modernization is a new tower, in a time without gods to please, attain, or punish, and that rather than the universal extension of freedom, justice, or prosperity, globalization reproduces instead difference and division, sundering anew communities and nations, separated by language, material wealth, technology, and militarized borders. Although *Babel* is promoted as a movie with a simple message of common humanity that transcends national borders, I would observe that, to the contrary, the film precisely *allegorizes* the perils of universal human community, demonstrating its brutal economy of representation, the labors of articulation and translation, and the violences of misreading—across and within national languages, between states and its citizens, parents and children, husbands and wives. It presents an *allegory* of the processes through which entitled communities have been recognized as the proper subjects deserving of human rights, whereas others are constructed as those from whom humanity must be protected, the multitude legible not as humanity but only as its violators. As *allegory*, it enlists the viewer in a critical framework through which we can interpret the processes of "globalization" as the promises of universality that mask the production of what Randall Williams has termed "the international division of humanity," and it instructs us to read in ways that might alter and reconceive the direction of those processes.

The film introduces several apparently distant stories that it slowly reveals to be related. It opens with the sale of a Winchester rifle to a Moroccan goatherd so that his young sons may kill the jackals attacking the herd; as the boys Yussef and Ahmed practice shooting, they dare one another to try to hit a vehicle in the distance. One shot hits an American woman traveling in a bus filled with French and British tourists passing through a small village called Tazarine, and she and her husband cannot return to their children in San Diego, whom they have left in the care of the undocumented Mexican housekeeper who has raised the children since they were infants. We are introduced to a deaf-mute high school girl in Tokyo and learn eventually that on a hunting trip in Morocco, her father had given the Winchester rifle as a gift to his guide. As the Moroccan village shelters the American woman until her embassy can send a helicopter to transport her to a hospital, the housekeeper brings the children to Tijuana so she can attend her son's wedding, where she is detained by the border patrol on the morning of their return. There are no facile continuities or discontinuities in the portrait of globalization that these linked but disconnected stories convey; industry, media, and technologies have profoundly altered publics and their intimacies, but they have also left particular conditions unchanged; the repetition of state violence toward, and forcible underdevelopment of, the subaltern poor of the global South reiterate the divides of nineteenth-century colonialisms. *Babel* suggests that if globalization promises universality through the social, political, or economic interconnection of worlds, it has not only failed, but also that the sites of encounter and exchange precisely pronounce the deepened exclusions of subaltern groups from representation.

Through the device of the Winchester—the U.S.-made "gun that won the West"—the film elaborates how reading and misreading threat and violence are historically critical operations in the legibility of an international division of human populations. The passage of the rifle would appear to be a metaphor for violence and its global crossings, yet the referential closure of this equation is from the start destabilized, opened, and reopened, in the world order allegorized in the film. The rifle is *not* a *metaphor* for violence, I would contend, but rather the *sign* of the opacity of violence, a figure stating that violence is not given to transparency, a figure whose role in the film is to introduce the question of the attribution of violence. By means of the rifle, we see that the distinction between who is violent and who must be protected from violence is central to the global economy of legitimate humanity and dehumanized humanity. From the nineteenth-century colonial state to the late-twentieth- to early-twenty-first century imperial nation-state, the state has exercised sovereignty through its monopoly on violence. This has meant not only that the state possessed the political and military power to determine the nature of the state of exception in which violence was necessary, but it has also consisted of a monopoly of biopolitical power "to make live" (*faire vivre*): the power to name the humanity entitled to protection in order to make live and, simultaneously, the power to "let die" (*laisser mourir*) those deemed "violent," named as those who threaten the state's sovereign power (Agamben; Foucault). What the state deems a "threat" may range from open dissent or revolution to the articulation of grief, the refusal of invisibility, silence, poverty, or hunger. In the political/juridical sphere of enfranchisement of the citizen in the nation, the "maternity" of the North American woman, Susan, who has been shot is recognized precisely as "endangered life," yet Amelia, the undocumented Mexican housekeeper who has raised her own adult son and now provides domestic care for Susan's children, is only legible as dangerously "illegal." The anxious French and British tourists are respected by the economic logic of development that recognizes the industrialized G-8 nations, yet the subaltern desert goatherds are either invisible or absurdly misread as "terrorists." The supranational global telecommunications order promises to transcend national and local linguistic particularity through extending sounds and images that travel across distances. "Japan" figures in the film as an exceptional national modernity that had once possessed technologies directed toward war and empire, but after U.S. postwar occupation demilitarizes and develops instead advanced information and communication technologies. Yet the irony for the deaf-mute subculture is that all of the communications technologies commonplace in Tokyo cannot ameliorate the sense of being cut off from the normative hearing world, which, Chieko comments, "thinks [or sic] we are monsters"; in the scene in Tokyo club, the pulsing sound of the dance music is cut periodically to dramatize Chieko's disconnection from audio-mediated sociality. The divisions are not exclusively enacted at national boundaries, but comprise the misreading of the agrarian world by the industrialized, rural life by the urban; the youth by the elders; and the speechless by those who speak.

Babel ends with several "speech acts" in which those who have been constructed as "outlaws" encounter and entreat the law. There are three linked scenes in which different subjects each attempt to speak to a representative of the law in whose terms they are not represented: Chieko has bared herself to the Japanese detective investigating the rifle; Yussef smashes the rifle before the Moroccan police and raises his arms in surrender; Amelia runs across the desert toward the Border Patrol, crying for help. These instances of embodied speech, beyond language, I would contend, are not seeking recognition from the law. Rather, their articulations are constituted as in excess of the terms of the law, whose agents view them as "in violation," as inhuman. These scenes, in which various agents of the law refuse these marginal subjects' attempts to speak, direct us as viewers toward the critique of the state and its monopoly on violence. I suggested earlier that the gun is *not* a *metaphor* for violence but more precisely the *sign* of its opacity; its appearance inaugurates an *allegory* in which violence becomes attributed to discrepancies of wealth, speech, force, modernization, and population. *Babel* implicates viewers in this attribution and instructs us that to represent globalization is to return continually to the impasse of deciding who is violent and who must be protected from violence.

In my discussion, I have observed that the detour to metaphor within the social sciences occurs at the point at which these studies confront the mandate of explaining globalization. In making a general distinction between the social scientific and cultural uses of *metaphor*, I differentiate between an instrumental use of *metaphor* as a practical, referential symbol, on the one hand, and its deployment as a principle of *allegory*, on the other. In the former, the use of metaphor is static; in the latter dynamic, one assumes a stable social totality, and the other invents an alternative from the ruins of historical loss of such totality. In ways that poststructuralist theory never could, the material conditions of globalization have brought the social sciences to epistemic crisis, revealing the limits, the occlusions, and the constructedness of disciplinary claims. We need not conceive this crisis as "failure," but rather as an opportunity for interdisciplinary collaboration. I am not in any sense arguing that it is inappropriate for empirical social sciences to resort to metaphor. Quite the opposite, my provocation is rather for the social sciences to take metaphors much more seriously. Instead of casting the superior "truths" of social science against the "fiction" of aesthetic works, perhaps there is much for the social sciences to draw from in the richer, developed critical future that one finds in culture and the humanities.

Notes

1. In the larger project from which this is drawn, I discuss sociology, political science, economics, and cultural studies in the U.S. university in order to connect the production of knowledge about globalization with contemporary U.S. geopolitical roles and desires.

2. James Clifford and George Marcus's *Writing Culture* marked a critical, self-reflexive turn in anthropology, accompanied by the work of cultural anthropologists such as Timothy Mitchell, Lila Abu-Lughod, Lisa Yoneyama, Lawrence Cohen, Lisa Rofel, Akhil Gupta, James Ferguson, Arturo Escobar, Saba Mahmood, Anna Tsing, and others. They have traced the history of encounter between forces of modernization and cultural practices outside the West, and their work suggests the importance of "other modernities" in the critique of Western modernity.

3. Weber analyzed modern industrial society in terms of its tendency toward rationalization, bureaucratization, specialization, the separation of public and private spheres, the waning of traditional ethics, values, and affective meanings, and the growing impersonalization of human life as well as the waning of collective sentiments. Whereas rationalization led to unprecedented growth in the distribution of goods and services, an aspect of democracy, Weber also observed that it led to an increasing division of labor, mechanization, and oppressive routine, which run counter to notions of freedom and democracy.

4. Williams reminded us of the genealogy of the concept of "culture" in eighteenth-century Europe, from the growing and tending of crops (as in "agriculture"), to the cultivation and civilization of the human person in civil society in the nineteenth century, denoting the *internal* reflection, discernment, and aesthetic judgment that was distinct from *external* social development. By the late nineteenth century, European colonial expansion gave rise to another meaning of "culture," established by modern study of anthropology, which studied non-Western cultures in Africa, Asia, and the Americas, in distinction from the modern West. Culture, in this modern anthropological sense, meant the values, expressions, and practices of a society; this anthropological sense contributed to sociological definitions of the components of modern Western national cultures. Two different meanings of "culture" continue today: culture in the sense of "high culture," in visual art, literature, or aesthetic culture; and culture in an anthropological or sociological sense, as "a way of life," a mode of social organization expressed in particular forms and practices that distinguish one group from another. The integration of these two genealogies permits us to study culture—as art, film, literature, and generally all practices of representation—as both drawing from and contributing to culture, in its social sense, as "a way of life." Such synthesis offers a way to bridge what is often perceived as a gap between the two meanings; this approach is what has been called cultural studies. See Chen and Morley; Grossberg et al.; and Hall.

Works Cited

Agamben, Giorgio. *Homo Sacer: Sovereign Power and Bare Life*. Stanford: Stanford UP, 1998.

Appadurai, Arjun. *Modernity at Large*. Minneapolis: U of Minnesota P, 1996.

Aristotle. *Poetics* 1457b.

Asad, Talal. *Genealogies of Religion: Discipline and Reasons of Power in Christianity and Islam*. Baltimore: Johns Hopkins UP, 1993.

Babel. Dir. Alejandro Gonzáles Iñárritu. Paramount Vantage, 2006.

Baldwin, David A. *Neorealism and Neoliberalism: The Contemporary Debate*. New York: Columbia UP, 1993.

Barber, Benjamin. *Jihad vs. McWorld*. New York: Times Books, 1995.

Bellah, Robert. *3*. New York: Harper, 1970.

———, ed. *Religion and Progress in Modern Asia*. Glencoe: Free Press, 1965.

Breckenridge, Carol A., and Peter van der Veer, eds. *Orientalism and the Postcolonial Predicament: Perspectives on South Asia*. Philadelphia: U of Pennsylvania P, 1993.

Burke, Kenneth. *A Grammar of Motives*. Berkeley: California, 1969.

Business Week. "The China Price." 6 Dec. 2004.

Calhoun, Craig. *Critical Social Theory: Culture, History and the Challenge of Difference*. Oxford: Blackwell, 1995.

Chakrabarty, Dipesh. *Provincializing Europe: Postcolonial Thought and Historical Difference*. Princeton: Princeton UP, 2000.

Chen, Kuan-Hsing, and David Morley, eds. *Stuart Hall: Critical Dialogues In Cultural Studies*. New York: Routledge, 1996.

Chow, Rey. *Woman and Chinese Modernity: The Politics of Reading Between West and East*. Minneapolis: U of Minnesota P, 1991.

Clifford, James. *The Predicament of Culture*. Cambridge: Harvard UP, 1988.

———, and George Marcus, eds. *Writing Culture: the Poetics and Politics of Ethnography*. Berkeley: U of California P, 1986.

Connery, Christopher. "Pacific Rim Discourse: The U.S. Global Imaginary in the Late Cold War Years." *Boundary 2* 21.1 (1994): 31–56.

Cumings, Bruce. Parallax Visions. Durham: Duke UP, 1999.

da Silva, Denise. "Towards a Critique of the Socio-logos of Justice: The Analytics of Raciality and the Production of Universality." *Social Identities* 7.3 (2001): 421–54.

Dirlik, Arif. "The Asia-Pacific Idea: Reality and Representation in the Invention of a Regional Structure." *Journal of World History* 3.1 (1992): 55–79.

Durkheim, Émile. *The Rules of Sociological Method*. 1938. Trans. Sarah Solovay. Glencoe: Free Press, 1950.

Ferguson, Roderick. *Aberrations in Black: Toward a Queer of Color Critique*. Minneapolis: U of Minnesota P, 2004.

Foucault, Michel. *"Society Must Be Defended": Lectures at the Collège de France, 1975–1976*. Trans. David Macey. New York: Picador, 2003.

Friedman, Thomas. *The World is Flat: A Brief History of the World*. New York: Farrar, Strauss, 2005.

Giddens, Anthony. *Capitalism and Modern Social Theory: An Analysis of the Writings of Durkheim, Marx and Weber*. Cambridge: Cambridge UP, 1971.

Gray, John. *False Dawn: The Delusions of Global Capitalism*. New York: New Press, 1998.

Greider, William. *One World Ready or Not: The Manic Logic of Global Capitalism*. New York: Simon and Schuster, 1997.

Gupta, Akhil, and James Ferguson. "Beyond 'Culture': Space, Identity, and the Politics of Difference." *Cultural Anthropology* 7.1 (Feb. 1992): 6–22.

Gourevitch, Peter A. "The Pacific Rim: Current Debates." *The Pacific Region: Challenges to Policy and Theory*. Ed. Peter A. Gourevitch. Newbury Park: Sage, 1989.

Grossberg, Lawrence et al., eds. *Cultural Studies: A Reader*. New York: Routledge, 1992

Hall, Stuart. "Cultural Studies: Two Paradigms." *Media, Culture, Society* 2 (1980): 52–72.

Hannerz, Ulf. "Scenarios for Peripheral Cultures." *Culture, Globalization, and the World-System*. Ed. Anthony D. King. Oxford: Blackwell, 1990.

Harvey, David. *The Condition of Postmodernity*. Oxford: Blackwell, 1990.

Irwin, Alexander et al. *Global AIDS: Myths and Facts, Tools for Fighting the AIDS Pandemic*. Brookline, MA: South End, 2003.

Johnson, Walter. *Soul by Soul: Life Inside the Antebellum Slave Market*. Cambridge: Harvard UP, 1999.

Juergensmeyer, Mark. *Terror In the Mind of God*. Berkeley: U of California P, 2000.

Kagan, Donald, and Frederick Kagan. *While America Sleeps: Self-Delusion, Military Weakness, and the Threat to Peace Today*. New York: St. Martin's Press, 2000.

Kahler, Miles, and Barbara Walter, eds. *Territoriality and Conflict in an Era of Globalization*. Cambridge: Cambridge UP, 2006.

Kapoor, Anish. *Marsyas*. London: Tate Publishing, 2002.

Keck, Margaret, and Kathryn Sikkink. *Activists Beyond Borders: Advocacy Networks in International Politics*. Ithaca: Cornell UP, 1998.

Keohane, Robert O., and Joseph Nye. *Power and Interdependence*. Glenview, IL: Scott, Foresman, 1989.

Keohane, Robert O., ed. *Neorealism and Its Critics*. New York: Columbia UP, 1986.

Lakoff, George, and Mark Johnson. *Metaphors We Live By*. Chicago: U of Chicago P, 1980.

Lemert, Charles. *Sociology After the Crisis*. 2nd ed. Boulder: Paradigm, 2004.

Levy, Marion. *Modernization and the Structure of Societies*. Princeton: Princeton UP, 1966.

Lowe, Lisa. "Immigrant Literatures: A Modern Structure of Feeling." *Literature on the Move: Comparing Diasporic Ethnicities in Europe and the Americas*. Ed. Dominique Marçais et al. Heidelberg: Carl Winter, 2002.

———. "Utopia and Modernity: Some Observations from the Border." *Rethinking Marxism* 13/2 (Spring 2001): 10–18.

MacPherson, C. B. *The Political Theory of Possessive Individualism: Hobbes to Locke*. Oxford: Clarendon, 1962.

Miyoshi, Masao, and Harry Harootunian, eds. *Learning Places: the Afterlives of Area Studies*. Durham: Duke, 2002.

Mudimbe, V. Y. et al., eds. *Open the Social Sciences: Report of the Gulbenkian Commission on the Restructuring of the Social Sciences*. Stanford: Stanford UP, 1996.

Ong, Aihwa, and Donald Nonini, eds. *Ungrounded Empires: The Cultural Politics of Modern Chinese Transnationalism*. New York: Routledge, 1997.

Oreskes, Naomi. "The Scientific Consensus on Climate Change." *Climate Change*. Ed. Joseph F. DiMento and Pamela Doughman. Cambridge: MIT Press, 2007.

Parsons, Talcott. *The Evolution of Societies*. Englewood Cliffs: Prentice-Hall, 1977.

Patton, Cindy. *Globalizing AIDS*. Minneapolis: U of Minnesota P, 2003.

Pellow, David Naguib. *Resisting Global Toxics: Transnational Movements for Environmental Justice*. Cambridge: MIT Press, 2007.

Preminger, Alex, ed. *Princeton Encyclopedia of Poetry and Poetics*. Princeton: Princeton UP, 1974.

Rafael, Vicente. "Cultures of Area Studies in the United States." *Social Text* (Winter 1994): 91–111.

Ritzer, George. *The McDonaldization of Society*. Thousand Oaks, CA: Pine Forge, 1993.

Robertson, Roland. *Globalization: Social Theory and Global Culture*. London: Sage, 1992.

Rodrik, Dani. *One Economics, Many Recipes: Globalization, Institutions, and Economic Growth*. Princeton: Princeton UP, 2007.

Said, Edward. *Orientalism*. New York: Random House, 1977.

Sassen, Saskia. *Globalization and Its Discontents: Essays on the New Mobility of People and Money*. New York: New Press, 1998.

Sklair, Leslie. *The Sociology of the Global System*. Herfordshire: Harvester Wheatsheaf, 1991.

Smith, Gordon, and Moisés Naím. *Altered States: Globalization, Sovereignty and Governance*. Ottawa: International Development Research Centre, 2000.

Taylor, Peter. *Modernities: A Geohistorical Interpretation*. Minneapolis: U of Minnesota P, 1999.

Wallerstein, Immanuel. *The Modern World-System*. New York: Academic Press, 1976.

———. *Capitalist World-Economy*. Cambridge: Cambridge UP, 1979.

Wapner, Paul. *Environmental Activism and Civil Politics*. Albany: SUNY P, 1996.

Weber, Max. *Economy and Society*. 3 vols. 1922. New York: Bedminster, 1968.

White, Hayden. *Metahistory: The Historical Imagination in Nineteenth-Century Europe*. Baltimore: Johns Hopkins UP, 1973.

Williams, Randall. "Appealing Subjects: Reading Across the International Division of Justice." Diss. U of California, San Diego, 2006.

Williams, Raymond. *Marxism and Literature*. Oxford: Oxford, 1977.

Yu, Henry. *Thinking Orientals: Migration, Contact and Exoticism in Modern America*. Oxford: Oxford, 2001.

Chapter Three

Crossing the Immigration and Race Border

A Critical Race Theory Approach to Immigration Studies

Mary Romero

Introduction

Largely in response to the civil rights movement of the 1960s and 1970s, scholarship in the sociology of race abandoned the conceptual framework of Robert E. Park, Ernest W. Burgess, and others who, during the 1920s and 1930s, had developed urban sociology at the University of Chicago. Using the city of Chicago as a "natural laboratory" for conducting urban social research, members of the Chicago School (Park; Park, Burgess, McKenzie, and Wirth; Thomas and Znaniecki; Wirth) focused their work on immigrants who settled in locales that recruited their labor. Adopting Simmel's social type of "the stranger" as an heuristic in their detached role as researchers, they studied immigrant populations moving into Chicago's "natural areas." Building on theories of social organization and conflict, Park and Burgess described immigrants' social experiences as being those of competition, conflict, or accommodation. Indeed, they saw these experiences as steps toward the inevitable process of assimilation.

One of the first major critiques of the Chicago School's theoretical framework on immigration was made by Blauner, who criticized: 1) its failure to recognize that race and ethnic groups persist as central entities in modern society; 2) its reduction of racism and racial oppression to economic, psychological, and other determining factors; 3) its focus on white prejudice while ignoring structural and institutional racism; and 4) its blanket application of the analogy of European immigrants to all racial minorities. At the same time, the mainstream sociology of race and immigration continued to rely on the white–black binary.

However, beyond the field of sociology, leading scholars in the humanities and social sciences attended to the larger significance of W. E. B. Du Bois's predication: "The problem of the twentieth century is the problem of the color-line—the relation of the darker to the lighter races of men in Asia and Africa, in America and the islands of the sea" (15). Openly embracing interdisciplinary approaches, some sociologists began reconceptualizing the sociology of race. Sociologists of color, in particular, were instrumental in developing new interdisciplinary programs, such as Chicana/o, Asian Pacific American, and African American studies. As race scholars moved toward analyzing the racialization process (e.g., Omi and Winant; Steinberg; Takaki), conceptual frameworks were developed to include groups identified in terms of ethnicity rather than race. Importantly, as "whiteness" became recognized as a social construct, other ways of racializing groups were also implemented (Ignatiev; Roediger). The assimilationist bias that framed previous Chicago-inspired research into ethnic and racial groups in the United States was challenged, and white middle-class assumptions were critiqued.

Although the immigrant analogy has not been entirely abandoned in sociology and research into racial attitudes, assimilation and levels of inter-marriage continue to flourish, and an increasing number of race scholars in sociology are particularly interested in analyzing the everyday practices of racism in face-to-face interaction (e.g., Bonilla-Silva; Bush), as well as in institutional settings (e.g., Oliver and Shapiro; Shapiro). In essence, many have heeded Derrick Bell's call "to 'get real' about race and the persistence of racism in America" (5).

Critical race theory (CRT) has provided an important conceptual framework and methodology for moving forward Bell's mandate. Sociologists concerned about race in the field of the sociology of crime, law, and deviance (e.g., Romero; Romero, and Serag; Russell; Schneider) and the sociology of education (e.g., Aguirre; Bernal; Ladson-Billings; Parker; Solórzano and Bernal) are particularly noted for their scholarship in CRT. These scholars have extended the concepts of micro- and macro-aggressions (Davis) and intersectionality (Caldwell; Crenshaw) and have theorized narratives and counterstories (Bell; Delgado; T. Ross; Williams; Yamamoto). Furthermore, using a CRT framework involves a commitment to antisubordination research agendas, social justice, and activism (Guinier and Torres; Matsuda; Valdéz; Valdéz, Culp, and Harris). CRT in sociology does not treat race merely as "a variable that can be controlled"; rather, it examines "the real impact that racism has had and continues to have within American society" (Yosso and Solózano 119).

In the writing that follows, I examine how critical race scholars have used interdisciplinary approaches in immigration research to conceptualize race and ethnicity not as inherent qualities, but as categories that have been socially constructed by law, public policy, and people's everyday practices. Rather than simply treating it as one variable among many, they place race at the center of immigration analysis. In addition, CRT scholars provide a model for using the sociological imagination in studying immigration that does not take the status quo for granted. Mari Matsuda describes this work as that of "progressive legal scholars of color who are attempting to develop a jurisprudence that accounts for the role of racism in American law and that works toward the elimination of racism as part of a larger goal of eliminating all forms of subordination" (331). Furthermore, CRT's focus on theory, praxis, and coalition building (Cameron; Cho and Westley; Guinier and Torres; Martínez; Romero; Yamamoto) offers crucial models for bridging the growing antagonism and increasing anti-immigration sentiment that impacts citizens and non-citizens in the global context.

In the next section I offer an overview of several mainstream approaches in the sociology of immigration and contrast them with CRT, and in particular with the newly emerging scholarship in Latina/Latino critical race theory, or LatCrit. Using my own research into immigration raids, I then demonstrate the potential of CRT's contributions to the sociology of immigration, especially with regard to its significance in keeping race (and its intersectionality with other forms of subordination) central to its analysis.

Master Narrative of Immigration in the United States

In response to the increased immigration of the 1960s, mainstream sociologists returned to the Chicago School approach and reinstated the sharp division between ethnicity and race. Attention focused on questions concerning assimilation, acculturation, intermarriage, and social mobility (usually based on cultural attributes rather than on legal, economic, or educational barriers or opportunities). Today, the field remains dominated by interest in the people who migrated to the United States before their early teens, or the 1.5 generation, segmented assimilation, social mobility, and other phenomena that perpetuate the myth of meritocracy and that distinguish among immigrants on the basis of whiteness (e.g., Alba and Nee; Portes; Portes and Rumbaut; Zhou and Bankston). The preoccupation with assimilation results in accepting white, middle-class standards as the norm and in regarding racialized groups as departing from the norm—that is, as deviant. Wildman and Davis explain how white privilege is concretely manifested:

> When we look at privilege we see several things. First, the characteristics of the privileged groups define the societal norm, often benefitting those in the privileged group. Second, privileged group members can rely on their privilege and avoid objecting to oppression. And third, privilege is rarely seen by the holder of the privilege. (574)

Focusing on assimilation not only conceals white privilege; it also frames research questions away from examining racial, economic, and political privilege among whites, ethnic Americans, and native- and foreign-born groups of color. Consequently, policy recommendations generated from the focus on assimilation maintain the status quo, ignore white privilege, and set the agenda to disadvantage racialized groups further.

Much recent literature on immigration has been dominated by the work of Alejandro Portes and Rubén G. Rumbaut and their colleagues. It is telling that, in their massive book *Legacies: The Story of the Immigrant Second Generation*, Portes and Rumbaut devote only about four pages to "the race question" and a paltry eight pages to the determinants of ethnic and racial identities. Throughout most of the book, they limit their discussion to more banal issues such as discrimination, acculturation, adaptation, ambition, countercultures, interaction effects, language acculturation, psychological well-being, and self-esteem.

This overly narrow perspective on acculturation and adaptation is consistent with Fordham and Ogbu's assertion that racial and ethnic minority students perform poorly in school because to do otherwise is "to act white." Whereas other educational scholars examine the ways that youth of color resist oppression (e.g., Bernal; Carter; Villenas and Deyhle), Fordham and Ogbu argue that resistance to white, middle-class culture (equated with educational success) is a form of oppositional culture. Portes and Rumbaut's conceptual framework restricts research questions by recognizing only one factor: the degree to which immigrants and their children embrace white, middle-class culture. An underlining assumption is that racial pride (which does not embrace whiteness) and cultural identification with communities of color are the causes of low academic achievement and lack of social mobility. Prudence L. Carter's recent study of student academic achievement points out that such research posits

> a position about these [minority] groups' perspectives on education that is not supported by many nationally representative surveys and other ethnographic studies. Not only has research shown that African Americans, for example, subscribe to the basic values of education as much as Whites do, or in some instances even more so than Whites do, but also there is insufficient evidence that a culture equating academic and socioeconomic mobility with Whiteness among Blacks and other so-called "involuntary minorities" exists. (8)

Analytic distinctions between race and ethnicity inherent in mainstream sociology's conceptualizations of immigration emerge even when immigrants' legal restrictions and economic circumstances are considered. For example, in their chapter on Nicaraguan children in Rumbaut and Portes's aforementioned volume, Patricia Fernández-Kelly and Sara Curran equate academic and economic failure with race and ethnicity: "Little over a decade after their arrival, Nicaraguan youngsters were already showing symptoms of decline—*a social darkening of sorts*" (128–29; emphasis added). Nicaraguan children who identify with black and Latino children are automatically seen as "emulating" an "adversarial culture." Not surprisingly, assimilationist researchers like Rumbaut and Portes and Fernández-Kelly and Curran do not call for structural changes, or even for collective action like the 2003 Immigrant Workers' Freedom Ride to Washington, D.C. Instead, their recommendations are focused on individual choices. Indeed, these studies support conservative policies such as advocating charter and private schools over public schools to avoid the racialization of second-generation youth. The underlying negative assumption that immigrants of color who identify with communities of color in the United States are doomed to fail reinforces racist stereotypes. There is an enormous ideological and theoretical gulf between immigration research and the sociology of race. Whereas mainstream sociology of race continues to dialogue with important interdisciplinary scholarship on racialization, examining how the "color-line" is maintained, reinforced, and transformed by everyday practices, immigration sociologists constrict their analyses by ignoring path-breaking scholarship that engages both race and immigration. It is regrettable that sociologists have disregarded the significant scholarship on immigration by critical race theorists. Indeed, it is rare to find any discussion of human rights or civil rights in the field. One outstanding exception is the research conducted into the increasing loss of human lives as failed immigration policies force migrants from Latin America to cross the border in the most desolate areas of the desert in the American Southwest (e.g., Cornelius). In contrast, immigration scholarship that draws on CRT identifies immigration as a key civil rights issue of the twenty-first century in the United States and a human rights issue worldwide. While working in the areas of CRT and LatCrit for several years, I became acutely aware of race as a glaring omission in immigration studies in sociology.

In the research on immigration raids by law enforcement agencies and other policing organizations, one is confronted with a literature that not only ignores but actually opposes racial politics and discourse. Recent research into crime and immigration neglects the issue of racial profiling, focusing instead on studies of geographical location; suspects' characteristics, such as level of education, behavior, and demeanor; and other police–citizen interactions and organizational concerns. Thus, in their research on the use of force in the arrest of immigrants in the United States, sociologists Scott Phillips, Nestor Rodriguez, and Jacqueline Hagan ignore issues of race and focus instead on changes in immigration legislation that require an increase of arrests and police use of force against all citizens. They do not consider institutional racism and factors like the number of police officers of color. Moreover, they make no attempt to engage with the immense sociological literature on race and crime.

I contend that a middle-class bias inhabits mainstream research, as it validates survey methodologies that are sensitive to only one population (e.g., illegal immigrants) and that fail to consider interactions between persons with different citizenship statuses. There is an unexamined assumption that poor, working-class, and lower-middle-class communities of color are segregated by citizenship status, and that these citizenship-status populations do not share the same homes and neighborhoods. The fact is that immigrants with different citizenship statuses frequently live in the same neighborhoods, share common employers, and patronize the same stores, restaurants, and nightclubs as other African Americans, Puerto Ricans, Chicanos/as, and Latinos who have been citizens all their lives. It is impossible to understand the effects immigration policies have on poor and working-class communities of color without the immigration scholarship of critical race theorists. Rather than divide populations of color into immigrants and citizens, concepts such as racial profiling emphasize connections in the treatment of all racialized groups and recognize citizenship status as a social construct.

CRT, LatCrit, and Outsider Scholars

CRT immigration researchers recognize that various forms of citizenship status stem from the delineation of rights, privileges, and penalties relative to property, taxes, welfare, and the freedom of movement across nation-states. The invention of passports, "green cards," and other identification documents was a crucial step in regulating people's movement, including their right to leave or return to their homeland as well as their ability to travel within their own country (Torpey). CRT reveals how racialized immigration laws and citizenship distinctions allow physical appearance to serve as a way of controlling certain racial and ethnic groups. Indeed, the simultaneous social construction of race and of the immigrant has been particularly noted by critical race legal scholars (Chang; Haney López; Hing; K. Johnson). In his widely read book, *White by Law: The Legal Construction of Race*, Ian Haney-López aptly captures the legal history of the construction of racial categories that specified citizenship privileges and restrictions. To his credit, he does not ignore immigration. Indeed, he regards the racial restrictions in the law of citizenship as an additional narrative and does not just treat race as an aspect of African Americans and other groups classified as minorities. Michael A. Olivas points to a few historical events that illustrate this shared racialized experience among people of color:

> Consider the immigration history and political economy of three groups whose United States history predates the prophecy for the year 2000: Cherokee removal and the Trail of Tears; Chinese laborers and the Chinese Exclusion Laws; and Mexicans in the Bracero Program and Operation Wetback. These three racial groups share different histories of conquest, exploitation, and legal disadvantage; but even a brief summary of their treatment of United States law shows commonalities of racial animus, legal infirmity, and majority domination of legal institutions. (11)

During the last two decades, the growing body of CRT literature has shown that racism in the United States can be fully comprehended only by studying the ways in which immigration laws have detrimental consequences for all racial minorities. LatCrit theorists, in particular, have begun to explore the transnational effects of domestic subordination (K. Johnson). In their review of U.S. immigration laws, cases, and trials, CRT and LatCrit scholars have analyzed the social construction of immigration status as well as the significance that race plays in maintaining and controlling immigrants and other minority citizens (Chang; Hing; K. Johnson). Among the most commonly cited are the 1882 Chinese Exclusion Act, the Gentleman's Agreement of 1907 between the United States and Japan, the 1923 U.S. Supreme Court case *United States v. Thind* (whereby immigrants from India were ruled to be ineligible for naturalization because they are not white), the 1924 national origins quota system, and the Immigration Act of 1965 (which limited the number of migrants from the Western Hemisphere). In his analysis of immigration laws, Kevin Johnson makes the connection between the legal construction and the social construction of "aliens" as the other:

> Fabricated out of whole cloth, the "alien" represents a body of rules passed by Congress and reinforced by popular culture. It is society, with the assistance of the law, that defines who is an "alien," an institutionalized "other," and who is not. It is a society, through Congress and the courts, that determines which rights to afford "aliens." . . . Like the social construction of race, which helps to legitimize racial subordination, the construction of the "alien" has helped justify the limitation on non-citizen rights imposed by our legal system. (154)

Robert Chang argues, "Examination of the immigrant allows us to observe the dynamics of racial formation as immigrants enter the political/cultural/legal space of the United States and 'become' differentially racialized as Asian American, Black, Latina/Latino, and White" (29). The treatment of persons identified as "alien," particularly those regarded as non-European, corresponds to the treatment of citizens of color in the United States. Under this paradigm, immigration law enforcement campaigns—such as Operation Wetback, Operation Blockade, Operation Hold the Line, and Operation Gatekeeper—are inextricably related to society's view of citizens of, in this case, Mexican ancestry. Concern about immigration to the United States is inseparable from stereotyping Mexicans as "illegal aliens" and socially constructing Mexicans as criminal, foreign, and the other. Although the law institutionalizes who is "alien," the social construction of immigrant status is not complete without policing and surveillance. The "show me your papers" inspection of passports, identification cards, and other forms of documentation, once associated with totalitarian regimes, is now routinely used in the United States to control access to social services, to authorize and regulate movement, and to single out specific racial groups for additional citizenship inspection (Caplan and Torpey).

Although branding and tattooing, or other forms of "writing on the body," are not used to distinguish between "aliens" and citizens, the practice of racial profiling demonstrates that citizenship status is inscribed on the body.[1] For instance, the U.S. Supreme Court decision in *United States v. Brignoni-Ponce* that "Mexican appearance" "constitutes a legitimate consideration under the Fourth Amendment for making an immigration stop" (K. Johnson 676) sanctions the immigration law enforcement use of racial profiling. Stigmatized as "aliens," Latinas/os and Asian Pacific Americans carry a bodily "figurative border" (Chang). Racialized immigration law–enforcement practices allow a person's appearance to serve as "reasonable suspicion" or "probable cause." This process of surveillance and citizenship inspection involves racial profiling; persons are identified on the basis of their social identity—for example, "Mexicanness"—rather than on the basis of specific behavior (Benitez; K. Johnson; Romero). Consequently, working-class Latinos are frequently the targets of racially motivated detentions and searches and thus are far more likely than middle-class whites to encounter abuse by the Immigration and Naturalization Service (INS) (Arriola; Benitez; Lazos; Vargas). The likelihood of mistreatment of Mexican immigrants and Mexican Americans increases with the routine use of racial profiling in citizenship inspections. As Kevin Johnson cautions, "Alien terminology helps rationalize harsh, perhaps inhumane, treatment of persons from other countries" (268). This is consistent with Dunn's finding that the "low intensity conflict doctrine," developed by United States military theoreticians during the 1980s, has been applied to the U.S.–Mexico border region. Nevins's account of hardships and the increasing control over human resources depicts the significant harms and diminished opportunities that communities along the border experience under Operation Gatekeeper.

My own work on immigration has been informed by CRT research into racialized law enforcement practices, particularly by the theoretical work of Katheryn Russell. Building on Peggy Davis's conceptualization of micro- and macro-aggressions and the law, Russell maintains that whereas micro-aggressions are racial assaults carried out on a personal level, macro-aggressions are "face group affronts" that are "not directed toward a particular Black person, but at Blackness in general" and may be made either "by a private individual or official authority" (139). Repeated micro- and macro-aggressions against a particular group not only routinize demeaning treatment, but simultaneously reinforce a racial hierarchy and minimize the extent to which injuries are experienced. Offended parties are denied their achieved status, and they experience "limit[ed] access to equal opportunities and fair dealings before the law" (Milovanovic and Russell xvi).

In their edited volume on petit apartheid, Milovanovic and Russell incorporate Georges-Abeyie's paradigm of grand and petit apartheid along with micro- and macro-aggressions to create a continuum of current practices of racial profiling with other "negative social factors and discretional decision-making by both criminal justice agents and criminal justice agencies" (x). Racial profiling, legitimated by the courts or official immigration campaigns, is an example of an overt and formal form of discrimination under petit apartheid. The continuum depicts petit apartheid as a system of legal control that ranges from covert and informal to overt and formal discriminatory practices. Russell identifies four characteristics of petit apartheid practices: 1) they occur largely outside of public view; 2) even when they take place within plain view, they are typically minimized or ignored; 3) they are likely to "proliferate where criminal justice personnel have high levels of unchecked discretion"; and 4) they "reflect and reinforce the racialized images of deviance that exist within society at large" (13).

As a theoretical construct, petit apartheid has been used to explain racial profiling in the war against drugs (Campbell; Covington), the regulation and policing of public space (Bass; Ferrell), the underrepresentation of persons of color in law enforcement (L. Ross), and the use of racial derogation in prosecutors' closing arguments in court (S. Johnson). These practices of petit apartheid demonstrate how nonverbal gestures, postures, and mannerisms are the most covert and informal forms of discrimination.

The four distinguishing features of petit apartheid practices are also evident in immigration law enforcement. Increased militarization along the U.S.–Mexico border occurs largely outside of the public view, and U.S. Border Patrol agents operate with a high level of unchecked discretion (Dunn; Massey, Durand, and Malone). Highly ritualized immigration inspection at border crossings and airports, particularly since 9/11, obscures the heightened levels of scrutiny and mistreatment of the racialized poor and working-class Latinos. Physical appearance as Latino, association with a work crew, inability to speak English or preference to speak Spanish, and proximity to the border are used as reasonable suspicion to justify investigatory stops. These practices select persons for citizenship inspection based on perceived "Mexicanness," and they reinforce the idea that Mexicans are foreigners, criminals, and inferior. Citizenship inspection targets racialized bodies and directs heavy surveillance at Mexican-American neighborhoods. Thus, the "police practice known as 'field investigations,' in which police interrogate persons who appear not to 'belong' to a given place" (Marx 323) is used against Latinos in immigration law enforcement. As suspected aliens become a physically identifiable "type," immigration surveillance reinforces the exclusionary use of urban public spaces and limits freedom of movement (Heyman; Weissinger).

Obviously, law enforcement agencies do not systematically record discriminatory practices because many such practices are legitimized, occur outside public view, and are not employed against the general white middle-class population. However, a source of rich data on micro- and macro-aggressions in immigration law enforcement can be found in witness narratives. In the section that follows I analyze three witness accounts collected by the Arizona State Attorney's office in its investigation of a series of immigration raids that targeted the Latino neighborhood in Chandler, Arizona, in 1997 (Romero; Romero and Serag).

Researching the Color of Immigration Enforcement: Witness Narratives

In response to community protest and accusations of civil rights violations, the Arizona Attorney General's office investigated a joint operation, conducted in the summer of 1997, by the Chandler Police Department and the Tucson Border Patrol Sector. Evidence collected by the local media and community leaders indicated that the joint operation was targeted at the predominately Mexican neighborhood within the Chandler city limits at work sites employing working-class Mexican men and at shops catering to a Spanish-speaking population. Detailed descriptions of micro- and macro-aggressions used in police field operations are interspersed throughout the witness accounts.

Racial profiling that encompasses cultural attributes does not merely target individual Mexicans and Mexican Americans, but rather "Mexicanness" in general. The computer-printed "Record of Deportable Alien" forms that were used during the law-enforcement operation and that were included in the final report of the investigation provide further evidence of the assumed profile that directed officers' use of discretionary citizenship inspection. Prior to being used in the field operation and filled out by the arresting officers, certain information had been typed in. For example, in the space requesting "Country of Citizenship," "Mexico and/or Mexican" was typed in beforehand; "BLK" was typed in for hair color, "BRN" for eye color, "MED" for complexion, "Laborer" for occupation, "MEX" for "Nationality of Minor Children," and "At Entry" was typed in the box requesting information on the "Length of Time Illegally in the U.S." These narratives reveal the "subtle, stunning, often automatic, and non-verbal exchanges that are 'put downs' " (Davis) resulting from using the amorphous designation "Mexicanness" as a basis of reasonable suspicion or probable cause.

Building on the work of LatCrit immigration theorists (e.g., Benitiez; Chang and Aoki; K. Johnson; Vargas), I coded the narratives into five patterns of immigration law enforcement that placed persons of Mexican or other Latino ancestry at risk before the law as follows: 1) making discretionary stops based on ethnicity and class; 2) using intimidation and other tactics intended to demean and subordinate the persons stopped; 3) restricting the freedom of movement of Mexicans but not of others in the same vicinity; 4) reinforcing stereotypes of Mexican as "alien," "foreign," "inferior," and" criminal"; and 5) limiting access to fair and impartial treatment before the law.

To illustrate the importance of placing race at the center of immigration research, I present here three narratives by and about outsiders who "resist the subordinate messages of the dominant culture by challenging stereotypes and presenting and representing people of color as complex and heterogeneous" (Montoya 244). The first narrative is drawn from an interview with Mr. Marlor, manager of the Southwest Supermarket located in the Chandler area. His store was targeted for citizenship inspection. He began by recounting the strategy that officers used in his store to separate his customers of Mexican ancestry by legal status. Officers requested his assistant manager, Nancy Rodriguez, to announce over the store's loudspeaker that all illegal aliens who were shopping should turn themselves over to law enforcement officers in the parking lot. Rodriguez, however, refused to make the announcement. Subsequently, the Chandler Police and U.S. Border Patrol set up a command center in the parking lot near the store and began stopping all customers who appeared Mexican. Customers who appeared white were not followed, asked for identification, or required to show proof of citizenship. Marlor was particularly upset about the following incident he observed:

> A man with two small children, about three to four years of age, was contacted by officers as he walked out of the store. The man talked to the officers as he walked to his truck. He opened the door on the passenger side of the truck and placed his children in the vehicle. He then walked around the truck to the driver's side. At this time a Border Patrol officer approached the passenger door and placed the wheel of his bicycle behind the door to prevent it from being closed. A Chandler police officer placed his bicycle wheel behind the driver's door in a similar fashion. The Chandler officer talked to the man for a few minutes, then began to try to pull him from the truck cab. The Border Patrol officer then rounded the cab and helped the Chandler officer. They pulled him from the cab, handcuffed him and placed him in a police van. The children were crying and very upset. An officer returned to the truck in about five minutes, stayed there for some time, then made a phone call. Later, another officer arrived and removed the children. In the meantime, a woman customer went to the truck and tried to comfort the children. They were left in the truck for a total of 15 or 20 minutes.

Because no robbery or other crime had been reported, the officers were clearly using this man's perceived "Mexicanness" as grounds for reasonable suspicion or probable cause. The officers' actions were not in response to any violent actions by the man, yet he was humiliated and demeaned in front of his children and other customers in the parking lot. His children witnessed that their father's physical appearance placed him at risk before the law and caused him to be treated as though he were inferior to the white customers, who were allowed to go about their business without citizenship inspection. Although citizens who leave children in cars in the summer can be prosecuted for child endangerment, this man's children were left by the officers in July's triple-digit temperature without apparent concern for their safety or fear of legal action against them.

Major immigration enforcement targets of the Chandler Police–U.S. Border Patrol joint operation were apartment complexes and trailer courts occupied by low-income Mexican Americans and Mexican immigrants. Police radio dispatch tapes indicate that vehicles leaving specific housing areas between 4:00 A.M. and 6:00 A.M. with persons identified as possibly migrant workers, landscapers, or construction workers were targeted for traffic enforcement by a spotter. (This is the only time officers recall using this strategy outside special Driving Under the Influence enforcement.) Forced entry into people's homes highlighted the level of intimidation and the limited access to fair and impartial treatment before the law that low-income Latinos experienced during the immigration raids. These incidents were particularly traumatic for children. In most cases, the house searches were the children's first encounter with law enforcement agents. Their firsthand observations involved witnessing their parents, grandparents, and other family elders humiliated and treated as criminals. The second narrative describes one of these house-to-house searches.

> On July 28, 1997, at approximately 11:00 P.M., B. and his family were sound asleep in a trailer owned by his brother-in-law. . . . The family was wakened by a loud banging on the front door and bright lights shining through the windows. When B. looked around, he saw two Chandler police officers, with an INS/Border Patrol agent behind them. All officers were bicycle officers. The officers demanded to be allowed into the trailer and when B. asked if they had the right to come in, he was told, "We can do whatever we want, we are the Chandler Police Department. You have people who are here illegally." Although B. denied that there were any undocumented aliens there, the officers insisted on entering the trailer, rousing everyone from bed. The family members were all in their sleep clothes, but the officers refused to allow them to dress. None of the children were United States citizens, and except for the brother-in-law, all the rest were legal aliens; the brother-in-law had entered the country legally but his visa had expired and he was in the process of getting it renewed. When the officers discovered that the brother-in-law did not have proper papers, they called a Chandler Police Department back-up vehicle and took him away in a patrol car. B. attempted to give his brother-in-law street clothes when the officers were taking him away, but the officers would not allow this and took him away in his sleep clothes. He was later readmitted to the United States with the

renewed visa he had been awaiting. The others were detained in the trailer for approximately ninety minutes; they were not searched but they were questioned even after they showed the papers demonstrating that they were legally in the United States. The police told B. that they had spoken with the park manager and he had given them permission to search the trailers, had given them a map, and had marked on the map where Hispanic residents lived. The four children involved in this incident are still fearful when someone knocks at the door of the trailer, and continue to be nervous when they see police officers on the street. . . . Most of the police visits occurred between 10:00 P.M. and 11:00 P.M. and were precipitated by police banging on doors and windows and shining lights through the windows. . . . Every night someone else was taken away.

The manner in which family elders were belittled, demeaned, and subordinated serves as a reminder that Latinos, whether U.S. citizens or not, are at constant risk before the law. Powerful messages involving their lack of rights and the unequal legal status of family members were delivered to the children. House searches teach children that association with loved ones who are not U.S. citizens may endanger their own safety.

The narrative above depicts forced entry into a home without a search warrant, reasonable suspicion, or probable cause based on observed illegal behavior of any of the persons residing in the trailer. Instead, the forced entry was based solely on the park manager's identification of the occupants as Mexican. Officers' unorthodox strategy for gaining entrance to homes, the process and length of time family members were questioned, and the refusal to allow them to get dressed are indicative of the various methods that law enforcement agents use with high levels of unchecked discretion. The possibility of officers restraining their behavior when making discretionary stops in parking lots, shopping areas, and other public places does not exist in these nighttime searches of private residents.

In the third narrative, F., the mother of three young children, presented a response to racial profiling and citizenship inspection that reveals how these law-enforcement techniques produce discord within the community and also weaken family ties. Having been publicly humiliated and rendered helpless in front of her children as she faced an officer's relentless citizenship inspection, F. is determined to protect her children from the same demeaning treatment.

The narrative gives an account of F. walking to her parked car outside the grocery store with her three daughters. Prior to being stopped and
questioned about her citizenship status by an officer, she had been speaking
in Spanish to her children. As do U.S. citizens who are requested by an
officer to show identification, F. assumed that providing her driver's license
was an appropriate response. The officer, however, refused to accept it as
adequate proof of citizenship and demanded another form of identification.
Consequently, she was forced into a desperate search in her car for a different document of identification. Completely subordinated to the officer's
discretion, F. and her daughters were detained in the July heat intensified
by the parking lot's blacktop and an increasing sense of mortification as
shoppers watched these suspected criminals. Her encounter with the officer became a public spectacle serving as a symbol of the overzealous and
draconian immigration law-enforcement practices adopted to stop illegal
immigration into the United States from Mexico. Reflecting on the degradation to which persons of Mexican ancestry who were caught in the
dragnet of immigration raids were subjected, F. realized that her American
roots, which reach back to before the Mexican-American War of 1846 to
1848, did not protect her from second-class citizenship—a citizenship status
whose rights and privileges are violated at the whim of public policy and
officers' unchecked discretionary use of power.

> F. feels that she has to watch what she wears and that she can-
> not look unkempt. The officer made her feel stereotyped on the
> basis of what she was wearing. She felt that she did not belong.
> A number of people were going in and out of the store and
> one couple looked at her. F. did not see anyone else stopped.
> The only time she has gone back to Chandler has been for the
> meeting [protesting the immigration raid] at the church. She has
> not gone back to the store because she does not feel welcome;
> she feels violated. This has also affected her plans to have her
> children spend some time with relatives in Mexico. She canceled
> their trip because she does not want to risk her children picking
> up a Spanish accent.

Prior to this traumatic encounter, F., like many middle-class Mexican
Americans, believed that immigration raids did not directly hamper the
freedom of movement of their targets or place them at risk before the law.
However, F. now realizes that the use of racial profiling places her family

at constant risk if they cannot cover their stigma, their "Mexicanness." As a dark-complexioned Mexican American, her physical appearance renders her vulnerable to the stereotype of "dirty Mexican" and "illegal immigrant." F. now makes conscious decisions about how to display clear visual signs of her middle-class status and avoids communities, shops, churches, and even relatives who might place her in danger of being treated as an immigrant or second-class citizen. Wanting to protect her children from the public spectacle of the degradation ritual performed in discretionary stops for citizenship inspection, F. is determined to eliminate any signs of their "Mexicanness." Quite probably, she will dissuade her children from playing outside in the sun and tanning darkly, from learning to speak Spanish to communicate with their grandparents and other family elders, or from gaining the cultural competence to participate in two cultures. Is it any wonder, then, that F. will probably place assimilation at the top of her list of mothering responsibilities?

Conclusion

My case study of the Chandler immigration raid demonstrates the importance of earnestly considering the concept of race in immigration research and recognizing the racialization of constructing citizenship in everyday practices. In this particular case, the racialization of "Mexicanness" was reinforced by selecting persons for citizenship inspection on the basis of their appearance, Spanish-speaking abilities, and location of residence. The use of racial profiling in immigration law enforcement mirrors similar questionable policing practices aimed at targeting blacks and Latinos in the policing of public spaces and in the war against drugs, as well as the targeting of Arab Americans in the war against terrorism. Like African Americans and Latinos, Mexican immigrants' physical appearance unfairly subjects them to reasonable suspicion or probable cause before the law.

Exemplified in the three narratives from the Arizona attorney general's report are instances of racial animus and legal infirmity commonalities in law enforcement practice that people of color experience in the United States, regardless of citizenship status. Like African Americans, as documented by the research, Latinos experience discretionary stops, intimidation, and restriction of movement that place them at risk before the law and reinforce a racial hierarchy. Public spectacles produced by racially profiling shoppers and motorists for citizenship inspection reflect and reinforce racialized images of deviance.

A CRT analysis of immigration leads one to consider several issues that are crucial to understanding the position of racialized groups. Within this framework, researchers can begin to explore the 1.5 generation's incentive to detach themselves from families and community and to erase any characteristics of their immigrant past in an effort to eliminate the likelihood that they will be humiliated, demeaned, and deprived of their civil rights by being racially profiled by police, teachers, and employers. Instead of recognizing experiences that shape racialized immigrants' identification with other racialized groups and the importance of their coalition building, an assimilation framework assumes that racial minorities are an adversarial culture and subordinates blacks, Chicano/as, and Puerto Ricans. However, CRT explains the ways in which the 1.5 generation's fate and their parents' fates are tied to other racialized groups. The Americanization process cannot be fully comprehended without identifying the construction of the "alien" and the ways we act upon all groups identified as "ethnic," "foreign," or "non-white." Race, ethnicity, and immigrant status are not mutually exclusive categories. Intersectionality becomes crucial in theorizing about the immigrant experience in a nation that has a history of social exclusion by race, class, gender, and citizenship.

Presenting a racialized immigrant counterstory to the master narrative of the assimilated immigrant not only challenges the myth of meritocracy, but it also exposes white privilege. Rather than accepting the majority domination of the legal, education, and media institutions and perpetuating cultural deficit models, research agendas that examine the consequences of this domination need to be established. Rather than proposing solutions that drive a wedge further into the gap between immigrants and U.S. racial minorities, counternarratives propose solutions aimed at eradicating racism and all forms of subordination. Sociologists of immigration must therefore abandon a research agenda narrowly focused on assimilation, acculturation, generational conflict, and social mobility and actively broaden their analyses to include issues of social justice. However, this cannot be achieved without acknowledging the growing antagonism and antiracist and anti-immigration sentiments that impact all persons of color residing in the United States, regardless of their citizenship status.

CRT and LatCrit's conceptualization of how political economy impacts both immigrants and citizens of color makes for a more comprehensive and nuanced understanding of racial antagonisms and of differences and similarities between immigrant groups, and it identifies barriers that influence their individual choices. CRT and LatCrit scholars have studied the relationship between civil rights and immigration laws and have identified the mirrored patterns of exclusion and deportation within the racial history of our country. As K. Johnson points out, "U.S. immigration law represents a national Rorschach test of the nation's civil rights sensibilities" (172).

CRT scholars have written on the significance of immigrants' organizing efforts with regard to issues of racial and economic justice based on civil rights discourse and strategies. By placing race at the center of their analysis and moving away from paradigms that hold whiteness as the norm, critical race theorists identify research agendas that incorporate collective actions taken by immigrant workers to improve their economic conditions and legislative proposals that support their struggle for economic justice. Instead of proposing recommendations and solutions that focus on individual choices, CRT has focused on both civil rights and human rights agendas. Consequently, communities of color, regardless of citizenship status, are not pitted against each other in proposed solutions but rather are seen as allies in the struggle to eradicate all forms of racism and all forms of subordination. CRT and LatCrit offer an ideal model for bridging the gap between immigration and race research in sociology.

Note

1. However, some critics have noted that nascent technologies like fingerprinting, retinal imaging, and facial recognition programs are coming very close to the practice of identifying the "other" by branding and tattooing.

Works Cited

Aguirre, Adalberto Jr. "Academic Storytelling: A Critical Race Theory Story of Affirmative Action." *Sociological Perspectives* 43 (2000): 19–39.

———. "The Personal Narrative as Academic Storytelling: A Chicano's Search for Presence and Voice in Academe." *International Journal of Qualitative Studies in Education* 18 (2005): 147–63.

Alba, Richard, and Victor Nee. "Rethinking Assimilation Theory for a New Era of Immigration." *International Migration Review* 3 (1997): 826–74.

Arriola, Elvia R. "LatCrit Theory, International Human Rights, Popular Culture, and the Faces of Despair in INS Raids." *University of Miami Inter-American Law Review* 28 (1996): 245–62.

Bass, Sandra. "Out of Place: Petit Apartheid and the Police." *Petit Apartheid in the U.S. Criminal Justice System: The Dark Figure of Racism.* Ed. Dragan Milovanovic and Kathyn Russell. Durham: Carolina Academic Press, 2001. 43–54.

Bell, Derrik. *Faces at the Bottom of the Well: The Permanence of Racism.* New York: Basic Books, 1992.

Benitez, Humberto. "Flawed Strategies: The INS Shift from Border Interdiction to Internal Enforcement Actions." *La Raza Law Journal* 7 (1994): 154–79.

Bernal, Delores Delgado. "Critical Race Theory, Latino Critical Theory, and Critical Raced-Gendered Epistemologies: Recognizing Students of Color as Holders and Creators of Knowledge." *Qualitative Inquiry* 8 (2002): 105–26.

Blauner, Robert. *Racial Oppression in America.* New York: Harper & Row, 1972.

Bonilla-Silva, Eduardo. *Racism Without Racists: Color-Blind Racism and the Persistence of Racial Inequality in the United States.* Lanham: Rowman & Littlefield, 2003.

Bush, Melanie E. L. *Breaking the Code of Good Intentions: Everyday Forms of Whiteness.* Lanham: Rowman & Littlefield, 2004.

Caldwell, Paulette M. "A Hair Piece: Perspectives on the Intersection of Race and Gender." *Duke Law Journal* 41 (1991): 365–96.

Cameron, Christopher David Ruiz. "The Rakes of Wrath: Urban Agricultural Workers and the Struggle Against Los Angeles' Ban on Gas-Powered Leaf Blowers." *University of California Davis Law Review* 33 (2000): 1087–1103.

Campbell, Jackie. "Walking the Beat Alone: An African American Police Officer's Perspective on Petit Apartheid." *Petit Apartheid in the U.S. Criminal Justice System: The Dark Figure of Racism.* Ed. Dragan Milovanovic and Kathyn Russell. Durham: Carolina Academic Press, 2001. 15–20.

Caplan, Jane, and John Torpey, eds. *Documenting Individual Identity: The Development of State Practices in the Modern World.* Princeton, NJ: Princeton UP, 2001.

Carter, Prudence L. *Keepin' It Real: School Success Beyond Black and White.* Oxford: Oxford UP, 2005.

Chang, Robert S. *Disoriented: Asian Americans, Law, and the Nation-State.* New York: New York UP, 1999.

Chang, Robert S., and Keith Aoki. "Centering the Immigrant in the Inter/national Imagination." *California Law Review* 85 (1997): 1395–1447.

Cho, Sumi, and Robert Westley. "Critical Race Coalitions: Key Movements that Preformed the Theory." *University of California Davis Law Review* 33 (2000): 1377–80, 1388–99.

Cornelius, Wayne A. "Death at the Border: Efficacy and Unintended Consequences of U.S. Immigration Control Policy." *Population and Development Review* 27 (2001): 661–85.

Covington, Jeanette. "Round Up the Usual Suspects: Racial Profiling and the War on Drugs." *Petit Apartheid in the U.S. Criminal Justice System: The Dark*

Figure of Racism. Ed. Dragan Milovanovic and Kathyn Russell. Durham: Carolina Academic Press, 2001. 27–42.

Crenshaw, Kimblé. "Demarginalizing the Intersection of Race and Sex: A Black Feminist Critique of Antidiscrimination Doctrine, Feminist Theory and Antiracist Politics." *University of Chicago Legal Forum* (1989): 139.

———. "Mapping the Margins: Intersectionality, Identity Politics, and the Violence Against Women of Color." *Stanford Law Review* 43 (1999): 1241–99.

Davis, Peggy C. "Law as Microaggression." *Yale Law Journal* 98 (1989): 1559–77.

Delgado, Richard. "Legal Storytelling: Storytelling for Oppositionists and Others: A Plea for Narrative." *Michigan Law Review* 8 (1989): 2411–41.

Du Bois, W. E. B. *The Souls of Black Folk.* New York: The Modern Library. (Original work published 1903, 2003.)

Dunn, Timothy J. *The Militarization of the U.S.–Mexico Border.* Austin: U of Texas Press, 1996.

Ferrell, Jeff. "Trying to Make Us a Parking Lot: Petit Apartheid, Cultural Space, and the Public Negotiation of Ethnicity." *Petit Apartheid in the U.S. Criminal Justice System: The Dark Figure of Racism.* Ed. Dragan Milovanovic and Kathyn Russell. Durham: Carolina Academic Press, 2001. 55–68.

Fernández-Kelly, Patricia, and Sara Curran. "Nicaraguans: Voices Lost, Voices Found." *Ethnicities: Children of Immigrants in America.* Ed. A. Portes and R. G. Rumbaut. Berkeley: U of California P, 2001. 127–56.

Fordham, Signithia, and John Ogbu. "Black Students' School Success: Coping with the Burden of Acting White." *Urban Review* 18 (1986): 176–206.

Guinier, Lani, and Gerald Torres. *The Miner's Canary: Enlisting Race, Resisting Power, Transforming Democracy.* Cambridge: Harvard UP, 2002.

Haney López, Ian. *White by Law: The Legal Construction of Race.* New York: New York UP, 1996.

Heyman, Josiah McC. "Putting Power in the Anthropology of Bureaucracy: The Immigration and Naturalization Service at the Mexico–United States Border." *Current Anthropology* 36 (1995): 261–87.

Hing, Bill Ong. *To Be an American: Cultural Pluralism and the Rhetoric of Assimilation.* New York: New York UP, 1997.

Ignatiev, Noel. *How the Irish Became White.* New York: Routledge, 1995.

Johnson, Kevin. " 'Aliens' and the U.S. Immigration Laws: The Social and Legal Construction of Nonpersons." *University of Miami International-American Law Review* 28 (1996): 263–92.

———. The Case Against Race Profiling in Immigration Enforcement. *Washington University Law Quarterly* 78 (2000): 676–736.

———. Race and the Immigration Laws: The Need for Critical Inquiry." *Crossroads, Directions, and a New Critical Race Theory.* Ed. Francisco Valdéz, Jerome McCristal Culp, and Angela P. Harris. Philadelphia: Temple UP, 2002. 187–98.

————. *The "Huddled Masses" Myth: Immigration and Civil Rights.* Philadelphia: Temple UP, 2004.

Johnson, Sheri Lynn. "Racial Derogation in Prosecutors' Closing Arguments." *Petit Apartheid in the U.S. Criminal Justice System: The Dark Figure of Racism.* Ed. Dragan Milovanovic and Kathyn Russell. Durham: Carolina Academic Press, 2001. 79–102.

Ladson-Billings, Gloria J. "Preparing Teachers for Diverse Student Populations: A Critical Race Theory Perspective." *Review of Research Education* 24 (1999): 211–47.

Lazos, Sylvia R. " 'Latina/o-ization' of the Midwest: *Cambio de colores* (Change of Colors) as *agromaquilas* Expand into the Heartland." *Berkeley la Raza Law Journal* 13 (2002): 343–68.

Martínez, George. "African-Americans, Latinos, and the Construction of Race: Toward an Epistemic Coalition." *Chicano-Latino Law Review* 19 (1998): 213–22.

Marx, Gary T. "Identity and Anonymity: Some Conceptual Distinctions and Issues for Research." *Documenting Individual Identity: The Development of State Practices in the Modern World.* Ed. Jane Caplan and John Torpey. Princeton: Princeton UP, 2001. 311–27.

Massey, Douglas S., Jorge Durand, and Nolan J. Malone. *Beyond Smoke and Mirrors: Mexican Immigration in an Era of Economic Integration.* New York: Russell Sage Foundation, 2002.

Matsuda, Mari J. "Voices of America: Accent, Antidiscrimination Law, and a Jurisprudence for the Last Reconstruction." *Yale Law Journal* 100 (1991): 1329–1407.

Milovanovic, Dragan, and Katheryn Russell, K., eds. *Petit Apartheid in the U.S. Criminal Justice System.* Durham: Carolina Academic Press, 2001.

Montoya, Margaret. "Celebrating Racialized Legal Narratives." *Crossroads, Directions, and a New Critical Race Theory.* Ed. Franciso Valdéz, Jerome McCristal Culp, and Angela P. Harris. Philadelphia: Temple UP, 2002. 243–50.

Nevins, Joseph. *Operation Gatekeeper: Theories of the "Illegal Alien" and the Making of the U.S.–Mexico Boundary.* New York: Routledge, 2002.

Olivas, Michael A. "The Chronicles, My Grandfather's Stories, and Immigration Law: The Slave Traders' Chronicle as Racial History." *Critical Race Theory: The Cutting Edge.* Ed. Richard Delgado. Philadelphia: Temple UP, 1995. 9–20.

Oliver, Melvin, and Thomas T. Shapiro. *Black Wealth/White Wealth: A New Perspective on Racial Inequality.* New York: Routledge, 1995.

Omi, Michael, and Howard H. Winant. *Racial Formation in the United States: From 1960s to 1980s.* New York: Routledge, 1986.

Park, Robert. *The Immigrant Press and Its Control.* New York: Harper, 1922.

Parks, Robert, Ernest W. Burgess, Roderick D. McKenzie, and Louis Wirth. *The City.* Chicago: U of Chicago P, 1925.

Parker, Laurence. "What's Race Got to Do with it? Critical Race Theory's Conflicts with and Connections to Qualitative Research Methodology and Epistemology." *Qualitative Inquiry* 8 (2002): 7–22.

Phillips, Scott, Nestor Rodríguez, and Jacqueline Hagan. "Brutality at the Border? Use of Force in the Arrest of Immigrants in the United States." *International Journal of the Sociology of Law* 2 (2003): 285–306.

Portes, Alejandro. *The New Second Generation.* New York: Russell Sage Foundation, 1996.

Portes, Alejandro, and Rubèn G. Rumbaut. *Ethnicities: Children of Immigrants in America.* Berkeley: U of California P, 2001.

———. *Legacies: The Story of the Immigrant Second Generation.* Berkeley: U of California P, 2001.

Roediger, David R. *Wages of Whiteness: Race and the Making of the American Working Class.* London: Verso, 1991.

Romero, Mary. "Afterword. Historicizing and Symbolizing a Racial Ethnic Identity: Lessons for Coalition Building with a Social Justice Agenda." *UC Davis Law Review* 33 (2000): 1599–1625.

———. "State Violence, and the Social and Legal Construction of Latino Criminality: From el bandido to Gang Member." *Denver University Law Review* 78 (2001): 1089–1127.

———. "Racial Profiling and Immigration Law Enforcement: Rounding Up of Usual Suspects in the Latino Community." *Critical Sociology* 32 (2006): 449–75.

Romero, Mary, and Marwah Serag. "Violation of Latino Civil Rights Resulting from INS and Local Police's Use of Race, Culture and Class Profiling: The Case of the Chandler Roundup in Arizona." *Cleveland State Law Review* 52 (2005): 75–96.

Ross, Lee E. "African-American Interest in Law Enforcement: A Consequence of Petit Apartheid?" *Petit Apartheid in the U.S. Criminal Justice System: The Dark Figure of Racism.* Ed. Dragan Milovanovic and Kathyn Russell. Durham: Carolina Academic Press, 2001. 69–78.

Ross, Thomas. *Just Stories: How the Law Embodies Racism and Bias.* Boston: Beacon Press, 1996.

Russell, Katheryn K. *The Color of Crime: Racial Hoaxes, White Fear, Black Protectionism, Police Harassment, and Other Macroaggressions.* New York: New York UP, 1998.

———. *Underground Codes: Race, Crime, and Related Fires.* New York: New York UP, 2004.

———. *Protecting Our Own: Race, Crime, and African Americans.* Lanham: Rowman & Littlefield, 2006.

Schneider, Christopher. "Integrating Critical Race Theory and Postmodernism Implications of Race, Class, and Gender." *Critical Criminology* 12 (2004): 87–103.

Shapiro, Thomas. *The Cost of Being African American: How Wealth Perpetuates Inequality.* Oxford: Oxford UP, 2004.

Solózano, Daniel G., and Dolores Delgado Bernal. "Examining Transformational Resistance Through a Critical Race and LatCrit Theory Framework: Chicana and Chicano Students in an Urban Context." *Urban Education* 36 (2001): 308–42.

Steinberg, Stephen. *The Ethnic Myth: Race, Ethnicity, and Class in America.* Boston: Beacon Press, 1981.

Takaki, Ronald. *Iron Cages: Race and Culture in 19th Century America.* Oxford: Oxford University Press, 1979.

Thomas, William, and Florian Znaniecki. *The Polish Peasant in Europe and America.* New York: Dover Publications, 1958.

Torpey, John C. *The Invention of the Passport: Surveillance, Citizenship and the State.* New York: Cambridge UP, 2000.

Weissinger, George. *Law Enforcement and the INS: A Participant Observation Study of Control Agents.* New York: UP of America, Inc., 1996.

Wildman, Stephanie M., with Adrienne D. Davis. "Language and Silence: Making Systems of Privilege Visible." *Critical Race Theory: The Cutting Edge.* Ed. Richard Delgado. Philadelphia: Temple UP, 1995. 573–81.

Williams, Patricia. *The Alchemy of Race and Rights.* Cambridge: Harvard UP, 1991.

Wirth, Louis. *The Ghetto.* Chicago: U of Chicago P, 1956.

Valdéz, Francisco. "Afterword. Theorizing 'OutCrit' Theories: Coalitional Methods and Comparative Jurisprudential Experience—RaceCrits, QueerCrits and LatCrits." *University of Miami Law Review* 53 (1999): 1265–1322.

Valdéz, Francisco, Jerome McCristal Culp, and Angela P. Harris. *Crossroads, Directions, and a New Critical Race Theory.* Philadelphia: Temple UP, 2002.

Vargas, Jorge A. "U.S. Border Patrol Abuses, Undocumented Mexican Workers, and International Human Rights." *San Diego International Law Review* 2 (2001): 1–92.

Villenas, Sofia, and Donna Deyhle. "Critical Race Theory and Ethnographies Challenging the Stereotypes: Latino Families, Schooling, Resilience and Resistance." *Curriculum Inquiry* 29 (1999): 413–45.

Yamamoto, Eric. *Interracial Justice: Conflict and Reconciliation in Post-Civil Rights America.* New York: New York UP, 1999.

Yosso, Tara J., and Daniel G Solózano. "Conceptualizing A Critical Race Theory in Sociology." *The Blackwell Companion to Social Inequalities.* Ed. Mary Romero and Eric Margolis. Oxford: Blackwell, 2005. 117–26.

Zhou, Min, and Carl L. Bankston III. *Growing Up American: The Adoption of Vietnamese Adolescents in the United States.* New York: Russell Sage Publications, 1998.

Chapter Four

Whiteness in a Red Room

Telling Stories and Legal Discourse in the Tribal Courtroom

Raquel Montoya-Lewis

[N]arratives invoke the right of the subordinated person to narrate—to interpret events in opposition to the dominant narratives, and to reinvent one's self by bringing coherence to one's life stories.

—Montoya, "Celebrating Racialized Legal Narratives"

During the course of the last twenty years, telling stories in a legal setting—legal narrative—has become a potent tool for critiquing the legal system and the assumptions that underlie it. Those assumptions, many have argued, prevent the legal system from creating and reflecting a socially just society. Critical race theorists have developed multiple ways in which narratives can be told: autobiographies (e.g., Williams; Bell), fictionalized dialogues (e.g., Bell; Richard Delgado), and outsider narratives (e.g., Montoya; Williams). Each of those narrative forms present critiques of the legal system that are, in a sense, extralegal. By their nature, they are forms of outsider knowledge, told using creative writing techniques but written to speak to the community of legal scholars. Critical race theory is an interdisciplinary undertaking, crossing the disciplines of social theory, legal theory and history, and storytelling.

In this article, I intend to focus on the autobiographical and outsider narrative forms of storytelling, the stories that tell the reader "how I experienced what happened." As a law student, lawyer, professor, and judge, I have found that telling my own story has made my ability to hear others that much more refined. During the last ten years, I have served as a tribal court judge for several tribal communities, having spent the most significant time on the bench in my own community, the Pueblo of Isleta,[1] and as a pro tem judge for the Lummi Nation.[2] In the tribal court setting, my ability to hear the stories of the parties in front of me is a critical component of providing a just result in each matter. However, that result is often diffi-cult to reach or, in fact, utterly unreachable, because of the legal structure surrounding the storytellers and the listener. More often than not, tribal courts have more flexibility than state or federal courts in determining what evidence is relevant to deciding the matter at hand. That flexibility, however, is limited by the construction (physical and psychological) of the courtroom, even when traditional methods of conflict resolution are employed.

In some ways, the tribal courtroom is the most receptive place for employing outsider narrative as a technique for helping the court to arrive at the most just result. Tribal courtrooms, however, have been significantly influenced by the federal and state court systems. Many use some form of federal or state rules of evidence or have their own modeled after the same. Many courtrooms use the same physical layout as standard courtrooms, with a bench at which the judge sits above the seating for the parties. None of this is surprising, because most formal tribal court systems had their gen-esis in the Courts of Indian Offenses, unarguably created by the federal government to ensure that the law of the dominant society. Despite this history, tribal courts have developed many ways to maintain the integrity of the tribe's own laws and methods of conflict resolution. The combination of tribal courts that employ both accepted and understood legal structures (e.g., reliance on written codes) and traditional law results a kind of colo-nized space, a place in which "red space" and "white space" intersect at a complex crossroads.

For most people, the tribal courtroom is neither a place they visit nor one they consider. Despite the fact that there are more than five hundred federally recognized tribes in the United States, as well as multiple tribes recognized by individual states, scholarly research and thought into the nature of the tribal courtroom is in its infancy.[3] Though many tribes in the United States are related in culture, language, and tradition, each has unique ways to resolve conflict and achieve justice. Most of those traditional means are rooted in the culture and language of each tribal community precontact. These traditional forms of conflict resolution, and the law that governs them, have been referred to as "customary law."

Tribal court criminal and civil jurisdiction is extremely complex, governed by United States federal laws, federal court decisions, tribal treaty rights, tribal constitutions, and tribal ordinances. Disputes between tribal members that originate on the reservation are generally within the tribal court's civil jurisdiction. Disputes between tribal members and nontribal individuals require a more complex analysis, requiring analysis of the nontribal individual's actions, tribal and federal law. Tribal court criminal jurisdiction is dependent on the parties involved, the nature of the criminal act, and the place where the act occurs.

Throughout the United States, tribal communities rely upon local, tribal court systems to resolve their disputes. Tribal court systems range from very small systems run by the head of the tribe[4] to complex systems with multiple levels (trial, appellate).[5] Many tribes have worked hard to create a judicial system that lawyers and laypeople, tribal members and non-Natives alike can negotiate smoothly. Many tribes have a codified system of laws (most often referred to as "tribal codes" or "tribal ordinances" that are adopted by the tribe's governing body) that range from providing comprehensive laws ranging from crimes, domestic relations, environmental protection, and probate to much less detailed codes that primarily focus on criminal laws.[6] In addition to these written codes, which are usually accessible to any tribal member or attorney practicing in that tribe's courts and sometimes available in a more public manner, customary law is also recognized and actively used by the tribal courts. Customary law is sometimes available in written form but more often is ascertained by the use of guidance from elders in the community or from the knowledge of the judge who may be intimately familiar with the customary law of the community.

Many tribal courts, therefore, attempt to blend custom and tradition with a codified system of laws (as well as some common law, which some tribal appellate courts produce). In so doing, the tribal judge is often called on to engage the use of narrative, either from the judge herself or from the parties. Because many parties in tribal courts are unrepresented, the judge must also be able to guide proceedings in a way that is more "hands on" than state or federal counterparts. Attorneys are also allowed some more freedom to develop the "story" behind the lawsuit. Thus, tribal courts can be incubators of new strategies, particularly those that employ the use of narrative, and a place in which the theoretical meets the practical. In that regard, it is also a place where it is possible to observe the ways in which the use of narrative in the framing of legal solutions to real problems can—and cannot—achieve a form of justice not available in the constraints of the U.S. courtroom.

On Defining the Theory and Practice of Narrative

The use of storytelling as a critique of the law, the legal system, and its assumptions has many critics, many of whom suggest that storytelling is anti-intellectual and lazy. As noted above, there are many kinds of storytelling, some of which are arguably more useful as tools for deconstructing the legal system than others. Narrative in and of itself can simply be another way of reinforcing the status quo (Ewick and Sibley). Ewick and Sibley argue that a key difference lies in recognizing hegemonic tales from subversive ones.

Because narratives are cultural productions, Ewick and Sibley argue, "our stories are likely to express ideological effects and hegemonic assumptions. . . . We are as likely to be shackled by the stories we tell . . . as we are by the form of oppression they might seek to reveal" (211). Thus, merely telling a story does not necessarily accomplish the goal of challenging the oppressive regime in which the story might be located. Rather, subversive stories must avoid being stories that can be used to generalize, because generalizing requires that we place the story into the general and, they argue, the hegemonic. Subversive stories, however, "do not aggregate to the general, do not collect particulars as examples of a common phenomenon or rule" (Ewick and Sibley 219). Instead, subversive stories stand out from the general, "juxtapose the particular and the private with the legal abstractions that are supposed to contain them" (Ewick and Sibley 219).[7]

In this article, then, I focus on two aspects of subversive storytelling: that of two particular people who appeared before me in my role as a tribal judge and my own story as the judge. In each of these instances, the stories are illustrative of the ways in which innovations in legal thinking and analysis can have "real world" impacts, but are limited by the nature of the hegemonic legal structure in which they function.

The requirement that subversive stories must focus on the particular raises problems, however. The effectiveness of social critique often lies in the ability of the reader/listener to understand the critique and then be able to apply it—to generalize from the particular experience. Failing that, the reader/listener accepts the story as merely anecdotal and therefore lacking.

In order for something to be true, it must be tested and subjected to the scientific method. The criticism of the narrative approach is, of course, coded by the cultural belief that all claims must be subjected to rigorous and repeatable testing. It is an easy answer to the stories, the narratives, that make us uncomfortable by their subversive nature.

In some key respects, it is the biographical form of storytelling that has the most relevance and applicability to what happens inside the courtroom. As the late Jerome Culp observed, "The most basic job of a lawyer is to convey a story that puts her client's perspective in its best light" (545). That is, it is the lawyer's job to 1) understand the client's story; 2) tell that story to an adjudicator; and 3) do it persuasively. It is the litigant's personal story and personal search for justice that typically brings him or her to the courtroom, particularly those who enter the courtroom as *pro se* litigants. A prevailing view of The Law, however, is that the remedy to each litigant's problem should be discernible through the application of certain rules, with certain outcomes. The law must be neutral. Thus, the only relevant story is the one with legally relevant facts, applied to a rule, with a definable outcome.

Perhaps no one is more subjected to the notion of neutrality and objectivity than the judge herself. Few judges discuss their decision-making process, though some scholars have studied it.[8] Although judges do discuss the reasons for their decisions on the bench, they are expected to present those decisions without reference to their personal history or emotions—indeed, the judges' "self" is expected to be excluded from the courtroom. Cold reliance on the law is demanded.

In the tribal court, however, that demand for neutrality is somewhat altered by the nature of the tribal community. For the most part, the tribal community knows the judge, the judge's family and family history, and/or where she lives. In communities where the judge is not drawn from the community itself, the judge is subject to a great degree of skepticism as someone who does not know the community's mores and history. Thus, the judge's story—her narrative—becomes a part of the tribal judicial system. It is sought by the community. This is another aspect of the significant differences between the tribal court and federal/state systems; it is an aspect that makes many new to tribal court practice uncomfortable, not simply with the difference in style, but also, I would argue, with the ways in which it illustrates the problems created by the demand for and expectation of neutrality.

The Courtroom as "White Space"

In their article "The Law of White Spaces: Race, Culture, and Legal Education," Peter Goodrich and Linda Mills define the law of white spaces as it relates to the law classroom as "the emotional and epistemic relationships between the white participants, the internal relationships that gained expression in the exclusion of students of color" (15). They posit that the dynamics between people who are white raise questions of race, arguing that "the white face of the racialized dynamic of institutional interaction is that of the silent assertion of the superiority of the norm" (18). In the context of the law classroom (as it is constituted by students and faculty) and legal scholarship, Goodrich and Mills argue that the unwillingness of the legal academy to confront the dominant (i.e., white) component of institutional racism creates the "white spaces."

Although Goodrich and Mills identify the law of white spaces specifically using the classroom as the example, the law of white spaces exists throughout the legal system (indeed, throughout U.S. society). As Goodrich and Mills and others have noted, knowing that law allows one to "get in the door" and, as Thomas Ross notes in his article "The Unbearable Whiteness of Being," "[g]etting through the door is pretty much all there is to it. . . . Once you're through that door, you need only perform in the ordinary and simply competent manner and keep out of trouble, and you succeed" (254). Although Goodrich, Mills, and Ross don't argue that simply being a white person acculturated to the law of white spaces is always successful in legal or social circles, they do assert that functioning and succeeding within the white spaces takes significantly less effort than it would for one not so acculturated—particularly people of color.

Performing in "ordinary" and "competent" ways means performing according to white norms. In my own observations of the law school classroom as both a student and faculty member, ordinary and competent means understanding and following those norms. Those norms are also so deeply ingrained in our understanding of the courtroom that we rarely question them. The law is power; the courtroom is the physical manifestation of that power.

As a lecturer in legal writing at a Southwest law school, I found myself in many situations where I recognized the "law of white spaces" and then enforced it. As is the case in most law school curricula, the law school had a required first-year oral argument. All the students regarded this piece of their law school education as a rite of passage to be feared.

Students presented their arguments as lawyers and in front of lawyers and, occasionally, judges. In one round, one of my students, a student of color for whom I had a great deal of respect and expectation, appeared for his oral argument in what were, in my mind, essentially street clothes. He dressed in khaki pants and a casual, white, long sleeved T-shirt. Seeing him come toward the room, I found myself panicking. "He can't go before the court dressed like that," I thought. I knew this student intended to argue in the simultaneous first-year oral argument competition, and I believed I had to tell him that he was dressed inappropriately so that he did not repeat the mistake.

I did so. "When you come back to argue in the competition," I said, "you need to dress appropriately—a suit, a jacket, something like that." The student slumped, all confidence and excitement for the coming argument gone. Though he managed to make the argument, he did so haltingly, so much so that the judges commented on his hesitancy.

Later, I apologized later for my timing in making the statement, an apology the student accepted graciously; he also said he was embarrassed to have been dressed inappropriately. As I have reflected on this awkward experience, I realize that it is a clear example of a violation of the law of white spaces by the uninitiated student. As one who has learned to move in those circles somewhat successfully, I felt it incumbent on me to inform the student that he failed to understand the occasion and failed to observe the proper courtroom decorum. I never apologized to the student for making the statement, but rather for the *timing* of it. I should have waited, I told him, until after his argument. I realized later that had I done so, telling him would have been unnecessary because one of the other attorneys in the room would have done so. Indeed, my own painfully similar first-year oral argument experience reflects this. Following one oral argument, one of the judges remarked that I did a reasonable job, despite "being short" and "nontraditional" (a remark I have never fully understood, though I assumed it to be an oblique reference to my being a person of color).

These simple incidences reflect the subtlety of the "law of white spaces." Lawyers are trained to see the courtroom as a formal place, where rules define conduct and argument. Dress codes are often explicit, but even when they are not, as in my example, they are enforced and reinforced. Initially, I saw my own reinforcement of an apparently nonracialized norm as an innocent reflection of the sterile requirements of the courtroom. In providing this feedback to the student, I sought to be helpful in socializing the student to the norms of the courtroom. Later, however, I realized that

I was reinforcing the superiority of the norm by telling this student that he should dress according to a norm created by and for the dominant, white society.

As I began to question this incident, I realized that the courtroom itself is unquestionably "white space." The physical layout of U.S. courtrooms relies on the English construction of the courtroom; the judge's bench high above the others in the room, the physical separation between the jury and the other parties, and the formalized nature of the trial embody the belief that the courtroom and its decision makers can be neutral, a decidedly "white" notion. Yet nearly all of the tribal courtrooms that I had seen replicated this physical layout and belief that the decision maker could be neutral. In an informal discussion with other tribal judges, all could recount having been recused from a case because of their knowledge of the families involved or other information about the parties that caused one or both of the parties to fear a bias on the part of the judge. This desire for neutrality diverges significantly from customary approaches to resolving conflict, in which community members who know the parties are sought out to assist in resolving disputes.

Thus, tribal courts stand at a crossroads between supporting, developing, and enforcing traditional, customary tribal law and approaches to conflict resolution and mimicking the courtrooms of the U.S. legal system. On the one hand, the tribal court is the perfect incubator for innovative approaches to legal problems; on the other, tribal courts need to maintain some degree of similarity to U.S. courtrooms, as required by the Indian Civil Rights Act,[9] and because of the viewpoint of many outsiders of tribal courts as unsophisticated "kangaroo courts."[10]

Courts at the Crossroads: Critical Race Theory in Practice

I have sat as a trial court judge on many kinds of cases. Cases involving the welfare of children have always been the most difficult, intellectually and emotionally. Most tribal court judges apply a "best interests" standard to the analysis of the care and custody of children, sometimes as required by tribal ordinance and others as an informal practice.[11] In state courts, cases involving child welfare are handled using the rules of evidence and other procedures that have the effect of restricting the way in which the "story" of the child and her history is presented. Here, I will present an analysis of the way I used an interdisciplinary approach stemming from the narrative tradition in a tribal court setting, followed by a discussion of the ways in which that interdisciplinarity succeeded and failed to promote social justice in this instance.

Cases involving children usually take one of two forms: child welfare (often referred to as "dependencies"), in which children are removed from their parents' care by a governmental agency, or child custody cases, in which the parents are disputing who should have primary caretaking responsibilities for the child(ren). In this instance, I presided over a complex case involving child custody (and more tangentially, child support payments).[12]

The case originated as a paternity suit brought by the alleged father of the child, a two-month-old baby boy. In this particular tribal court, formal paternity procedures are not codified, so the court generally uses state court procedures to determine paternity tests, including ordering DNA tests. DNA tests were conducted and the plaintiff was determined to be the biological father of the child. A hearing was held to formalize that finding. After reviewing the file, I walked into the courtroom, expecting to see the mother and father of the child.

Instead, the courtroom was filled with several people, some of whom I knew and some of whom I did not. Initially, I asked that the mother and father identify themselves. After that, the father asked to address the court.[13] He began by telling me that he wanted to explain the situation and the reason for the many people's presence in the courtroom. I allowed him to proceed.

He conceded that he was the father of the child and that he intended to provide for the child financially. He also stated that he wanted to be a part of the child's life, but did not intend to continue his relationship with the child's mother. The conception of the child resulted from an adulterous affair. Following his statement, a woman sitting to his left asked to be heard. She introduced herself as the father's wife and told the court that although she was angry with her husband and the affair that resulted in this child, she wanted to be a mother to the child and be a part of his life.

Following this exchange, the mother of the child addressed the court and said that she wanted his father to be a part of his life and that she believed it would be beneficial to the child to have the parties working together to raise the child. The mother's father then asked to address the court. Prior to making his statement, he noted that my presence on the judicial bench was not a traditionally accepted role for women in the tribal community,[14] but that he believed I would act in the best interests of the child. He also stated that he was ashamed of his daughter's conduct but looked forward to helping to raise the child.

None of the parties in this instance was represented by an attorney. The tribal code had a small set of provisions addressing domestic relations law and provided authority for the court to establish child support obligations. In general, the court used state court guidelines for addressing child custody matters. Most matters involved the mother and the father of the child; in this instance, although it was possible to limit the proceedings to the father and the mother of the child, it was apparent that there were at least two other parties who intended to have a role in the child's life and wanted a voice in the court proceeding.

Thus, at this stage of the case, I had two choices in front of me: 1) limit the participation of the parties to the mother and father and adhere to state court procedures to determine custody, visitation, and support or 2) allow the matter to proceed with all the interested parties participating and use a more traditional (and informal) process. This particular court required cases involving children to be closed to the public; it became necessary for me to determine who constituted "the public" and who constituted "the parties."

I chose to proceed using a less formal approach and saw my role become more like that of a mediator than a judge. At the outset, I identified the mother, father, maternal grandfather, and father's wife as parties to the matter and then closed the proceedings to anyone other than court personnel. I asked the parties to identify the role they wished me to play in the case. After some discussion, they chose to use me as a guide toward helping them find resolution to the custody and visitation issues that had arisen. The child resided with the mother, and the father wished to have an active role in the child's life.

I sat with the parties at tables, without the judicial robe. I asked each of the parties to talk about what the best possible outcome of the case would be and suggested that, based on each person's ideal view of the future, we develop a consensus-based plan to address each person's concerns. The concerns centered around four main issues: 1) The mother wanted to continue to work and she wanted her son to reside with her; 2) The father wanted to be an active part of the child's life and he also wanted to continue to work; 3) The father's wife did not work, and wanted to be a part of the child's life; and 4) The father's income was very limited, and his ability to provide financial support for the child was equally limited. In facilitating the discussion that followed, I began by acknowledging the painful complexity to resolving the case. I asked that the parties put aside the affair that had resulted in the birth of the child and focus on the child. Each of them agreed to do so.

The resulting agreement answered each of the concerns raised. The father's wife suggested that she provide child care for the child during the mother's work hours, thus allowing the mother to return to work and the father to provide support for the child that was not financial in nature. The father often worked from home and would be available to provide breaks for his wife, as well as be an active part of the child's daily routine. Each of the parties began to see the maternal grandfather's role as key in helping them to develop a working relationship with each other. As the elder male in the family, his traditional role was to provide that guidance, and the process allowed him to do that.

I entered the agreement as a formal court order, substituting the provision of child care for a dollar amount of child support. I appointed the maternal grandfather as the person to whom disputes would be addressed. I also reserved the right to the parties to bring the matter back into court should the agreement fail.

The parties proceeded with the agreed order for about one year. At approximately this time, the mother began to have misgivings about having her son spend so much time with the father and the father's wife. The problems were brought to the maternal grandfather, who made several attempts at resolution. Following those unsuccessful attempts to resolve the issues, the matter came back to the court.

After some informal discussion with the parties, it became clear that they had lost the ability to work together; both sought custody and the mother sought financial child support. The parties requested that I hold a hearing on the record and enter a formal parenting plan after hearing from each of the parties. In sum, they sought a judicial resolution to their conflict and were no longer interested in pursuing the matter through the informal and more traditional process. I asked each of the parties whether they would prefer to have a new judge brought in to make those decisions, but they all agreed that they wanted someone who knew the case and the parties well. I agreed to proceed and the next hearings took place on the record, in the courtroom, with witnesses presented to support each side's view of the best interests of the child. Ultimately, I decided that the mother should retain primary physical custody of the child, established significant weekly visitation with the father, ordered a financial child support obligation on the part of the father, and ordered shared, joint decision making for the mother and father of the child. Future disputes about the court order were heard by the court.

This case demonstrates both the promise of the use of narrative in a courtroom setting as well as its limitations. Through the use of narrative, I was able to understand the circumstances associated with this complex familial unit. It is extremely unlikely that the father's wife and the maternal grandfather would have been provided with an opportunity to be heard in a state courtroom.[15] Both of these individuals held important facts about the case and would continue to serve in important roles in the raising of the child. Given the application of the rules of evidence, it is likely that much of the story with regard to the conception of this child would not have survived a challenge on evidentiary grounds. Similarly, most state court child support obligations are derived from a mathematical formula, with little or no room for modification by the court. The creative use of child care to meet that obligation is unlikely to see the light of day in a state court proceeding that must follow the statutory provisions closely.

By using the narrative approach as a judge, I became an active participant in the conversation between the parties. As a result, I became a part of the story of the case. By hearing from all the parties, I felt I was more accurately informed and then better able to craft a reasonable solution to the case. Because the parties had come up with that solution, their investment in maintaining it seemed to be likelier.

Ultimately, however, we all resorted to standard courtroom practices when that creative approach failed over time. Rather than continue to attempt to employ a traditional approach to the case, the parties essentially gave up that possibility and resorted to having the judge decide the case in as standard a manner as possible. Although that responsibility is part of the role of a judge, it is an odd position in which to find oneself after working to use alternative means of resolution. By returning to the courtroom and donning the judicial robe and demeanor, I wore the cloak of neutrality. That cloak, however, did not remove that which I had learned through the narrative process.

At the stage of the proceedings that resulted in the return to standard courtroom practice, I found it necessary to disclose on the record the nature of my prior involvement in the matter. At the time, I was concerned that if the case eventually would be heard by a new judge,[16] she would need to know that the case initially had used a traditional process. Following that disclosure, I resorted to citations to relevant statutory provisions in state law, wrote heavily cited opinions and orders, and held the parties in contempt of court (and assessed fines) when they failed to follow court orders.

In so doing, any of the work done early on in the case to bring a customary and decidedly "outsider" approach to the case unraveled. Although my continuing to act as the judge in the case violated standard courtroom procedures because I knew more about the case from informal, off-the-record, traditional methods than I did from the courtroom proceedings, the resulting decisions I made in the matter did not deviate particularly from a standard resolution to the case. The orders and opinions I wrote in the case cited to state and tribal codified law. Any judge who heard domestic relations cases would have recognized the standards I applied to the facts of the case and could determine the logical, "neutral" method by which I resolved disputed issues.

Thus, the narrative arc of this particular case follows a peculiar line from a consciously applied attempt to use a form of outsider knowledge in an outsider environment, the tribal courtroom, to a formalized, state court–like proceeding using state court procedures and laws. In this instance, all of the parties except for me had lived in this tribal community their entire lives. The tribal language was the primary language spoken in their homes. The tribal courtroom was the only courtroom any of them had been in prior to this hearing. All of them were willing to leave the courtroom to employ a traditional, customary practice that used me as a kind of mediator and the maternal grandfather as the elder appointed to resolve disputes. Although my presence on the bench was not a traditionally accepted role for a woman, in other respects, the position I took early in the case was a traditional one.

After the failure of that process, though, the parties chose to return to the courtroom and use it in as standard (and as Ewick and Sibley might say, as hegemonic) a way as is possible in the tribal courtroom. All of the players in this case, including me, used the "neutral" state court standards and procedures for determining the issues in the case. Although I could have persisted in applying the customary process, doing so without the consent of the parties, which they withdrew on its failure, would not have worked and would have provided obvious grounds for recusing me from the case or appealing the ultimate outcomes.

The resolution of the case was not different from outcomes one sees in state courts. The solutions were not particular to the parties, nor did the solutions use the flexibility the tribal courtroom provides. Though this may be a failure of imagination on my part as the judge (and perhaps the parties), the fact that we resorted to an imposed, dominant system to resolve the dispute and deemed that the "fairest" way to proceed when the traditional process failed demonstrates how the context of the courtroom shapes the arc of the case.

Currently, a wide-ranging debate about the role and nature of tribal courts exists among its judges. For some of us, the tribal courtroom is a place where we choose to work because it allows us the ability to use multiple means to resolve disputes and allows us to reach a just result as well as a legally correct one. Because tribal courts can establish their own processes and methods (within the limitations prescribed by the tribe's governing body), they can serve an important role in developing alternative means of reaching a resolution. For others of us who strive to be seen as equal to state court judges, the flexibility and, sometimes, the informality of the tribal courtroom prevent that recognition. Thus, we stand between two worlds: the world in which tribal custom and tradition prevails, perhaps unaffected by dominant processes, and the world in which the rule of law prevails, ignorant of the society in which it sits and of the full stories of the people who seek the court's guidance.

The example discussed here shows how the "norm of whiteness," the law of white spaces, intervenes even in an environment that consciously attempts to exclude it. Some would see this as an argument for the return to traditional, customary means of dispute resolution without reliance on a court system to solve disputes when the customary means fail. However, returning to such a process seems unlikely and could violate the federal laws that apply to tribal courtroom processes. In addition, it might provide additional argument for those who seek to limit the jurisdiction of tribal courts to tribal members only, a limitation that would seriously damage the ability of tribes to act as sovereign entities.

As the dockets of tribal courts become full of more legally complex matters,[17] the absence of traditional processes becomes apparent. The kinds of complex civil matters that involve contracts, dissolutions of marriage involving determinations of property distribution like retirement accounts, and civil lawsuits on a variety of other claims appear to be answered only by dominant legal processes, statutes, and precedent. Thus, the attempt to blend outsider knowledge and interdisciplinary approaches with formalized courtroom procedures is rife with the potential to reproduce the very problems the tribal courtroom has the opportunity to avoid.

Notes

1. Located in New Mexico, about fifteen miles just south of Albuquerque, the Pueblo of Isleta has approximately 3,500 enrolled members. See also United States

Census 2000, PHC-T-18, American Indian and Alaska Native Tribes in the West Region 2000, <http://www.census.gov/population/cen2000/phc-t18/tab005.pdf>.

2. The Lummi Nation is located about ten miles northwest of Bellingham, Washington, and has approximately 4,500 enrolled members, about 75 percent of whom live on or near the reservation, <http://www.lummi-nsn.gov>. See also United States Census 2000, PHC-T-18, American Indian and Alaska Native Tribes in the West Region 2000, <http://www.census.gov/population/cen2000/phc-t18/tab005.pdf>.

3. Two researchers/practitioners have largely built the field: Christine Zuni-Cruz, professor of law at the University of New Mexico, and Nell Jessup Newton, chancellor and dean, University of California Hastings College of Law. Professor Zuni-Cruz created the online *Tribal Law Journal*, http://tlj.unm.edu/, and has written about her work both as a tribal lawyer and judge, as well as director of the Southwest Indian Law Clinic at the University of New Mexico School of Law. Professor Newton's extensive analysis of the work of tribal courts, "Tribal Court Praxis: One Year in the Life of Twenty Indian Tribal Courts," remains a seminal piece analyzing how tribes integrate tribal law, custom, and tradition into court systems.

4. Leaders of tribes are referred to by many different appellations, including chief, governor, and tribal chairperson. I refer to those holding such positions as "heads" in this article to avoid confusion.

5. The largest and most complex system is the Navajo Nation's tribal court system. A detailed overview and history of that system is available, <www.navajocourts.org>.

6. For the most complete collections of tribal codes, see the National Tribal Court Clearinghouse, www.tribal-institute.org, and the National Indian Law Library run by the Native American Rights Fund, <www.narf.org/niil>.

7. Ewick and Sibley specifically reference the work of Patricia Williams in this discussion.

8. See Conley and O'Barr.

9. "The Indian Civil Rights Act of 1968," Title 25, *United States Code* Sections 1301 to 1303, requires the tribal courts to provide criminal defendants with speedy and public trials, due process rights, including the right to counsel (though not one provided at the tribe's or government's expense), and limits the tribal courts' ability to assess fines to not more than $5,000 per offense and not more than one year in jail per offense.

10. For a comprehensive discussion of the history and practice of tribal courts, see Nell Jessup Newton's article.

11. For example, the Zuni Tribe's Children's Code (Title IX, Section 9-2-1, 2006, of the Zuni Tribal Code) requires that the best interests of the child be ascertained by assessing the following factors:

A. *A child's need for love, nurturing, protection and stability*. A child must have a safe and nurturing home environment offering emotional support and comfort; the basic needs of food, clothing, and shelter; reasonable medical care and protection from danger, violence, or exposure to harmful conduct including drug or alcohol abuse.

B. *A child's need for family*. A child must have connection to loving family members for guidance and nurturing. Although not all children have the benefit of family care, nothing can replace the primary role of loving parents and family in a child's life.

C. *A child's need for identity and development*. A child must develop self-identity and awareness of his or her unique role within the larger community, including the child's cultural community. This is done by participation in cultural activities, speaking one's native language, and having opportunities and encouragement to pursue education and enrichment.

D. *A child's need for happiness*. A child cannot be happy unless his or her primary needs are met; but a child also needs opportunities for play and recreation, leisure time and other activities the child enjoys, and possession of toys and other personal items of importance to the child.

12. The case discussed here was closed to the public. I have changed some key identifying information in order to protect the anonymity of the parties.

13. Neither of the parties was represented by attorneys.

14. In every instance when a tribal elder participated in courtroom proceedings as witnesses, plaintiffs, or defendants, he began his participation by reminding me that I was not in a traditionally acceptable role.

15. In fact, recent a U.S. Supreme Court decision held that grandparents did not have standing to proceed against the parents for visitation rights. This decision has been read to prevent grandparents from having standing to challenge child custody decisions in most instances. See *Troxel v. Granville*, No. 99-138. Supreme Court of the United States, 5 June 2000.

16. Often child custody disputes like this one last until the child reaches the age of majority.

17. Tribes are now including in complex contracts that all disputes be resolved in tribal courts. In addition, courts in many tribes hear other types of complex civil and, to a lesser extent, criminal matters.

Works Cited

Bell, Derrick. *Confronting Authority*. Boston: Beacon Press, 1996.

———. *Faces at the Bottom of the Well*. New York: Basic Books, 1993.

Conley, John M., and William M. O'Barr. *Rule versus Relationships: The Ethnography of Legal Discourse*. Chicago: U of Chicago P, 1990.

Culp, Jerome. "Autobiography and Legal Scholarship and Teaching: Finding the Me in the Legal Academy." *Virginia Law Review* 77 (1991): 539–59.

Delgado, Richard. "Rodrigo's Final Chronicle: Cultural Power, the Law Reviews, and the Attack on Narrative Jurisprudence." *Southern California Law Review* 68 (1995): 545–75.

Ewick, Patricia, and Susan S. Silbey. "Subversive Stories and Hegemonic Tales: Toward a Sociology of Narrative." *Law and Society Review* 29 (1995): 197–226.

Hitchcock, Jeff. *Lifting the White Veil.* Roselle, NJ: Crandall, Dostie & Douglass Books, 2002.

Goodrich, Peter, and Linda Mills. "The Law of White Spaces: Race, Culture and Legal Education." *Journal of Legal Education* 51 (2001): 15–39.

Montoya, Margaret E., "Celebrating Racialized Legal Narratives." *Crossroads, Directions, and a New Critical Race Theory.* Ed. Francisco Valdes, Jerome McCristal Culp, and Angela P. Harris. Philadelphia: Temple UP, 2002. 243–51.

Newton, Nell Jessup. "Tribal Court Praxis: One Year in the Life of Twenty Indian Tribal Courts." *American Indian Law Review* 22 (1997): 285–355.

Ross, Thomas. "The Unbearable Whiteness of Being." *Crossroads, Directions, and a New Critical Race Theory.* Ed. Francisco Valdes, Jerome McCristal Culp, and Angela P. Harris. Philadelphia: Temple UP, 2002. 251–58.

Sando, Joe S. *Pueblo Nations: Eight Centuries of Pueblo Indian History.* New Mexico: Clear Light Publishers, 1992.

Troxel v. Granville, No. 99-138. Supreme Court of the United States. 5 June 2000.

United States Code. "The Indian Civil Rights Act of 1968." 25 USC Secs. 1301–1303. 1968.

Williams, Patricia. *The Alchemy of Race and Rights: A Diary of a Law Professor.* Boston: Harvard UP, 1991.

Zuni-Cruz, Christine. "(On the) Road Back In: Community Lawyering in Indigenous Communities." *Clinical Law Review* 5 (1999): 557–88.

———. "Tribal Law as Indigenous Social Reality and Separate Consciousness [Re]Incorporating Customs and Traditions Into Tribal Law." *Tribal Law Journal* 1 (2000).

———. "Children's Code," Title IX *Zuni Tribal Code* Section 9-2-1, 2006. "Children's Code," Title IX Zuni Tribal Code Section 9-2-1. 2006.

Chapter Five

An Emergent Extradisciplinarity

Worlding Arabs, Activist Representation, and the Example of Ahdaf Soueif

Mrinalini Chakravorty

Recent efforts by Arab scholars toward an extradisciplinary understanding of the crises of representation and power in the Middle East can best be grasped by situating the rise of the academic discipline of Middle Eastern Studies in the West as a specific historical byproduct of American geopolitical formations and imperial investments. (Neo)Orientalist representational practices that govern political and cultural studies of the Middle East within U.S. institutions of higher learning and information derive directly from the tensions of the Cold War and the indeterminate and nonaligned status of the Arab world after the Second World War. Edward Said has pointed to the transformation of colonial cartographies of division and conquest into new forms for explaining conflict between the Arab and Western worlds.[1] Said contends that these (neo)Orientalist modes of structuring knowledge about Arabs along fixed cultural cartographies, seemingly mapped through empiricist claims within discourses of political science (Samuel Huntington) and area studies (Bernard Lewis), rematerialize the imaginative fantasy of an earlier Orientalism onto the present to sustain latent stereotypes of radical otherness about Arabs.[2] The goal of writers who live in what Ahdaf Soueif has called the "common ground" or "Mezzaterra," the "ground valued precisely for being a meeting point for many cultures and traditions," is to find a way around the durability of these separatist habits and methods for thinking about the everyday struggles of war and social conflict in Arab

society that move beyond disciplined ways of knowing the world in their
attempts to negotiate cultural difference (*Mezzaterra* 23, 6).

Worlding Extradisciplinarity:
A Brief History of Its Emergence

The era of the Cold War marked the birth of area studies within the
Western academy. As a protracted conflict, which was in many ways different from previous armed engagements, the Cold War acted as the catalyst
for extending U.S. hegemonic interests in various geopolitical areas of the
world. The establishment of area studies signaled the state-sanctioned and
hence institutionalized effort at leveraging knowledge, gathered through
both covert and open strategies, about discretely parceled areas of the globe
that were unaligned with either of the powers in order to exert control
over these foreign areas or markets and thus amass global power. The
fields of research generated by area studies played a crucial role in securing knowledge in the service of state interests. Because of the alliance of
the state and the academy at the level of the formation of various area
studies programs, it follows that such shared interests hold at the level of
dissemination as well. In this sense, area studies have served the purpose of
creating bodies of knowledge about the non-West while also processing and
producing Western-centered scholarship and interpretive approaches. From
the American perspective, the Cold War was invested in remapping and
reshaping geopolitical terrains around a decidedly nationalist U.S.-centered
axis of power. As critics Harootunian and Miyoshi note, the provinciality
of this method for legitimating disciplinary claims amounts to "a strategy
of trench warfare deployed by scholars of area studies" (8). Such an over-
emphasis on national boundaries, with a bias toward American dominance,
that motivated the founding logic of certain areas of study within the U.S.
academy is useful in thinking through our present disciplinary alignments
insofar as these geopolitical investments continue to be mirrored in our
academic compulsions to remain area bound.[3]

Of course, equally importantly, particularly in the waning years of the
Cold War, the academy saw the rise of several interdisciplinary programs
such as women's studies, various ethnic and race studies, and cultural studies,
which sought quite deliberately to challenge the fixed boundaries around
which power in the academy traditionally circulated. These programs were
premised on oppositional discourses of resistance that attempted to draw

attention to, in order to critique, the founding premises on which more traditional disciplinary circuits of power were historically formed. If "area studies has today become the beleaguered fortress housing the traditional disciplines as if nothing has changed in the last fifty years," Harootunian and Miyoshi rightly contend that "cultural studies has attempted to blur the boundaries of disciplines and even dissolve them" (8). Rather than parcel out fields of knowledge, these interdisciplinary programs sought to traverse disciplinary boundaries, drawing on multiple perspectives and weaving together diverse methodologies and epistemological practices. The resistance methodologies of these activist fields of study were directly concerned with repudiating occidental ethnocentrism and furthering social justice and a politics of equity in representations as the primary concerns of knowledge production.[4]

I contend that certain activist discourses have emerged, and continue to evolve, in response to the provinciality of area studies, as well as to accelerate the modes of interdisciplinarity loosely designated as cultural and gender-sexuality studies that render the practice of deliberately extradisciplinary forms of representation. In my formulation, extradisciplinarity goes beyond all manner of academic disciplines, ratcheting up the premise of interdisciplinarity by moving beyond institutionalized systems of knowledge, bridging into coherence academic and nonacademic discourses and modes of knowledge production—for example, journalistic and creative. The Middle Eastern situation is not unique in this context, but rather is one instance among others (e.g., Chinese, Soviet) in which new (non)academic modes are coming into being within a specific attempt to redefine areas of scholarship that account for the modes of historical and cultural production from which they somewhat antagonistically emerge. If, as Rey Chow suggests, cultural studies proceeds by way of four discursive yet discrete initiatives foregrounding "Orientalism-critique, investigations of subaltern identities, minority discourse and culture-as-hybridity," extradisciplinary strategies of representation fuse these various modes of inquiry with (non)academic forms of cultural production in an effort to underscore the arresting political stakes that determine the fissures in the everyday life events and experiences of particularly vexed social communities (Chow 104-06). In this sense, extradisciplinary work forsakes the easy categorical distinctions Chow makes between different aspects of cultural studies and invigorates instead and repeatedly the necessary interplay of world and text as the common ground for articulating all culturally nuanced claims. Even as the discipline of cultural studies may be carved to reflect certain divides between anti-Orientalism, subaltern studies, minority discourse, or hybridity, extradisciplinary practices retain the core premise of cultural studies as a mode for recognizing counterhegemonic designs within cultures as essentially unstable and not contingent on particular institutionalized processes for reading the terrain of the discipline.

Rather than offer general comments about the possibilities of extradisciplinarity with regard to Middle Eastern studies within Western academia, I would like to focus on particular habits of scholarship that produce the Middle East as a particular kind of sublime commodity in the West at large. This, together with a consideration of tactical strategies in response to such scholarship that originates both within the academy and within particular disciplinary structures, as well as from external sources, will, I hope, provide a fuller scope of the possibilities held by extradisciplinary modes of engagement. One of the more pervasive modes of studying the Middle East has been through the lens of what Edward Said has theorized as Orientalism. Those few who have written against the grain of disciplinary Orientalism have had to represent the subjects, conflicts, and struggles of the Middle East through a deliberately oppositional discourse.[5] Said, writing about the context of Islamic and Middle Eastern Studies in the United States, has focused on the "antithetical scholarship" that orients this counter-discursive effort to generate "the kind of knowledge produced by people who quite consciously consider themselves to be writing in opposition to the prevailing orthodoxy" (Covering Islam 149). The attempt by Arab activist writers such as Ahdaf Soueif, Ghassan Kanafani, Tayeb Salih, Hanan Al-Shaykh, Talal Asad, Edward Said, George Antonius, and others to reorient readers toward a complexity of problems that condition Arab lives certainly seeks to escape a tendency to place Arabs in unitary, or even binary, molds within the Western imaginary. Ironically binaristic in their own opposition against entrenched practices of disciplinary Orientalism, these extradisciplinary modes of drawing portraits of the Arab world ultimately eschew neat binaries between this and that world, or this or that field of knowledge. This move toward extradisciplinarity ultimately directly calls into question, or, to use Said's terms, offers a "dissenting configuration" to the ideologically hardened cult of "expertise" and narrowly confined "interpretive communities" that, for Said, control and disseminate knowledge about Arabs in the West (Covering Islam 152, 141, 41).

The argument Said makes in his early study, Covering Islam (1981), of the impact of U.S. academic structures in media coverage and study of the Middle East is worth considering briefly to arrive at a sense of the turns against disciplinary orthodoxy that Arab writers who transgress disciplinary bounds and even forsake them altogether are routinely compelled to make. Noting that the rise of Middle East studies in the United States is part of a tripartite and symbiotic structure—university, government, and corporations—whose interests since the 1970s have been interdependent, Said makes the point that most public (academic, governmental, and economic) knowledge about this region has been dominated by a self-perpetuating group of experts primarily interested in preserving the terms of their own employment rather than assessing the value of their methodology (chapter 3). This lack of self-reflexivity, together with the rising demand in recent years for media sound bites about specific areas of the Middle East directly related to U.S. commercial and military interests, generates a body of knowledge severely limited in scope.

Counter to this, activist Arab writers attempt to initiate less myopic and more integrated representations that reconcile Arab lived experience not on the basis of disciplinary ideologies often working in concert with imperialist aims, but in more autonomous terms. The tension here is that the representation of specific local and pan-Arabic cultural, social, historical, and political sentiments and responses are remarkable precisely because of their traditional exclusion from disciplinary mechanisms of the West. In effect, what is then actively produced through representation is an expanded notion of what Said calls a "community of interpretation" that, although opposing the dominant order, also goes beyond reproducing itself simply by restaging a conflict between dominance and minority (41).

I mark the type of extradisciplinarity I am describing as going beyond Said's description of "interpretive communities" because his formulation of various disciplinarily different knowledge producing and consuming communities seems somewhat polemically entrenched in its logic of opposition. Said writes, "In other words, what we are dealing with here are in the widest sense communities of interpretation, many of them at odds with one another, prepared in many instances literally to go to war with one another, all of them creating and revealing themselves and their interpretations as very central features of their existence" (41). Said's emphasis on the interpretive manner in which culture produces meaning is important, and although the oppositional element is key in discerning culturally conditioned positions, some activist Arab writers are seeking to move beyond this structured antagonism. Activist representations that are deliberately extradisciplinary reveal the ways in which cultural representations are conditioned by, and respond to, economic and political factors that govern, for example, literary and journalistic expression. In their work, these writers seek to expose underlying circuits of control that are exerted on cultural production about the Middle East within literature and the press, even as these are often presumed to be unregulated.

Extradisciplinary Texts and Contexts: Unruly Alliances in the Work of Ahdaf Soueif

The particular example of Ahdaf Soueif's work captures the kind of activist writing that risks disciplinary betrayals in the interest of securing a place for new cultural productions that mediate between intellectual and physically anchored political expressions and experiences. For example, Soueif writes of marginalized Arab collectivities that have been historically excluded by interpretive communities preoccupied with reproducing already affirmed institutional interests. Soueif's fiction (*Sandpiper*, *The Eye of the Sun*, *Map of Love*, *I Think of You*) constitutes an inter- and extradisciplinary overlay whose design is all the more marked in the allied historical, political, and journalistic compasses of her work (as the editor of *I Saw Ramallah* and author of *Mezzaterra: Fragments from the Common Ground*). My argument is that the fictional worlds Soueif invokes, the historical and political registers of her writing, along with the institutional contexts in which she writes—as an Anglophone Arab novelist in London and as a journalist writing on Palestine—open up possibilities for understanding disciplinary limits, disciplinary privilege, and the kind of forced exclusions that disciplined inquiries often generate. The dazzling scope of her work, which ranges from careful fictional portraits of struggle to textured analysis of historical conditions, where the mainframes of history are bypassed in favor of rarely glimpsed counterhistories, suggests an ethics of activism that trumps disciplinary interests that cohere narrowly in the separate studies of literature, history, and politics.

What Soueif's work represents instead is a mode of activist scholarship that invokes collective experience and struggle as sites for critiquing provincial disciplinarity and the kinds of authority it assumes. If disciplinarity broadly emphasizes a singularity of both authorial perspective and subject material, Soueif's work offers a deliberately unbounded subjectival perspective that troubles any overt isomorphism between institutional and identitarian allegiance. Rather, she points us toward those moments of careful transfer and translation within and between disciplinary knowledges and dominant and marginalized cultures that produce alternative discourses for recognizing the claims of the dispossessed. What often results is a startling upset of expectations wherein historically conditioned social and cultural allegiances are shown to be increasingly inadequate in capturing the possibilities inherent in new alliances that have begun to emerge.

To draw out these unexpected alliances, Soueif often melds literary, journalistic, and political strategies, merging the tools of each discipline while also using each against itself and the others. To this end, Soueif's extradisciplinarity involves repeatedly citing testimony from Israeli soldiers in her letter to Prime Minister Tony Blair to make her case about the atrocities being carried out on the ground in Palestine ("Do Something"). Despite her admission that before her trip to Palestine in 2000, she had never "seen," "spoken" with, or "wanted" to meet an Israeli, Soueif is careful to document all those "Israeli characters who stand like heroic figures against the current. The wise men of Rabbis for Peace, the soldiers who are refusing to serve in the occupied territories. Scholars like Ilan Pappe or historian and one-time deputy mayor of Jerusalem, Meron Benvenisti, who warned, in *Ha'aretz* on 15 August of 'the possibility of a mass transfer of Palestinians in case of war in Iraq.' The members of the Gush Shalom . . ." (*Mezzaterra* 29, 112). In addition to these explicit recognitions of the complexity of the struggle over Palestine that destabilizes stable identity claims for being on one or other side of the political conflict, Soueif's account of the Palestinian crisis "quotes heavily from these young men [Israeli servicemen]" precisely to question any credibility gap that may be attributed to her because of her identity as "a UK citizen of Egyptian origin" (99). Soueif's persistent efforts to include in her work on Palestine myriad examples of counter-identity such as "Jews who fought with the PLO," "calls for help from Israelis," motivational distinctions between career Israeli soldiers and reservists based on "small acts of kindness," and the risks borne by the "refuseniks" or conscientious Israeli objectors who denounce their compulsory military service to the state reflect the restrictive economy of how the conflict is generally bounded along nationalistic, religious, and ethnocentric lines (61, 100, 153, 157).[6] In short, her inclusion of the often stifled voices of Jewish dissidence to Israeli state actions attests to the uselessness of these divides that in fact are routinely expended by those in the conflict zone.

Before returning to a consideration of Arab collectivism in her fiction, I want to dwell for a moment on Soueif's work as a political journalist in Palestine.[7] Writing for *The Guardian*, her reports from the West Bank in particular and Palestine in general eschew any semblance of objective reporting and revolve instead around documenting the constant state of siege under which Palestinians live. Soueif is primarily concerned with capturing the forced militarization of Palestine as a collective cultural experience—she repeatedly details the unrelenting military violence that conditions daily life in Palestine and the kinds of militant insurgencies this produces in response. However, her reports from the war zone also evidence echoes of the types of commonplace collective translation and critique of disciplinary autonomy that instantiate Palestinian recalcitrance.

Alongside vignettes of life in Gaza—checkpoints every two miles near settlements, the seam zone, blocked access to Birzeit university, farms laden with harvest where farmers are not allowed without permits that divest them of their claims to the land, the snaking metallic "security fence" with the state-sanctioned death threats posted along it—Soueif gives us portraits of people, the students, families, militants, and even Israeli soldiers who strive for normalcy in this climate of force. Among the myriad details she invokes is the following one of a wall on the periphery of Manger Square, Bethlehem. Soueif writes: "On the walls in the street the portrait of Edward Said has taken its place alongside the pictures of Christine Saada, the 10-year-old girl shot in her father's car in March, and Abed Ismail, the 11-year-old boy killed by a sniper in Manger Square" ("Waiting Game" 2). I will return to this collage of portraits to consider the manner in which this citation makes legible a politics of Arab resilience to imperialism that turns precisely on an undisciplined play of juxtaposed historical, literary, and political registers to invoke a social scene of resistance and dominance that cannot be wholly recuperated into any singular discourse.

My objective here is not to take inventory of the manifold disciplinary transgressions Soueif and her readers are forced to make in her variously oriented representations of the Arab situation. Neither is it to simply herald a sort of wandering scholastic eclecticism and to suggest that Arab resistance to dominance can only be understood in terms of an accumulation of uncoordinated and haphazard social processes. To the contrary, I suggest that Soueif's concurrent explorations of the political, cultural, and economic oppressions of Arabs through divergent modes of representation strategically point to the uneven logic of expansion by which Western modernity imposes its coercive and, in this sense, unitary authority over the non-West. Considering the intertexts between Soueif's fictional and nonfictional worlds brings to crisis the legitimacy of the Western modernizing project that, although entrenched in institutional authority (of governments, nations, and universities), all the while bolsters its power through the capture of markets and by its logic of commodification.[8]

The situation that Soueif describes in her travelogue from the West Bank thus illuminates the complex interplay of forces that inscribe domination in the Middle East. Consider, for example, that in addition to citing the occurrence of the images of Said and the two child casualties, Soueif's article details the trauma and nonautonomy of West Bank farmers cut off from their fields and produce, the rapid and excessive militarization of the seam zone, the aggressive construction of an impenetrable wall by the Israeli government, the rubble and blockades that impede access to schools for younger students in Jerusalem al-Quds and for college students at Birzeit University, and the illogical and scripted surveillance of all movement within the occupied territories ("Waiting Game" 2). What, we may ask, is so critical about Soueif's making the overt policing of movement, the control of produce markets, and the search and seizure of students in the West Bank contingent on one another? What is the connection between these scenes of military discipline and the disruption of everyday life being drawn here? How are responses to these dispersed scenes of subjugation to be read as provisional and multiple forms of resistance to a dominant order for Palestinians? If, as Soueif notes, "[g]etting to class here is an act of resistance and at the university the Kamal Nasser Auditorium is full," then what is the scope and strategy of this resistance if, as she also affirms, in class, "[n]o one wants to talk about the occupation. For three hours, these students and their teachers want to talk literature, theatre, music. And they want to do it in English" (2). The echo between this scene in Birzeit and the one of student solidarity at Cairo University at the end of the Six Day War between Egypt and Israel, which Soueif describes in *The Eye of the Sun*, is not to be missed: "Participation. Life," Soueif writes. "Students from Egypt, Libya, Sudan, Algeria, Morocco, Iraq, Jordan, Palestine, Syria and Yemen all sit round the same table. News of unrest comes from the universities of Europe and the United States. Poetry and Politics. Never mind the defeat. Never mind the 'Setback' and Sinai and what remained of Palestine gone. The young have a voice and the voice shall be heard. Bassam, the Palestinian, and Hani, one of the Harley-Davidson boys, both play the guitar and the campus rings to songs of exile and yearning" (97). These two moments of representation elaborate a careful intertextual rendering of measures of dominance, and practices of resistance, of claims of national security and quotidian solidarity, of the language of literature and its political-artistic expression that work in concert, albeit within vastly different interpretive communities, to refashion the field of action and agency for the dominated.

Key to this refashioning is an interrogation of traditional modes of reading and representation allowed within disciplinary domains (academic and otherwise), and an engaged critique from within (e.g., the nation, the university, the media) that relies on an unruly calibration of scenes and circumstances that are typically regarded as the domain of this or that discipline proper or as events unconscripted by disciplinary measures. Certainly through the vignettes of Palestinians under siege she presents in a mainstream British newspaper and in her fiction, Soueif begins the task of posing such a challenge, which, because of its unruliness, can begin to reconstitute the way in which Arab opposition to the West is generally received.

Once again, this strategy produces unexpected consequences. Soueif's writings can viewed as tracing the myriad complexities of power and contestations to power that link various Arab societies and social practices. The building of the "security wall" on the West Bank in this sense figures as a historical, political, economic, social, and cultural act that is stimulated by a complex set of factors none of which can be fully assimilated to any unitary disciplinary context. Hence, within the same logic that captures the impossibility of daily Palestinian life, it also becomes impossible to read all Israelis generically as the authors of the violence perpetrated by the Israeli state. The wall in her work thus serves as a metaphor—physical, political, and literary—of the impossible conditions under which both Israelis and Palestinians continue to exist. Soueif recounts her first encounter with the wall in the West Bank: "On this, our first morning here, we drive up through the West Bank to see Israel's 'security fence'; a monster barrier of steel and concrete that separates farmers from their land and refugees from their hard-earned homes. Brute technology hacking away at a living body of land and people. It rears up into a giant wall to block the sunset and the evening breeze from the people of Qalqilya, then spreads itself out to swallow great stretches of land cultivated over hundreds of years. . . ." (*Mezzaterra* 139). This impassable front, as Soueif's numerous references to it make clear, is at once a historical reminder of the military conflict and nationalist fervor of the Six Day War of 1967 between Egypt and Israel described vividly in Soueif's novel,[9] an instantiation of present-day political struggles between Israel and Palestine over the occupied territories (Gaza and the West Bank), land disputes, and the right of return.[10] The wall is an economic barrier that facilitates free passage for some while curtailing it for others[11] and a physical reminder of social and cultural assumptions that continually hamper any attempt at peace in the region. But equally, it is a reminder of the injury perpetrated on the Jewish diaspora and the unspeakable trauma that resulted from an attempt to seal off geopolitical and cultural terrains. Seals, as Soueif also insists on reminding us, can be broken. She quotes her taxi driver remarking on the wall: "They build the wall and now everybody is talking about the wall. The wall is just a wall. It was built and it can be removed. The real questions are the borders, the settlements, Jerusalem and the refugees" (*Mezzaterra* 144). The wall, we are reminded casually, is a harsh manifestation of manufactured differences that can be managed and even undone. It is the figurative transformation of this physical obstruction into various other psychic, social, and material differentiations that remain intractable and continue to compound the violence of its initial erection.

Socially and culturally, the wall is the very symbol of the "threat" and "primitivism" with which Palestinians are aligned in the imagination of the Israeli state. In Soueif's argument, the wall is being built to both keep suicide bombers out of Israel and so to mark a protective zone between Israel and those who threaten its citizens, and to discourage nomadic and outmoded ways of land use that are deemed inconsistent with the region's technological and modern outlook. The Palestinians, on the contrary, see the wall as the cause of impoverishment and a ruse to any peace process initiated by Israel. For example, chief Palestinian negotiator Saeb Erakat has pointed to its strategic effect of cutting the West Bank off from Gaza and its tacit appropriation of more than eight percent of the West Bank for Israel at a time when, according to the "Roadmap for Peace," Israel is being very publicly lauded for pulling out of Gaza and four settlements of the West Bank. The wall masks, according to Erakat and others, the fact that more than 120 illegal settlements remain militarily shielded in the West Bank, and the structure itself bifurcates Palestine, making it impossible to construct a continuous autonomous zone for its people.

Such a textured consideration of even a singular sociopolitical occurrence in the Middle East, where each thread of reference is cited without regulatory designs, is antithetical to disciplinary representations that typically consider emergent representations only within well-drawn contours of the field. Unrestricted by stale rules of examination, objectification, and dissemination, Soueif presents an array of vignettes on Arab life that deliberately disorder narrowly disciplined perspectives and produce alternatively oriented representations that, although articulated as disciplined by some overarching narratives, gain meaning and legibility through lenses that are decidedly extradisciplinary. It is difficult, for example, to define the genre of Soueif's *Mezzaterra: Fragments from the Common Ground* as nonfiction or essays on culture in the loosest sense. It is a compilation of work ranging from travelogues to political manifestoes to activist letters, as well as editorials, cultural commentaries, book reviews, eulogies, and meditations both intensely subjective and global about the effects of difference in our world. In form and as well as voice, the book's forceful critique of a unitary orientation toward conflicts in the Arab world is possible only because of the ever-shifting outlines and multiple tones in which it makes its claims: It is both terse and poetic, journalistic and metaphoric, a mosaic, complete and in fragments, of the worlds in which Soueif dwells.

The Booker-nominated *In the Eye of the Sun*, one of Soueif's early novels, begins a similar project of an unruly critique that breaks the rules of disciplinarity and its attendant forms of allegiance. Written in English and published in London, it consolidates its trenchant critique of Americanization in the Middle East with a scathing portrayal of Egyptian nationalism and a concerted effort to reconsider majority Arab opinions toward disenfranchised Arabs in their midst. For Soueif, it seems as important to launch an internal, Arab response against superficial capital accumulation and modernization as to recognize the ways in which the possession and flow of capital, of oil money, magnifies interdependencies and creates alliances between Arabs.[12] The circumstances of the dispossessed and their strategic exclusions from dominant social orders serves as the location for Soueif's undisciplined politics. And one of its tactical aims seems to be to reorient all forms of representation (literary, cultural, historical) to enable the predicament of the exploited, and the terms of their often unarticulated and unrepresented resistance, to be more thoroughly disseminated. It is not insignificant that Soueif emphasizes the fact that the students at Birzeit hold forth in English!

Soueif's novel traces the life of a young Cairene, Asya al-Ulama, through her formative years in Nasser's Egypt, her life as a student of literature and linguistics in England, and her subsequent return to Cairo.[13] Asya's coming of age is a coming to recognition of the scars of dislocation and migration. Asya's friendship with Noora and Noora's Palestinian lover Bassam instantiate the kind of collective convergence of identifications beyond political and cultural borders with which the novel is concerned. Bassam's songs of "exile and yearning" punctuate the narrative of *In the Eye of the Sun* and offer a narrative counter focus to Asya's immediately Egyptian experiences of nationalism. Bassam is Palestinian, and he lives in Cairo as an emblem of Arab unity regarding the disenfranchised status of Palestine. At the same time, Bassam's liminal position within Egyptian society emerges as the condition for negotiation that makes Pan-Arabism in this novel the basis of an identity that is constantly in the making. Asya's Egypt may seem inflected by the nationalisms of Nasser and Sadat, but Asya's lived experience of Egypt, a place with many who are out of place, bears witness to the fragility of nationally "imagined communities" in the Arab political context.

Bassam's presence within Soueif's novel stirs Asya to sustained contemplation on the plight of the *Abdel* (dispossessed), a contemplation that is all the more important for its gyre-like logic, seeing Bassam as wholly other, seeing him as herself, and then expanding outward into a kaleidoscopic awareness of the multitudes around her who are without a sense of permanent belonging. At a study session, Soueif writes of Asya's preoccupation with Bassam: "Asya closes the book gently and glances at Bassam. She had wondered since she had met him—what was it *really* like to be him? To be so displaced?" (233). To this question, Asya has no immediate answer, and Soueif's tactic here is to place Bassam elsewhere in Asya's thoughts, at least for the moment: "He was born in 1949; one year after the partition and the war. He'd grown up in Nablus and since 1967 his family—and he in the summer holidays had been living under occupation" (233). This, then, is a movement in representation toward origins; for Asya to understand Bassam, he needed first to be identified as Palestinian, someone born into a state of dispossession that Asya, as Egyptian, has never experienced. Yet his proximity to her, moving as he does in her circles, makes Asya go further: "Actual physical occupation. What would that be like?" she asks, and ventures, "To have people, the Israelis themselves, stop you and say, 'Sorry. You can't come in here any more. You are banned'" (233).

This, it seems, is the political moment, opposing disempowered Arabs to Israeli aggression in Asya's still-youthful ruminations. Asya here "others" herself, for a time imagining herself in Bassam's place, without place, and is able to next enunciate a politics of Arab unity. Momentarily, this becomes a way for Asya to see herself, Bassam, and countless others in a place of political vulnerability.

Bassam, Asya realizes, appeared to her almost . . . maimed. One of the bruised people. All those bruised people: Palestinians, Armenians, Kurds, and of course the Jews themselves. . . . What *can* be done? (234)

There is a shift in Asya's new expression of Pan-Arab solidarity. The inclusion in this list—"Palestinians, Armenians, Kurds"—of "Jews" is important because Asya here recuperates Pan-Arabism from becoming

religiously divisive, and foregrounds instead a certain pathos of displacement, an empathy toward the "maimed" and "bruised" as sufficient grounds
for unity and action. And regardless of religious affiliation, Soueif makes
refugees the source of political impetus, without at the same time completely
dissociating, or ignoring, historical specificity. Palestinians, Armenians,
Kurds, Jews, all have very distinct experiences of unrootedness, and for
Asya, their historical differences must be acknowledged in any attempt to
think of them together, to ponder the active question, "What *can* be done?"
Asya will have none of what Djait has called the "abstract humanity" of
European colonialism that "consider(s) peoples as blocs of static, homogenous
humanity with no roots in the earth, unaffected by time" (31). Hers is an
activist's call. On a meta-narrative level, *In the Eye of the Sun* makes the
unstable circumstances of this refugee an ever-present lens through which
its protagonist is compelled to view the world.

The novel's intermittent gaze on Bassam and Noora's life together—disowned from Noora's family, Bassam working precariously for the
Voice of Palestine—shapes the political ethos of Pan-Arabism within it
(233). Bassam's forceful deportation from Egypt becomes a way for Soueif
to implicate representations of displacement in representational critiques
of American influence on the Arab region. On her return to Egypt from
England, Asya tells of Bassam's last night in Egypt:

> . . . . Bassam is gone. Picked up the night of Camp David and
> given twenty minutes to pack a bag and then driven off into the
> night leaving a distraught Noora. . . . As far as anyone could tell
> he would not be able to come back for a long time—perhaps
> not ever. (775)

The year is 1980, and Asya returns to a very different Egypt, one
that is no longer nonaligned; Sadat is very much in the American camp,
and politically, it seems Egypt has swerved clear of Nasserian visions of
"Socialism, Arab Unity, The Palestinian Cause" with which the novel
opened (17). Still, Asya's attachments are with Bassam and Noora, and the
novel keeps open the need to interrogate the kind of national politics that
seek to write them out of Egypt's history. As Amin Malak notes, "What
is particularly engaging about the heroine, Asya, is that her sharp political
sensitivity extends beyond Egyptian nationalist concerns to embrace other
dispossessed peoples of the Middle East such as Kurds, Palestinians, and
Armenians" (146). This "sharp political sensitivity" characterizes Soueif's
call to consider Arab unity beyond national borders.

In the Eye of the Sun represents Arab experience as change, as a confluence of histories that formally exposes nation and religion as interdependent, inchoate forms of belonging. People's stories in *In the Eye of the Sun* are the prisms through which narratives of national and international politics are refracted. Egypt, within Soueif's novel, becomes the conflicted site of modernity because the very space of the novel, the space where the novel narrates the nation, is fractured by the contradictory experiences Soueif's characters have of Egypt. The stories of Bassam, Dada Zeina, Asya, Saif, Lateefa, Deena, and Muhsin jostle for prominence amid the other, fragmentary accounts of Egypt's encounter with colonialism and American imperialism.

Soueif's narrative is textured by the crisis moments in Egypt's history, such as the Suez Crisis of 1956, the Arab-Israeli colonial conflict of 1967, and the *Pax-Americana* of the Sadat years.[14] But these crisis moments of Egyptian history, between Nasser and Sadat, are perceived only through the filters of their representation—in the media, in this novel, and by the reaction of the people who inhabit the space of *In the Eye of the Sun*. The effect is the absence of a mega-national narrative. In its place, the coming together of divergent collectives (exiles, migrants, women, the *fellaheen,* the *effendiya*, students) always at odds with any attempt to write Arab history in terms of singular national development suggests a radical rethinking of the place of the nation and of History proper for Arabs. What Soueif's account suggests is that even a schizophrenic history of Egypt, from one crisis to the next, as one nation's reactions to colonialism or imperialism, is an inadequate way to historicize Arab representation. Opened up instead are new histories, new diplomacies, modern spaces of cohabitation between Arabs, within and without particular national bounds, which make urgent a politics of regional coalition.

Coda: *Reworlding*, an Ethics of Extradisciplinarity

The unruly methodology that I am pointing to in recent Arab attempts such as Soueif's to address Western imperialist involvement in the Middle East, as well to alter the course of dominant representation of Arabs as wholly conditioned by a certain primitivism of religion and attitudes hostile to modernity, involves collapsing the all-too-neat separations between political, historical, and cultural frames of reference. The effect of such a deliberately disruptive tactic is that it allows representations of the Arab situation to be multiply nuanced by various discursive and material effects, and Arab responses to be understood as conditioned by but intractable to governing modes of exploitation.

If, as Said has noted, the Orientalist management of knowledge about the East, the "imaginative geographies" of the West that for so long textualized and worlded the Orient, conditioned and continue to condition the ways of being Arab in the world,[15] writers such as Soueif represent alternatives. Recognizing, as Said does, that to a large extent, "the modern Orient [also] participates in its own Orientalizing," Soueif focuses on collectives of migrants, of women, of workers, whose very representation breaks the molds of such internalized Orientalism and shows the monolithic idea of identities circumscribed within fixed communities of belonging, or disciplined as such, as always already ineffectual, as always already fragmented.

In closing, I want to return briefly to those images on the walls in Bethlehem that Soueif describes in her writings on Palestine to consider the stakes of reading Arab collective agency as a particular confluence between the disciplines of literature, history, and politics. What does it mean for Soueif, writing on Palestine, writing as a Booker nominee in *The Guardian*, to invoke Edward Said, Egyptian-Palestinian-American, literary critic and theorist from Harvard and Columbia, and an activist-scholar in his own right, alongside those child victims of violence—Christine Saada and Abed Ismail? More importantly, how does the "portrait of Edward Said" on walls in Palestine, beside the portraits of children all too routinely chalked off as collateral damage, signify a new way of conceiving collective activism against power? Perhaps it is the beginning of a new arrangement of the ethical obligations between scholar and subaltern that is being inscribed here. It is a deliberately etched relationship between the intellectual subject and the unforgiving politics of subjection for these and other of the region's youth that need extending. A relationship that would extend the realm of intellectual engagement to think and act in consideration of the terms of troubled humanity evoked by these clearly sentimentalized images of the victims of political violence. Troubled because their legibility in some places (e.g., in the West, within the academy) through the portrait of the intellectual's struggle is an ultimately nonsensical understanding of the terms of humanity these children no doubt possess.[16] At the same time, it points to the particular attempts by a Said or a Soueif to act on behalf of those who remain largely unrecognizable and the extended symbolic and even perilous circulations of their own selves that these scholars are willing to risk.[17]

In *The World, the Text, and the Critic*, Said himself articulates the necessity for such excess, extratextual intellectual engagements with the world when, in his quarrel with American literary theorists of the 1970s and 1980s, he insists that "texts are worldly" and that post-structuralism was too fast retreating "into the labyrinth of textuality" (4, 3). Although his call for literary critics to engage with texts as if they are "a part of the social world, human life, and . . . the historical moments in which they are located and interpreted" may seem mundane today, he can be credited with making one of the first efforts at staving off disciplinary solipsism (4). If, as a result of his own reaction to the Six Day War and his previous, almost simultaneous attempts at writing about the Middle East in *Orientalism*, *The Question of Palestine*, and *Covering Islam*, Said found it necessary to insist on the direct relevance of textual worlds to historical ones, the imperative towards the text's worldliness also has served to expose the ways in which the world itself continues to be textual, as inhabited, understood, and contended through forms of representation.[18]

I will end with the suggestion that this collage, and its reference in the Western media by Soueif, conjures up precisely the kinds of commonplace critiques and subversions of disciplinary privilege that occur every day on the street. Her work effectively demonstrates the need to conjoin seamlessly journalistic, historical, and fictional worlds that preserve within each the sure traces of the other discourses often presumed to be mutually set apart because of disciplinary attitudes toward the relevance of factual, verifiable claims. I will add also that such moments of signification as suggested by the collage and inscribed within activist representations of Palestine as instanced by Soueif are weighted as counter-historical and countercanonical calls that bend the ideological weight of disciplinary knowledge regulated solely through institutional power. What Soueif, crisscrossing the bounds of fiction and history, legitimacy and marginality, and legibility—Edward Said's image—and illegibility—the images of the children, Christine Saada and Abed Ismail—confronts are the more urgent questions of violence, torture, and rights that make up the collective Arab experience. Disciplinarity in this regard becomes a secondary discourse whose limits can and should be persistently breached.

Notes

1. My sincere thanks to Joe Parker for extending me the opportunity to present my work in the conference on "Interdisciplinarity and Social Justice" that he organized at Pitzer College in 2005. Aside from Joe, I am also grateful to the

other editors, Ranu Samantrai and Mary Romero, for their suggestions on an earlier draft. For intelligent editing as well as critical and undisciplined conversations on this paper, I thank Leila Neti and Lindon Barrett.

In the "The Clash of Ignorance?," for example, Said famously critiques Samuel Huntington's reductionist models for identifying Muslims in terms of a flattened cultural jihadism. In "Impossible Histories: Why the Many Islams Cannot be Simplified," Said expands his critique to more fully include the work of Bernard Lewis, whose work so directly influenced Huntington's "jihad vs. mcworld" history of post–Cold War global politics.

2. (Neo)Orientalism as empire and expansionism in the Arab world from antiquity to contemporary times is meant to be suggestive of linkages between prior representations of Arab sovereignty and their deployment in modernity. Questions of representation for the Middle East in this moment are also troubled by the urgency of war, brutality, and American imperial ambitions in the region, and this term is deployed particularly to be attentive to such current repressive structures of dominance. Equally, the term can be used to demarcate the efficacies of counter-narratives and subversive practices that world the Arab situation in difference from (Neo) Orientalist stereotypes.

3. See Ravi Arvind Palat's argument in "Fragmented Visions: Excavating the Future of Area Studies in a Post-American World" that the formation of area studies programs is "thoroughly impregnated with the geopolitical conditions of its conception" that was geared almost exclusively toward "U.S. ascension to a position of global hegemony" (65). Additionally, Palat describes the reductive effect of such modes of knowledge production that insist on cartographic unity among peoples and in regions where in fact much more diverse and various local conditions routinely prevailed. Beyond this, Palat historicizes area studies as a particular mode of inquiry that acquires empirical knowledges about the non-West in order to facilitate a transition from older colonial economies to the more flexible monopoly economies of globalization. In order to enable such a transformation, he notably argues that area studies have to pretend to a certain catholicity of interests while remaining entrenched in microlevel analyses that promotes a totalized split between the West and the non-West.

4. Rey Chow, in "Theory, Area Studies, Cultural Studies: Issues of Pedagogy in Multiculturalism," makes the case that the premise of interdisciplinarity that cultural studies represents is a "kind of dangerous supplement to poststructuralist theory" that in itself repeats the play against the fixed significations of structuralism, and the dislocation of the sign that according to Rey despite its "fundamental epistemological subversiveness" remained restricted to high European theory (106). It is this sense of risk that extradisciplinary attempts to consider the predicament of writing Arab identity embrace in order to continue the play of signification post-structuralism inaugurated in theory.

5. Saree Makdisi, in "Postcolonial Literature in a Neocolonial World: Modern Arabic Culture and the End of Modernity" describes the era of the Nahda, or enlightenment, in which Arab thinkers contended with the dualisms of colonialism. His reading of Tayib Salih's *Season of Migration to the North* articulates the difficulties of reading literary efforts at blurring such dualisms when they have so pervasively influenced debates about traditionalism and westernization, culture and modernity in only recently decolonized postcolonies.

6. In her letter to Tony Blair, "Dear Mr. Blair," first published in *The Guardian* in 2002, she primarily quotes Israeli soldiers' testimonials to evidence the implacable situation of the occupation of the West Bank. Israelis in effect become witness to the horrors inflicted on Palestinian families, the heroism of the women, the normativization of violence that the conflict generates, the abject conditions enforced by continued military assaults, as well as the voices through which the desperate demands for rights by Palestinians continue to proliferate: "But still, as Tamir Sorek, sergeant first class, army intelligence, writes: 'The deprived [Palestinian] habitants are still desperately demanding their rights. The obvious facts that their uprising includes hideous assaults against innocent privileged [Israeli] people do not subtract from the legitimacy of their claim for freedom from non-elected rule.' How is that for straight moral thinking? Do something to stop the occupation, Mr. Blair" (*Mezzaterra* 100).

7. For fuller discussions of Ahdaf Soueif's fiction, see my essay on *The Eye of the Sun*, "To Undo What the North Has Done," a brief part of which is offered by way of example in this article. Wail S. Hassan's article, "Agency and Translational Literature" also offers a nuanced critique of the multiple and uneven grounds of transnational metaphors deployed in Soueif's other significant novel.

8. Middle Eastern newspapers frequently note the exceptional wealth disparity in the Arab region. In "Riding for a Fall," Wael Gamal of *Al Ahram* writes of the poverty line in the Middle East based on two reports—"Working out Poverty" from the International Labor Office, and "The World Wealth Report (2003)" issued by Merrill Lynch and Cap Gemini Ernst and Young, which measure "key trends and developments in the global HNWI [high net worth individuals] market." "The Middle East," writes Gamal, bringing these two status reports together, "is a stark example on both sides. 'The number of people in the Middle East living at or below the $2 a day line rose from $50 million to nearly $70 million in the 1990s,' the ILO report said. At the same time, according to the HNWI report, 'the number of HNWIs increased by 4.7 percent—nearly double the international rate—to 300, 000 . . . to reach $1.1 trillion." However, this type of comparative economic analysis, which considers both social, and corporate, "wealth management" type findings under one rubric to arrive at the bigger picture is rare. Most economic reports ignore labor-based reports that allow for conclusions such as the ones Gamal supports: "There is no safety net and little state support. After all the

poor do not cause poverty. Poverty is the result of structural failures and ineffective economic and social systems. It is a product of inadequate political responses, bankrupt policy imagination and insufficient international support.... The work of the poor is largely invisible. Far too much of women's work is still uncounted and undervalued." Instead, what is perpetuated are policies of trade liberalization and tariff reduction that, although purporting to be aimed at reducing economic disparity, continue to focus on a corporate system too centered on individuality, and profit generation, that is, on the maintenance and regeneration of HNWI. Social change is hence made dependent on an ethos of individuality that merely uses the rhetoric of change and communitarianism to stabilize the status quo, the domination of world markets by the West according to Western conservative market principles. See, for example, the implementation of the Egypt-EU Association Agreement of 2002 and the World Bank's "2003 Trade Investment and Development" report for the MENA [Middle East and North Africa] region, both of which facilitate a lowering of tariffs within Arab countries and an opening up of Arab markets to foreign import and export, and Egypt's entry into the Patent Cooperation Treaty in September 2003, which checks all Egyptian innovation against a standard of Intellectuality, and Intellectual rights established by the American market system.

9. Historically, the West Bank is land belonging to Palestinians, and considered previously to be a part of Jordan that has been occupied by Israel since the conflict of 1967. Ironically, the recent Israeli withdrawal from Gaza returns the responsibility for civic control to Jordan, which has assumed the task of training and deploying a Palestinian police force to maintain some semblance of stability in the area.

10. The presence of the wall has been justified by Sharon's government as an essential feature of Israeli security and border patrol. Conversely, the Palestinians make the case that the wall annexes more land in the West Bank to Israel, protects and encourages illegal settlements, and further stifles the chances for successful Palestinian autonomy by separating and isolating parts of the West Bank completely from Israel, Jordan, and Gaza. The unresolved logics here speak to the disparate and almost completely incommensurable political concerns on either side.

11. Soueif's writings from Palestine routinely invoke the way in which restrictions on movement such as the one posed by the wall and difficulty in negotiating military blockades and arbitrary zoning regulations cost those whose lives remain curtailed by the wall their livelihood, leading to a cycle of impoverishment and desperation for these many, and lucrative profiteering (e.g., new construction projects, greater land resources), for some select few.

12. I would note again, as I have in my other piece on Soueif's fiction, Soueif's strategic compromise here, as against more critical works such as Ghassan Kanafani's *Men in the Sun*, which takes a much more stringent view against the oil-rich states. Kanafani's novel represents the experiences of Palestinian workers who attempt to cross into Kuwait, without papers for work, in the hope of a better life. The novel has a dark end: The workers die of heat and suffocation when

their truck, driven by an Iraqi human trafficker, is unexpectedly held up at a customs checkpoint. Kanafani's conclusion here is about the impossibility of a collective Arab experience, given the manner in which colonial borders between Arab states are still rigidly enforced by Gulf states that, in Kanafani's account, make it impossible for rich Arabs to identify, or aid those other, dispossessed, poor Arabs, outside their borders. Soueif's novel avoids such neat divisions and thus offers a singularly apocalyptic commentary on the Arab experience.

13. The following reading of *In the Eye of the Sun* is excerpted from my "To Undo What the North Has Done." I return to these passages because they seem particularly relevant to demonstrating the break with isomorphic identity politics that Soueif's form of extradisciplinarity engenders.

14. For more on the Suez crisis, see Khalidi and Owen.

15. See Said's *Orientalism*.

16. See Judith Butler's "Violence, Mourning, Politics" in *Precarious Life*, where she predicates the question of humanity itself (to the extent that one must ask, "[W]ho counts as human?" in thinking about global violence) on the extent to which we fail ourselves when we refuse to recognize the humanity of others and hence to publicly mourn them. Butler's critique of Freud's sense of mourning as a private incorporation and replacement of the lost other and her contention that in fact grief must be a public incorporation of the extent to which "we are undone by each other" and our own humanity remains "in the thrall" of others whose loss must be openly grieved in order to confirm our common human conditions is aptly situated in the context of what she shows to be ungrievable, and hence dehumanized Palestinian lives are deliberately excised from our public discourses (22).

17. Hence the uproar at Columbia University regarding Edward Said's having thrown a stone in the general direction of soldiers guarding the Israeli–Lebanese border during his 2000 visit to Lebanon, the numerous protestations at San Francisco State University about memorializing his image, as well as the various posters of this academic on the walls of Gaza and the West Bank.

18. To this end, Said's critique of Derrida, and indeed of post-structuralists such as de Man and Foucault, as stuck in a hermetic textuality that "forfeits an active situation in the world" (*World* 146) can be said to restore Derrida's often quoted claim on textuality, "*Il n'y a pas de hors-texte,*" to its fullest sense: to account for the various ways in which the textuality of the world itself always supplements the intellectual's endeavor, or that limited world of valuation drawn from that which is literally written or authored (Derrida 158).

Works Cited

Butler, Judith. "Violence, Mourning, Politics." *Precarious Life: The Powers of Mourning and Violence*. New York: Verso, 2006.

Chakravorty, Mrinalini. "To Undo What the North Has Done: Fragments of a Nation and Arab Collectivism in the Fiction of Ahdaf Soueif." *Arab Women's Lives Retold: Exploring Identity Through Writing.* Ed. Nawar Golley. New York: Syracuse UP, 2007.

Chow, Rey. "Theory, Area Studies, Cultural Studies: Issues of Pedagogy in Multiculturalism." Ed. Harry D. Harootunian and Masao Miyoshi. *Learning Places: The Afterlives of Area Studies.* Durham: Duke UP, 2002. 103–18.

Derrida, Jacques. *Of Grammatology.* Trans. Gayatri Chakravorty Spivak. Baltimore: Johns Hopkins UP, 1976.

Djait, Hichem. *Europe and Islam: Cultures and Modernity.* Berkeley: U of California Press, 1989.

Egypt-European Union Association Treaty. Ratified by the EU in Brussels, 25 June 2001. Confirmed in Egypt by Presidential Decree No. 335/2002.

Gamal, Wael. "Riding for a Fall." *Al Ahram Economy* 646 16 July 2003 <http://weekly.ahram.org.eg/2003/646/ec4.htm> (2008)

Harootunian, Harry D., and Masao Miyoshi, eds. *Learning Places: The Afterlives of Area Studies.* Durham: Duke UP, 2002.

Hassan, Wail S. "Agency and Translational Literature: Ahdaf Soueif's *The Map of Love.*" *PMLA* 121.3 (2006): 753–68.

Khalidi, Rashid. "Consequences of the Suez Crisis in the Arab World." *Suez, 1956: The Crisis and Its Consequences.* Ed. Roger Louis and Roger Owen. Oxford: Oxford UP, 1989. 377–92.

Makdisi, Saree. "Postcolonial Literature in a Neocolonial World: Modern Arabic Culture and the End of Modernity." *Boundary* 2 22.1 (1995): 85–115.

Malak, Amin. "Arab Muslim Feminism and the Narrative of Hybridity: The Fiction of Ahdaf Soueif." *Alif: Journal of Comparative Poetics* 20 (2000): 140–83.

Moran, Joe. *Interdisciplinarity.* London: Routledge, 2002.

Owen, Roger. "Egypt and Europe: from French Expedition to British Occupation." *Studies in the Theory of Imperialism.* Ed. Roger Owen and Bob Sutcliffe. London: Verso, 1972.

Palat, Ravi Arvind. "Fragmented Visions: Excavating the Future of Area Studies in a Post-American World." *Beyond the Area Studies Wars: Toward a New International Studies.* Ed. Neil L. Waters. Hanover: UP of New England, 2000.

Said, Edward W. "Clash of Ignorance?" *Nation.* 273.12 22 Oct. 2001: 11–14.

———. *Covering Islam: How the Media and the Experts Determine How We See the World.* New York: Pantheon Books, 1981.

———. *The World, the Text, and the Critic.* Cambridge: Harvard UP, 1984.

———. "Impossible Histories: Why the Many Islams Cannot be Simplified." *Harper's* July 2002: 69–74.

———. *Orientalism.* New York: Vintage Books, 1979.

Soueif, Ahdaf. *In the Eye of the Sun.* New York: Anchor Books, 1992.

————. *The Map of Love*. London: Bloomsbury, 1999.

————. "Do Something" in G2, Comment and Features Section of *The Guardian* 3 Apr. 2002: 4 <http://www.guardian.co.uk/books/2002/apr/03/israelandthe-palestinians.politics> (2009).

————. "The Waiting Game" in Comment and Features Section *The Guardian*. 24 Nov. 2003: 2 <http://www.guardian.co.uk/world/2003/nov/24/israel> (2009).

————. *Mezzaterra: Fragments from the Common Ground*. London: Bloomsbury, 2004.

World Bank. "2003 Trade, Investment, and Development in the Middle East and North Africa: Engaging with the World." *MENA Development Report*, Washington D.C. 2003.

Section II

Critiques of Interdisciplinary Fields

Chapter Six

Cultural Studies

Justice, Values, and Social Class

Patrick Brantlinger

Wherever you find injustice, the proper form of politeness is attack.

—T. Bone Slim of the IWW

Cultural studies examines how people are classified (or "classed") and how they classify the world around them. In its initial phase in Britain in the 1960s, it focused on the relations between social class and cultural value; its emphasis on justice was unmistakable and remained so as it added both race and gender to its New Left agenda. From the outset, moreover, cultural studies has served as a counter-discourse to the modern "science of value"—that is, to economics in its dominant, capitalist mode.

The seminal texts of the cultural studies movement—Raymond Williams's *Culture and Society*, Richard Hoggart's *The Uses of Literacy*, and E. P. Thompson's *The Making of the English Working Class*—all treat culture as classed and emphasize the active role of workers in its production and consumption, even as they also stress the rise of industrialized mass culture. After the establishment of the Birmingham Centre for Cultural Studies in the early 1960s, these concerns remained central in, for example, the analysis of "subcultures" (Hebdige; Gelder and Thornton). This was a variation on the themes of "class fractions" and mass culture, from which emerged the interminable debate about whether the mass media can be genuinely "popular" in the sense of democratic or are merely "mass"—conformist, ideological, and antidemocratic.[1]

Hoggart's and Thompson's books belong to a lengthy tradition of labor history in Britain; they are both versions of "history from below" (Brantlinger 112–18). Williams's *Culture and Society* takes a different tack; it is a literary study dealing mainly with canonical nineteenth- and early-twentieth-century writers, and to that extent it pursues a top-down approach. But Williams stresses the many ways in which the writers he examines turned "culture" into a critical tool for analyzing and challenging social class inequality and economic orthodoxy, as in Dickens's *Hard Times* and Elizabeth Gaskell's *Mary Barton*. In the tradition Williams surveys—itself a principal source of cultural studies—culture was typically viewed as transcendent, rising above what Matthew Arnold saw as the "anarchy" of material competition and class conflict. For Arnold, high culture—at once aesthetic and ethical—was to be the modern substitute for religion and the arbiter of all values, including economic ones.

Needless to say, Arnold's faith in high culture seems naive today. Nevertheless, from our postmodern standpoint, characterized in part by what Fredric Jameson calls "the disappearance of class" (*Signatures* 35), it is possible to look back with a certain nostalgia to nineteenth-century Britain or France, when social class demarcations were clear and when all cultural values were arranged in hierarchies marked by class—aristocratic, bourgeois, proletarian. In *The Origins of Postmodernity*, Perry Anderson notes that, starting in the nineteenth century, cultural modernism, in its confrontation with capitalism and economics, "could appeal to two alternative value-worlds, both hostile to the commercial logic of the market and the bourgeois cult of the family. . . ." An aristocratic perspective "offered one set of ideals against which to measure the dictates of profit and prudery. . . ." By contrast, the "emergent labor movement" also opposed bourgeois hegemony and unregulated capitalism, seeking "its solution in an egalitarian future rather than hierarchical past" (103). Today, cultural values and the grounds of class conflict are much less certain, in large measure because of the blurring or obscuring of class boundaries and definitions. Both Anderson and Jameson are well aware that class has not really disappeared in postmodern societies. Nevertheless, the aristocracy is nonexistent in the United States and has almost disappeared in Europe. And the postmodern condition involves a significant degree of "social homogenization," which, Jameson notes, is often explained in terms of "the embourgeoisement of the worker, or better still, the transformation of both bourgeois and worker into that new grey organization person known as the consumer" (36). Meanwhile, what has become of that very Victorian and Marxist notion of class conflict?

Postmodernism as a Declassed and Deconstructed Condition

Jameson's homogenized, "new grey organization person" is not so new. He or she was as much a modern or even Victorian person as a postmodern one. Between the 1870s and World War I, the old Marxist threat of the revolutionary "masses" acquired a very different meaning. No longer threatening revolution or even economic redistribution, the new idea of the "masses" referred to petit-bourgeois or even classless conformists, the empty-headed individuals who were steered into lives of mediocrity and acquiescence in their lot partly by prosperity (consumption) and partly by ideology (advertising, religion, education—Louis Althusser's Ideological State Apparatuses [ISAs]). Instead of revolutionary values, the new masses were the bearers of no values whatsoever—José Ortega y Gassett's mindless millions in *Revolt of the Masses*, T. S. Eliot's "hollow men," Karl Čapek's "robots." These "masses" are no different from Herbert Marcuse's "one-dimensional men" of the 1960s or Jean Baudrillard's postmodern "silent majorities." Whereas the earlier discourse about the robot-like masses points ahead to theories of the postmodern, both versions either implicitly or explicitly blame large-scale economic factors on producing nonindividuals who are all "mass" or mass-produced because they can't think for themselves. It hardly matters, moreover, whether the economic factors involve communism, socialism, or capitalism. In all three versions of modernization, patterns of intellectual and cultural "distinction" are eviscerated or disappear altogether through the collapse of older structuring principles—or at least through the new "mass" inability to recognize the operation of those structuring principles. From a Marxist perspective, for the mindlessness of the new gray masses, you can substitute the view that they have no class consciousness, which is close to Thomas Frank's conclusion in *What's The Matter With Kansas?* Conservative Kansans, Frank writes, even blue-collar, low-income ones, believe that you choose what class you belong to just as you choose "hairstyles or TV shows" (26).

In many dystopian visions of modern and now postmodern society, people herd together in gray gulags—kind of like Kansas in the winter—where they wait to die or be slaughtered in future wars. This dismal picture of what the lives of ordinary (mass) individuals are like in modern or postmodern society perhaps expresses little more than intellectual disdain and stereotyping (Niethammer). Yet it was also a picture that helped Hannah Arendt, Theodor Adorno, and many others understand how emergent democracies gave way to totalitarianism, as in the case of the Weimar

Republic. That recent theories of the postmodern often echo this dystopian view is an indication of the power of the mass media to overwhelm processes of cultural "distinction," dumbing down the masses; but it is perhaps also due to the willingness of many intellectuals to abandon questions of social justice in favor of the very discourse about "the masses" that allows them seemingly to transcend (or escape from) the cultures they purport to analyze. In short, although "the masses"—in the United States, at least—may be both anti-intellectual and lacking in intellectual sophistication, postmodern theorists are often equally and perversely anti-intellectual, in part because they fail to grapple with the problem of how cultural "distinction" is organized and operative in today's societies, in part because they underestimate their fellow citizens, including workers, and in part because they do not believe that class warfare is happening.

Capitalist economics helped give birth to Jameson's "new grey organization person known as the consumer." Social class categories are based on production, not consumption. This is historically the case, although Pierre Bourdieu's "reflexive sociology" shows how patterns of consumption are closely related to class and even class fractions. But starting in the 1870s, with the economists' turn away from labor theories of value and to the theory of marginal utility (or price theory emphasizing consumption rather than production), economics has promoted the notion that all actors in the marketplace operate on equal terms. This is perhaps the key version of the illusion of classlessness under capitalism, which has its echoes in several prominent theories of postmodernism, including Baudrillard's. Yet given this apparently hegemonic view, how can anyone explain the now widespread notion that, as CNN's Lou Dobbs states, there is "a war on the middle class"? If there is only one happy class of united, prosperous, middle-class Americans, who or what could possibly be waging class war against us? There is no aristocracy, and it surely can't be the working class, which seems to have nearly disappeared from the myriad flat screens of postmodern American culture. When was the class war that eliminated the working class? But the main threat of the war against the middle class is that it will drive its bourgeois members straight into the working class or worse—into a "jobless future" when work itself disappears (Aronowitz). Given the subprime mortgage crisis, people's homes are also disappearing. Presto-change-o, the alleged classless condition in which we all belong to the middle class may devolve into a condition of classlessness in which everyone except CEOs is jobless and homeless.

In addition to the modernist and now postmodern theme of the mindless masses, and beyond the shift in orthodox economics from production to price theory and consumption, a third source of the illusion that class has vanished from postmodern culture is postmodern culture itself. The pop art of Andy Warhol and Roy Lichtenstein presents us with images of commodified images, including stars and soup cans, cartoons and ads. Once again, what is stressed is consumption, available for everybody. Furthermore, various theories of the postmodern condition celebrate or at least announce the downfall of cultural hierarchies, the complete relativization of values, and the vanishing of class conflict into Baudrillard's "silent majorities"—that is to say, into the indiscriminate and apolitical masses. According to Baudrillard, there is no longer any "reality," only "hyperreality" consisting of "simulacra," or image-copies without originals (*Simulations*). His postmodern conception of value as sheer contingency mirrors, perhaps intentionally, what neoliberal economics has to say about it: "The entire strategy of the system lies in this hyperreality of floating values," writes Baudrillard. "It is the same for money and theory as for the unconscious. Value rules according to an ungraspable order: the generation of models, the indefinite chaining of simulation" (Baudrillard, *Selected Writings* 122). This is similar to what Gianni Vattimo, in *The End of Modernity*, has to say about the postmodern "dissolution of truth into value": "Truth . . . reveals itself to be 'a value which dissolves into itself,' or, in other words, no more and no less than a belief without foundation" (Vattimo xlviii).

In *The Postmodern Condition*, Jean François Lyotard famously argued that today, all metanarratives of emancipation, including the Marxist metanarrative of emancipation from social class exploitation and inequality, are no longer credible; postmodern culture instead consists of micronarratives and a global swirl of incommensurate language games. No doubt poststructuralist theory helped give birth to Lyotard's version of the postmodern condition. On the one hand, there is Lyotard's metanarrative about the untenability of all metanarratives; on the other, there is Foucault's poststructuralist metanarrative about the modern, disciplinary diffusion of power—it is everywhere, it apparently needs no ruling class or headquarters or economic base—and it both creates and distributes value and serves as its own tautological explanation.

For Jacques Derrida, too, the question of value is indeterminable. In *The Politics of Friendship*, Derrida writes: "[D]arkness is falling on the value of value" (81). Derrida's analyses of value are, he would have been the first to admit, "spectral," because all values are "spectral." This point of view is rendered all the more spectral, because in *Specters of Marx*, Derrida quite implausibly claims that "deconstruction" is an "attempted radicalization of Marxism" (92). But Derrida nevertheless insists that even though Francis Fukuyama might declare "the end of history" via the triumph of capitalism and liberal democracy, neither the need for social critique nor the goal of social justice has disappeared. Derrida echoes the Frankfurt theorists when he asserts that, like Marxism, deconstruction is "heir to a spirit of the Enlightenment which must not be renounced" (88). His deconstructive understanding of the "spectral" rootlessness or indeterminacy of value is, however, scarcely different from that of neoliberal economics, and therefore from Baudrillard's and Fukuyama's ends-of-history notions.

By downplaying or ignoring actual social classes and class conflict, post-structuralism, some versions of postmodernism, and neoliberal economics leave the question of value up to market forces. This mirroring of the neoliberal embrace of global capitalism renders it difficult, if not impossible, for post-structuralism to be the "radicalization of Marxism" that Derrida was hoping for, and both Lyotard and Baudrillard abandoned Marxism long ago for "the ecstasy of communication." Nevertheless, some other theorists of postmodernism have not abandoned Marx and his central problem of social class and class conflict. I have in mind Jameson, Perry Anderson, David Harvey, Terry Eagleton, and—though at an abstract remove—Jürgen Habermas. Jameson's analyses of postmodernity view it as "the logic of late capitalism"; Harvey is agreeing when he relates it to the transition from the Fordist mode of production and the Keynesian welfare state to the mode of "flexible accumulation" or transnational corporate capitalism and neoliberal, "free market" economics.

Neither Jameson nor Harvey is under any illusion that workers today form a potentially revolutionary class. For a Marxist, Jameson has little to say about social class, although that is in part a reflection of the postmodern condition. When Jameson does address social class as a category, it is to indicate how "groups" like ethnic minorities or even the homeless have replaced class in others' social analyses and, more importantly, to indicate how postmodern culture occludes class divisions and class conflict. Postmodern culture typically flattens cultural values into a faux-populist mishmash—a version of what Jameson refers to as deliberate depthlessness—a commodified, mass-mediated grab bag with something for everyone (if you can pay for it). For Jameson, moreover, if postmodern culture expresses class interests, it is as "the 'consciousness' of a whole new class fraction," one "variously labeled as a new petit bourgeoisie, a professional-managerial class, or more succinctly as 'the yuppies'" (*Postmodernism* 407). Perry Anderson similarly argues that the historical bourgeoisie, just like the historical proletariat, has now been complicated, fragmented, and decentered nearly out of existence, so that there is nothing any longer for an antibourgeois aesthetic or political avant-garde to target. And, arming himself with thorough analyses of both capitalism and traditional Marxism, David Harvey writes about the downsizing and deskilling of the labor force, along with the weakening of trade unionism from the recession of 1973 forward.

These Marxist theorists of the postmodern condition understand that neither the capitalist class nor the working class, either nationally or internationally, has or will disappear in the foreseeable future. According to Terry Eagleton, "If it is a mistake of some Neanderthal Marxists to imagine that there is a single agent of social transformation (the working class), it is equally an error of new-fangled postmodernists to imagine that this agent has now been outdated by the 'new political movements'" (60). Eagleton probably has in mind the claim that Ernesto Laclau and Chantal Mouffe make in *Hegemony and Socialist Strategy* that "the new social movements" seeking environmental sustainability and justice for racial minorities, women, and gays have displaced the industrial proletariat as the agent of historical progress. Except for environmentalism, which involves a different form of economic redistribution than does social class inequality, the other "new social movements" appear to demand adequate cultural recognition as their version of social justice. However, as Nancy Fraser contends, "justice today requires both redistribution and recognition" (2). Obviously, if they have slipped out of view in mainstream American culture, the growing ranks of the new working class also demand both recognition and redistribution.

A key role of "populist" or "yuppified" postmodern, mass-mediated culture is simply to occlude both the working class as a potential agent of social and cultural change and the capitalist class as its opposition, and in so doing to put a smiling face on that all-pervasive source of contemporary power, namely capitalism or, as its true believers like to call it, "the free market." As I have already done, Eagleton also notes that some varieties of supposedly radical current theory help with this mystification: "We now find ourselves confronted with the mildly farcical situation of a cultural left which maintains an indifferent or embarrassed silence about that power which is the invisible colour of everyday life itself, which determines our very existence [and] decides in large measure the destiny of nations. . . . It is as though almost every other form of oppressive system—state, media, patriarchy, racism, neo-colonialism—can be readily debated, but not the one which so often sets the long-term agenda for all of these matters," namely capitalism (22–23). That is at least partly because, as Anderson contends, although "late capitalism [has] remained a class society," the configuration of the classes has drastically changed, both in their internal and in their external relations. "On a world scale—in the postmodern epoch," Anderson writes, "no stable class structure, comparable to that of an earlier capitalism, has yet crystallized. Those above [in the class hierarchy] have the coherence of privilege; those below lack unity and solidarity. A new 'collective labourer' has yet to emerge. These are the conditions," Anderson concludes, "of a certain vertical indefinition" (62). In other words, there is still a hierarchy of social classes, now globalized, though it is less well defined than it used to be.

Although social classes have arranged themselves in many different ways throughout history, there has never been and never will be a classless society. Class, caste, or status systems are themselves both cultural value hierarchies and sites of class struggle, operative even in those societies—the United States or the People's Republic of China, for instance—that claim to be relatively classless or egalitarian.[2] Even the simple societies that Marx and Engels identified as practicing "primitive communism" have structures of authority and value based on age, gender, kinship, and often wealth or property. Indeed, as anthropologists have repeatedly demonstrated, the value hierarchies of so-called primitive societies frequently are highly elaborate. Moreover, all versions of cultural value and classification are incoherent when detached from the economic factors that shape them, including class conflict.

To return to the interesting notion of "the war on the middle class," in the nineteenth century, the European bourgeoisie virtually eliminated the aristocracy. Thus, who or what is driving members of today's bourgeoisie into the working class, or perhaps eliminating both classes altogether? And if both of these major classes are eliminated, who, then, will be the consumers who flock to the markets to buy the goods produced by an apparently totally automated, jobless, globalized, and classless capitalism? Will the ultimate triumph of capitalism indeed be the end of history? Or will Charlie Chaplin escape from the gears of the gigantic machine of capitalist, industrial production and rediscover himself as a rebellious worker—or at least as a sweet and sentimental, albeit unemployed and homeless consumer, with little wherewithal to consume anything? I will try to answer these questions in the second part of this essay, in which, however, instead of the modern Little Tramp, I will trot out the postmodern Chicken Little—W., that is, George Bush the Second.

Class Warfare? That's Not How We Think

During a press conference in January 2003, a reporter asked W. about his plan for boosting the economy by a tax cut "weighted toward helping the wealthiest Americans." W. replied: "I understand the politics of economic stimulus, that some would like to turn this into class warfare. That's not how I think."[3] Apparently, that's not how millions of Americans think either. Even when class warfare is clobbering us, we don't know what it is. According to the pundits, watching the news about Hurricane Katrina's devastation of New Orleans awakened Americans to the poverty in our midst. If it takes a catastrophe to alert us to something so obvious, then we really have been asleep at the switch. And if we aren't aware of poverty, then "class warfare" can't be how we think.

It is true that a lot of the poor are literally invisible: out of sight, out of mind. With the highest incarceration rate in the world, a huge number of citizens in the United States disappear. More than 2.3 million Americans, most of them poor and about half of them black, are behind bars. Furthermore, it doesn't seem likely that most prisoners think that way, either. People arrested for drug dealing or petty street crimes don't typically see themselves as waging class warfare. Many Americans appear to believe that wealth and poverty are natural, God given, and earned. If you're rich, you deserve your money; if you're poor, you deserve your poverty. Government, in any case, can't, won't, or shouldn't do anything about it. And besides, aren't almost all Americans (excluding prisoners) middle class? That's what the reporter who questioned W. suggested: The tax cut would help "the wealthiest," but not "middle income" Americans. He did not mention the working class, the poor, or prisoners, perhaps because these huge populations have also become almost unthinkable to the rest of us.

But if "class warfare" is unthinkable in American culture, why did W. choose that phrase to respond to the reporter? Among ways to spin his response, three seem obvious. First, W. wished to paint the opponents of his tax cuts into a corner identified as left wing, extremist, perhaps communist. Second, he is a pseudo-egalitarian, faithful to trickle-down Reaganomics: he believes that whatever benefits the rich and the corporations will (eventually) benefit the "middle income" people and maybe even the poor. (But supposedly the poor are poor because they deserve to be so.) And third, "class warfare" names a type of turmoil that W. believes the

United States, in contrast with other parts of the world, has outgrown or never even experienced.

There is also a fourth, less obvious way to interpret his comment: "Class warfare" has never gone away; it is now everywhere evident in American culture and society, as in Lou Dobbs's version—"war on the middle class." The first three "spins"—the ones W. probably believes—are thinkable only because of ideological mystification. That a president of the United States can express all three of them in one sentence, confident that millions will agree with him, suggests how thoroughly the concept of class warfare has been rendered un-American in the postmodern United States. Of course, the concept carries a lot of European, and more specifically Marxist, baggage. *The Communist Manifesto* begins with the claim that "the history of all hitherto existing society is the history of class struggles" (Marx 473) and ends with the famous revolutionary battle cry: "Workers of the world, unite! You have nothing to lose but your chains!" Whether W. knows this is not important; he knows how to use "class warfare" to tar and feather his critics as un-American, if not explicitly communist. Waging preemptive warfare in Iraq is OK. But "class warfare" is "not how I think" because it's just not American to think that way.[4]

Even if it is not how W. thinks, what does he think "class warfare" is or was? Is he thinking of Robin Hood, perhaps, who stole from the rich and gave to the poor—long ago and in an un-American country? Probably not, but as Senator Paul Wellstone used to say, W. is acting like Robin Hood in reverse by stealing from the poor and giving to the rich (Krugman 279). Although he didn't use the phrase "class warfare" (W. did), the reporter was right: W.'s tax cuts amount to top-down class warfare. Assuming the cuts remain in effect from 2001 to 2011, the wealthiest 20 percent of the nation will be getting 65.7 percent of the rebate; the rest—80 percent of us—will be getting the rest, 34.4 percent. During these years, the poorest 20 percent will receive $21.8 billion, which sounds pretty good until contrasted with the amount the richest 20 percent will rake in: $1,133.3 billion—that is, more than a trillion dollars. Of that staggering amount, more than half—$578.5 billion—will go to the wealthiest one percent of the nation. That wealthiest one percent already owns 33 percent of the nation's wealth, and the richest 20 percent owns 83 percent of it, while the poorest 18 percent are, well, worthless—they own zero or negative wealth.[5] After all, what is the benefit of a tax cut to those who pay no taxes? It isn't zero, but negative, because cutting taxes means cutting programs that benefit the poor.

The tax cuts swell W.'s record-breaking deficit, which then becomes the excuse to gut social programs. Funds for student loans, Medicaid, food stamps, child care, and low-income housing were all axed in the budget passed by Congress on December 21, 2005. "That Republicans had the nerve to ram through such a budget a week before Christmas," wrote Eyal Press in *The Nation*, "vividly illustrates that when it comes to so-called class warfare, it is the right that is on the offensive" (4). And then there is the assault on Social Security. The Congressional Budget Office reports that Social Security will be solvent until 2052 and that it can easily be stabilized long after that. But W. has preemptively proclaimed its bankruptcy by 2027. This is just one more instance of what Paul Krugman has called the Bush administration's "world-class mendacity" (xxxvi). Social Security is apt to go broke only because, if enacted, W.'s privatization scheme will keep billions from going into the trust fund, thus compounding the currently nonexistent crisis.[6]

Today's class warfare of the rich against the poor, devastating much of the middle class in the process, has been going on at least since President Reagan busted PATCO, the air traffic controllers' union, in 1981. Organized labor has been in a tailspin ever since. In 1973, 24 percent of the workforce was unionized; by 2001, the number had fallen to 13.5 percent.[7] As Robert Perrucci and Earl Wysong wrote in *The New Class Society*, the gains in social welfare and civil rights made in the 1960s and 1970s caused "panic among the U.S. capitalist class," which fought back: "The superclass response was a concerted, large-scale mobilization for total class war" (70). They quote Reagan's budget director David Stockman: "The Reagan Revolution required a frontal assault on the American welfare state" (71). As Bill Moyers writes: "Our business and political class . . . declared class war twenty years ago, and it was they who won. They're on top" (Moyers 12).

W., of course, will have none of this: As far as he thinks, to accuse the rich of class warfare is to foment class warfare where none exists. Nevertheless, he knows which side of the bread to butter. At a fundraiser in 2000, W. said: "This is an impressive crowd, the haves, and the have mores. Some people call you the elite. I call you my base." From time to time, W. displays his economic expertise by uttering versions of the number-one axiom of latter-day economics—that is, of Reaganomics: Growth is good, and ultimately good for everyone. So what if growth can sometimes be cancerous? Who disputes that sacrosanct law of economics espoused by such powerful figures as Alan Greenspan and the late Milton Friedman? Here is one of W.'s versions of it: "We ought to make the pie higher." W. uttered that gem, worthy of Little Jack Horner, on February 15, 2000; two years later, regarding his energy policy, he declared: "We need an energy bill that encourages consumption." Growth is good: keep the engines humming, the oil rigs gushing, and the bombers bombing. But who does higher pie benefit the most? Those at the top of the pie, of course.

   In addition to the seemingly self-evident goodness of economic growth, there is also the notion that whatever is good for corporations is good for everyone. And there is a corollary: the product of a corporation may not be made in postmodern America (and probably isn't), but if it is bought in America, it is still good for America. True, the pundits occasionally fret about the mushrooming trade deficit, especially with regard to China. Also true, scandals like the Enron blowout put a dent in the notion that corporations are good for us, but what is the alternative? After Wal-Mart has driven the little guys out of business in your hometown, what is next? Shopping at Wal-Mart, of course. And shopping, we know, is good for the economy—even, since 9/11, a patriotic duty. Furthermore, after GM and GE and all the rest have downsized and outsourced American jobs, where are new jobs popping up? Why, of course, Wal-Mart to the rescue! Writing about Wal-Mart's role in today's "corporate race to the bottom," Barbara Ehrenreich notes how it has helped to swell "the ranks of the thirty million Americans—nearly one worker in four—who work full-time for less than a poverty-level wage" (51). The excuse for all the union busting, downsizing, and outsourcing is always some version of "It's the economy, stupid!" The pressure on corporations exerted by globalization and competition is so great, say their hucksters, that they can't behave in any other way—even as CEO salaries and perks skyrocket and many of the megacorporations outstrip the economies of entire nations (Wal-Mart is currently the twenty-second-largest economic power in the world). This is just how competition works under "free market" capitalism, we are told. When corporations win, everyone wins. Doesn't every American schoolchild learn that the "free" in "free market" or "free trade" means democracy? In *Capitalism and Freedom*, Friedman, Reagan's favorite economist, taught us that "the organization of the bulk of economic activity through private enterprise operating in a free market" is "a necessary condition for political freedom" (4). Beyond a bare minimum of defense and law enforcement, government should stay its hand—otherwise it is interfering with both economic and political freedom. Friedman is justly famous also for declaring that "there is no free lunch," but that's another story.

   According to economic orthodoxy, in a free society, corporations should be just as free of government "interference" (i.e., "regulation") as individuals. This is how W. thinks, just like Milton Friedman, only without the math: As he stated shortly before he became president, "Entrepreneurship equals freedom." Everyman his own CEO. As Molly Ivins says, W. "is a wholly owned subsidiary of corporate America" (xvi). And of course, if you are going to give tax cuts to individuals, then you ought to give tax cuts to corporations. They are defined by American law as "persons." So the federal government has been giving them approximately $170 billion a year in tax rebates to help them out. According to Vijay Prasad: "Even though Enron [paid no] taxes from 1996 to 2000, it received a net tax rebate of $381 million—$278 million alone thanks to GWB's tax cut" (51). Meanwhile, through lobbying, campaign donations, and the privatization of once-public jobs, corporations have virtually bought up what remains of government.

Are most Americans concerned about any of this? Perhaps more so than we were six years ago when, reviewing a number of opinion polls, Everett Ladd and Karlyn Bowman reported in USA Today that "the nation says NO to class warfare." According to Ladd and Bowman, "With the bulk of society describing itself . . . as middle-class, polarization is not pronounced." Obviously class warfare cannot occur if we all belong to one big, happy class. Another reason why "Americans tolerate great differences in wealth" is that we "believe that opportunity is broadly present" (Ladd and Bowman). But if opportunity means the chance to move out of poverty or the working class into the middle or upper classes, there is much less of it today than there was at the end of World War II.

The notion that almost everyone belongs to the middle class was fueled by 1950s and 1960s prosperity. During those decades, many with working-class jobs could self-identify as middle class on the basis of income, ownership (homes, cars), pensions (including Social Security), and the prospect of sending their kids to college. Besides, it is comforting to believe that we are just like everyone else—at home in the heartland. But since the mid-1970s, that version of the American dream—everyone able to join the great middle class—has steadily eroded. In a 1998 poll by the National Opinion Research Center, 45 percent of the respondents identified as working class and 5 percent as "lower" class. According to Perrucci and Wysong, however, the vast majority of Americans—roughly 80 percent—now belong to what they call "the new working class" (29). Still, the belief persists that most Americans believe we all belong to the middle class.

The belief also persists that, compared with all other countries, the United States has the most dynamic economy and the greatest prosperity. That may be true if the comparison is with countries in Latin America, Africa, and parts of Asia, but not with regard to other "developed" countries.

The nation-states of western Europe and also Japan, Canada, Australia, and New Zealand now all enjoy living standards as high as or higher than ours.[8] Health care serves as an example: The countries with "interventionist economies" all have national health insurance plans. But today more than 46 million Americans have no health insurance. Furthermore, the United States does not rank in the top twenty among nations in either life expectancy or infant mortality rates. Michael Moore's *Sicko* tells it like it is.

Despite the facts, W. and apparently most Americans do not think class warfare is happening. Perhaps that is because workers and the poor have been so thoroughly deunionized, downtrodden, outsourced, and generally blindsided that they have already lost the class war.[9] Furthermore, after the Cold War and the era of McCarthyite red-baiting, who is willing to talk openly about class warfare unless it is how W. does it—as a way of attacking his opponents?[10] Otherwise, "That's not how I think." But if W. were ever to think about it, he might wonder if Marx was right to claim that class struggle is the main engine of history. When have there ever *not* been conflicts between classes regarding power, money, scarce resources, and cultural values? What is exceptional about America today is not that it lacks classes or class conflict; it is instead that mainstream culture typically softens or erases social class as a major factor in determining American values, including economic and governmental policy. This has been the main ideological victory in America's class warfare so far—the success that the mass media, bolstered by orthodox economics, have had in convincing the public of the relative insignificance of social class as a factor in our lives. It is precisely this version of the ideology of classlessness that cultural studies must continue to oppose if social justice is to remain one of its primary values.

Marx's prediction that the ultimate outcome of class warfare would be a classless utopia was wrong, but that does not mean he misinterpreted the past. The communist regimes of eastern Europe and the USSR failed not just because they were totalitarian and inefficient, but also because they continued to be wracked by class conflict—think of Solidarity in Poland, for example, which began as a trade union movement among dock workers in Gdansk. If all "hitherto" history can be understood in terms of "class struggles," on what basis can anyone assume that such struggles aren't occurring in the United States? No one would ever be crazy enough to claim that the United States is in fact the classless society that the USSR failed to become. Further, if communism didn't end class conflict in Russia and eastern Europe, will W.'s tax cuts do the trick in the United States?

That's an unfair question, I realize: W. was not saying that his tax cuts would end "class warfare"; he was just saying that "class warfare" is "not how I think." Nor is it how a number of theorists of postmodernity think, either. For Derrida in *Specters of Marx,* the question of value turns into a dance of the commodities, similar to that in Marx's reflections on commodity fetishism at the start of *Capital*: "One watches for the signals, the tables that turn, the dishes that move...." (*Specters* 99). But to many postmodernists, today's values would not seem so "spectral" if they considered how transnational capitalism is creating new patterns of social class domination throughout the world.

Despite the obfuscating efforts of the mass media, of neoliberal economists, and of some theorists of the postmodern condition, class struggle continues to shape American culture. It is through such struggle that the values of everyday life are organized, but also that the hope for social justice arises—the hope, that is, of rearranging our common life together in less unequal, more democratic ways. Neoliberal economics, political conservatism, and corporations now rule the postmodern world, and in the United States, at least, the working class seems to have been effectively silenced. But silence does not mean that it has disappeared. As Richard Sennett and Jonathan Cobb long ago argued in *The Hidden Injuries of Class*, "To speak of American workers as having been 'bought off' by the system or adopting the same conservative values as middle-class suburban managers and professionals is to miss all the complexity of their silence and to have no way of accounting for the intensity of pent-up feeling that pours out when working people do challenge higher authority" (251).

There are signs that American workers are beginning to challenge "higher authority" in new ways. Trade unionists teamed up with environmentalists, feminists, Native Americans, and many other activist organizations in the Battle of Seattle in 1999. Efforts to unionize the factories of the Maquiladora are now being made on both sides of the border. Many workers' organizations, including unions, have participated in all of the meetings of the World Social Forum and at the American Social Forum held last August in Atlanta. Two summers ago at the Midwest Social Forum in Milwaukee, many of the sessions focused on labor. The rights of labor are also being promoted by a growing number of NGOs, including Jobs with Justice, ACORN, United Students against Sweatshops, Global Exchange, and the Living Wage campaign. The reinvigoration of the labor movement now depends on its articulation, at both the national and the international levels, with many other activist movements in the fight against transnational corporate power. The current struggle for greater equality, freedom, and prosperity for all, represented by the World Social Forum, should be a primary focus for contemporary cultural studies because its primary value has been and should continue to be social justice for all. "Another world is possible."

Notes

1. Though the original emphasis of cultural studies in the works of Williams, Thompson, and Hoggart was clear about social class, starting in the 1970s there was a movement away from class issues toward those of race and gender and also toward what Jim McGuigan has called "cultural populism." Because both race and gender are linked in many ways to social class, however, emphasizing these categories did not necessarily detract from the earlier emphasis on social class. But, as McGuigan argues, it is in the "populist" direction that the critical edge of cultural studies, focused on social justice, tends to get lost in celebrations of mass culture: Whatever the common people enjoy must necessarily be democratic and deserving of recognition. This is a position hard to distinguish from the very economism that insists markets are infallible and the customer is always right.

2. Echoing Pierre Bourdieu, John Frow writes: "The primary business of culture is distinction, the stratification of tastes in such a way as to construct and reinforce differentiations of social status which correspond, *in historically variable and often highly mediated ways*, to achieved or aspired-to class position" (his italics). Frow continues: "Whereas in highly stratified societies culture is closely tied to class structure, in most advanced capitalist societies the cultural system is no longer organized in a strict hierarchy and is no longer *in the same manner* tense with the play of power" (85; his italics).

3. Quotations from W. are from Jacob Weisberg, ed. "The Complete Bushisms," <http://slate.msn.com/id/76886/>.

4. Whenever the issues of inequality and poverty are raised, other conservatives also like to accuse their opponents of fomenting class warfare. In 1997, Lawrence Summers, then–Deputy Secretary of the Treasury, called those pushing to abolish the estate tax "selfish." He was attacked by GOP apparatchnik Ken Khachigian for indulging "in the rhetoric of class warfare and view[ing] with socialist passion the opportunity to confiscate another's wealth." Quoting Khachigian's remark in "The Real Class War," Michelle Cottle also cites "a seniors' association . . . calling for Summers to be fired for promoting 'class warfare' and the tenets 'of the Communist Manifesto.' " As Cottle points out, "Conservatives love to fling around terms like 'socialist' and 'class warmonger' whenever someone suggests that policy makers tend to favor rich, influential special interests" (13).

5. For these and related figures, see the Web site of Citizens for Tax Justice, <http://www.ctj.org>.

6. How much W. really understands or cares about "saving" Social Security seems evident from a number of his comments about it. On November 3, 2000, for example, he opined: "They want the federal government controlling Social Security, like it's some kind of federal program."

7. The year 1973 is also the starting date for the rise of what Naomi Klein calls "disaster capitalism." In that year, neoliberal economists from the University of Chicago helped the new Chilean dictator, Augustus Pinochet, inaugurate "free market" reforms in that country, dismantling its welfare state. Seven years later, Reagan in the United States and Margaret Thatcher in Britain began their assault on labor and so-called "big government" in favor of private enterprise.

8. As *The State of Working America* notes, "Supporters of the U.S. model generally acknowledge the relative inequality in the United States but argue that the model provides greater mobility, greater employment opportunities, and greater dynamism than do more interventionist economies. The evidence, however, provides little support for this view" (Mishel 431). On the contrary, "poverty is deeper and harder to escape in the United States, and much less is available in the way of adequate social policy relative to other" developed countries.

9. Many books and articles have been written to explain what might be called the unmaking of the American working class. In addition to Sennett and Cobb, whom I quote later in this essay, see also Mike Davis, *Prisoners of the American Dream*.

10. I have, of course, already mentioned several exceptions, such as Barbara Ehrenreich and Bill Moyers. There is also the redoubtable CNN pundit Lou Dobbs, whose *War on the Middle Class* takes up the issue precisely because economic inequality is now eroding bourgeois—and not just working class—living standards. "Even writing the words 'class warfare' makes me uncomfortable," Dobbs says, but he insists it is nevertheless an accurate description of what is happening in the United States today (23).

Works Cited

Anderson, Perry. *The Origins of Postmodernity*. London: Verso, 1998.

Aronowitz, Stanley, and William DiFazio. *The Jobless Future: Sci-Tech and the Dogma of Work*. Minneapolis: U of Minnesota P, 1994.

Baudrillard, Jean. *Selected Writings*. Mark Poster, ed. Stanford: Stanford UP, 1988.

———. *Simulations*. New York: Semiotext(e), 1983.

Brantlinger, Patrick. *Crusoe's Footprints: Cultural Studies in Britain and America*. New York: Routledge, 1990.

Cottle, Michelle. "The Real Class War." *Washington Monthly* 29: 7/8 (July/Aug. 1997): 12–17.

Davis, Mike. *Prisoners of the American Dream: Politics and Economy in the History of the U.S. Working Class*. London and New York: Verso, 1999.

Derrida, Jacques. *The Politics of Friendship*. Trans. George Collins. London: Verso, 1997.

———. *Specters of Marx: The State of the Debt, the Work of Mourning, and the New International*. New York: Routledge, 1994.

Dobbs, Lou. *War on the Middle Class: How the Government, Big Business, and Special Interest Groups Are Waging War on the American Dream and How to Fight Back*. New York: Viking, 2006.

Eagleton, Terry. *The Illusions of Postmodernism*. Oxford: Blackwell, 1996.

Ehrenreich, Barbara. "Earth to Wal-Mars." James Lardner and David A. Smith, eds. *Inequality Matters*: 41–53.

Fraser, Nancy. *Justice Interruptus: Critical Reflections on the "Postsocialist" Condition*. New York: Routledge, 1997.

Friedman, Milton. *Capitalism and Freedom*. Chicago: U of Chicago P, 1962.

Frow, John. *Cultural Studies and Cultural Value*. Oxford: Oxford UP, 1995.

Gagnier, Reginia. *The Insatiability of Human Wants: Economics and Aesthetics in Market Society*. Chicago: U of Chicago P, 2000.

Harvey, David. *The Condition of Postmodernity*. Oxford: Basil Blackwell, 1989.

Hoggart, Richard. *The Uses of Literacy: Changing Patterns in English Mass Culture*. Boston: Beacon Press, 1961.

Ivins, Molly, and Lou Dubose. *Shrub: The Short but Happy Political Life of George W. Bush*. New York: Vintage, 2002.

Jameson, Fredric. *Postmodernism: or, The Cultural Logic of Late Capitalism*. Durham: Duke UP, 1991.

———. *Signatures of the Visible*. New York: Routledge, 1992.

Klein, Naomi. *Shock Doctrine: The Rise of Disaster Capitalism*.

Krugman, Paul. *The Great Unraveling: Losing Our Way in the New Century*. New York: Norton, 2004.

Ladd, Everett, and Karlyn Bowman. "The Nation Says No to Class Warfare." *USA Today Magazine*. 127:2648 (May 1999): 24–27.

Lardner, James, and David A. Smith, eds. *Inequality Matters: The Growing Economic Divide in America and Its Poisonous Consequences*. New York: The New Press, 2005.

Lyotard, Jean-François. *The Postmodern Condition: A Report on Knowledge*. Trans. Geoff Bennington and Brian Massumi. Minneapolis: U of Minnesota P, 1984.

Marcuse, Herbert. *One-Dimensional Man: Studies in the Ideology of Advanced Industrial Society*. Boston: Beacon Press, 1964.

Marx, Karl, and Friedrich Engels. *The Marx-Engels Reader*. Robert C. Tucker, ed. 2nd ed. New York: Norton, 1978.

McGuigan, Jim. *Cultural Populism*. New York: Routledge, 1992.

Mishel, Lawrence, Jared Bernstein, and Heather Boushey. *The State of Working America: 2002/2003*. Ithaca: Cornell UP, 2003.

Moyers, Bill. "Which America Will We Be Now?" *Nation* 273:16 (19 Nov. 2001): 11–14.

Niethammer, Lutz. *Posthistoire: Has History Come to an End?* Trans. Patrick Camiller. London: Verso, 1992.

Perucci, Robert, and Earl Wysong. *The New Class Society: Goodbye American Dream?* 2nd ed. Lanham: Rowman and Littlefield, 2003.

Prasad, Vijay. *Fat Cats and Running Dogs: The Enron Stage of Capitalism*. Monroe: Common Courage Press, 2003.

Press, Eyal. "Ruling Class Warriors." *Nation* 282:3 (23 Jan. 2006): 4–5.

Sennett, Richard, and Jonathan Cobb. *The Hidden Injuries of Class*. New York: Vintage Books, 1973.

Thompson, E. P. *The Making of the English Working Class*. New York: Vintage, 1963.

Vattimo, Gianni. *The End of Modernity*. Trans. John R. Snyder. Baltimore: Johns Hopkins UP, 1991.

Weisberg, Jacob. "The Complete Bushisms: Updated Frequently." *Slate* 2 Feb. 2004 <http://politics.slate.msn.com>.

Williams, Raymond. *Culture and Society*. New York: Columbia UP, 1983.

Chapter Seven

The Other Inters

Augmenting Academic Disciplinarity to Make Things (Happen)

Alexandra Juhasz

An Inter-duction

I know and use interdisciplinarity as a set of inherited, tested, and productive methods that allow me to work across, between, or among otherwise isolated academic, artistic, and activist traditions in the hopes of better understanding (and then changing) cultural conditions that matter to me. However, although interdisciplinarity is potentially radical, in that it pushes scholars and institutions to consider and then refashion systems of knowledge production and dissemination, like any method or structure, it is not in itself ideological. Social justice is quite specific in its politics: a cluster of historically linked commitments to particular movements, theories, outcomes, and methods, of which interdisciplinarity is merely one. In this chapter, I will suggest that for interdisciplinarity to function as an effective component of social justice work, it is critical to expand our theories and practices concerning the *inter* to include other inters, including inter-locations, inter-languages, inter-practices, and inter-standards. It is difficult to combine these four inters, so it is rarely done—facilitating movement between the academy and other worlds while speaking in languages and engaging in actions and activities that fall outside the norms of our training and employment and academia's traditions of validation. Thus I am keen to share here a small but seminal tradition of a linked body of theoretical

writing and political art making, what I call *media praxis*, that has focused
on the complex questions and acts of the many inters. The interdisciplinary
tradition of *media praxis*, which I cull from my interdisciplinary field of
media studies, has much to teach us in that it demonstrates how to move
across, between, and among the academy and the nonscholarly world while
wielding accessible modes of communication exhibited through a range of
activities and products that are judged on their own terms, and in particular,
on their effects on campaigns for social justice.

In my recent work, I have been committed to locating an *ethical media
praxis*.[1] These writings, films, and practices that I study and link—discrete
works of a theorized media practice committed to world and self changing—are central to my field, yet are usually left unassociated, unlinked, not
interrelated. This lack of recognition evidences, as I hope my biographical
musings below will demonstrate in greater detail, that my field, although
imminently suited to model movements between people, places, and practices
in the name of politics, is not nearly as interconnected as I had hoped, and
as scholars in other fields might imagine. For reasons I will detail soon,
which perhaps are familiar to those of you in other fields, even the newer
interdisciplinary fields born in tandem with the movements for social justice of the 1960s did not prove to be as radical as their initial aims or the
progressive players who people them. Film studies as an academic discipline
and procedure for training and vetting is rarely a *praxis*, even as it studies
objects and methods that are. Theory and practice are taught in tandem
in merely a handful of select and marginal settings (Pitzer Media Studies,
where I teach, is one of these). And although the majority of professors and
students in the field claim to be "political" and often situate themselves and
their work in and around ideas of social justice, this has not radically remade
the work and workings of my interdisciplinary field. An (inter)discipline
like any other, media studies is not a model for the best ethical and political
possibilities of interdisciplinarity for social justice, even though it should
be in that we mostly stay put in the isolated places, procedures, practices,
and politics of the academy that houses and pays us.

In the following two-part presentation, I will exhibit two ways of
knowing and saying what we might learn about the four further-inters
from, first, a personal and then a theoretical consideration of the interdisciplinary tradition of *media praxis*. In part 1, I do not set out to provide a
complete or even an accurate history of my young field (fortunately, there
is a recent spate of writing looking at the field's formation that has been
highly informative to my thinking here[2]), nor do I engage in traditional

scholarly writing or research authoritatively validating my claims about the politics and social justice concerns of the early years of the interdisciplinary fields I describe. Rather, I attempt to create the feelings, moods, and personal motivations that brought me and many others to interdisciplinarity and other tactics within the academy in pursuit of social justice as experienced during a period when it seemed that the academy just might be remaking itself toward such ends. This section is my private, but perhaps demonstrative and sometimes political, story of scholarly experiments, disappointments, and obstacles toward academic labor in pursuit of social justice. In part 2, I partake in more traditional academic writing about more traditional academic research to explain what I have deduced from one such scholarly project toward social justice. I hope this split structure contributes to my overall project by both modeling the effects of engaging multiple vernaculars and ways of knowing and marking how method and style create signs of expertise as well as their willful abandonment. And I hope my inter-duction to the ideas of *media praxis* commences an interaction with scholars in other interdisciplines.

Part I: A Private History Toward an Ethical Media Praxis

In the early to mid-1980s, I was a college student at an elite New England liberal arts college that had only quite recently gone coed. That place was cold, gray, and super-preppy; its traditions of beer swilling and erudite, stoic athleticism were both compelling and repulsive to this budding feminist from the hinterlands of Colorado. I entered the academy at an exciting time—repulsion and attraction, tradition and its destruction all evident and in lively play—when the radical, interdisciplinary fields called into being in the 1960s and 1970s (women's, ethnic, film studies) began to evidence early manifestations of professionalization, institutionalization, and sedimentation. From where I entered, these ways of thought, and the places and people associated with them, seemed legitimate, sanctioned, and downright cool: they had offices, acolytes, and textbooks; esteemed professors discussed the newest independent art, the trickiest continental theory, and uncharted realms of unseemly practices, personal experiences, and visions of a better world. At my small, secluded college, a strong and exuberant minority of scholars and students set about calling for new traditions by challenging the old ways of college, scholarship, and disciplines. The resultant battles about how and what to think and what we might need (or demand) to do so (departments, professors, radical methods, safe spaces) were hard-won and probably as often lost. My beloved feminist teacher and mentor was refused tenure, it seemed, for driving to work from a point midway between her job and her husband's (she is now an esteemed full professor at Yale); I sat on the committee that brought women's and gender studies to the college. At this time, and perhaps even more excitingly, I learned from and participated in the early tremors of what would be a later batch of radical interdisciplinary fields (queer, media, and cultural studies) as they began exhibiting signs of their emergence. For example, two of my closest friends wrote undergraduate theses on gay or lesbian themes in literature, both firsts supported by radical gay and lesbian professors inventing the field.

At the same time, I often joined with progressive students and faculty on campus who were organizing around the lived experiences of community members who felt disenfranchised by the elitist, old-guard, preppy values of the institution: its tail-gate parties, its faculty with only one female full professor, and endless tokenization. We formed a support group for gay and lesbian students (one year, my friends Jim and Hali were the only out gay students at the entire college, so there weren't enough "gay" students or faculty to form a group on their own). We demanded sexual harassment policy with sit-ins, then successfully closed down the fraternities, with their hundred-plus-year histories of exclusion and bad behavior. I like to say that I learned to be an activist at Amherst College; and I believe that it is true. In this safe, wealthy, conservative, and isolated institution—where infractions were glaring and support was plentiful (intelligent, political professors; guilty, deep-pocketed administrators)—we named problems, and then their solutions were often forthcoming. I have also long traced my commitment to the inter to this time and place, for here, my developing political commitments were buttressed by elegant bodies of thought and their equally eloquent spokespeople who together were focused on interdisciplinary questions and their associated world changes.

But with hindsight, I realize that our practices of idea and world changing, or in the terms of this volume, interdisciplinarity and social justice, although intellectually and politically linked, were not fully integrated. The inter was evidenced in new relations between academic traditions but was not functioning as a path that connected these new ways of knowing to alternative methods, places, or goals of doing. For we fought about ideas in class; later, we "hit the streets" and other real-world sites like the president's office, faculty meetings, or the town commons to combat policies and practices. Although each sphere certainly informed the other, there was a decided break in setting, protocol, language, tactics, and forms of affirmation between our intellectual-political work and our material-political work. I do not recall anyone noting or caring about this rupture in the inter.

However, thinking back, I find that I was already making small gestures toward opening or perhaps connecting these different avenues of ideological action, as others must have been as well. I was keen to trouble what constituted the proper voice, method, and practice for the many audiences and goals we hoped to reach. I was ready to learn what might be the effect if we shook things up. Thus, in my senior year, emboldened by the theoretical challenges of feminist film theory and the lived changes exhibited in lesbian-feminist Western Massachusetts, I stepped far outside my comfort zone as smart-girl, book-girl, girl-intellectual and took an art class (at Hampshire, of course!); a film class, to be exact. I touched material that I had considered only with my mind and eyes; I stretched timidly to express myself through abstraction and affect rather than rhetoric alone. And then I pushed my Amherst professors (who readily agreed, although this was most likely the first such request) and dared to turn in my first super-8 film (about film's relation to memory and desire) and my first black-and-white video (about the unique and interrelated power of the sound and audio tracks) as assignments for my academic classes. Of course, it wasn't far—although it felt like forever—to move across campuses, between ways of knowing and among technologies of communication. I am well aware that this stretch, although personally monumental, is almost embarrassingly mundane, especially situated as it was in this particular location of privilege and safety. But we might want to consider these glaring inconsistencies of scale (something so small feeling so significant) as some of the definitive terms and struggles of self changing within the academy—itself a fundamental first step toward world changing, or social justice.

Ever Onward to Theory and Praxis

This work felt exciting and potentially important, and I was driven to continue such pursuits. So, immediately following my undergraduate education, I went on to graduate school in New York City in the field of cinema studies, because I hoped that this was an intellectual location likely to support and further my burgeoning commitment to integrating the doing and thinking of something in the name of changing something else. Namely, I decided that I wanted to think about and make film in the pursuit of feminist politics. Quickly, my life and times brought me to AIDS as well. Cinema studies, a relatively new discipline with strong and evident ties to the Marxist, feminist, antiracist, and post-structuralist political/intellectual traditions of cultural studies in England and women's studies in the United States, was a lucky bet. However, by the mid-1980s, and because of the all-too-predictable restrictive effects of disciplines and the conservative institutions that house them, the political nature of all of these interdisciplines, although still formative ideologically (in the disciplines' sense of themselves and what they stood for) were not being as richly evidenced through a consistent tradition of related intellectual, institutional, or social practices. Yes, I stretched my institution to allow me to make media about and for movements for social justice as my "academic" work. But my program, and discipline, were never so organized. Yes, I found those loving professors and supportive administrators who were open to my (at that time) relatively unique requests to make intellectual videos for academic assignments and to use my AIDS activist political video project as my doctoral research (although not my dissertation—I still had to write a regular 250-page opus in addition to my extensive real-world art activities). But, really, we were asked to learn this radical interdiscipline like any other: through the academy's tried-and-true structures of training, expertise, performance, judgment, and tradition (no matter how short-lived). No one seemed to mind that much. This was the 1980s, after all, the sixties no longer, and even the most radical of my feminist, queer, Marxist, antiracist professors and fellow students had quieted down, not in the sense of their words, but surely in their actions and activities, at least on campus.

Beyond the times themselves and the effects of a growing and ever-more-sanctioned body of work and workers, there was another significant contributor to this sense of calcification, one that against its own stated interests served to tame the once-radical interdisciplines that had been organized around social justice, interdisciplines that had been initially hell-bent on rethinking the production and dissemination of knowledge within higher education, that had been founded on a linking of the interpretation and changing of culture because of stated ideological commitments. At least as I experienced it, it was a particular form of disciplining the interdisciplines that coincided with the American academy's discovery and subsequent headlong, giddy pursuit of "theory" as an isolated, invigorating, thought-and-political object in its own right. And really, given how hard and new it was and that it was expressed through specialist languages from intellectual traditions in which none of us were (initially) trained (philosophy, psychoanalysis, semiotics), we had to work really hard at it. It became difficult to find the time and energy for anything else; it felt good to master it; it explained some of the political concepts that we wanted to understand; and, as an ancillary bonus, it authorized our interdisciplines through a (new) master's language, although oddly enough, this was one thing that most of the radical interdisciplines had set out to challenge. Let's face it, it's hard to ever do your work at the mocked and substandard margin. But there I was, repulsed and enthralled again; supported and held back in my inter-aims.

Frankly, I am finding this rather hard to express with subtlety, and that feels scary. I imagine it might sound like I'm engaging in a knee-jerk reaction to "theory," which is anything but the case. I do hope my commitment to "theory" will be evidenced in the second part of this essay, for the invigorating tradition of media praxis attests to just how "theory" is a necessity for our social justice work, in and out of the academy. But theory, quite simply, is not politics—particularly social justice work—until it is made material through practice in interconnected places, through multiple vernaculars, actions, and outputs. In fact, in isolation, even the most radical political theory that is set to thinking the opposite can serve to close doors between disciplines, among and between specialist and nonspecialist audiences and across the divide that separates where and how we work in the academy from the social justice work that we are committed to in the world.

Of course, the call to praxis—to integrate theory, practice, and politics—is not mine, nor is it new, or even radical, that is to say, in its idea form, as theory. In fact, this was precisely what I was being taught by my radical professors and teachers (at this time I was also attending the Whitney Independent Studio program, where my instructors were world-renowned conceptual artists) who were engaged in the decade(s)-old intellectual, institutional, and political project at the heart of the interdisciplines. What I now come to understand as idiosyncratic about my experience was not the desire to engage in praxis, but my interest for this to be realized within an integrated professional practice where all aspects of this work (ideas, artistic expression, real-world application) were equally valued and supported. Quite simply, the intellectual scaffolding for a media praxis far predates the institutional one; or, to state it another way, it seems easier to change ideas than institutions.

On Institutions, Favored Practices, Neo-Liberalism, and Nostalgia

What I found as a graduate student attempting to engage in undersupported inters, and what I still find, is that the institutional needs for the evaluation of employees and their labor and practices, the professional demands for specialization, and the individual's interests in or capabilities to be poly-vocal are all strong forces limiting such movements toward social justice across, between, and among. As we all know, the academy and its humanities and social science disciplines are sites where we are paid to think, write, and talk, using standardized methods and vocabularies, referring to and being authorized by similarly structured traditions, with our result being words spoken or written. We are trained, and then go on to mark our expertise, precisely through the ways that our language is removed from common parlance, casual thinking, and daily practices. Furthermore, most people are drawn to the academy, and academic labor, precisely because we are good at, and like, speaking in and thinking through rarified, intellectual, special-ized language. We are smart people who are rewarded for how quickly and adeptly we master and mobilize such traditions. Meanwhile, other ways of knowing, through the touch and feel, the sensuous engagement with the material world of humans and objects, falls outside what we might do. As intellectuals, we are, by definition, neither artists nor activists: Both are similarly formalized, professionalized languages and traditions, albeit based as often in experiential, accessible, and affective structures as theoretical ones. These separate traditions are also fields of distinction. When we also choose to work as artists or activists, these are activities that occur in isolated spheres, using a separate vernacular, practices that are construed by those who judge our work as hobbies. We produce our real work in conversation with but not across, between, or among such spheres because the inter would demand multiple trainings and intelligences, varied practices, products, and modes of evaluation, not to mention the truly radical possibilities of undo-ing, rethinking, or combining such forms of discipline.

Certainly the picture that I draw, for means of demonstration, is much too rigid. It is at once absurd but also somehow true. We all know plenty of professors who are poly-vocal in their classrooms, publications, and political actions, who expertly combine and interact. However, it is my contention that such individuals do so by struggling, usually alone or with a small group of allies, against the disciplinary procedures of their institutions and fields. Each inter-act is exceptional, like my own, spelled out above; there is little institutional, structural, or even social support. To go inter is to go it alone; on our backs we carry our inter-load until we tire. Of course, one can build a tradition and even a field from such isolated practices (this is evidenced in my *Media Praxis* project discussed below), just as we all build alliances of like-minded colleagues. However, I attest that this group, and its histories, traditions, and needs, remains marginal, isolated, and embattled within the academy during, or because of, the changing nature of our work in this profession in this country and during the last few years.

As the public sphere in America shrinks in direct proportion to the gains of the market, so that the academy becomes one of the last places where one can actually engage in pursuits beyond capital, the academy itself becomes increasingly regulated by the logic of the market. Now workers within our industry have even less freedom to engage in the inventive practices of praxis, and those few who remain capable of doing so (because of tenure or other waning forms of institutional support) are reduced to quaint holdouts enacting what is perceived as a politically correct but retrograde vision of a better world (and academy) that never did come to pass. We serve as the institution's conscience: wacky hippie holdouts, angry scholars of color, hip queer activists, groovy women-of-colorists, aging socialists. You know the cast of characters: we strange but noble bedfellows, sometimes aligned, other times fighting over the same tired piece of pie, while the rest of our colleagues and students treat us as quaint nostalgic specters, dying out fast, and necessarily appeased and quieted until we stop reproducing. The ideas we stand for are beyond debate, holy even: Who among us could be against social justice, interdisciplinarity, or personal dignity? Meanwhile, the institution questions, challenges, and then quietly closes down the inter-spaces we had tentatively unlocked. Talk to graduate students uncertain they will ever have a job, let alone tenure, and it is understandable why adventurous attacks against structural discipline become more and more anomalous.

On Doing, Making, Teaching, Process, Ethics, and Inter-Action

So what is left? First, there is always teaching. If one considers that praxis means an integrated doing and thinking toward world and self changing, the classroom can be constituted as an ideal site for doing and talking, as well as a stable place from which to depart. Across American higher education, there are exciting models for community-based learning with growing traditions of their own. At its best, this pedagogy is inter in all the ways I have mentioned, forging alliances across, between, and among critical thinking, accessible language, lived experience, social justice, multiple locations, complex communities, and a range of practices that are most appropriate for the task(s) at hand. This kind of teaching is exhilarating and exhausting.

Then there is interaction. Maintaining across a career the kinds of pedagogic invention necessitated by social justice work demands another kind of inter: that we need to work with and teach each other. Models of collaboration that emphasize the unmaking or sharing of expertise and power are critical to engaging in such work. Thus conversations that unthink the rhetoric of specialization are key, just as are practices and theories that unmake the sanctified art or intellectual object. Artists need to teach scholars, and activists need to instruct intellectuals. The members of communities with whom we interact, when leaving the academy, need to teach us their local knowledge. However, the process of engaging as we must across, between, and among places, ways of knowing and speaking, and their varied practices, and always with real-world ends in mind, alters (and makes much more difficult) the logic of our academic labor and training. There are different stakes when varied groups of people engage together in projects for social justice. Thus we must think about and then engage in ethical behavior that takes into account power differences within, between, and across the classroom and the people and places of the outside world. This, in turn, raises questions of process: How we teach, what happens in the classroom and world, and how we interact are as important as what we teach; in fact, they are often what we teach. Here, our interdisciplinarity must be augmented by traditions of radical pedagogy with their own histories and theories that emphasize critical thinking, power sharing, and ethics.

As an uncertain conclusion, I would like to raise a few questions that have been critical lately in my classroom as I attempt to engage an ethical media praxis with my students and across, between, and among our starting place in the academy and the activist communities within which we also are members.

Perhaps you have the specialist knowledge to help me think these through. Then, we need to talk. I will happily share what I know about video (see below). I find these questions troubling:

What counts for the *doing* part of the praxis equation if one's primary labor is thinking and talking?

Because the academy is without question in and of the world, is change within this institution—its classrooms, traditions, disciplines—and/or within the realm of ideas, world and self changing in its own right?

In the end, are these merely question of technologies (the word, the pen, the camera, the computer); output (lecture, paper, book, video, Web site, action); intention (interaction with my production leads to contemplation or action); audience (whom do I want to hear me?); or affirmation (how will I be judged and by whom)?

Although I am not yet satisfied with my own answers, I have found a hundred-year history of media praxis to be quite informative about such questions. Some of what I have learned as student and practitioner of this tradition is what follows.

Part 2: Media Praxis

I have been working for several years on a project called *Media Praxis: A Radical Website Integrating Theory, Politics, and Production* (www.mediapraxis. org), which is an online interactive archive of media and theory by committed artists, intellectuals, and activists making use of the best writing and media work from the hundred-year history of the media arts to consider the role of digital media in contemporary social change. Here's Jean-Luc Godard raising the gauntlet:

JLG: Art is a Special gun. Q: How do you explain the camera as a gun? JLG: Well, ideas are guns. A lot of people are dying from ideas and dying for ideas. A gun is a practical idea. And an idea is a theoretical gun.

Theorists and makers of Third Cinema, Octavio Getino and Fernando Solanas, give us a production tip:

The cinema of revolution is at the same time one of destruction and construction: destruction of the image that neo-colonialization has created of itself and us, and construction of a throbbing, living reality which recaptures truth in its expression.

And philosopher and filmmaker, Trinh T. Minh-ha, keeps the boys in check:

> The socially oriented filmmaker is thus the almighty voice giver (here I, a vocalizing context that is all-male), whose position of authority in the production of meaning continues to go unchallenged, skillfully masked as it is by its righteous mission.

On this site, many more inspiring, thoughtful, and self-aware words from linked traditions of revolutionary media are supplemented by and connected to a range of information, including contextual information written by scholars, images, and words from related political projects and links to living communities of authors and artists bent on considering and using digital media toward social justice. At its core, the site is a repository of media theory written by film, video, and digital producers engaged in changing the world. "You couldn't stay neutral in Madrid," theorizes Joris Ivans about his resulting filmic (and related distribution and organizing) methods connected to his film, *Spanish Earth*, which documents the delinquencies of the Spanish Civil War. On the Web site, Ivans will share space with ethnographic film scholar and maker David MacDougall, who, sixty years later, while living and working with Australian aborigines, writes about and makes media keen to keep the offenses of cross-cultural power relations in our sight lines: "The real crime of representation is representation itself."

As is true for MacDougall (and perhaps less so for Ivans), most of what can be read here already has been canonized in textbooks of the discipline of media studies—from Sergei Eisenstein to Laura Mulvey, Maya Deren to David MacDougall—but these seminal theoretical productions have heretofore been considered in isolation from each other: as either the hallowed words of a great director allowing scholars access to behind-the-scenes minutiae, or as part of a national or genre tradition. When I understand them as part of an unheralded tradition of media praxis, these voices speak as they have not before, among and to other political filmmakers, as well as to the discrete historical/political movements from which they were initially produced; they speak across time, between regions, and among radical philosophies and practices. Thus, for example, the experimental films and ideas of the New American Cinema of the 1940s to 1960s, set to jettison middle-class conformity, seem impossibly far away from the ethnographic theories and films of the 1970s and 1980s, set to revision the world's primitives, which already seems more than a lifetime away from the contemporary concerns generated by neoliberal globalization. Yet by realizing affinities across political, global, and chronological landscapes, a picture of cinema and of cinema history emerges that is optimistic, anti-corporate, agitational, intelligent, and as often as not gendered female and multicultural. Although many theoretical traditions are mined (structuralism, psychoanalysis, feminism, critical race, postmodern), the centrality of Marxist thinking within this tradition is notable, especially considering its absence elsewhere in contemporary cultural production and conversation.

Yet posting these texts together and learning from their affirming allegiances and dramatic debates is an intradisciplinary project of merely the first order. Cementing the legitimacy, value, and power of this as a theoretical tradition is merely the first step. On the Internet we can move beyond text, and thus past contemplation, and the reification of great words and images on a screen. Thus this new technology furthers the work of the inter (as might a classroom) because it creates a context for reading, writing about, and viewing political media as a step toward action and interaction and, ideally, better-informed media making. When I teach with the site it serves to both evidence and inspire *praxis*, the organic integration of theory (thinking) and practice (doing) when one's aims are political (changing).

Since cinema's invention, artists committed to social transformation have engaged in *media praxis*: the using and theorizing of various media toward world and self changing. Although I understand this to be a radical tradition in that it directly refers to what Marx, in *Theses on Feuerbach*, calls "revolutionary practice," the project of interpreting and changing the world, my Web site is equally radical in that it makes a demand on my self-consciously (and self-righteously) interdisciplinary discipline, media studies, to account for theoretical and political consequences of the highly enforced boundaries it continues to raise—between theory, practice, and politics—even as the field was founded on a radical critique of the traditional disciplines. In other words, although cinema, and later, media studies, like women's or race studies, was founded in a 1960s challenge to disciplinary and institutional structures and hierarchies—openly contesting *who* might make a proper academic, *what* she might properly study, and what questions she might rightfully ask—there are some structures and hierarchies that have remained too unseemly to breach. In my highly interdisciplinary field, one that could be said to be largely invented and populated by feminists and other politicized scholars who look to popular culture to ask of it questions about power, injustice, and ideology, we have all but disavowed praxis. Bringing praxis to the fore of the analytic and practical project—making a commitment to a linked doing *and* thinking of social justice—is the aim of this essay and my career's body of work.

Marx calls for "sensuous human activity" as well as contemplation, "changing of circumstances" and "self-changing"—production in real life and within the life of the mind that creates change in consciousness and lived conditions. *Feuerbach*, and the theoretical legacy it produced, fosters the hopeful position that some human activity might not simply reproduce but could transform social existence in society. The legacy of a philosophy of praxis has emboldened filmmakers throughout cinema's hundred-year history to include media work as revolutionary practice within larger struggles for social transformation. Although all of the arts have seen great works produced through an integrated practice and theory—praxis—the history of the media arts has most neatly paralleled the political, technological, and economic demands of modern and postmodern revolution. In 1922, Lenin informed his minister of culture, "You must remember that of all the arts for us the most important is the cinema." But early Soviet cinema is not the exception, even as it is the most heralded of such convergences; rather, the explicit linking of art, culture, revolution, and philosophy has inspired a great many of the seminal works and theories of media history.

Media Praxis demonstrates that a pursuit of revolutionary practice within the media has been an ongoing experiment and inspiration responsible for many of the decisive ideas and works of film history. By linking these texts, I vehemently attest to an ongoing project, indebted to Marxist theories of ideology, that links culture, theory, and politics in the twentieth century through mediation technologies. In the process, I tell other stories: of field formation, the institutionalization of knowledge production, and the delegitimization of the ideas of media producers, even within the very field that honors them. Also told is the often-silenced story of a modernity that was just as political as it was aesthetic, that was text *and* earth bound.

I have organized the Web site (as well as the class that inspired it) into ten chronological moments where media is theorized as a vital component of political struggle. For those who are not film scholars, I believe you will surely recognize these revolutionary moments, if not their associated film traditions. The tradition begins with the years shortly after the Russian revolution, then moves to the Popular Front in France, Germany and the United States in the 1930s, the beatniks and underground denizens of American bohemia in the 1940s and 1950s, the decolonization of the Third World in the 1960s, France and the United Kingdom in 1968, feminism and the black Atlantic of the 1970s, AIDS in the 1980s, and cyberspace bringing us up to the present. The collection of theory I draw differs from others in ways that demonstrate how even the new academic interdisciplines, like media studies, maintain certain restrictions that limit their clearly stated commitments to social justice.

For instance, *Media Praxis* demonstrates a filmmakers' ontology of film: what filmmakers know and learn about the medium they shoot, edit, and project because they engage in its sensuous activity. Writing in neither interviews nor memoirs, the theory of practitioners challenges the distinction typically drawn between those capable of and qualified to make systematic claims about the media (its theorists) and those whose ruminations are about the particular, daily, and technical (its producers). I am not the first to note that this bifurcation, in and of itself, leads to a "theoretical crisis." The founding of media, cultural, and minority studies in the 1960s and 1970s was rooted in an energizing political and theoretical investment in practice, daily activity, the personal, and the political. "Now I think the true crisis in cultural theory, in our time, is between this view of the work of art as object and the alternative of art as a practice," writes Raymond Williams in the 1950s in "Marxist Cultural Studies," one of the theoretical contributions that led to the invention of cultural studies. He continues: "What this can show us here about the practice of analysis is that we have to break from the common procedure of isolating the object and then discovering its components. On the contrary we have to discover the nature of a practice and then its conditions."

A significant number of the writers in the media praxis tradition seek to understand less the isolated object, the aesthetics and formal structures of film, than they do the nature of its practice and its conditions: what happens when it is made, seen, and used and how to do this effectively in pursuit of real-world goals. Certainly, if one makes film with a social rather than a monetary or aesthetic goal, its "self-changing" capacities—to enable makers and viewers to see and know the world and themselves differently—require the greatest attention. Thus, in this writing, the film object is often refracted through theories of collective production and radical reception. Theories and practices bent on transforming receivers of culture into its producers are as ubiquitous as analyses of who is authorized, educated, and entitled to produce a society's art and ideas. In this way, political-economic considerations regarding access to both authorship and media education are also definitive. Celebrations and concerns about technology abound. Writes Dziga Vertov: "Kino-eye as the possibility of making the invisible visible, the unclear clear, the hidden manifest, the disguised overt, the acted non-acted; making falsehood into truth." The role and nature of the personal, pleasure, and the political is also addressed. Here is avant-garde filmmaker Jonas Mekas:

> The park scene, and the city scene, and the tree—it's all there, on film–but it's not what I saw the moment I was filming it! The image is there, but there is something very essential missing. I got the surface, but I missed the essence. At that time I began to understand that what was missing from my footage was myself: my attitude, my thoughts, my feelings in the moment I was looking at the reality that I was filming.

Feminists then made collective and political this move towards the personal. Laura Mulvey writes:

> The alternative is the thrill that comes from leaving the past behind without simply rejecting it, transcending outworked or oppressive forms, and daring to break with normal pleasurable expectations in order to conceive a new language of desire.

Across time, a growing concern with identity (politics) can also be seen, as can a move toward politicizing what we now call globalization, as movements for social justice become increasingly conceptualized cross-culturally. Says Pratibha Parmar, "As Asian women we have to place ourselves in the role of subjects creatively engaging in constructing our own images based both in our material and social conditions and in our visions and imaginations." Although the film movements from the first half of the century are rooted in local, often national struggles for change in what might be understood as the base, a noteworthy change occurs in the sixties, when cross-cultural, global, or mobile identity-based (and thus superstructural) politics of representation and personal liberation take dominance.

Yet all of the theory in this tradition depends on the Marxist philosophical assumptions that cultural production can contribute to social change, that popular culture is a viable site of education and action, and that the media are the realm where ideology is active and adaptable. "The open secret of the electronic media, the decisive political factor, which has been waiting, suppressed or crippled, for its moment to come," writes Hans Magnus Enzenberger, "is their mobilizing power." Most of these theorist-filmmakers attempt to prove how the media are ideal for this work and how the artist-intellectual is the worker best suited for this kind of labor toward the struggle. The writing is also supremely self-referential: theorizing praxis itself (how do ideas exist in an action, and how is this related to the project of radical pedagogy?); calling into question the conditions, apparatuses, forms, and processes of the authors' production; questioning their roles as bourgeois intellectuals and/or trained artists. Not surprisingly, a dialectical approach organizes much of the thought found here: base/superstructure, form/content, truth/obstruction. Sergei Eisenstein explains: "In *The Strike* we have the first instance of revolutionary art where the form has turned out to be more revolutionary than the content. . . . [This is] established in formal terms through the construction of a logical antithesis to the bourgeois West, which we are in no way *emulating* but which we are in every way *opposing*." Following the lead of the Soviets, most of these theorists argue for radical engagements with form and content. This debate, as is also true in media studies more generally, is often waged through opposing commitments to montage or (socialist) realist practices. Thus, theories of realism, documentary, and truth abound.

Some years later, deconstruction joins the theoretical landscape and serves to expand or empty out such binary conflicts. Peter Wollen suggests:

The cinema cannot show the truth or reveal it because the truth is not out there in the real world waiting to be photographed. What the cinema can do is produce meanings, and meanings can be plotted, not in relation to some abstract yardstick or criterion of truth, but in relation to other meanings.

Then Kobena Mercer and Isaac Julien add race, nationality, and ethnicity to the deconstructed configuration:

What is in question is not the expression of some lost origin or some uncontaminated essence in black film-language but the adoption of a critical voice that promotes consciousness of the collision of cultures and histories that constitute our very conditions of existence.

Later yet, gender-radical and cyber-guru Rosanne Allacquere Stone blows the subject apart:

The boundaries between the subject, if not the body, and the
"rest of the world" are undergoing a radical refiguration, brought
about in part through the mediation of technology.

Who better to theorize the nature and rationale of a practice than
its practitioners? And why is this most obvious truism such a bitter pill?
When considering the writing of the "great" theorist/makers of film history, cinema studies at once embraces their messy, hands-on, ideologically
motivated practice, but only as a kind of romantic fetish, not as a viable
or learnable practice. But what is threatened here? Perhaps for the majority of film scholars whose ideas about film come from their heads alone,
there is the fear that their theories will be proven inadequate in the field.
"The dispute over the reality or non-reality of thinking that is isolated
from practice is a purely *scholastic* question," cautions Marx. Perhaps for
the discipline, one that moved so quickly from margin to center, its legacy
of both partisan politics and hands-on practice must be closeted like so
much dirty linen. Serious academic disciplines must claim a theoretical,
not a political lineage at their core. Just as women's colleges maintain the
most thoroughly functional closet in academia (if you think we have too
many lesbians here, you're right, so we're all going to live and work painfully maintaining we don't, at great cost to us individually, but to benefit
the institution we love), cinema studies has ever-so-subtly secreted away
its direct debt to the intellectual-practitioner who is inspired by moral
indignation and political crusade.

Yet dreams of political and social change (of the world and academia)
were fundamental to the field's formation, not just to the films and writings
it considers. Leftists, feminists, and others engaged in and emboldened by a
Marxist, post-structuralist critique of education, the arts, and culture created
new fields that challenged what could be studied, by whom, and for what
ends. That, for instance, a *woman* professor could engage in *dialogue* with
female students about a *popular* film to help them see how *sexism* is structured into the very ways of looking of our culture, so that these students
could imagine and *remake* themselves as men and women, was in its time
radical media praxis. In one of a series of anthologized essays in *Reinventing
Film Studies*, an anthology dedicated to remembering and rethinking the
formation of this academic field, Tessa Perkins points to the repression of
such messy beginnings: "In this crisis both the contributions of theory and
the place (or not) of politics have played a significant role—to the extent
that some wish, to all intents and purposes, to abandon both, and others

are determined that the former should cleanse itself of all contamination by the latter, fantasizing, perhaps, that a pseudoscientific objectivity will emerge from the funeral pyre." But thirty years later, as cinema and media studies enter their maturity, it seems that the proper place of, and relation between, theory, practice, and politics has been settled. Cinema and media studies are, first, scholarly, in that they apply pseudoscientific theories to texts; then political, in that a relation between text and culture is foundational to the field; and only nominally practical, in that media scholars will occasionally consider the work of making media (by its producer) as itself related to the texts under scrutiny, whereas consideration of any practical component to their own work would be, of course, taboo.

I strive to challenge media studies' tautological advancement toward theory abstracted from politics and practice. I look beyond what political artists think of their craft and medium to what they express about politics, ideology, and culture. Again, this murking up of roles and specialties, although attractive to postmodernists and even interdisciplinarists in the abstract, remains surprisingly threatening to scholars in the flesh. For a discipline that formed itself around the breakdown of more traditional boundaries, objects, and methods of study, there is a remarkable clarity in the production and maintenance of our education. Fears abound: about vocational training, soft thinking, creativity. (Media Studies students on the 6th Floor, Film Production above; scholars at the Society for Cinema and Media Studies, makers at the College Art Association.) Even as our materialist forefathers fought for a link to everyday activity, our bosses in the academy want work created in the traditional, removed ways. In another essay from *Reinventing Film Studies*, Gill Branston provides the answer: "Oddly, such very contemporary emphases meld with the histories of Western academic theorizing. . . . This is echoed in the gendered and classed language with which 'theory' is often justified: said to possess 'rigor,' 'proper distance/objectivity' as opposed to the 'emotion' and 'instinct' of raw encounters with the object of study."

Such conservative tendencies for a field that heralds its birth as revolutionary! In the same collection, Geoffrey Nowell-Smith writes, "The revolution which took place in film studies in the 1970s was, to use the jargon of the time, highly over-determined. It had a significant political dimension, spun off from the radicalism of 1968. Philosophically it vaunted its materialism, in opposition to idealism of every kind." I came to my graduate education in cinema in the 1980s, drawn to this revolutionary field "representing the point at which theory, politics and the academy intersect." It was these intersections that distinguished the field, its method and objects; this linkage that made media and cultural studies so exciting, relevant, and radical; this association that is ever more repressed within an ever more institutionalized discipline.

In the 1980s, I was a graduate student at NYU and an AIDS activist video maker. I was supported to write my dissertation about a media movement in which I was an active participant. In that work, *AIDS TV: Identity, Community and Alternative Video*, and in later projects where I made and theorized feminist or queer film as part of those political movements, I also place myself as a participant in the very tradition of media praxis I map in this article. I also do so in my teaching and program building, where I ask my students to think about, make, and use media in ways and places that matter. I name my place, and that of my students and institution, in this history not to mark our prowess, but quite the opposite, for media praxis focuses on what we theorize and learn about the media when commitment and engagement are more valued than artistic genius. I make video—along with teaching, scholarly writing, and organizing—to speak with different audiences, in multiple settings, using a range of tactics, so as to address real-world conditions that matter to me. To do so, I have been enabled by those who have done such work before me; I want to imagine participating in communities that continue to make such ideas and tactics relevant to our times and needs by learning from and adapting the prescient work of the past.

Yet in conclusion, although I will attest that my field has in many ways tried to closet me, as perhaps your field has closeted you, my field has as often supported me, as I hope yours supported you. This contradiction, and blurring of the boundaries I initially set out as calcified, seems important to consider. For I do work at an institution that has supported my interests in moving from theory to production to politics, and it has allowed me to take my students and program with me. And for the past twenty years I have made low-end media about feminist issues from teen sexuality to black lesbian identity that have been carefully linked to both social justice movements that can make use of these images and a scholarly community that considers committed media practices. Where I work, I have built, along with my fellow theorist-practitioner colleagues, a distinct program in media studies. I am most proud of my program's founding philosophies: a commitment to the integration of theory and practice; to an interdisciplinary approach to media studies; to teaching our students the nonindustrial histories, applications, and values of the media; and a prioritizing of local and international community-based media.

Thus I cannot rightfully lambaste my discipline, or even the now-institutionalized interdisciplines, but instead I will signal the ways that the academy, and the theory and practices it upholds, both enable and restrain work committed to understanding and contributing to social justice. To denounce the academy in its totality would be false, unproductive, and diminishing of the project of praxis, one that includes the doing *and the thinking*. However, to celebrate the contesting of academic knowledge systems through the creation of our newer interdisciplines would be equally limited in that it fails to recognize what boundaries have become legitimate to break, like those across fields, and what boundaries are still taboo: those involving our bodies and the lives they lead in a world connected to but much bigger than our philosophies.

I hope *Media Praxis*, and this essay about it, will prompt us to know media theory and history not as something written on paper, the mark of some distant other's formidable mind, but as a thing that was made to be used and remade by us, in our world, toward what matters most. I want the theorizing that has been born from sensuous human engagement with the medium to be granted the central place it deserves in the history of the interdiscipline of media studies, and to also cross out of this discipline to enable those with other skills and expertise to learn from these impassioned, intelligent practices. This because I want to pass on and *make use of* the great and interlegacy of "revolutionary practice," a hundred-year-old project of interpreting *and* changing the world, so that present-day theorist makers can learn from and expand on these magnificent ideas to then contribute to the real-world changes that we all know must happen here, and soon, in this radically media-saturated world in great need of a counter, intelligent, angry, and artful media praxis.

Notes

1. Please see my teaching/research/action Web site <www.mediapraxis.org>.

2. Some of these recent publications on the history of film studies include Christine Gledhill and Linda Williams (2000), Dana Polan (2007), and B. Ruby Rich (1998).

Works Cited

Branston, Gill. "Why Theory?" *Reinventing Film Studies*. Ed. Christine Gledhill and Linda William New York: Arnold, 2000: 18–33.

Getino, Octavio, and Fernando Solanas. "Towards a Third Cinema." *New Latin American Cinema*. vol. 1. Ed. Michael Martin. Detroit: Wayne State UP, 1997: 33–58.

Gledhill, Christine, and Linda William, eds. *Reinventing Film Studies*. New York: Arnold, 2000.

Godard, Jean-Luc. Audio interview. *San Francisco Express Times* 14 Mar. 1968: 8–9.

Ivans, Joris. *The Camera and I*. New York: International Publishers, 1969.

Lunacharsky, Anatoli. "Conversation with Lenin, II: Newsreel and Fiction Film." *The Film Factory: Russian and Soviet Cinema in Documents*. Ed. Richard Taylor. Cambridge: Harvard UP, 1994.

MacDougall, David. *Transcultural Cinema*. Princeton: Princeton UP, 1988.

Marx, Karl. "Theses of Feuerbach." *The German Ideology*. New York: International Publishers, 1970. (Originally published 1947.) 121–23.

Mekas, Jonas. "The Diary Film." *The Avant-Garde Film: A Reader of Theory and Criticism*. Ed. P. Adams Sitney. New York: Anthology Film Archives, 1987: 190–98.

Mercer, Kobena, and Isaac Julien. "Introduction: De Margin and De Center." *Screen* 29.4 (1988): 3–10.

Minh-ha, Trinh T. "Documentary Is/Not a Name." *October* 52 (Spring 1990): 76–97.

Mulvey, Laura. "Visual Pleasure and Narrative Cinema." *Issues in Feminist Film Criticism*. Ed. Patricia Erens. Bloomington: Indiana UP, 1991. 34–47.

Nowell-Smith, Geoffrey. "How Films Mean, or from Aesthetics to Semiotics and Half-Way Back Again." *Reinventing Film Studies*. Ed. Christine Gledhill and Linda William. New York: Arnold, 2000. 8–17.

Parmar, Pratibha. "Hateful Contraries." *Queer Looks*. Ed. Martha Gever, John Greyson, and Pratibha Parmar. New York: Routledge, 1993. 289–93.

Perkins, Tessa. "Who (and What) Is It for?" *Reinventing Film Studies*. Ed. Christine Gledhill and Linda William. New York: Arnold, 2000. 76–96.

Polan, Dana. *Scenes of Instruction: The Beginnings of the US Study of Film*. Berkeley: U of California P, 2007.

Rich, B. Ruby. *Chick Flicks: Theories and Memories of the Feminist Film Movement*. Durham, NC: Duke UP, 1998.

Stone, Roseanne Allacquere. "Will the Real Body Please Stand Up?" *The Cybercultures Reader*. Ed. David Bell and Barbara Kennedy. New York: Routledge, 2000. 504–25.

Vertov, Dziga. *Kino-Eye: The Writings of Dziga Vertov*. Ed. Annette Michelson. Berkeley: U of California P, 1984.

Williams, Raymond. "Base and Superstructure in Marxist Cultural Theory." *Media and Cultural Studies: KeyWorks*. Ed. Meenakshi Durham and Douglas Kellner. London: Blackwell, 2001. 152–65.

Wollen, Peter. "Godard and Counter Cinema: *Vent D'Est*." *Movies and Methods*. Ed. Bill Nichols. Berkeley: U of California P, 1985. 499–507.

Chapter Eight

The Ethico-politics of Dedisciplinary Practices

Joe Parker

An ethical and political problem for those in the academy becomes visible when we consider the long-term social effects of postsecondary institutions of learning. Many have argued from different perspectives that the social effects of the academy are to preserve and even exacerbate social hierarchies and inequalities (Althusser; Apple; Bourdieu; Foucault, *Order*; Messer-Davidow; Messer-Davidow in this volume). If we support the honorable virtues of equality and justice, then how might we respond to the apparent complicity for those of us in the academy with these antiegalitarian hierarchies?

To develop academic practices that refuse this complicity, I draw on Michel Foucault's analysis of the academy as a site for instilling docility and ease of governability (Foucault, *Discipline* 30, 159, 181–83, 199–201, 215, 299; Foucault, *Order*; Noujain; Burchell). In exploring approaches to social justice that refuse determination by the disciplinary apparatuses of the modern academy, I develop briefly an analysis of three approaches to what, following Foucault, we might call dedisciplinary academic practices, as discussed shortly. The first is based on Foucault's *Discipline and Punish*, whose critique of modern knowledge practices has been influential in a wide range of disciplinary (philosophy, literature, history, art history) and interdisciplinary fields (postcolonial studies, feminism, queer studies) in its reconsideration of the importance of modern conceptions of power. The second approach examines Joan W. Scott's *Gender and the Politics of History* as a major extension of Foucault's historical work on the topic of gender, focusing on ways in which Scott's interdisciplinary work has been appropriated back under the modern power/knowledge regime. The final approach I

175

examine is Gayatri Chakravorty Spivak's interdisciplinary reconstruction of comparative literature in her 2003 volume *The Death of a Discipline*. Spivak's comparativist practice of interdisciplinarity links a language-centered deconstructivist analysis to social justice concerns shaped by feminism and Marxism and centers on reconstituting the relation of the writing and teaching self with her Others. Taking these three approaches as sources of critique of dedisciplinary practice suggests specific ways to approach interdisciplinary work that critically engage with complicities of the academy with inequality and injustice. Before turning to these dedisciplinary practices, I review Foucault's critique of discipline as it applies to academic work.

Dedisciplinarity within a Foucauldian Critique of Interdisciplinarity

A Foucauldian view of disciplines finds them to be mechanisms for objectification and subjection, a way to "analyse space, break up and rearrange activities" of the body that subjects them to an hierarchical economy of subjection interrupting horizontal solidarities and constituting the body as both subject visible for regulation and productive social participant (*Discipline* 157, 172, 178–81, 187). Foucault argued that the establishment of these disciplines installed the bourgeoisie as the politically dominant class in eighteenth-century France through the double-edged combination of a formally egalitarian juridical framework of the representative parliamentary regime (guaranteeing rights and freedoms and the authority of all) that also guaranteed the docile submission of bodies to diffused modern formations of power/knowledge (26–27, 222). The double sense of the term "discipline" as both an academic field and a larger social mechanism instilling docility and limits to power/knowledge that many have noted (Gore; Hoskin and Macve 107; Kondo 25–27; Messer-Davidow et al.; Shumway and Messer-Davidow 201–222, 211–12) provides a frame for rethinking the relation between interdisciplinarity and social justice.

From this perspective, the social effects of incremental changes in the academy resulting from the emergence of interdisciplinary fields may be usefully compared with the effects of reforms in the penal system, another major site of the modern disciplinary regime. Foucault noted that persistent critics of the modern penal system argue that the penal apparatus consistently fails to reduce legal offenses through repression, yet the criticisms are consistently accompanied not by the abolition but by the maintenance of the penal system through reform programs. Foucault concluded that what is served by this failure is that the prison and punishment more generally are "not intended to eliminate offences, but rather to distinguish them, to distribute them, to use them; that it is not so much that they render docile those who are liable to transgress the law, but that they tend to assimilate the transgression in a general tactics of subjection" (272). Foucault made similar comments in his later work on the failure of social attempts to eliminate child sexuality, in which "[t]he child's 'vice' was not so much an enemy as a support [...] to proliferate to the limits of the visible and the invisible ... power advanced, multiplied its relays and its effects ... penetrating further into reality...." (*Sexuality* 42). By examining some specific power effects of this distributional economy of subjection and differentiation, a Foucauldian perspective suggests that the emergence of interdisciplinary fields as part of such a reform movement would not be sufficient to change the power effects of the modern academy. According to this perspective, if it wishes to be something other than part of a general tactics of subjection that advances modern power/knowledge relations, interdisciplinarity must instead become something substantively different from a modernist reform of the objects of knowledge, tools and methods, protocols and theoretical foundations of the modern academy.

Foucault's analysis of discipline suggests why this is so. Through the disciplinary generation of visible, intelligible objects of power/knowledge, such as the delinquent, Foucault finds the prison system to have succeeded in naming and placing in full visibility a form of illegality that has multiple important social effects. The first social effect is the generation and regulation of a grid of intelligibility based on differences between delinquency (through courts, police, prisons) and social norms (through schools, workplaces, heteronormative families). By rendering visible a specific type of illegality, the general economy of subjection isolates it as a limited object of regulation, thereby rendering it less politically and economically dangerous to the structure of power than were the widespread forms of popular illegalities (refusal of taxation and conscription; popularly forced sales of products at "fair" prices; confrontations with political authorities; prohibited labor coalitions and associations) that characterized the frequent upheavals of France in the mid- to late eighteenth and early nineteenth centuries (*Discipline* 273–77). Isolated from popular illegalities, delinquency becomes an agent for the illegalities of dominant groups (277, 279, 282ff.), so that people are no longer fighting the authorities but instead are fighting the law itself (274). Thus popular illegalities are constricted through the disciplinary regime as delinquents in their prisons are divided from students in school and from productive youth in the workplace, interrupting potential horizontal solidarities and delimiting the population that is willing to join in illegal or illicit behaviors, however popular.[1] The tactics dividing delinquents from the poor include the moralization that, according to Foucault, serves the profit and power of the bourgeoisie: the rules of property, thrift, docility at work, stability of residence, the heteronormative family, and so forth (278–86). The intelligibility of objects of power/knowledge in this way divides modern society into a hierarchically differentiated field of compulsory objectifications limiting illegalities, supporting norms, and disrupting horizontal solidarities in support of modern forms of moralization that are still widely practiced in the modern academy.

A second social effect is seen in the docility and productivity of the bodies of those subjects successfully subjected to the apparatuses of the normative institutions. The effectiveness of this subjection may be seen when comparing those bodies in such normative sites as schools, families, the military, and the workplace with those bodies subjected to the apparatuses of institutions contrasted with the normative, such as asylums and prisons. The docility is produced on a day-to-day basis through the repeated enforcement of what Foucault termed a "micro-physics of power" (26) administered through the pervasive apparatuses and mechanisms at work consistently across the multiple institutions that make up the disciplinary regime. These apparatuses make up a "micro-economy of perpetual penalty" (181) in the academy, where Foucault emphasized the hierarchizing effects of examinations and the fields of surveillance constituted in academic settings, just as they are at work in such sites as the medical clinic, the conjugal household and the orphanage, the factory and the military barracks, the asylum as well as the prison.

A third social effect is seen in the separation out, isolation of, and rendering visible of a small, isolated, and thus useful illegality as only one part of a general economy of illegalities, some of which are deemed illegal and subjected to surveillance and some of which are not. This rendering intelligible selected parts of the general economy of illegalities that defines the modern limits of tolerance for some illegalities, "of giving free rein to some, of putting pressure on others, of excluding a particular section, of making another useful, of neutralizing certain individuals and of profiting from others," results in the distribution of illegalities into a general economy or tactics of disciplinary subjection (272). The tolerated illegalities are those actually practiced by the bourgeoisie, of which Foucault mentions police surveillance, secret infiltrators, and sociologists who use police data (280–85) while also discussing nineteenth-century workers' newspapers' emphasis on thefts on the stock exchange or starvation and murder by exploitation (287–88). These illegalities are not subjected to surveillance and the carceral, instead continuing apace or expanding under a power/knowledge regime colonized by the dominant illegality. Under this regime of truth, the knowledges of subjugated groups, most obviously prisoners but also other groups, are also obscured, as they are overshadowed by the internal and other forms of surveillance given to the objects of knowledge rendered visible by modern forms of power/knowledge.

Foucault's analysis highlights how modern constitutions of intelligibility render visible only a limited range of objects of knowledge while simultaneously rendering invisible the domination at work in the modern power/knowledge regime. The consequent grid of intelligibility produces "a whole horizon of possible knowledge" (277) that produces specific aporias for modern knowledge and obscures subjugated knowledges and the power effects of knowledge (disruptions of horizontal solidarities, internalized surveillance, bodily docilities and productivities). It was the naming and betrayal of the erasure of these power effects that was behind Foucault's development of the term "power/knowledge" (27, 187–88). In sum, a Foucauldian perspective on the social effects of the academy centers on complicity with (or refusal of) social divisions that disrupt horizontal solidarities (between delinquents and the poor or visible and obscured groups), with the erasure of subjugated knowledges ("Two Lectures" 84) and tolerated illegalities (such as police brutalities, the drug trade and prostitution, or murder by exploitation), with modern moralizations (virtues of private property ownership, bodily docility, heteronormative family stability), and with the rendering docile of bodies in the modern economy of subjection.

Some have argued that interdisciplinary work, particularly in fields deriving from social justice movements, may be able to counter the disciplinary effects of the apparatuses consolidating and enforcing established twentieth-century academic fields (Blacker; Gore; Shumway and Messer-Davidow 213–18). Yet interdisciplinary fields linked to social justice through the social movements from which they have emerged have struggled with the pressures toward subjection within the modern disciplinary regime. They find that the apparatuses of the disciplinary regime persistently bring them back into the episteme and the complicit ethico-politics of modern academic practices through the multiple mechanisms of the academic publication industry, the hierarchizing classroom, hiring practices dependent on disciplinary graduate training, and other sites for the subjection of modern subjects to the power/knowledge regime of which Foucault was so critical. Resistance to and critique of the double sense of disciplinary tendencies resulting from this pressure are found scattered through the academic literature, but the news from these fields is not encouraging in women's studies (Allen and Kitch; Blee; Coates, Dodds, and Jensen; Messer-Davidow), Asian American studies (Nakatsu 8–9; Liu; Wong), and other interdisciplinary fields. From a Foucauldian critique, these forms of interdisciplinarity may carry out their business, expanding slowly, certainly, but still hopefully toward the promised rights and forever deferred equality of modernity, but they do so with the burden of legitimation and complicity with the brutal effects of the microeconomy of perpetual penalty and with the everyday illegalities and moralizations of normative social groups.

Foucault identified social practices that successfully refused these disciplinary apparatuses in considering how philosophers and historians might respond to power/knowledge not as an interdisciplinary encounter but as the "common labor of people seeking to 'de-discipline' them selves" ("Poussière" 39; qtd. Goldstein 3). Foucault develops his notion of dedisciplining in an essay presented for the same events as those just quoted, in which he emphasized his own search for knowledge centered on "the will to discover a different way of governing oneself through a different way of dividing up true and false" ("Method" 82). In this sense, the ethico-politics of dedisciplining are found not only in the politics of constituting the truth and falsehood of the object of knowledge but simultaneously in the ethics and politics of the constitution of the self. Comparable perspectives may be found in Foucault's earlier work, in which, for example, he evaluated scientific knowledge produced as "a new object, calling for new conceptual tools, and for fresh theoretical foundations . . . a true monster, so much so that [modern knowledge] could not even properly speak of [it] . . . [unlike someone] committing no more than a disciplined error" (*Archaeology* 224). Although some have used this characterization as a description of Derrida and other post-structuralists, in considering interdisciplinarity, we may take it as a constructive program for more than disciplined errors: for social justice work that rejects the modern power/knowledge grid in order to produce the monstrosities of new objects of knowledge with new tools on fresh foundations.

I now turn to brief evaluations of attempts at articulating social justice and interdisciplinary academic work by three authors, Foucault, Scott, and Spivak, in terms of the practice of dedisciplinarity, that is, the pursuit of new ways of governing the self and others through the refusal to be determined by disciplinary mechanisms and modern apparatuses that divide true from false. I will take up this question in terms of Foucault's own subjection to modern disciplinary apparatuses in four ways: three defined by specific regulatory sites that modern academics inhabit (publication, classroom teaching, and the individualized body); and one defined by mechanisms managing the relation between different sites. This last mechanism is the most important in a Foucauldian analysis and is perhaps the best obscured and most difficult to render visible in the modern power/knowledge regime, as it deals with the overall operation of the general economy of subjection and the overall distributional economy of the body discussed above. My discussions of Scott and Spivak will return to these different sites where relevant and where material is available in order to examine critically each approach to draw conclusions about the limits and strengths of a dediscíplinary approach to interdisciplinarity and social justice.

Limits to Foucault's Dediscíplinary Practices

Michel Foucault's work may be considered interdisciplinary in a number of ways not limited to the intersection of philosophy and history, including critiques of the natural sciences and of the academy more generally (*Order*; "Polemics" 386–88). Whereas *The Order of Things* became a major statement for growing non-Marxist left concerns with social justice, Foucault engaged with social justice concerns from 1966 to 1968 while teaching in Tunis and particularly from 1971 in many social justice issues: antiracism; immigration; opposition to U.S. interventions in Vietnam and the Gulf area; public awareness of prisoner views on society; gay liberation; labor issues in Poland; the health effects of toxic pollution; profit margins in the pharmaceutical industry; the limited range of political perspectives in the French mass media; and more generally with the role of the intellectual in society (Macey 257–323ff.). This political work is not seen directly in his academic teaching and publication, however, but came to public attention through other forms of writing.

In Foucault's engagement with the apparatuses of modern discipline through academic publication, his use of philosophical critique in writing history returned the protocols of twentieth-century history writing to its roots in European historiography before it became subject to modern European natural scientific truth claims. The enlightenment writings of Edward Gibbon, Hegelian historians, and the historical philosophy of

Nietzsche were characterized by an infusion of history with philosophy and morality. Foucault's histories did not escape conventions of earlier European historical writing, including an emphasis on white males and the archive, but it breaks with the discipline in refusing to affirm the social order of the historians' own day as a telos of history. In dystopic characterizations of the modern, Foucault's work joins other critiques of modern claims to a politically neutral, scientific objectivity that happens to ratify the social practices and humanist beliefs of modern Euro-American domestic and transnational social order (Feierman; Spivak, "Race" 38; Hartman 6).[2] The power effects of history written as refusal of modern Eurocentric narratives is key in a dediscipinary approach to social justice practices in the academy, for it shifts the focus of agency away from institutions supporting established social norms and toward ways to refuse subjection, domination, and objectification.

There are several clearly identifiable gaps in Foucault's relation to social justice concerns for which he was criticized, the best-known being his exclusive focus on French history, a persistent failure of interest in gender and race difference with implications for colonialism and imperialism, and his unwillingness to work at the forefront of the gay and lesbian movement. Foucault's emphasis on France reifies and subtends the claim of nation-states to a totalizing sense of identity for its citizens, so that his work toward a refusal of legitimating the state did not prevent him from falling into a subjection to the state in this way. Foucault also was charged with a certain racism during his lifetime for his focus exclusively on a seemingly whites-only France, criticisms answered in part with closer attention to his lectures (Stoler) and the publication of some of his lectures (*Society*). His work has also been extended to incorporate important studies of colonization, as in the writings of Edward Said and Ann Laura Stoler, and to the topic of gender by many, to which we return below.

When we turn to evaluating Foucault's dediscipinary practices in the classroom, however, we see less success at refusal of the apparatuses of the academy. Foucault persuasively critiques the traditional classroom mechanisms of the examination, of grading differentials, and of bodily docility (*Discipline* 170–94), yet inside the lecture hall and seminar room Foucault's engagement with the apparatuses of modern technologies of the body seems to have closely followed social norms with the exception perhaps of his participation in specific, localized disturbances while he was teaching at Vincennes.

A third site for evaluating Foucault's dedisciplinary work, questioning the degree of subjection of the body to modern discipline, is not one that is part of the traditional academic evaluation process. His subjection to the general economy of the body is seen in his stable residence with a lifetime partner in the fixed home that modernity demands, in commuting bodily from residence to places of stable employment adored by modernity, and in the docility of remaining quietly seated while reading his archival documents. There were a few exceptions, such as his teaching in North Africa and his travels to Iran while researching a series of journalistic reports (Macey 406–10) and to Japan, where he experienced Buddhist meditation at Koryu-ji temple in Kyoto (Macey 401–14). None of these exceeds the bodily economy of modernity significantly, however, just as leaving the archive or the university campus does not guarantee any release from modern disciplinary regulation.

There are three significant ways in which Foucault refused the modern docility of the body that require brief comment. The most direct example is his well-known rejection of the heterosexual activities of the body and his historical research into the uses of pleasure and the cultivation of the self that resists subjection (Macey 446–49, 468–70). From biographical records, some have surmised that Foucault was also experimenting with anonymity and the body later in life, and in this way he was not only refusing the sexual monogamy demanded by the record-keeping machinations of the modern state and morality but may also have been exploring the limits of bodily responses (Macey 425–27). A second is his refusal of the bodily role as parent and head of the heteronormative household, which must be understood in terms of his study of the family in collaboration with the historian Arlette Farge (Macey 450–54). Finally, his willingness to enter jail not only as a researcher but also as an incarcerated person also shows how he underwent subjection to the modern state apparatus of the penal system in ways that have been very important in numerous modern social movements.

The final place of subjection to disciplinary apparatuses and their participation in general economies of subjection is less easy to identify but very fruitful for the present purposes: his entanglement with mechanisms working to manage the distribution of bodies between sites, what was termed above the distributional economy of subjection and differentiation. Through his Prison Information Project and his writing on the history of sexuality, Foucault worked to bring the experiences and knowledge of two groups who were excluded from public purview in normalized society (Macey 268–69). By rendering these subjects into visibility, Foucault built bridges across social divisions that modern disciplinary mechanisms worked to generate and enforce, facilitating horizontal solidarities that modern disciplinary effects work to disrupt. Interventions in modern distributional economies of visibility and legibility of this sort are among the most suggestive and effective for social justice and organizing concerns from a dedisciplinary Foucauldian perspective.

Joan Wallach Scott's Dedisciplinary Practices and Their Limits

Joan Wallach Scott of *Gender and the Politics of History* is operating in a Foucauldian vein at the intersection of an academic discipline, history, and an interdisciplinary field, women's studies or feminism. By constituting her work and the governance of herself and others in terms of a single academic discipline, she is subjected to comparatively strong pressures to subject herself to the disciplinary protocols of history. Despite these pressures, Scott carries out a series of skirmishes in which she attempts to change the subjects of history from the masters of neutrality to histories critically aware of the present-day power effects of the historian's construction of the past (7–8). In this refusal of the protocols of the discipline of history, Scott works to render visible the contested processes by which categories such as gender come to regulate societies, thereby destabilizing a truth regime anchored in the biology of gender difference in order to carry out political interventions (xi, xiii). Scott gives considerable attention to the academic discipline of history, working to make its limits and its politics visible for investigation rather than accepting them as uninterrogated determinants for work (8). In this way, Scott articulates her academic work with social justice concerns almost exclusively through feminism and the women's movement, focusing on gender and particularly on the workplace.

   An evaluation of Scott's dedisciplining practices centered on the site of academic publication finds that she rejects the normative exclusion of the working women in historians' narratives of the early history of capitalism in France, England, and elsewhere, instead clearly indicating the subtle ways in which men's work as well is gendered (75, 89). By succeeding in institutional terms in this struggle, such as through her appointment at the Princeton Center for Advanced Studies and prolific publication with

prestigious university presses, Scott has not only been successful in changing the discipline of history but also in furthering gender studies beyond
the frame of French history.

An inquiry into the status of race in Scott's constitution of objects of
knowledge, as in Foucault's work, unearths several aporias in Scott's dedisciplining practices. In *Gender and the Politics of History* and more recent
publications (*Parité*; *Only Paradoxes*), she follows Foucault in limiting the
object of knowledge to the territorial boundaries of the modern French
nation-state, and some modes of subjection to the modern racialized truth
regime occur, as was the case in the previously discussed work of Foucault.
For example, Scott writes in *Gender and the Politics of History* about France
in the 1830s to 1850s, yet she overlooks entirely the consolidation of modern
racial categories in these same decades following on the Haitian Revolution threatening French claims to democracy and universal egalitarianism
(Dubois).[3] France also carried out a racialized overseas expansion during
these decades in Algeria in the 1830s, established naval bases to suppress
the slave trade in Gabon in 1839 and in Tahiti in 1843, and pursued treaty
ports in China in the 1840s and 1850s, in New Caledonia in 1853, and in
Saigon in 1859. This history of antislavery struggles, colonial expansion, and
emerging race-based categories for differentiating and legitimating social
hierarchies not only reconstitutes the colonized populations, but also consolidates new modes of power for the dominant racial group, including the
women and men whom Scott studies (Cherniavsky; Spivak, "Race"; Young).
In her more recent work in which she considers the topic of race explicitly,
she emphasizes public opinion and government policy and overlooks how
the body might be constituted by racialized groups as modes of resistance
and agency (*Veil*, 42–89). In her study of the veil prohibition controversies
in *The Politics of the Veil*, the body is almost completely erased, as if there
were only veils to lift and to outlaw without a gendered and racialized
body for them to cover. In this way, Scott subjects herself and her others to
modern, racialized inequalities and constructions of the body as historically
constituted through practices of imperialism and colonization.

The legitimacy of universalist claims implicit in modern forms of
political sovereignty is precisely what Foucault's notion of dedisciplinary
practice encourages us to critique. The unthinking subjection by the writing
subject to the implicit, naturalized claim of the workers Scott examines to be
French citizens is destabilized and interrogated when the horizon of analysis
is opened up to question the limits of France by including the transnational.
What were the relations to the construction of the nation France of the

mixed-race and maroon children of French merchants and bureaucrats in French Guiana or Gabon? Why is the labor of those in the territories annexed by the French during the period Scott considers (Algeria, Tahiti, New Caledonia, Saigon) not considered by Scott? Similar blind spots are found in Scott's *Parité: Sexual Equality and the Crisis of French Universalism*, in which she considers the abstract individual that provides the foundation for the republic while overlooking late eighteenth-century struggles about whether women, Jews, and blacks were to be included (Offen 282). By subjecting herself to the universalized terms of the modern nation-state, Scott constructs "a whole horizon of possible knowledge" that occludes the race-based forms of domination in France and renders the governing of self and others in her work complicit with modern inequalities constructed through the modern power/knowledge regime.

It is also important to examine the distributional economy of subjection and differentiation in Scott's case. Her entanglement with mechanisms working to manage the distribution of bodies between sites, sending some to penal institutions and others to be students or teachers, is clear from her affiliation with an elite academic body, as it is for all three of my case studies. She has written critically about the weakening of affirmative action practices in U.S. postsecondary education, a modest mechanism for attempting to redirect the racialized and class-stratified flow of bodies into the academy ("Governance"). Scott has found effective ways to render into visibility the politics of the historical struggles excluding women workers and artisans and political agents from histories of the early modern period, excluded despite the best of intentions by the egalitarian commitments of historians such as E. P. Thompson (*Gender* 75, 107). This interrogation of the limits of visibility renegotiates not only the limits of specific objects of knowledge but also the claims to universal surveillance and truth of the modern truth regime.

Gayatri Chakravorty Spivak: Destabilizing the Limits of Dedisciplinary Practices

Gayatri Chakravorty Spivak, like Scott, has responded to Foucault's critique of modern disciplinary knowledge in developing interdisciplinary research and teaching, but Foucault remains less central to her work than to Scott's. Spivak explicitly describes her own work in contested relation to interdisciplinarity, problematizing interdisciplinary work in the humanities ("Marginalia") while arguing for interdisciplinarity construed as an ethical supplement to the social sciences centered on close analysis of agency in texts of the global South ("Culture Studies" 280; *Death*). Spivak consistently frames her interdisciplinary approach around the intellectual and social movements of deconstruction, Marxism, and feminism so that "each of these things brings the other to crisis. And that's how it ought to be: serious crisis" ("Violence" 138). Such crises in this approach to interdisciplinary work are not moments of weakness or confession but productive interrogations of a theoretical perspective (e.g., feminism) by a social movement (e.g., the women's movement) ("Violence" 139).[4]

Spivak construes justice in a way that diverges from traditional social movements, aligning herself with post-structuralist rejections of metanarratives that tell how social justice is to be achieved to emphasize instead what is left out when a narrative is constructed, as in narratives of social change and resistance ("Academic Freedom"; "Post-modern" 18–19). In one of her reflections on Foucault's notion of power/knowledge, she agrees with Derrida that deconstruction itself is "justice," in its emphasis on the subject centered without closure in the act, the decision, the affirmation rather than as an exposure of error or of some pathology of logocentrism. In this way, Spivak affirms a responsibility toward the Others who are often subordinated through the disciplinary hierarchies instilled by modern power/knowledge, a responsibility enacted not simply by reversals of hierarchies but through their displacement, even as she recognizes the "anguish that knowledge must suppress difference as well as differance, that a fully just world is impossible, forever deferred and different from our projections, the undecidable in the face of which we must risk the decision that we can hear the other" (*Critique* 199). It is through the careful political practice of strategic essentialism that she works with deconstruction and feminism and Marxism to practice a responsibility to the radically Other that is both impossible and necessary ("Subaltern Studies" 214–26), even as she has moved away from strategic essentialism toward an emphasis on ethics in more recent work. Spivak prefers to renegotiate the ethics and politics of movement practices and objectives rather than go along with those activists she sees as "resolutely anti-intellectual communalist political activists whose slogan seems to be 'if you think too much about words, you will do no deeds'" ("Marginalia" n. 14, p. 49).

In evaluating how Spivak's work may be seen as dedisciplinary, I begin with her approach through deconstruction to the disciplinary apparatuses of academic publication, working with considerable success to destabilize and displace many of its fundamental assumptions and practices. Although she has published regularly with very well-respected journals and presses in several fields both in the United States and internationally, she also persistently refuses the terms with which academic publication is supposed to make sense and divide the true from the false. The most fundamental way in which Spivak refuses the basic assumptions of the modern academy is in the insistence that we cannot know the wholly Other ("Power/Knowledge" 38), a marking of the limits of modern forms of knowledge and of the limits of appropriation of the subaltern into modern intelligibility and power/knowledge. This becomes, in *Death of a Discipline*, an emphasis on comparativist work not as defined in terms of an Other whose social conditions need to be studied or alleviated or whose poverty requires help or who requires anthropological diagnosis (*Death* 50), but as learning from below through teacher-training work with indigenous peoples and association with counterglobalizing networks in the global South (*Death* 28, 35–36; "Righting Wrongs"). This learning from below is grounded in imagining what is not known in the metropole, based on careful textual readings of culture of the global South, a perspective and an agency from below that interrupts the universalist knowledge of the disciplines (*Death*, 49–50).

The way in which this presents a new mode of governing the self and Others is seen in Spivak's presentation of herself not as expert but as learning how to be at home in the cultural idiom of the place of the global South, a literary skill as opposed to the academic or health professional or nongovernmental organization (NGO) representative who learns language with social science fluency (*Death* n. 12, 106). This learning does not grow from some automatic affinity she has with the global South because of deterministic affiliations through national or cultural identities but through Spivak's lengthy commitment to work in the global South (some ten years as of 2003), a major point of difference with Scott and Foucault.[5] The new comparativist practices she proposes construct forms of responsibility to the global South through attention to the politics of Othering that refuses to demystify the global South as Other, instead preferring to "surpris[e] the historical" through staging unexpected maneuvers toward collectivities (55–56) and thereby refusing fixed conceptions of the Other in generating the collectivities that are required for a politics. Spivak's emphasis on the politics of comparisons of global South and North facilitates her refusal of the terms that modern constructions of alterity provide, thereby producing new collective/Other configurations of social relations that may facilitate justice in social relations.

The implications of Spivak's dedisciplinary practices for the boundaries of true and false are found in her deployment of deconstruction. She persistently returns self-reflexively to a critique of the academy, as in her summary of "[a] careful deconstructive method . . . displacing rather than only reversing oppositions (such as between colonizer and colonized) by taking the investigator's own complicity into account. . . ." (*Critique* 244). Thus the disruption of the claim to fixed, noncontradictory universal meaning in modern academic writing also consistently displaces the universalist modern narrative frame by repeatedly inserting the writing subject's own ethically and politically troubled positioning into the picture. We see an application of this principle to the university classroom in a brief statement of the title of her essay collection regarding metropolitan teachers with origins in the global South, such as her own origins in Bengal: "[R]adical teachers at universities . . . should attend to the nature of the institution that is their contractual space—and not ignore their obligation by claiming a spurious marginality. . . . I believe the teacher, *while operating within the institution*, can foster the emergence of a committed collectivity by not making her institutional commitment invisible: outside in the teaching-machine" ("Marginality" n. 2, 294; emphasis in original). Through problematizing middle-class status and affiliation with the academy, the teacher can work even while in the institution toward a responsible politics and perhaps foster an ethics of organized political commitment of self and Others by betraying his or her own complicity and thereby displacing totalizing claims to oppositional practices, such as decolonization. This refusal of such binarisms as colonizer/colonized renegotiates the means by which alterity is produced, rejecting the subject as the source of a fixed alterity or as part of a dialectic of affirmation of one and a negation of the Other (*Death* 73). By reducing the degree to which the self may be formed and governed through such identifications and their inevitable alterities, Spivak is taking aim not only at the disciplinary mechanisms of the academy, but also at the fundamental way in which the ethical and political are construed.

Spivak's interest in language does not deter her from a certain precisely targeted dedisciplining of the body, centering on refusals of the ways in which modern constitutions of race and gender make claims on bodies. For example, in discussing young, white, male undergraduate students, Spivak encourages them to refuse a determinism or an essentialism based on skin color (chromatism) or genitalia (genitalism) based on "an *historical* critique of your position as the investigating person" ("Multi-culturalism" 62; emphasis in original). Her own persistent refusal of attempts to be rendered marginal in the academy is closely comparable to this practice, as she rejects attempts to subject her to such hierarchies as margin/center or colonizer/colonized through their claims at rendering her intelligible. This practice is what Spivak terms "negotiation," meaning "try[ing] to change something that one is obliged to inhabit" as a form of intervention, a practice that seems closely comparable to Foucault's notion of dedisciplining.

Spivak is well-known for her intervention in our final topic for dedisciplining: mechanisms that work to manage the distribution of bodies between sites, or the distributional economy of subjection and differentiation. Her persistent emphasis on the subaltern renders visible the object of knowledge that remains perhaps unavoidably at the margin of the objects of knowledge that the modern disciplinary regime wishes to isolate and highlight (*Critique* 140–146, 268–76; *Death* 16–17, 32; "Speak?"). In this area, her work is closely comparable to Foucault's emphasis on the tolerated illegalities that remained obscured when delinquency was isolated from among other illegalities and highlighted in order to render it manageable. In the case of the subaltern, the modern power/knowledge regime tolerates the presence of the subaltern in the shade of objects of knowledge that it would rather domesticate when studying the global South, such as the metropolitan migrant of whom Spivak is so critical. Through displacing the normative from the center in the workings of these mechanisms, what she sometimes terms the white educated male as unacknowledged universal, she attempts to render intelligible the subaltern even as she subjects herself and the subaltern to the terms of power/knowledge relations that attempt to silence the subaltern.

Conclusion

In closing, we may return to the problem faced by many interdisciplinary fields as they are pressured through multiple disciplinary mechanisms back into the complicit ethico-politics of modern social hierarchies and bodily docilities. Foucault, Scott, and Spivak have all been successful in dedisciplinary practices that pursue what Foucault characterized as "analyz[ing] the connection between ways of distinguishing true and false and ways of governing oneself and others" ("Method" 82), even as they all have certain complicities that remain. First, all three give attention to objects of knowledge obscured and displaced to the margins by the modern disciplinary regime: prisoners, gay men and lesbians, contested conditions for women's work, the subaltern. Second, Foucault and Spivak are particularly effective at constituting spaces for building horizontal alliances disrupted by the modern power/knowledge regime, particularly of the poor and students with delinquents in the case of Foucault, and of the comparativist with the Others and subalterns of modernity in the case of Spivak. Finally, there was significant attention paid to the dedisciplining of the body by Foucault in terms of sexuality and docility and by Spivak in her attention to refusing attempts at making racialized, gendered, and marginalizing claims on the body.

Justice, one of the central terms under which this paper is written, seems troubled by the operations of these authors. Foucault's notion of justice seems to refuse any easy closure, centering itself in a critique of modernity even as he carried out many of the traditional practices of the social activist: participating and founding social movements; contributing to public debates; writing for general audiences; confronting political authorities and being imprisoned. The academy is still sorting out its response to Foucault's emphasis on what in social justice movements was once considered the private sphere, including not only sexuality but also the body in a broader array of practices and settings. His focus on the body as a site for domination of the subject interrupts the turn away from the body toward claims to objectivity that erase the observing (presumed white, male, straight, bourgeois) subject in modernity. This disruption of the erasure of the body from visibility may be one of his most important contributions. Spivak's emphasis on the limits and erasures of justice seems designed to produce a restless political and ethical practice that will never settle easily into any single academic discipline or social movement, and she has paid the price for this approach through the resistance of many in several fields to respond seriously to her work. This displacement comes with the promise that the resulting movement will produce new solidarities and flexibilities that strengthen multiple social movements as modernity works to appropriate and subject them to its terms.

Scott's work may serve as a warning about the pitfalls of dedisciplinary work. She erases the construction of her own subjectivity in a manner that follows Foucault in his historical writings, but she does not problematize her own subjection in a manner comparable to that achieved by Foucault in his interviews. She also overlooks the centrality of the body and follows Foucault in neglecting the comparative across the divide of the global South and global North. As a result, Scott's notions of justice are more readily appropriated into modernist notions of economic and social equity than are those of Foucault and Spivak, suggesting that attention to the self-reflexive, to the body, and to the comparative are important components of dediciplinary practice.

Foucault's more general argument regarding justice in *Discipline and Punish* centers on the ways that the disciplinary regime disrupts links between multiple social conflicts. In the decades around 1800, popular struggles against political regimes were linked with resistance to increasing industrialization and the effects of recurring economic crises. The multiple-issue solidarities that developed aimed to do more than extract concessions from the state or change specific policies: They aimed to change the very structure of power (*Discipline* 273–75). According to this view, it is the horizontal solidarities disrupted by the modern disciplinary regime that threaten the modern power/knowledge regime (219, 273–78, 285), such as between the poor and the delinquent or the student and the incarcerated, and it is to reinvigorating comparable solidarities from our own day that a dediciplinary practice must give its attentions. Foucault participated in many efforts to produce unexpected solidarities in his activist work, though not in his historical writings. Spivak's emphasis in *Death of a Discipline* centers on the generation—not in traditional forms of activism outside the academy but within the limits of the modern academy—of collectivities that surprise both its participants and its history, a practice that seems prototypical for dedicplinarity.

Foucault tells a delightful story at the end of his Illegalities and Delinquency section in *Discipline and Punish* that may illustrate the possible life of a dediscipled academic. In 1840, at the very beginning of the modern penal system in Foucault's rendering, a child of thirteen without home or family testified in a court that named him as a delinquent. When asked by the court about the offenses under which they rendered him intelligible, a local newspaper captures how he reformulates each offense:

> What is your station in life?—My station: to begin with, I'm thirty-six at least; I don't work for anybody. I've worked for myself for a long time now. I have my day station and my night station. In the day, for instance, I hand out leaflets free of charge to all the passers-by. . . . I turn cart-wheels on the avenue de Neuilly; at night there are shows; I open coach doors, I sell pass-out tickets; I've plenty to do.—It would be better for you to be put into a good house as an apprentice and learn

a trade.—Oh, a good house, an apprenticeship, it's too much trouble. And anyway the bourgeois . . . always grumbling, no freedom. (290–91)

The practices of indiscipline without being fixed in definite relations of domination are what the failure of discipline looks like: no single station; no fixed home; a vanished family; a roving, wheeling body; no compulsory insertion; no intelligible identity.

For those of us who work in the academy, it is as if we are constantly if subtly and implicitly being queried by our colleagues and, most importantly, by our own internalized self-surveillance and discipline, just as this free-spirited youth was being queried by the court. Finding ways to reply, as this boy did, not only to our colleagues and our internalized discipline but also to the various mechanisms and apparatuses that so persistently ask us to discipline ourselves would help dediscipline ourselves and our others. These dedisciplined practices become relations to social justice only through a future that is as yet indeterminate, through those we impact in our refusals and our limited freedoms, through the politics of our governability and that of our others, through what we write and where we do our work, through the erased horizontal solidarities that we build, and through the prohibited multi-issue collaborations we constitute. It is in these relations that interdisciplinary work has its social justice or power effects, and although dedisciplinarity certainly has its pitfalls, it may also render visible aspects of academic work that are both politically troubling and ripe for new practices.

Notes

1. Such observations in Foucault's *Discipline and Punish* echo later observations in *The History of Sexuality* about the open transgressions, shameless discourse, and "tolerant familiarity with the illicit" of seventeenth-century French sexual practices (3), popular illegitimate behaviors that became likewise incarcerated not in the prison but in the modern home and the conjugal family.

2. Thanks are due to Leila Neti for bringing Hartman to my attention.

3. We see these emerging theories most notoriously in one of the foundational texts for European white supremacist racial theory, J. A. Gobineau's *Essay on the Inequality of the Races*, published in the mid-1850s (Young 15, 99–101).

4. Spivak follows Derrida in directing this conception of interdisciplinarity as a productive bringing to crisis at Foucault's interdisciplinary linking of

philosophy and history mentioned above, for example, by arguing that the problem
with Foucault's early work in *Madness and Civilization* is one of "not yet having
brought each other to the crisis that this new politics of practice must assiduously
cultivate" ("Power/Knowledge" 38).

    5. Foucault's teaching in Tunis and journalistic research in Iran were inter-
ventions of shorter duration, a year or two, whereas his travels to Japan seemed
much more in the vein of other major poststructuralists who have dabbled in an
exoticized Asia, such as Roland Barthes (Barthes) and Julia Kristeva (Kristeva).
With the exception of essays in her edited volumes, I have not found evidence of
work by Scott on topics outside the global North.

Works Cited

Allen, Judith A., and Sally L. Kitch. "Disciplined by Disciplines? The Need for
    an *Interdisciplinary* Research Mission in Women's Studies." Feminist Studies.
    24.2 (Summer 1998): 275–99.
Althusser, Louis. "Ideology and Ideological State Apparatuses." *Lenin and Phi-
    losophy and Other Essays*. Trans. Ben Brewster. London: New Left Books,
    1971. 127–86.
Apple, Michael. *Ideology and Curriculum*. Boston: Routledge & Kegan Paul, 1979.
Barthes, Roland. *Empire of Signs*. Trans. Richard Howard. London: Jonathan
    Cape, 1983.
Blacker, David. "Intellectuals at Work and in Power: Toward a Foucaultian
    Research Ethic." *Foucault's Challenge*. Ed. Popkiewitz and Brennan. New
    York: Teacher's College, Columbia UP, 1998. 348–67.
Blee, Kathleen. "Contending with Disciplinarity." *Women's Studies on Its Own: A
    Next Wave Reader in Institutional Change*. Ed. Robyn Wiegman. Durham:
    Duke UP, 2002. 177–82.
Bourdieu, Pierre. *Homo Academicus*. Trans. Peter Collier. Stanford: Stanford UP,
    1988 (1984).
Burchell, Graham, Colin Gordon, and Peter Miller, eds. *The Foucault Effect: Stud-
    ies in Governmentality with Two Lectures by and an Interview with Michel
    Foucault*. Chicago: U of Chicago P, 1991.
Cherniavsky, Eva. *Incorporations: Race, Nation, and the Body Politics of Capitalism*.
    Minneapolis: U of Minnesota P, 2006.
Coates, Jacky, Michelle Dodds, and Jodi Jensen. " 'Isn't Just Being Here Political
    Enough?' Feminist Action-Oriented Research as a Challenge to Graduate
    Women's Studies." *Feminist Studies*. 24.2 (Summer 1998): 333–46.
DuBois, Laurent. *Avengers of the New World: the Story of the Haitian Revolution*.
    Cambridge, MA: Belknap Press, 2004.
Feierman, Steven. "African History and the Dissolution of World History." *Africa
    and the Disciplines: The Contributions of Research in Africa to the Social Sci-

ences and the Humanities. Ed. Robert H. Bates, V. Y. Mudimbe, and Jean O'Bau. Chicago: U of Chicago P, 1993. 167–212.

Foucault, Michel. *The Archeology of Knowledge & the Discourse on Language*. Trans. A. M. Sheridan Smith. London: Tavistock, 1972.

———. *Discipline and Punish: The Birth of the Prison*. Trans. A. M. Sheridan. New York: Pantheon Books, 1977 (1975).

———. *The History of Sexuality: An Introduction, Volume 1*. Trans. Robert Hurley. New York: Vintage Books, 1990 (1978).

———. *The Order of Things: An Archaeology of the Human Sciences*. New York: Vintage Books, 1970.

———. "Polemics, Politics, and Problematizations: An Interview with Michel Foucault." *The Foucault Reader*. Ed. Paul Rabinow. New York: Pantheon Books, 1984. 381–90.

———. "La poussière et le nuage" (Dust and Mist). *L'Impossible Prison: Recherche sur les système pénitentaire au XIXe siècle* (The Impossible Prison: Studies in the Nineteenth Century [French] Penitentiary System). Ed. Michelle Perrot. Paris: Éditions du Seuil, 1980.

———. "Questions of Method." *The Foucault Effect: Studies in Governmentality with Two Lectures by and an Interview with Michel Foucault*. Ed. Burchell, Graham, Colin Gordon, and Peter Miller. Chicago: U of Chicago P, 1991. 73–86.

———. *"Society Must Be Defended": Lectures at the Collège De France, 1975–1976*. New York: Picador, 2003 (1997).

———. "Two Lectures." *Power/Knowledge: Selected Interviews and Other Writings, 1972–1977*. Ed. Colin Gordon. New York: Pantheon Books, 1980. 78–108.

Goldstein, Jan. "Introduction." *Foucault and the Writing of History*. Ed. Jan Goldstein. Cambridge, MA: Blackwell, 1994. 1–15.

Gore, Jennifer. *The Struggle for Pedagogies: Critical and Feminist Discourses on Regimes of Truth*. New York: Routledge, 1993.

Hartman, Saidya V. *Scenes of Subjection: Terror, Slavery, and Self-Making in Nineteenth-Century America*. New York: Oxford UP, 1997.

Hoskin, Keith W., and Richard H. Macve. "Accounting and the Examination: A Geneaology of Disciplinary Power." *Accounting, Organizations, and Society*. 11.2 (1986): 105–36.

Kondo, Dorinne. "(Un)Disciplined Subjects: (De)Colonizing the Academy?" *Orientations: Mapping Studies in the Asian Diaspora*. Ed. Kandice Chuh and Karen Shimakawa. Durham, NC: Duke UP, 2001. 35–40.

Kristeva, Julia. *About Chinese Women*. Trans. Anita Burrows. New York: Marion Boyars, 1986.

Liu, John M. "Asian American Studies and the Disciplining of Ethnic Studies." *Frontiers of Asian American Studies*. Pullman: Washington State UP, 1989. 271–83.

Macey, David. *The Lives of Michel Foucault*. New York: Pantheon, 1993.

Messer-Davidow, Ellen. *Disciplining Feminism: From Social Activism to Academic Discourse.* Duke UP, 2002.

Messer-Davidow, Ellen, David R. Shumway, and David J. Sylvan, eds. *Knowledges: Historical and Critical Studies in Disciplinarity.* Charlottesville: UP of Virginia, 1993.

Nakatsu, Penny, "Keynote Address." *Tool of Control? Tool of Change? Proceedings of the National Asian American Studies Conference II.* San Jose: n.p., 1973. 3–10.

Noujain, Elie Georges. "History as Genealogy: An Exploration of Foucault's Approach to History." *Contemporary French Philosophy.* Ed. A Phillips Griffiths. Royal Institute of Philosophy Lecture Series, 21. New York: Cambridge UP, 1987. 157–74.

Offen, Karen. Rev. of *Parité: Sexual Equality and the Crisis of French Universalism,* by Joan Wallach Scott. *History.* 92.2 (Apr. 2007): 281–82.

Scott, Joan Wallach. "The Critical State of Shared Governance." *Academe.* 88.4 (July/Aug., 2002): 41–48.

———. *Gender and the Politics of History.* Rev. ed. Gender and Culture. New York: Columbia UP, 1999 (1988).

———. *Only Paradoxes to Offer: French Feminisms and the Rights of Man.* Cambridge: Harvard UP, 1996.

———. *Parité: Sexual Equality and the Crisis of French Universalism.* Chicago: U of Chicago P, 2005.

———. *The Politics of the Veil.* The Public Square Book Series. Princeton: Princeton UP, 2007.

Shumway, David R., and Ellen Messer-Davidow. "Disciplinarity: An Introduction." *Poetics Today.* 12.2 (Summer 1991): 201–25.

Spivak, Gayatri Chakravorty. "Can The Subaltern Speak?" *Wedge.* 7/8 (Winter/ Spring, 1985): 119–30.

———. *A Critique of Postcolonial Reason: Toward a Theory of the Vanishing Present.* Cambridge: Harvard UP, 1999.

———. *Death of a Discipline.* The Wellek Library Lectures in Critical Theory. New York: Columbia UP, 2003.

———. "Explanation and Culture: Marginalia." *The Spivak Reader.* Ed. Donna Landry and Gerald MacLean. New York: Routledge, 1996. 29–52.

———. "Marginality in the Teaching Machine." *Outside in the Teaching Machine.* New York: Routledge, 1993. 53–76.

———. "More on Power/Knowledge." *Outside in the Teaching Machine.* New York: Routledge, 1993. 25–52.

———. "Negotiating the Structures of Violence." *The Post-Colonial Critic: Interviews, Strategies, Dialogues.* Ed. Sarah Harasym. New York: Routledge, 1990. 138–51.

———. "The Post-modern Condition: The End of Politics?" *The Post-Colonial Critic: Interviews, Strategies, Dialogues*. Ed. Sarah Harasym. New York: Routledge, 1990. 17–34.

———. "Race before Racism: The Disappearance of the American." *boundary 2*. 25.2 (Summer 1998): 35–53.

———. "Questions of Multi-culturalism." *The Post-Colonial Critic: Interviews, Strategies, Dialogues*. Ed. Sarah Harasym. New York: Routledge, 1990. 59–66.

———. "Righting Wrongs." *Human Rights, Human Wrongs: The Oxford Amnesty Lectures 2001*. Ed. Nicholas Owen. New York: Oxford University Press, 2003. 168–227.

———. "Scattered Speculations on the Question of Culture Studies." *Outside in the Teaching Machine*. New York: Routledge, 1993. 255–82.

———. "Subaltern Studies: Deconstructing Historiography." *The Spivak Reader*. Ed. Donna Landry and Gerald MacLean. New York: Routledge, 1996. 203–35.

———. "Thinking Academic Freedom in Gendered Post-coloniality." *The Anthropology of Politics: A Reader in Ethnography, Theory, and Critique*. Ed. Joan Vincent. Malden: Blackwell Publishers, 2002. 452–59.

Stoler, Ann Laura. *Race and the Education of Desire: Foucault's History of Sexuality and The Colonial Order of Things*. Durham, NC: Duke UP, 1995.

Young, Robert J. C. *Colonial Desire: Hybridity in Theory, Culture and Race*. New York: Routledge, 1995.

Wong, Cynthia Sau-ling. "Denationalization Reconsidered: Asian American Cultural Criticism at a Theoretical Crossroads." *Amerasia Journal*. 21.1–2 (1995): 1–27.

Chapter Nine

The Limits of Interdisciplinarity

The Case of Chicano Studies

Michael Soldatenko

As Chicano and Chicana activists challenged academic knowledge in the 1960s and 1970s, most agreed that traditional academic disciplines were inadequate to explain the Mexican American condition. For many, the methods and methodologies of the humanities and social science disciplines served to either erase or stereotype Mexican Americans; their epistemic frameworks dismissed or created a caricature of the Mexican American. For the majority of Chicano(a) activists, to escape these academic confines and break the epistemic hold of the "American" university was to turn to some expression of interdisciplinarity. Unfortunately, this turn did not result in the intended goal of rupturing disciplinary bonds or providing a foundational challenge to American education and its support to American exceptionalism. Instead, the interdisciplinary turn reproduced the intellectual apparatus of the American academy, and by so doing reasserted the subordination of the Mexican American.

In this essay I will explore how early Chicano(a) activists framed Chicano studies through their adoption of interdisciplinarity. They used "interdisciplinary," "multidisciplinary," and "transdisciplinary" to suggest the same concept: the avoidance of disciplinary control and the endeavor to establish an activist intellectual framework. I will also show how the institution corralled the potential disruptive aspects in Chicano studies and used interdisciplinarity to control and manage Chicano studies, like all the ethnic studies. In Chicano studies, interdisciplinarity simply became another tool in the management of a potentially oppositional site in the academy.

Therefore I will also explore the relationship between U.S. academic disciplines and interdisciplinarity.

Chicano Studies and Interdisciplinarity

Let me trace how early Chicano studies and interdisciplinarity became one and the same. In July 1968, the southern California chapters of United Mexican American Students (UMAS) organized a one-day conference at the University of South California. The conference focused on developing an effective Chicano organization on college campuses, building on the recent high school walkouts in Los Angeles. The activists discussed a wide variety of issues, such as admissions, curriculum, funding, Mexican American studies, bridge programs, liaisons with black student organizations, the autonomy of UMAS chapters, and ties to the United Farm Workers. When dealing with curricular issues, the UMAS students called for relevant, interdisciplinary, and problem-solving courses (UMAS). Chicano(a) campus activists used the notion of interdisciplinarity to challenge traditional disciplinary practices and reject their research about the Mexican American as biased. For the majority of Chicanos(as), the use of interdisciplinarity somehow promised an approach that could open up the research and interpretation of being Mexican American in the United States. What exactly this meant was left for further discussion.

We can establish an idea of how some Chicanos(as) perceived how Chicano studies and interdisciplinarity came together by looking at the presentations at the Summer Institute of Chicano Studies at California State College, Long Beach. The Summer Institute's editorial committee wrote:

> The goal for Chicano Studies is to provide a relevant education. This learning is preparing the Chicano student with a different political, social, and cultural perspective than the society at large has traditionally imposed so that he can be prepared to work and live for the purpose of changing established institutions that have failed to meet the needs of the Chicano community. ("El Concilio" v)

Some of the essay writers endeavored to structure the curricular side of nascent Chicano studies. Manuel Guerra suggested that the best way to explore this unique subject was through an interdisciplinary study of the

Mexican American; in the process, scholars would provide Chicano studies with its own specialization and categorization (8). Julius Rivera adjoined that the goal of Chicano studies programs was to correct academic distortions, achieve academic recognition, educate both Anglos and Chicanos(as), link up with the community, become a magnet for activists, and (again) apply an interdisciplinary model. Sergio Elizondo advanced: "The main point made here is that we, as Mexican Americans, can no longer tolerate anyone to pretend that the study of Mexican Americans is an object of curiosity any longer" (4).

Chicano studies, these authors would agree, needed to develop alternative approaches to the problems of the barrio and the students' relationship to the community because the goal of Chicano studies had to be the transformation of the barrio.

> [I]n higher education the academic world has not intellectualized the problems of the barrio and the nature of these problems and their possible solutions have remained outside the current of thought of American life. (Guerra 9)

> The emergence of Mexican American studies as a distinct, legitimate and transcendental academic and scholarly discipline is more important to the Mexican American for its philosophical import. (Elizondo 3)

For most of the writers, the American philosophy of education was inconsistent with the values of the Chicano movement. "We must recognize that that which we seek in Chicano Studies call for radical change in the university," wrote Lopez (14). Underlying this perspective was the assumption that the Chicano(a) could not leave the barrio or La Raza (Sánchez 1). For this reason, Chicano studies had to focus on community action; Chicano studies needed to provide techniques to resolve community concerns: "[W]e need that information [new type of research] to be used by *us* in the implementation of programs to solve specific programs by *us*" (Elizondo 4). And the only way to subvert the limits imposed by traditional disciplines was to engage in interdisciplinary practices.

Many early Chicano studies scholars turned to internal colonialism as the paradigm of Chicano studies as a nascent discipline. In an essay for *Aztlán*, Tomás Almaguer translated Chicano cultural nationalism into the internal colonial model (7). Although Almaguer's essay was not the first to use the internal colonial model, his work demonstrated how the model had become "central to the evolution of the 'concept of Chicano Studies' because internal colonialism provided a theoretical, a 'social scientific,' explanation for Chicano Studies' ideological role" (Contreras 283). The model was developed by a wide variety of scholars like Mario Barrera, Carlos Muñoz, Charles Ornelas, and Rodolfo Acuña (Barrera, Muñoz, and Ornelas). In the following years, the internal colonial model, with an increasingly Marxist tinge, became the alternative perspective in order to engage in activist research (García 27; Muñoz, *Quest* 30; Muñoz, *Youth* 148).

An example was the 1974 special issue of *Aztlán* (vol. 5), edited by Carlos Muñoz (1). In this issue, Mario Barrera pointed out how political scientists continued to use myths and stereotypes in their analysis of the Mexican American. He pointed out that Chicano(a) scholars faced cooptation if they remained close to their academic field of training: "There is great temptation to accept the assumptions of the profession and the funding agencies, since this makes it much easier to work in that environment" (23). Therefore, Chicanos(as) needed an interdisciplinary model based on an historical perspective:

> [S]ubstituting Chicano political scientists for Anglo political scientists will not in itself provide a meaningful discipline. A re-definition of the study of politics, which will challenge existing approaches at their theoretical and methodological base is needed to develop effective strategies for change and alternative conceptions of a just society. (24)

Barrera argued that to avoid the failures of social science, the scholar needed to turn to internal colonialism as a way to understand the Mexican American situation. He suggested that the internal colonial model offered an escape from disciplinary constraints and allowed for an explication of the contradictions of American society. What he left undeveloped was the relationship between internal colonialism and interdisciplinarity. Although he suggested that an historical perspective offered some resolution to the empiricism of social science, he was not clear regarding how an interdisciplinary model could avoid the epistemological constraints of academic practices.

But the internal colonialism did not last as the paradigm of Chicano studies. Both liberal disciplinary challenges together with Marxism disrupted the aim for a Chicano studies research paradigm. Any close reading of these scholars reveals significant theoretical differences that resulted from their particular understanding of capitalism, colonialism, internal colonialism, and race. These differences, which I cannot trace here, as well as the challenges by other perspectives, often led these thinkers to reduce the internal colonial model to some expression of interdisciplinarity (Soldatenko). Practitioners of the model resorted to the claim that by using an interdisciplinary approach, they could avoid disciplinary blind spots and narrowly defined intellectual practices. Thus interdisciplinarity became the "radical break" sought by Chicano studies.

Some Chicano(a) scholars agreed that the only way to understand the Mexican American condition and devise a political response was to comprehend the structures that created domination. The key was to analyze the institutional mechanisms by which dominant groups maintain their power and privilege (Rocco 561). A fusion of internal colonialism and Marxism became the preferred manner to describe the American system of domination. These scholars further assumed that this framework necessarily resulted in an activist program. With this approach, Chicano scholarship brought together theory and praxis. The internal colonial model with its structural methodology therefore was not an academic (or bourgeois) enterprise and did not seek academic answers; it was a revolutionary program. The explication of U.S. capitalism would help disentangled the Chicano(a) from the academy's structure and rules of operation and prepared him/her for practical political action. In this manner, interdisciplinarity also could stand as a method to explore the structures of American oppression and assist in the development of an activist political engagement. Interdisciplinarity thus imagined would reveal the contradictions in the U.S. social and political structures and prepare the revolutionary agenda to make a new order.

Many Chicano studies scholars believed that their analysis could exist outside the academic structures of knowledge. In a revealing footnote, Almaguer asserted that social science has always been an ideological tool meant to distort history, mystify reality, and justify oppression (52–53). Therefore, there was no good social science; all social science was ideological. He implied that the internal colonial model could exist outside academic knowledge and therefore could avoid ideological confusion. The internal colonial model was not part of bourgeois ideology. For most of these writers, the model was the result of the correct application of a theory that could truly explain the Mexican American condition and provide a real basis for change. For instance, Muñoz, in his dissertation, wrote that the scholar must provide a critical analysis aimed at the construction . . . of a responsible ideology that can become a foundation for the development of viable strategies for social change in the urban barrios and the creation of alternative institutions conducive to the decolonization of Chicano America. (11)

Muñoz added that the only way to reach this conclusion was to escape disciplinary bonds. Only an interdisciplinary approach could help Chicanos(as) understand the Mexican American condition: "For it is my belief that Chicano Studies, due to its interdisciplinary scope as opposed to any traditional discipline, has the potential to more adequately deal with the questions that are underscored in this study" (16).

Because interdisciplinarity became the link between the nonacademic revolutionary hope of Chicano studies and the internal colonial model/ structural methodology as an academic practice, Chicano(a) scholars found themselves defining interdisciplinarity as central to the epistemological revolution within the academy. Interdisciplinary work was perceived to avoid the limits of traditional social science and humanities and thereby provided a method, methodology, and epistemological revolution to Chicano studies scholarship. Even for those scholars who were unsure of their own views on internal colonialism or a structural methodology, interdisciplinarity was a code for Chicano studies research *in toto*. For example, Carlos Ortega accepted Muñoz's challenge to develop a discipline of Chicano studies with its particular paradigm. Yet for Ortega, internal colonialism in any of its configurations was "too narrow, deterministic and unsatisfactory." Rather, he saw a different paradigm on the rise. The new paradigm that marked the "uniqueness" of Chicano studies was "its interdisciplinary and comparative focus" (xi).

In an early essay, Juan Gómez-Quiñones argued that Chicano history "will call for rigorous interdisciplinary research and innovative methodology" (1). Although he acknowledged the tentative nature of his postulations, he asserted that Chicano history needed a conceptual framework that juggled the relationship among culture, economics, psychology, sociology, and history of the Mexican American—as expressed by various disciplines. Earlier, Chavarría had claimed that Chicano studies had to take in all of the diversity of the Mexican American experience (175). Thus he maintained a balance in his historical practice between his modified colonial perspective and interdisciplinarity. Chavarría left the impression that the best interdisciplinary practice was found in history (177).

Institutionally, we find the same push for interdisciplinarity. For instance, when we look at the early years of the Chicano studies program at the University of California, Berkeley, Chicanos(as) proposed a curriculum that would continue the "growth in Chicano Studies towards permanence without rigidity, towards academic excellence without academic ossification" (Hernandez-Chavez et al. i). For the authors, this curriculum was a rejection of the dominant Anglo value system that excluded all things Mexican American, especially their culture. Chicano studies would rectify this imbalance. "Here the perspective is an 'objective' one in the sense that what is discovered is true only as it is cut free of bias, no matter what source its springs from." To achieve this goal, Chicano studies had to rely on a strong interdisciplinary structure linking the social sciences, humanities, and the arts (1–3). At the University of California, Los Angeles, we encounter a similar institutionalization of interdisciplinarity. When the Mexican American Cultural Center introduced its curriculum to the Academic Senate for its approval, it sought to establish an interdisciplinary and interdepartmental major in Chicano studies (Mexican American Cultural 2). The Center's curriculum would be interdisciplinary, with special emphasis in three areas of study—the humanities, education, and social science.

From the first articulation of Chicano studies, the demand for autonomy and self-determination in academic work was expressed as a desire to use an interdisciplinary studies approach. To engage in traditional disciplinary work would not allow Chicanos(as) to control their intellectual work or produce scholarship that was for the community. The only manner to engage in research by Chicanos(as) for Chicanos(as) was to practice interdisciplinary work. But what did this mean? Was interdisciplinary work a particular method that brought together different disciplines to focus on a particular topic? Was it a methodology that could be unfolded within a discipline that allowed other disciplinary methods to bleed into the research program? Was it an epistemological vision that potentially went beyond all disciplines?

Faced with the biased or nonexistent academic knowledge of the Mexican American, many Chicano(a) campus activists argued that the social sciences and the humanities could not provide an understanding of the Mexican American condition. Academic disciplines lacked the epistemic paradigms and the methodological tools to understand the Mexican American experience. Thus many early Chicano studies scholars who wished to engage the academy, distrusting their disciplinary training, turned to what they thought stood outside the academic boundaries. Interdisciplinarity, multidisciplinarity, and transdisciplinarity were the answer to their intellectual quest. Moreover, this seemed to create an academic practice that allowed for direct social and political intervention in racist America. Whether or not one accepted internal colonialism, Chicano studies practitioners found it easier to postulate interdisciplinarity as the solution to the limits of academic work. This interdisciplinarity became the epistemic and methodological approach of nascent Chicano studies.

Interdisciplinarity as Part of the Hidden Curriculum

What few early Chicano(a) scholars realized was that interdisciplinarity could not provide an escape from academic intellectual or administrative practices. They did not recognize that interdisciplinarity was simply another alternative disciplinary practice and part of the hidden curriculum (Margolis). Chicano(a) campus activists and academics therefore could not use interdisciplinarity to escape the constraints of the academy. For this reason, Chicano studies never became an oppositional force to the epistemic practices or a revolutionary tool in the transformation of the political, economic, and social structure. Rather, interdisciplinarity served to corral and control Chicano studies and its practitioners. Why was this the case? What were the necessarily limits to interdisciplinarity?

Disciplines and interdisciplinary are complimentary parts of the American academic enterprise (Frodeman and Mitcham).

> The usual response to the problem of "the collapse of the disciplines" has been to promote interdisciplinary teaching and scholarship. But interdisciplinarity is not only completely consistent with disciplinarity—the concept that each academic field has its own distinctive program of inquiry—it actually depends on that concept. (Menand, "Marketplace" 52)

Disciplinary boundaries serve to confine particular methods, methodologies, and epistemologies together with an agreed-on set of assumptions and practices (Stanley and Wise). These boundaries allow disciplines to claim institutional and intellectual control of particular academic spaces. Moreover, the acolytes patrol the discipline, overlapping with departments, to make sure practitioners successfully manipulate its procedures and remain faithful to its creed and loyal to other adherents. "Disciplines/disciples fiercely defend their space, patrol boundaries, and regard those who either intrude or disrupt with suspicion" (Bird 467). Disciplines serve to preserve a particular expression of the curricular status quo. This defense of disciplinary parochialism also accounts for claims on other disciplines' territories by the use of favored tropes of the aggressive discipline—a form of disciplinary imperialism (Sayer 2).

These U.S. disciplinary practices matured in the post–War World II era as part of the reconfiguration of U.S. higher education and the American college system. One can read the construction of the system of majors, electives, general education requirements, departments, and other tools together with the consolidation of disciplines. Earlier expressions of the American college had allowed for a different articulation of the college system with a different and greater flexibility to the disciplines. Therefore the contemporary American college education that emerged from the debates of the 1930s and 1940s is tied to the establishment of the disciplines, with their particular limitations (Rudolph; Lucas; Boyer; Brubacher and Rudy; Veysey). We should further add that U.S. higher education was linked to the development of the Cold War (Menand, "Undisciplined" 55) and American exceptionalism (Ross).

This mid-century revolution of American higher education that gave us the discipline simultaneously created the need for interdisciplinary research and teaching. Frodeman and Mitcham, following Heidegger, argue that "the disciplinary formations of modern science set the stage for further interdisciplinary interactions—and thereby new disciplinary formations" (507). Klein notes the central role interdisciplinarity played in the general education reform movement and the great book debates. Almost from the start, the link between a discipline and department did not hold up, especially in light of how different colleges and universities defined administrative functions. Furthermore, the intellectual rationale for a discipline was constantly in flux, given changes in philosophical, methodological, and technological practices. The sciences, for example, moved to construct zones where disciplines/departments either created new interdisciplinary fields or formed mushier disciplinary boundaries by creating multiplicities of subfields that could appear in different departments. Thus different departments shared the subfield of biophysics or created interdisciplinary disciplines like neuroscience, biochemistry, or cybernetics. In the humanities and social sciences, similar disciplinary/interdisciplinary structures were fashioned. Some argue that today the advancement of knowledge occurs in these new subfields and new disciplines.

Many 1960s radicals thought that interdisciplinary work could avoid the nature of the disciplines, in particular their disciplining of its adherents. Moreover, interdisciplinarity was seen as part of a radical politics (Bird 467). Bird's research on women's studies highlights the way feminists thought of interdisciplinarity as holistic in opposition to discipline's particularism (469). Yet it became apparent to feminists that the hope inspired by interdisciplinarity faded. Thus Bird concludes, "My interviews suggest that rather than the system, either inside or outside the academy, knowledge was reined in and brought back into the intellectual and physical spaces that constitute traditional disciplines" (474). One could add that interdisciplinarity reinforced the parochial nature of disciplines (Frodeman and Mitcham 507).

Like the disciplines, interdisciplinarity was simply one of the many tools to sustain and manage U.S. academic practices. One might add that interdisciplinarity was central to the creation and preservation of disciplinary boundaries and order. It is both ironic and tragic that Chicano studies activists turned to interdisciplinarity as a way to construct their academic space. Maybe this was a case of Audre Lorde's warning about trying to build an autonomous and critical space with the master's tool (99).

Simultaneously, interdisciplinarity was the preferred institutional mechanism to control nascent women's and ethnic studies programs. When student and community protest forced institutions to construct ethnic studies programs, administrators channeled these desires into institutionally acceptable structures. For example, the University of California, Berkeley, effectively disrupted the hopes of the Third World Strike. As UC Berkeley's Chancellor Roger Heyns noted in his request to UC President Charles Hitch,

> With proper planning the Ethnic Studies curricula should be interdisciplinary in the best sense; and, with proper institutional controls and safeguards against political and ideological abuse, they may provide us with a highly instructive model for undergraduate education on a broad front. ("Memo" 2)

In other words, interdisciplinarity was an institutional operating system that provided the façade of avoiding disciplines and operating outside administrative and academic senate structures. But as can be seen in Heyn's remarks, interdisciplinarity was another institutional practice—with its established hierarchy and rules. In this same memorandum, he stressed that the ethnic studies center would proceed "at every stage in accordance with the principles and procedures" required by the institution ("Memo" 3; "Chancellor's Report"). Given this control, Hitch accepted the new programs, including Chicano studies (Hitch; Heyns, "Statement").

In the end, nascent Chicano studies was stillborn. Activists' belief that it had avoided disciplinary boundaries and could engage in activist research was soon revealed to be mistaken. The hope that interdisciplinarity could provide the epistemic and methodological break was not the case. Simultaneously, the belief that an interdisciplinary program could form a parallel organization to institutional academic practices was also revealed to be false. The Chicano studies program in all its manifestations found interdisciplinarity to be another academic structure to manage Chicano studies.

An Afterward: The Need for Unruliness

Frodeman and Mitcham, building on the work of Julie Thompson Klein, hope for a "critical interdisciplinarity" that could replace disciplines by turning to a global, humanist, free-ranging, and practical knowledge (508). They argue that only a critical interdisciplinarity can circumscribe current disciplinary overproduction. Even scholars who feel that interdisciplinarity has fallen victim to the institution and mirrors the preexisting structure see possibilities. Ethan Kleinberg, for example, writes that interdisciplinarity programs can resist "the temptation of total autonomy and independence lest they become isolated fortresses each beholden to their own particular methodology, ideology, or canon" (10). The current success of interdisciplinary programs in American colleges, they believe, speaks well of the possible success of a critical interdisciplinarity.

Today, institutions promote their programs or colleges by calling attention to their interdisciplinary curriculum and/or institutions (Kleinberg). As Davis points out, the contemporary American college system sells their institution to a new generation of consumers by tempting them with innovative "interdisciplinary programs." Some judge that the era of the disciplines has come to an end: "[T]he traditional disciplines have by now almost all been co-opted" (Menand, "Undisciplined" 54). But they do not see this as a negative. In a paper for the British Sociological Association, Andrew Sayer states, "I believe we should celebrate rather than mourn the decline of disciplines" (2). Menand advances, "The collapse of disciplines must mean the collapse of interdisciplinarity as well; for interdisciplinarity is the institutional ratification of the logic of disciplinarity" ("Marketplace"

12). For some, from this collapse something new has arisen: postdisciplinary studies. Sayer defines postdisciplinarity as the point at which "scholars forget about disciplines and whether ideas can be identified with any particular one; they identify with learning rather than with disciplines" (5). He adds that this really suggests a return to *pre*-disciplinary studies. Menand proposes that versions of interdisciplinary programs were attempts to be antidisciplinary because of their view that the disciplines were arbitrary. He then states that antidisciplinarity was an academic "phase of postdisciplinarity" ("Marketplace" 11).

Yet questions remain. We need to explore whether a critical interdisciplinarity or postdisciplinarity can achieve the hope that many of us had in the 1960s to break the control of the hidden curriculum. Does the division between a critical and an instrumental interdisciplinarity, for instance, really provide a space to not only save intellectual and radical work but also rescue Chicano(a) studies? Unfortunately, it seems that this is another example of *plus ça change, plus c'est la même chose*.

I believe that we cannot salvage interdisciplinarity from U.S. higher education and its hidden curriculum. From my perspective, the concept of interdisciplinarity, as well as multidisciplinarity, transdisciplinarity, crossdisciplinarity, pluridisciplinarity, and on, is beyond redemption. "*Le seul trait commun à tous les 'interdisciplinaristes' tient à ce qu'inter est au minimum interruption (de l'interruption), beaucoup plus qu'intersection*" (Dubreuil 6). Rather, we need to find a way to demolish the American college system that is incapable of escaping its Cold War vision of orientalism and American exceptionalism. The disciplines and their interdisciplinarities must go, as they are both central to contemporary American higher education.

Unfortunately, I am not ready to present a solution regarding what can replace the discipline/interdisciplinary structure. Initially, I thought a discussion/debate about concepts like undisciplined, postdisciplinary, predisciplinary, and antidisciplinary might serve as a start. But then I found myself back on the turf of academic institutions, with their particular rules and limitations. Then I recalled my earlier reading of Paul Feyerabend and his call for an anarchist methodology.

> The attempt to increase liberty, to lead a full and rewarding life, and the corresponding attempt to discover the secrets of nature and of man entails, therefore, the rejection of all universal standards and of all rigid traditions. (20)

This rejection might move us away from the American educational system as it now exists. This may allow us to play with a multiplicity of intellectual perspectives and tools—some not legitimated by the academy. For this reason I prefer to think of Laurent Dubreuil's use of *"l'indiscipliné"* as unruliness (6). Maybe what we need is a good intellectual free-for-all, an intellectual carnival that abandons academic constraints yet allows us to reason beyond boundaries. So instead of more interdisciplinarity, we need more unruliness.

Works Cited

Acuña, Rodolfo. *Occupied America*. San Francisco: Canfield Press, 1972.

Almaguer, Tomás. "Historical Notes on Chicano Oppression: The Dialectics of Racial and Class Domination in North America." *Aztlán* 5.1 and 5.2 (1974): 27–56.

Almaguer, Tomás. 1971. "Toward the Study of Chicano Colonialism." *Aztlán* 2.1 (1971): 7–21.

Barrera, Mario. "The Study of Politics and the Chicano." *Aztlán* 5.1 and 6.2 (1974): 9–26.

Barrera, Mario, Carlos Muñoz, and Charles Ornelas. "The Barrio as an Internal Colony." *Politics and Peoples in Urban Society*. Ed. Harlan Hahn. Beverly Hills: Sage Publications, 1972: 281–301.

Bird, Elizabeth. "Disciplining the Interdisciplinary: Radicalism and the Academic Curriculum." *British Journal of Sociology of Education* 22.4 (2001): 463–78.

Boyer, Ernest L. *College: The Undergraduate Experience in America*. New York: Carnegie Foundation, 1986.

Brubacher, John S., and Willis Rudy. *Higher Education in Transition: A History of American Colleges and Universities*. New Brunswick: Transaction Publishers, 1997.

Chavarría, Jesús. "A Précis and a Tentative Bibliography on Chicano History." *Aztlán* 1.1 (1970): 133–41.

Chicano Coordinating Council on Higher Education. 1970. *El Plan de Santa Bárbara: A Chicano Plan for Higher Education*. Santa Barbara: La Causa Publications.

Contreras, Raoul. *The Ideology of the Political Movement for Chicano Studies*. Diss. University of California, Los Angeles, 1986.

Davis, Lennard J. "A Grand Unified Theory of Interdisciplinarity." *Chronicle of Higher Education* 53.40 (2007): B8-B9.

Dubreuil, Laurent. 2007. "Defauts de saviors." *Labyrinthe: Atelier Interdisciplinaire* 27 (2007): 13–26.

Elizondo, Sergio D. "Critical Areas of Need for Research and Scholastic Study." *Epoca* 1.2 (1971): 1–7.

Feyerabend, Paul. *Against Method*. London: Verso, 1975.

Frodeman, Robert, and Carl Mitcham. "New Directions in Interdisciplinarity: Broad, Deep, and Critical." *Bulletin of Science, Technology and Society* 27.6 (2007): 506–14.

García, Mario. 1974. "Internal Colonialism and the Chicano." *La Luz* 3.8 (1974): 27–28.

Gómez-Quiñones, Juan. "Toward a Perspective on Chicano History." *Aztlán* 2.2 (1971): 1–49.

Guerra, Manuel H. "What Are the Objectives of Chicano Studies?" *Epoca* 1:2 (1971): 8–12.

Hernandez-Chavez, Eduardo et al. "A Proposed Curriculum for an A.A.B. Major in Chicano Studies." UCB Ethnic Studies Library Archives Chicano Studies Box 5, 1971.

Heyns, Roger W. "Chancellor's Report on Ethnic Studies." *Daily Californian* 8 Apr. 1969, 1–2.

Heyns, Roger W. "Memo." UCB Ethnic Studies Library Archives Chicano Studies Library Box 3, 1969.

Heyns, Roger W. "Statement by Chancellor Roger W. Heyn." UCB Ethnic Studies Library Archives Chicano Studies Library Box 3, 1969.

Hitch, Charles L. "Memo." UCB Ethnic Studies Library Archives Chicano Studies Library Box 3, 1969.

Klein, Julie Thompson. *Interdisciplinarity: History, Theory, and Practice*. Detroit: Wayne State UP, 1990.

Kleinberg, Ethan. "Interdisciplinary Studies at a Crossroads." *Liberal Education* 94.1 (2008): 6–11.

López, Manuel I. "The Role of the Chicano Student in the Chicano Studies Program." *Epoca* 1.2 (1971): 13–17.

Lorde, Audre. "The Master's Tools Will Never Dismantle the Master's House." *This Bridge Called My Back: Writings by Radical Women of Color*. Ed. Cherríe Moraga and Gloria Anzaldúa. New York: Kitchen Table 1981. 98–101.

Lucas, Christopher L. *American Higher Education: A History*. New York: St. Martin's Press, 1994.

Margolis, Eric, ed. *Hidden Curricula in Higher Education*. New York: Routledge, 2001.

Menand, Louis. "The Marketplace of Ideas." American Council of Learned Societies, Occasional Paper No. 49. 2001. 13 Sept. 2008 <http://archives.acls.org/op/49_Marketplace_of_Ideas.htm>.

Menand, Louis. "Undisciplined." *The Wilson Quarterly* 25.4 (2001): 51–60.

Mexican American Cultural Center. "Steering Committee Meeting Minutes." UCLA CSRC Library Collection, 1970.

Muñoz, Carlos. "Politics and the Chicano: On the Status of the Literature." *Aztlán* 5.1 and 2 (1974): 1–7.

Muñoz, Carlos. *The Politics of Chicano Urban Protest: A Model of Political Analysis*. Diss. Claremont Graduate School, 1973.

Muñoz, Carlos. "The Quest for Paradigm: The Development of Chicano Studies and Intellectuals." *History, Culture, and Society: Chicano Studies in the 1980s*. Ed. Mario García and Francisco Lomelí. Ypsilanti: Bilingual Press, 1983: 19–36.

Muñoz, Carlos. *Youth, Identity, Power: The Chicano Generation*. London: Verso, 1989.

Ortega, Carlos F. 1997. "Introduction: Chicano Studies as a Discipline." *Chicano Studies: Survey and Analysis*. Ed. Dennis J. Bixler-Márquez et al. Dubuque, IA: Kendall/Hunt Publishing Comp, 1997: v-xiv.

Rocco, Raymond. "A Critical Perspective on the Study of Chicano Politics." *Western Political Quarterly* 30.4 (1977): 558–73.

Rochin, Refugio I. "The Short and Turbulent Life of Chicano Studies." *Social Science Quarterly* 53.4 (1973): 884–94.

Rivera, Julius. *On Chicano Studies*. Washington, D.C.: Chicano Studies Institute, 1970.

Ross, Dorothy. *The Origins of American Social Science*. Cambridge: Cambridge UP, 1991.

Rudolph, Frederick. *Curriculum: A History of the American Undergraduate Course of Study Since 1636*. San Francisco: Jossey-Bass Publishers, 1989.

Sánchez, Lionel. 1970. *La Raza Community and Chicano Studies*. Washington, D.C.: Chicano Studies Institute, 1970.

Sayer, Andrew. 1999. "Long Live Postdisciplinary Studies! Sociology and the Curse of Disciplinary Parochialism/Imperialism." Department of Sociology, Lancaster University. 5 Dec. 2003. 15 Sept. 2008 <http://www.lancs.ac.uk/fass/sociology/papers/sayer-long-live-postdisciplinary-studies.pdf>.

Soldatenko, Michael. *Chicano Studies: The Genesis of a Discipline*. Tucson: University of Arizona Press, 2009.

Stanley, Liz, and Sue Wise. "Method, Methodology and Epistemology in Feminist Research Processes." *Feminist Praxis*. Ed. Liz Stanley. London: Routledge, 1990: 20–60.

"United Mexican American Student Conference 1968." UCLA CSRC Library Collection.

Veysey, Laurence R. *The Emergence of the American University*. Chicago: U of Chicago P, 1965.

Interdisciplinary Claims to Social Justice

Chapter Ten

Whiteness Studies and the Paradox of Particularity

Robyn Wiegman

Let me begin with the story of two museums. A number of years ago, in Laurens, South Carolina, John Howard built one in the old Echo Theater. "The World's Only Klan Museum," blared the marquee. Inside, there were robes and books, confederate flags, pocket knives, "White Power" sweatshirts, even T-shirts declaring "It's a White Thing. You Wouldn't Understand." In Alabama, the Birmingham Civil Rights Institute is located across from the Sixteenth Street Baptist Church, site of multiple bombings in the 1960s, including the now-famous one that killed four black girls. Inside the museum are replicas and remnants from the period of official segregation: public bathrooms marked "white" and "colored," pieces of a yellow school bus, a segregated street scene. In the gift shop, patrons can purchase African American history books, posters, postcards, T-shirts emblazoned with the image of Dr. Martin Luther King. When the local authorities in Laurens tried to deny Howard a business license to sell souvenirs in the Redneck Shop, he responded with legal action.[1] For both Howard and his civil rights lawyer, the existence of the Alabama museum established the legal precedent for the Klan Museum, guaranteeing Howard's right, in his terms, to display pride in being white.[2]

So many of the characteristics of U.S. racial discourse in the 1990s are exhibited in John Howard's story. Most notably, the language of civil rights is mobilized to protect whiteness, which is cast not only as a minority identity, but also as one injured by the denial of public representation. In this scenario, whiteness is revealed as embodied and particular, which left critics have long proposed as the means to disempower white supremacy as a whole. But Howard's case was settled out of court in his favor, and the shape of white identity formation well into the twenty-first century has remained simultaneously injured and powerful. What then is the relationship between disembodied universals and embodied particulars for thinking social justice and race today?[3] To answer this question, this essay advances three interrelated claims about whiteness. The first is historical: that the distinctiveness of southern white supremacist identity since the Civil War hinges on a repeated appeal to the minoritized, injured "nature" of whiteness. To be injured—by the economic transformations of Emancipation, by the perceived loss of all-white social spaces, by the reformation of a national imaginary of white citizen-subjects—provides the basis of white supremacist collective self-fashioning, which has and continues to function by producing the threat of its own extinction as the justification and motivation for violent retaliations.[4] The second claim is theoretical: To the extent that critical race theorists have assumed that the power of whiteness arises from its appropriation of the universal and that the universal is opposed to and hence devoid of the particular, we have failed to interpret the tension between particularity and universality that characterizes not simply the legal discourse of race (where early documents enfranchise the "white person"), but the changing contours of white power and privilege in the last three centuries. Apartheid structures, both slavery and Jim Crow segregation, indeed universalized whiteness through the entitlements of the citizen-subject, but they also simultaneously mobilized a vast social geometry of white particularity, as the declarative warning "For Whites Only" ominously suggested. While the post-segregation era has put such white supremacist particularity to the test, new and quite powerful strategies of particularization have emerged. The ways in which white power has and continues to reconstruct itself in the context of segregation's demise leads to my third and final claim. But first, I need to tell you more about Howard's story.

In Laurens, a multiracial town of about ten thousand people, Howard was not a popular man. Everyone wanted him and his museum out. This was a town with a violent history. "For decades," Rick Bragg writes, "a piece of rotted rope dangled from a railroad trestle, just outside this little town, a reminder of the last lynching in Laurens County. It was back in 1913, but people still talk of the black man wrongly accused of rape, and the white mob that hanged him." The lynch rope was not removed until 1986 when the trestle was destroyed, which means that when Howard opened his museum, little more than a decade had gone by without the public display of violent white supremacy. Although no whites were moved in the course of seventy-three years to undo the master sign of their privilege, its resurrection in the downtown Klan Museum was met with an outpouring of white alarm. Why one response and not the other? One answer has to do with the politics of social space: The museum was located in the center part of town, whereas the lynch rope hung outside the town, along the road to and from Laurens's historically black section. The lynch rope thus signified the panoptic power of whiteness—always present but never fully visible; the Klan Museum, on the other hand, embodied white supremacy in an open, public display, implicitly fixing it in narratives of local and national violence. To protest the museum meant, for whites, protesting the particularizing pact between segregationist ideologies and white embodied identity. It also meant participating in—indeed actively forging—a counter-whiteness whose primary characteristic was its disaffiliation from white supremacist practices.

My third claim involves the disaffiliation that might be thought of as the pedagogical lesson for whites of civil rights reform, when the transformation from segregation to integration reconstructed not only the materiality of black life in the United States, but also the national imaginary of race and race discourse within which white identity since the 1960s has been reconfigured. Integration, no matter how failed in its utopian projections of a nation beyond race division, nonetheless powerfully suspended the acceptability of white supremacy's public display, so much so that the hegemonic formation of white identity by the end of the twentieth century must be understood as taking shape in the rhetorical, if not always political, register of disaffiliation from white supremacist practices and discourses. This does not mean that racism and white supremacy have been dissolved or that their consequences today are less damaging, exclusive, or exploitative than they were under official national segregation. Rather, by the late 1990s, segregationist practices and their Klan-esque defenses would come to serve as the referential framework for cultural references to white supremacy in general, which enabled many white Americans to join efforts to undo civil rights reform without acknowledging their contributions to ongoing reconfigurations of white power and privilege.

This essay proceeds as an analysis of white racial formation in the aftermath of segregation by juxtaposing two different and politically contradictory engagements with white identity in order to deliberate on the fraught nexus of universality and particularity that constrains and constructs what George Lipsitz once called "the impossibility of the antiracist white subject."[5] I begin by looking first at the film that one month before the Oklahoma City bombing garnered best picture honors for 1994. In *Forrest Gump*, the symptomatic anxieties of late-twentieth-century white racial formation are set into play, with the narrative performing a series of strategic reinventions of a post-segregationist antiracist whiteness—what I call liberal whiteness—as a means to rejuvenate "America" in the aftermath of social upheaval and crisis for its entrance into a transnational capitalist order. Although the film's overall trajectory is of the most reactionary political kind, it fulfills the cultural desire to forget what we do not know how to remember by remembering in haphazard and incoherent ways the images of racial trauma and social dissent that we cannot yet forget—the physical violence that attended desegregation, the street protests of the sixties, the bloodbath of the Vietnam War, and the murder of national political leaders. Through its use of television images and in the passive construction of our model spectator—Forrest Gump, who neither can nor wants to "know"—the film participates in the contemporary struggle to reform whiteness by moving its protagonist through a range of antiracist positions. In so doing, *Forrest Gump* offers a provocative vantage point from which to consider the emergence in the 1990s of the academic project of whiteness studies, with its emphasis on white particularity and political disaffiliations from white racial power.[6] By reading the film as a precursor to further discussion of whiteness studies, this paper explores the emergent disciplinary apparatus that might be said to have produced and defined self-conscious attempts to establish the study of whiteness as an academic field. Call it, if you will, an analysis of the compulsion to form a disciplinary endeavor called whiteness studies in the first place.

Back to the Future

At the Civil Rights Institute in Birmingham, Alabama, visitors begin their tour by taking a seat on one of the narrow white benches that fill a rather small, darkened room behind the admissions booth. As the lights fade, an entire wall comes to life with documentary footage narrating the history of the state and its long and bloody battle to desegregate.[7] When the documentary ends and the lights return, the movie screen wall rises dramatically to reveal the space of the museum on the other side. Every visitor to the museum must walk through that screen, so to speak, into rooms and corridors that contain artifacts of the material culture of segregation and the fight to undo it. At nearly every turn, there are more screens—a mock 1960s storefront where boxy televisions broadcast images of encounters between Freedom Fighters and the police; a video wall where multiple contemporary television's juxtapose racist commercials, political interviews, and the speeches of Martin Luther King. In a grand gesture where history and the present meet, the visitor is positioned in front of a picture window that looks out onto the Sixteenth Street Baptist Church across the street.

Forrest Gump, you might remember, is set at a bus stop, and one of its main technological innovations is its clever insertion of the protagonist into nationally recognizable television scenes. In the most famous instance, Gump becomes a participant in George Wallace's failed attempt to block black entrance to the University of Alabama following the court order to desegregate. Positioned initially as a member of the crowd, Gump symbolically joins the students when he retrieves one of their dropped books; in the spatializing logic of segregation, Gump is here a race traitor. He crosses the lines of racial demarcation, disengaging from a white racist social body to join the black students, but the innocence of his action crucially depoliticizes the scene. It is this kind of race trait-ing that most characterizes the film, as Gump's movement in personal moral terms not only displaces the necessity of conscious identifications as precursors to collective political action, but also consigns the entire realm of the "historical" to television, which installs a consumptive spectator as the ultimate witness—and postracist subject—of political change itself.

In its extraction of Gump from the legacy of southern segregationist identity, the film, we might say, de-essentializes the relationship among white skin, white privilege, and white racism, answering (or so it seems) the clarion call of contemporary theory to render race a social construction. But *Forrest Gump* can only imagine a nonessentialist whiteness by shifting the signification of segregation from emblem of black oppression and white material privilege to a form of white injury. This shift enables segregation to serve not only as the historical form of white particularity that must be disavowed, but also as the means for crafting a liberal whiteness that is now, rhetorically speaking, kin to blackness. The film's preoccupation with the resignification of segregation is apparent at the outset, as the narrative tellingly offers a black woman to serve as the bus stop audience for the childhood portion of Gump's tale.[8] Without recognition of the meaning of her only words, "my feet hurt," Gump remembers his first pair of shoes, or I should say, he remembers through his *desire for* the woman's shoes his own personal history of mobility as a series of restrictions. The first was physical, as Forrest was forced to wear leg braces to correct his curvature of the spine; the second was social, as Forrest endured ridicule and exclusion because of his physical and mental disabilities. If the analogy between segregationist racialization and Forrest's restricted mobility, ostracism, and physical "difference" isn't clear, the narrative locates the scene of Forrest's social exclusion on a school bus where his classmates eagerly refuse him a seat. (Later in the film, he will again be refused a seat on a bus by his fellow inductees in the army.) These scenes perform two functions: They rewrite segregation as a discourse of injury no longer specific to black bodies, which installs whiteness as injury, and they define that injury as private, motivated not by a social system but by the prejudices and moral lacks of individuals who seem simply not to know better. That Forrest can "know better" without ever *knowing* is of course the deep irony of this film; from this anti-epistemological position, he gets to utter the sentimental punch line: "I may not be a smart man, but I know how to love."

If *Forrest Gump* is a liberal white rendition of the history of segregationist apartheid, if the film can be said to be a walk through the archive of popular national memory, its project does not end with white occupation of injury. That would be a version of Howard's story. *Forrest Gump* has a more pedagogical mission: to demonstrate that difference and injury, even intellectual deficiency, are not impediments to the "American" way of life. The plot thus advances through scenes in which Forrest gains mobility, thereby exchanging injury for liberation and transcendence. As a kid being chased by his classmates, he magically breaks free of his leg braces; as a teenager being harassed by boys in a truck with a confederate flag license plate, his flight across a college football field results in a scholarship and an All-American athletic career. In Vietnam, his ability to run saves his life and the lives of others, and in the film's oddest and longest segment devoted to mobility, Gump spends three years running from shore to shore, redrawing the boundaries of the nation's geographic identity and demonstrating that no region (no state, no neighborhood, no city street) is off-limits or out of reach. All of this mobility critically recasts the segregationist history of the bus stop, even though that too must be left behind. In the final segments of the film, Forrest discovers that he doesn't need the bus to get where he is going, as he is only blocks away from his destination, where marriage, the domestic scenario, and, miraculously, a completed paternity ("Little Forrest") await. He can easily walk there.

In his exodus from the bus stop and its symbolic evocation of national struggle and racial strife, Gump is extricated from the public domain of the political in favor of an insulated private and domestic realm. Such a movement inscribes the cultural logic of what Lauren Berlant calls today's "intimate public sphere" where the family "usurps the modernist promise of the culturally vital, multiethnic city . . . [and] public life . . . [becomes] ridiculous and even dangerous to the nation" (5). That the family is imagined and indeed popularly imaged as white underscores the conservative racial agenda of this new public intimacy; in the case of *Forrest Gump*, it gives to the protagonist's incessant movement a final resting place: in the last scene, outside his ancestral home on an Alabama country road, the white father will board his now motherless but perfectly intelligent son on a school bus where, the film promises, little Forrest will never be denied a seat. This resolution, in which a sentimentalized white paternity ensures the survival of the nation-as-family, is predicated on Gump's celebrated failure to cognitively or narratively register the events he witnesses—predicated, that is, on Gump's native inability to forge anything but the most narcissistic and personalized of identifications, first with the mother who bore him and later with the child who utopicly doubles him. The film's commitment to a protagonist unable to read the historical archive through which he is moving demonstrates the prevailing assumption of the Reagan years during which, as Berlant states, "[the normal American] sees her/his identity as something sustained in private, personal, intimate relations; in contrast, only the abjected, degraded *lower* citizens of the United States will see themselves as sustained by public, coalitional, non-kin affiliations" (185).

The shift to the private and familial carries a certain risk, however, for a film whose protagonist is a southerner, an Alabaman, and the named descendent of the founder of the Ku Klux Klan, Nathan Bedford Forrest. Under these conditions, too much familial intimacy risks sustaining a white identity that the film is sentimentally invested in undoing, the identity, that is, of the overtly racist American: the white southerner. As I have already suggested, liberal whiteness is characterized by its disaffiliation from segregationist forms of white identity and identification. For this reason, the first flashback narrative of the film, told to the black female witness, features Gump's Confederate hero ancestor, a man who was born in poverty but grew rich as a slave trader and planter and who garnered both fame and shame during the Civil War as a brilliant, unconventional battle tactician who incited his men to massacre surrendering black troops

at Fort Pillow. But the film's Nathan Bedford Forrest is ludicrous, not powerful; in Gump's mind, he would "dress up in . . . robes and . . . bed sheets
and act like . . . ghosts or spooks or something." Gump's mother chose the
name to remind her son that "sometimes people do things that just don't
make no sense." The film's parable of naming displaces the intimate family relations that attach Gump to a genealogy of masculine aggression and
segregationist white supremacy, and in so doing it importantly diffuses any
feminist reading of the violence of patriarchal forms of inheritance.[9] As if
to emphasize this point, the patronymic, Forrest, is shifted to Gump's first
name, and the repetition of the line "My name is Forrest, Forrest Gump"
continually reminds us of this foundational displacement. In the liberal
white fantasy of *Forrest Gump*, the descendent of the founder of the Klan
can emerge at the end of the twentieth century shorn of his damaged
patriarchal inheritance, which is to say that the intimacy of familial, personal relations has now been successfully separated from the past and tied
instead to a prototypically American future. In the process, white power
and privilege are displaced from any inherent relation—historically, ideologically, politically—to white skin.[10]

The liberal whiteness formed from these narrative displacements
offers a subtle but telling commentary on one of the most volatile issues
of the 1990s, affirmative action. In "Whiteness as Property," Cheryl Harris distinguishes between corrective justice, which seeks "compensation
for discrete and 'finished' harm done to minority group members or their
ancestors" and distributive justice, which "is the claim an individual or
group has to the positions or advantages or benefits they would have been
awarded under fair conditions" (1781). According to Harris, the goals of
affirmative action—to address the harms done to those minoritized by racial
(or gendered) oppression—are undermined when corrective justice is the
interpretative frame, because not only is the harm assumed to be finished,
but also the practices through which harm has been done are individualized,
confined to those who perpetrated it and the one who endured it. In this
context, whites can claim to be innocent and therefore in need of counter-
legislative protection because they have not individually perpetuated harm.
This is the logic of Bakke as well as of California's Proposition 209, and of
course it is the model of compensation being worked out in *Forrest Gump*.
Gump's mother, you might recall, supports her family by running a room-
ing house at the old plantation that is the ancestral home in Greenbough,
Alabama, a narrative convenience that renders the family's historical connection to the economics of slavery if not deficient, at least not materially

advantageous. Whatever harm slavery inflicted is finished, and the privileges of economic gain that garner for white identity a material advantage have been narratively swept away. This does not mean that Gump will have no racial debt to pay, but that his debt is, first, not historical, not about the ongoing economic privilege of whiteness as a material effect of slavery and segregation, and, second, not collective, not about a social identity enhanced and protected by the law as an economic investment.

What, then, is Gump's debt? And why must there be a debt at all in a film so clearly devoted to the fantasy of humanist transcendence? To answer these questions, we need to consider Gump's accumulation of wealth and to return, in time, to the issues of shoes, specifically the red and white Nike running shoes that serve as visual cues of the diegetic present time of the film. Gump's accumulation of wealth has two primary forms: shrimp and computers. The shrimping business is borne of an interracial male confederation with Bubba, who gives Forrest a seat in the film's second passage through the scene of the school bus and who also gives to Gump all his knowledge about the shrimping business. When Bubba dies in the Vietnam War, Gump returns to the South and to shrimps, only to make it big when a hurricane conveniently destroys every other boat in the black-owned industry. Gump's knowledge is quite literally African American knowledge, but the conversion of that "labor," if you will, into accumulation is effected through nature, not society. Any debt to be paid is thus a personal one arising from Gump's friendship with Bubba and not from the material advantages accorded to whiteness as an economic privilege. In this parable of the economics of contemporary black–white relations, the debt to be paid by Gump to Bubba's family—of half the profits of the shrimp business—is defined not by hierarchy or history, but as an honor to intimate male friendship.

What is significant about *Forrest Gump*, of course, is its inability to imagine the black male as surviving the trauma of the racial history that Gump will supersede.[11] This is especially striking because the other form of debt that the film imagines for Gump is likewise borne of a male friendship and features Gump playing a role of compensation that has likewise been detached (in the film) from the responsibilities of the state: In his relationship with Lieutenant Dan, whose patriotic family has lost a son in every war since the Revolution, Gump both rescues and redeems the multiply injured white Vietnam veteran. Not surprisingly, this redemption is thematized through mobility as Lieutenant Dan, initially disabled by the loss of his legs in the war, comes finally to walk again (albeit with artificial limbs) in his last appearance in the film. Set at Gump's wedding to his childhood love Jenny, the symbolic reconstruction of Lieutenant Dan's traumatized white male body is accompanied by his own heterosexual completion as he announces his impending marriage to Susan, an Asian American woman. Whereas Jenny has functioned as the traumatized female body who is rescued through Gump but not saved because she *is* contaminated sexuality, Gump's ability to save Lieutenant Dan is figured as a restoration of masculinity via the agency of interracial heterosexuality.

But there is more to Susan's appearance than the predictable circulation of woman as emblem of a rejuvenated masculinity. Susan is the only person of Asian descent in a film that devotes significant narrative time to the Vietnam War and its aftermath, yet the film's commentary on the war is never able to reverberate beyond the sphere of intimate private relationships among U.S. men. Gump's debts, after all, are to black and white American men, which confines the racial discourse of the film to the traumatic resolutions of antiblack white supremacy. Susan evokes both a history and racial discourse of which the film has no mechanism or motive to speak, even as it requires her presence as both witness and accomplice to Lieutenant Dan's remasculinization.[12] Her insertion into the scene of heterosexual intimacy privatizes the national narrative of war in Southeast Asia, thereby displacing the economics of accumulation that have followed U.S. interventions in the region. I am referring here to the significance of Gump and Lieutenant Dan's investment in Apple Computers, which belongs to an industry whose transnational circuits of production and distribution are indelibly linked to postwar capitalist expansion in Southeast Asia. If the Vietnam War cost Lieutenant Dan his legs, his economic mobility is nonetheless enabled by it, as is Gump's, yet it is precisely this phenomenon that the film's thematic focus on segregation, mobility, and the resurrection of a privatized U.S. nation occludes. In moving the sites of the accumulation of wealth from shrimping to computer investments, *Forrest Gump* depicts without commentary capital's contemporary mobility from local, regional forms of industry to transnational practices of production and exchange.

With this in mind, we can return now to the opening scene of the film, where a feather floats gently from the sky to land on Gump's red and white Nike running shoes. As the first material detail offered of the protagonist, Gump's running shoes are simultaneously his signature and personal trademark, evincing not simply his hard-won physical mobility, but also his symbolic ability to move beyond the detritus of historical trauma.[13] Moreover, the Nike shoes "ground" Gump's magical movement in an unconscious relation to a commodity that itself had become associated in the 1990s with the worst aspects of transnational modes of production. In the context of media revelations about Nike's exploitative working conditions in Southeast Asia, the corporation's commodity presence in *Forrest Gump* seems quite overtly engaged in a project of resignification. Through Gump, Nike can seek the reification of all material relations that is the effect of Gump's mode of narration, which means participating in the film's celebration of the detachment of state from nation. This celebration is demonstrated in two moves: first, in the way that the televisual archive that Gump moves through works to disavow the power of presidents and other state leaders, and hence to undermine not simply the authority but also the value of contestation at the level of the state; and second, in the way the film endorses the "shore to shore" logic of nation as geographical entity that underlies Gump's seemingly motiveless three-year run across the United States.[14] With the state represented as the site of traumatic instability, loss of decorum, or simple comic incomprehensibility, the nation arises in illustrious geographical wholeness. Transporting Gump there, beyond the historical problematic of the bus stop, are his Nike running shoes; their resignification as a private commodity relation fulfills Nike's own corporate fantasy of an innocent (that is to say nonexploitative) historicity.

In the figure of the shoes, then, lies the film's investment in the simultaneous transnational accumulation of capital in the aftermath of imperial war and the reinvigoration of a national symbolic, rescued now through the individual's pedagogical identification with the commodity (and conversely, the commodity's identification of the individual). As Gump is marked quite literally first and foremost by the trademark, the trademark becomes the film's earliest mechanism for ascribing to Gump a particularizing identity. It is, importantly, an identity that situates him from the outset beyond the specific national contestations of the bus stop, beyond any recognition or reception of the lingering meaning of the black woman's utterance, "my feet hurt." Gump's debt, after all, has been paid; compensatory justice, imaginable only at the individual level, has been achieved; all that remains is the telling of the tale. If, in the film's formula, that telling takes shape as a walk through the archive of segregation and black–white racial relations, Gump's innocence, that is, his rescued whiteness, "stands" on his inexhaustible and dematerialized relation to the commodity.[15] As Gump declares about his chocolates, "I could eat about a million and a half of these."

White Studies in Forrest Gump's America

Forrest Gump's celebration of the white race traitor who defies the logic of segregation and the history of southern racism in order to participate innocently in the new order of global capital is certainly a far cry from the ideals of whiteness studies, which focuses on an object of study whose power and privilege it hopes to critically undo. Yet even as the popular and the academic move toward different political goals, they both begin their projects of rearticulating a post-segregationist white identity at the site of the historical. In *Forrest Gump*, this entails rendering the history of violent white power incomprehensible, if not comic—the Klan leader, remember, liked "to dress up in . . . robes and . . . bed sheets and act like . . . ghosts or spooks or something." Thus refunctioning the present as the origin for a new America no longer held in grief or guilt to a violently unredeemable past, the film confirms the ideological architecture of the contemporary anti-affirmative action movement. That is, it offers a white subject who becomes "particular" through a claim to social injury, thereby affirming not only that all historical racial debts have been paid (and hence that the historical is itself irrelevant), but also that there is finally no privileged linkage between the protocols of universality and white racial embodiment. At the same time, of course, Forrest Gump, like John Howard of the Klan, can only be injured as a white (and male) subject from the symbolic location of the universal, because it is the negation of the expectation or actuality of privilege that makes social injury for whites conceivable in the first place. By this, I mean that only from an implicit and prior claim to the universal can the particularity of white injury (and I am tempted to say the particularity of white identity) ever be articulated. Passing as a minoritized subject through the "non-sense" of the historical, the white subject thus reclaims its power on the far side, we might say, of civil rights reform.

Whiteness studies, by contrast, turns with urgency to the historical to serve as the critical construction site for constituting a post-segregationist antiracist white subject. In four regularly cited texts—David Roediger's *The Wages of Whiteness* and *Towards the Abolition of Whiteness,* Theodore Allen's *The Invention of the White Race*, and Noel Ignatiev's *How the Irish Became White*—social historians chart the effects of industrialization and with it wage labor on the racialization of ethnic immigrants in the nineteenth century. In so doing, they locate whiteness not in the epidermal "reality" of white skin, but in complex economic and political processes and practices. Key to the demonstration of the historical construction of whiteness is the story of the Irish who left their homeland as racialized subjects of British colonial rule to become white in the course of nineteenth-century U.S. life. As W. E. B. Du Bois determined nearly a century ago in *Black Reconstruction*, whiteness emerges as the compensatory psychological and public "wage" that enabled various groups, especially the Irish—often called the "black Irish"—to negotiate a social status simultaneously distinct from and opposed to that of the slave or ex-slave. For Roediger, this negotiation is a tragic failure of insurgent class-consciousness, because much of the force behind the discursive racialization of the Irish as black arose from their large occupation of unskilled and domestic labor. "[W]hiteness was a way in which white workers responded to a fear of dependency on wage labor and to the necessities of capitalist work discipline" (*Wages* 13). By paying close attention to the Irish's own struggle against the negative racialization that accompanied their lower-class status in the United States, Roediger demonstrates how "working class formation and the systematic development of a sense of whiteness went hand in hand for the U.S. white working class," so much so in fact that the very meaning of "worker" would be implicitly understood as "white" by the end of the century (8).

Whereas some scholars disagree with Roediger's tactic to emphasize the Irish's active pursuit of white identity—Allen, for instance, says the Irish were "bamboozled" by the ruling class (199)[16]—much of the work in the proliferating archive of whiteness studies depends for its political force on the disciplinary legacy of labor history put into play by Roediger. Taking conscious political action and the centrality of the subject as an agent and not simply as an object of history, labor history, Roediger explains, "has consistently stressed the role of workers as creators of their own culture [and therefore] it is particularly well positioned to understand that white identity is not merely the product of elites or of discourses" (*Abolition* 75–76). In this retrieval of the historical as the site of human agency, Roediger jump-starts, we might say, the critical project of imaging an antiracist white subject in the present, because if whiteness is historically produced and if its production requires something more than the physical characteristic of skin color, then whiteness as a form of political identification, if not racial identity, can be abolished. Citing James Baldwin, in a line that has become a banner for whiteness studies as a field, Roediger glosses, "As long as you think you are white, there's no hope for you" (185).[17]

This emphasis on the active process of "unthinking" whiteness as a structure of power and privilege is certainly a compelling counter to the unconscious white subject celebrated in *Forrest Gump*, and it offers, through

the political project mapped by labor history, a means to refunction working class struggle as cross-racial alliance. But once the theoretical precepts
of labor history become installed as the governing disciplinary apparatus
of whiteness studies—that is, once the historical retrieval of agency and
the story of pre-white ethnics who choose whiteness in the tense interplay
between race and class come to define the possibility of the antiracist white
subject—the field begins to generate a range of contradictory, sometimes
startling effects. The most critically important include: 1) an emphasis on
agency that situates a theoretically humanist subject at the center of social
constructionist analysis; 2) the use of class as the transfer point between
looking white and believing you are white; 3) a focus on economically
disempowered whites, both working class and poor, as minoritized white
subjects; and 4) the production of a particularized and minoritized white
subject as a vehicle for contemporary critical acts of transference and transcendence, which often produces a white masculine position as discursively
minor. Each of these effects must be examined further in the context of
the contemporary academy, where the assault against affirmative action has
been aggressively pursued in a climate of employment scarcity and corporate
downsizing. Such economic constrictions are crucial to understanding why
the critical apparatus being forged in whiteness studies bears the unconscious trace of the liberal whiteness its reclamation of history so strenuously
seeks to disavow. For in the particularity of the pre-white ethnic, whiteness
studies reverses the historical process of white construction, offering for
the contemporary white subject a powerful narrative of discursively black
ethnic origins. History, in other words, rescues contemporary whiteness
from the transcendent universalism that has been understood as its mode of
productive power by providing pre-white particularity, which is reproduced
as pre-white injury and minoritization.

To trace the critical turns I have narrated above, where the social
construction of whiteness is located at the historical origin of "discursive
blackness," I want to begin with a brief passage at the end of Roediger's
introductory comments in *Towards the Abolition of Whiteness*. Here, in
an economist language of investment and divestiture, Roediger hopes to
inspire working-class whites to give up the compensatory psychological
and public wage of whiteness by forging class-based political identifications
with people of color:

> [W]e cannot *afford* to ignore the political implications [that]...
> whites are confessing their confusion about whether it is really

worth the effort to be white. We need to say that it is not *worth* it and that many of us do not want to do it. Initiatives [should] . . . expos[e] how whiteness is used to make whites settle for hopelessness in politics and misery in everyday life. . . . Our opposition should focus on contrasting the *bankruptcy* of white politics with the possibilities of nonwhiteness. We should point out not just that whites and people of color often have common economic *interests* but that people of color currently act on those *interests* far more consistently . . . precisely because they are not burdened by whiteness. (16–17; emphasis added)

Casting whiteness as the burden that prevents working-class whites from identifying their real interests, Roediger differentiates identity from identification in order to redirect the investments in whiteness toward political allegiances with those designated as "nonwhite." Such identificatory mobility is central to the social constructionist project, countering what we might think of as the political and theoretical *immobility* of an essentialized subject. For when looking white and being white are collapsed, white identity becomes saturated with, if not wholly indistinguishable from, political identifications with white supremacy. To pry apart this essentialized relation, Roediger emphasizes the mobility of political identifications. Working-class whites need to "cross over" there, to trade against the faulty essentialist confederacy between white power and white skin, in order to discover the class "interests" that are already theirs. By using class as the mechanism for this transportation, Roediger's critical model passes through the pre-white ethnic to a complex citing of cross-racial economic affinities to secure a future of post-white working-class struggle.

In the context of my conversation about the trope of mobility in *Forrest Gump*, the theoretical moves articulated here reverse the political investment but not the spatializing logic that accompanies the popularized race-traitoring white subject in the post-segregationist era: It is the white subject who crosses the segregationist boundaries of both knowledge and political identification, whereas people of color remain politically identified with the social margins where the relation between race and class is more intimately—one hesitates to say, more essentially—interested. The force of social construction as a theoretical vocabulary for agency thus posits the agency of people of color as an effect of their social position as marginal; hence identifications and identities are identical. For the antiracist white subject, it is the incommensurability between racial identity and political identification that bears the fruit of the constructionist enterprise, enabling a claim to particularity that rewrites the universal as a burden that must be shorn. Marked as the difference within whiteness, the antiracist white subject becomes particular by asserting a political difference from its racial "self." Roediger names this difference "nonwhiteness," and in so doing, not only reconvenes an essentializing elision of white with racist, but also demonstrates how overwritten is the antiracist subject by universal privilege itself. After all, the white subject's claim to nonwhite particularity can only be asserted from the position of the universal, as it is in the space of the universal and never the particular that the theoretical mobility of political identification by definition takes place. This is not to charge Roediger with the failure to provide us with a seamless model of the antiracist subject, but to remark on the way that the desire to combat white privilege seems unable to generate a political project against racism articulated from the site of whiteness itself.[18]

It is not a surprise, therefore, that the activist quasi-academic journal *Race Traitor* locates its antiracist project in "abolish[ing] the white race from within" (2). Troping the emphasis on conscious agency drawn from labor history and finding political sustenance in individual narratives of race traitoring, the various authors collected in *Race Traitor* posit white abolitionism as necessary to "solving the social problems of our age" (10). In the opening editorial to the Routledge volume that collects the first five issues of the journal, editors Noel Ignatiev and John Garvey describe the *Race Traitor* project: "The existence of the white race depends on the willingness of those assigned to it to place their racial interests above class [or] gender. . . . The defection of enough of its members . . . will set off tremors that will lead to its collapse. *Race Traitor* aims to serve as an intellectual center for those seeking to abolish the white race" (9–10). Guided by the principle *"treason to whiteness is loyalty to humanity"* (10), *Race Traitor* envisions treason on a number of fronts, from verbal retorts to racist jokes or commentaries to interracial marriage to cross-racial identifications in politics, fashion, and music. "What makes you think I am white?" is the quintessential race traitor question, and its deployment in the face of the police is one of the most heralded abolitionist acts. As Garvey and Ignatiev write in "The New Abolitionism":

What if the police couldn't tell a loyal person just by color? What if there were enough people around who looked white but were really enemies of official society so that the cops couldn't tell whom to beat and whom to let off? . . . With color no longer serving as a handy guide for the distribution of penalties and rewards, European-Americans of the downtrodden class would at least be compelled to face with sober sense their real condition of life and their relations with humankind. It would be the end of the white race. . . . (105-06)

In this way, *Race Traitor* joins Roediger in constructing a model of the mobile antiracist subject whose conscious political production not only particularizes whiteness by citing its power, but does so to craft for economically disenfranchised whites a generative and ultimately antiracist class politics.

If this description of *Race Traitor* suggests a coherent intellectual and activist project, it is important to stress that contributions to the journal vary widely in political content. This is due in part to the collective nature of the journal and to its mediation between activist and academic political sites. It is also a consequence, it seems, of the difficulties that abound in transposing nineteenth-century antislavery abolition into the paradigmatic site for constructing a late twentieth-century antiracist subject. By affirming as heroic and antiwhite the work of such abolitionists as John Brown, leader of the failed slave revolt at Harper's Ferry, *Race Traitor* reinscribes the centrality of white masculine leadership even as it posits such leadership as historical evidence for the abolition of the white race. "How many dissident so-called whites would it take to unsettle the nerves of the white executive board? It is impossible to know. One John Brown—against a background of slave resistance—was enough for Virginia" (13). Overly drawn to masculine models of armed retaliation, *Race Traitor* effectively evacuates altogether the feminist trajectory of nineteenth-century abolitionism, reproducing instead the white male rebel as the affirmative subject of antiracist struggle. Such affirmation, situated in the context of essays about the Irish and pre-white immigrants, symptomatically demonstrates the oscillation between universal privilege and minoritized particularity that characterizes not only the history of white subject formation in the United States, but also the critical apparatus of whiteness studies itself.

Race Traitor's implicit response to its own critical contradiction of abolishing whiteness in a frame of white masculine heroic narrativity is to situate the African American as the quintessential American. Ignatiev writes, "The adoption of a white identity is the most serious barrier to becoming fully American.... [T]he United States is an Afro-American country.... Above all, the experience of people from Africa in the New World represent the distillation of the American experience, and this concentration of history finds its expression in the psychology, culture, and national character of the American people" (18, 19). Thus, defining the abolition of whiteness as the precondition for becoming American, Ignatiev retrieves an American exceptionalist logic that displaces the historical white subject as the national citizen-subject for a narrative of national origin cast now as black.[19] In so doing, a metaphorical "America" of national longing supplants the materialist "America" through which state violence—physical, economic, and ideological—has guaranteed the juridical privileges of whiteness. Leaving aside the many ways this formulation eradicates a range of groups and experiences, it is significant to note how important to *Race Traitor* is the resignification of the nation as part of a reclamation of the "human." "It is not black people who have been prevented from drawing upon the full variety of experience that has gone into making up America. Rather, it is those who, in maddened pursuit of the white whale, have cut themselves off from human society" (19). The abolition of whiteness reclaims the democratic possibility of human sociality, itself a characteristic of the resignified nation.

My focus on the language of nation and national identity is meant to recall the ideological work of *Forrest Gump* and its mobile protagonist whose fantastic projection of a post-segregationist America entailed the literal and symbolic remapping of the American territorial nation. In Gump's claim to what Berlant calls "the normal," the white male subject reconstructs itself on the grounds of a fabled sentimentality, with all state-based debts paid and a reproductive future of politically uncontaminated subjectivity guaranteed. In *Race Traitor*, the editors seek not so much the normal but the "ordinary" as the contrast to the state: "[T]he ordinary people of no country have ever been so well prepared to rule a society as the Americans of today" (4). This is because, in Ignatiev's words, "few Americans of any ethnic background take a direct hand in the denial of equality to people of color" (16–17). The conscious agency that defines the becoming white of the pre-white ethnic is strategically dissolved in the present, where the ordinary person is theoretically divested of taking a committed interest in the perpetuation of white racial privilege. Indeed, whiteness, although the object under investigation and ultimate destruction, is exteriorized to such an extent that the conscious agency heralded as necessary to undo it has no theoretical hold on the interior constitution of the subject. In contrast with Roediger's work, there is here no psychological depth to whiteness as a social construction, merely an interpretative inscription based on skin that can be consciously refused.

The construction of the antiracist subject in *Race Traitor* thus goes something like this: Whiteness is understood as the consequence of a universalizing pact between white skin color and white club privilege, one that deprives white people of both a positive relation to humanity and to American national identity. White supremacy is less an effect of individual activities and ideologies than the consequence of institutions of state power, which themselves alienate the ordinary citizen who is neither directly nor enthusiastically involved in the oppression of people of color. In this way, *Race Traitor* assumes, as does Roediger, that cross-racial class alliance is the locus of more urgent and identifiable political interests for the majority of whites, though *Race Traitor* is dedicated to the possibility of a "minority" of traitors—not, as in Roediger, a mass class movement—to perform the work of abolishing white supremacy. This work involves making whiteness visible as a racial category by interrupting the "natural" assumption that people who look white are invested in being white. Race traitors must thus mark whiteness as a racialized particular in order to perform their disaffiliation from the universality that underwrites the category, where such performance is understood as the necessary claim to an antiracist subjectivity. This is, it seems to me, the performative force of the race traitor question, "What makes you think I am white?" which simultaneously and paradoxically refuses the position of the universally unmarked by ultimately claiming to no longer be marked by it. In asserting the particularity of white racial identity as preamble to refusing it altogether, the race traitor passes through both the universal and the particular in order to found a new minority of former white people. Counting on the power of individual disavowal of the juridical white subject of state power, *Race Traitor* reimagines an empowered humanist subject whose intent to repeal its own whiteness is consecrated as the central practice of antiracist struggle.

In her contribution "White Savagery and Humiliation" in White Trash: Race and Class in America, Annalee Newitz is especially critical of the reliance on self-consciousness that udnerwrites the new abolitionism. When *Race Traitor*, for instance, asserts its aim to abolish the white race by hailing those who are dissatisfied with the terms of membership in the white club, Newitz questions the self-congratulatory mode that enables whites "to critique themselves before anyone else does" (149). From her

perspective, the problem with the abolitionist project is its spectaculariza-
tion of white humiliation as a mode of political insurgency, because it is
finally the specter of self-destruction that enables the abolitionist's heroic
refashioning. As a counter-strategy, Newitz seeks to disaffiliate white racial
identity from the practices and institutions of white supremacy:

> We are asked [by the abolitionists] to demonize whiteness
> rather than to deconstruct it. . . . Social problems like unequally
> distributed resources, class privilege, irrational prejudice, and
> tyrannical bureaucracy which we associate with whiteness are
> just that—*associated* with whiteness. . . . They are not essential
> to whiteness itself, any more than laziness and enslavement are
> essential to blackness. . . . Informing whites that their identities
> are the problem, rather than various social practices, makes it
> sound like whites should die rather than that white racism should.
> The ideologies of white power which make some white people
> socially destructive are the symptoms of American inequality
> and injustice, not its principle causes. (149–50)

Disembodying white racial power by differentiating it from identity, Newitz
pursues a de-essentialized whiteness, one that can hold its own, so to speak,
in the same grammatical gesture as the anti-essentialist analysis of blackness.
In the process, the empowered privileges of whiteness and the stereotypes
that degrade blackness take on an analytical equivalency as whiteness is
situated as an identity object in need of the same resignification that has
accompanied civil rights and black power struggle over and in the name
of blackness. "While whiteness is undeniably linked to a series of oppressive social practices, it is also an identity which can be negotiated on an
individual level. It is a diversity of cultures" (148). Such diversity points
toward the possibility, as Newitz writes with co-editor Matt Wray in the
anthology's introduction, of "a more realistic and fair-minded understanding of whiteness as a specific, racially marked group existing in relation to
many other such groups" (5).[20]

The desire for a critical paradigm that can approach both black and
white on quite literally the same terms—in a mode of theoretical equal
opportunity—shapes *White Trash* at a number of levels. For instance, when
the editors write that whiteness is "an oppressive ideological construct that
promotes and maintains social inequalities, causing great material and psychological harm to both people of color and whites" (3), they inadvertently

construct a mutuality-of-harm hypothesis that powerfully appends whites to the harmed position of people of color. This move co-joins the rendering of "white trash" as "not just a classist slur—it's also a racial epithet that marks out certain whites as a breed apart" (4). The double reading of "white trash" as classist and racist is fundamental to *White Trash*'s articulation of itself as an antiracist project:

> Our anthology is intended as an intervention in this field [of whiteness studies], offering a critical understanding of how differences within whiteness—differences marked out by categories like white trash—may serve to undo whiteness as racial supremacy, helping to produce multiple, indeterminate, and antiracist forms of white identity. (4)

But how does one arrive at a notion that the class oppression that poor whites experience is also a racial oppression and, further, that the very category of "white trash" can serve as a model of antiracist forms of white identity?

Wray and Newitz begin by noting that the term has been traced to African American origins, being deployed by slaves as a mode of insult and differentiation in relation to white servants. This origin story, they write, "in the context of black slavery and white servitude speaks to the racialized roots of the meaning of ["white trash"]" (2). Racialized in what sense? As a mechanism of institutional power? As a force of subordination? The authors don't say, and it is in this failure to explore the nexus of power embedded in the origin story that allows "white trash" to be cast as a racialization with minoritizing effects. The consequences of these critical moves are multiple: The insistence on "white trash" as a minoritizing racialization simultaneously disarticulates racism from institutionalized practices of discrimination based on a group's designated racial status, while crafting for poor whites a position structurally comparable to that of the racial minority. In so doing, an antiracist project for whites is inaugurated at the site of a harmed and discriminated whiteness. As the editors declare at the outset: "Americans love to hate the poor. Lately, it seems there is no group of poor folks they like to hate more than white trash" (1).[21] In an important contrast with *Race Traitor* and the critical tradition offered by labor history, the elucidation of the white permanent and working poor does not function here to establish a mobile antiracist white subject who can transfer, through the interestedness of class position, identification from the wages of whiteness to collective antiracist struggle with people of color. Instead, the model forged in *White Trash* is one in which the psychological wages of whiteness defined by Du Bois and taken up by Roediger are supplanted by emphasizing whiteness as a material privilege—and one whose security has decidedly lessened: "As the economy and unemployment figures in the U.S. worsen, more whites are losing jobs to downsizing and corporate restructuring, or taking pay cuts. While it used to be that whites gained job security at the expense of other racial groups, whiteness in itself no longer seems a sure path to a good income" (7). In the context of the introduction's larger and at times deeply contradictory framework, the above assertion functions to produce the power of whiteness as a fully (and seemingly only) materialized economic relation; hence when material advantage does not exist, one becomes a racialized minority, albeit within whiteness. In measuring the comparable worth of marginality in this way, *White Trash*'s intervention into whiteness studies produces, we might say, a white identity formation that has no compensatory racial debt to pay. What generates this compulsion for a minoritized whiteness that is not "expensive" to people of color? Or more precisely, why does the production of a minoritized whiteness become the seemingly necessary precondition for an antiracist project? Part of the answer to this question is lodged, as this essay has been suggesting, in the contradictions between universality and particularity that characterize contemporary post-segregationist racial formation, especially as particularity has become the invested sign for the creation of antiracist equalities. But particularity is not essentially anti-essentialist, nor does it guarantee the white subject's disaffiliation from the powers and pretensions of universality. Indeed, to render whiteness the object of study from within the province of a humanist subject now hyperconscious of itself thus mistakes the way that even radical traditions within modern knowledge formations are not innocently prior to but decisively and unpredictably implicated in the histories and inequalities of racial asymmetries and oppressions. The political project that generates knowledge formations and the political consequences of their generation cannot be unequivocally coordinated, which is to say that the social construction of white racial identities and ideologies that is the object of study in whiteness studies arises in the context of ongoing historical processes. These processes have reworked the relation between universality and particularity that constitutes the negotiated hegemony of white power and made possible new and powerful attacks on civil rights legislation—all as part of a contradictory reconfiguration of the public discourse of race and white racial identity in the post-segregationist era. Far from operating as the opposite or resistant counter to the universal, then, the particular is the necessary contradiction that affords to white power its historical and political elasticity. In this context, the political project for the study of whiteness entails not simply rendering whiteness particular but engaging with the ways that being particular will not divest whiteness of its universal epistemological power.

Notes

1. For information on the original Laurens controversy regarding the Klan Museum, see Bragg (1:16) and Baker (A3).

2. That being white is here a transaction of "race" into a money-making business lends further credence to George Lipsitz's suggestion that white identity primarily constitutes itself through propertied investments, whether literal or imaginary. See both Lipsitz and Sanchez.

3. On citizenship, abstraction, and the promise of the universal, see especially Warner.

4. For an analysis of the language of victimization in the documents of white supremacist organizations in the 1990s, see Daniels.

5. Personal communication, 1997. My thanks to George Lipsitz for his thoughtful and thorough consideration of the issues raised in this paper.

6. On whiteness studies, see Allen; Daniels; Fine, Weis, Powell, and L. Mun Wong; Frankenberg; Hill; Ignatiev; Ignatiev and Garvey; Lopez; Lott; Pfiel; Roediger (1991, 1994); Saxton; Segrest; Ware; Wray and Newitz.

7. On the history of black resistance to public transportation segregation in Birmingham during World War II, see Kelley.

8. As the red, white, and blue buses intermittently obstruct the camera's view of the bus stop, Forrest's narrative advances from his early childhood through his college career, his tour in Vietnam, his various business adventures that render him a millionaire, and back to the film's final resting place, the heterosexual reproductive domestic sphere. Each person who listens to Gump is keyed by race and gender to the significant events of his narrative: The black woman hears the story of Gump's physical and mental difference, the discriminatory treatment received by him, and his final transcendence of the leg braces; the white women each hear portions of the romance narrative, which culminates in Gump's marriage to Jenny; and the white male listens to the episodes of war and economic accumulation. Notable here are the absence of the black male as an audience and the schematic representation of race as a singularly black–white affair.

9. For the most extensive reading of *Forrest Gump* in the context of feminist analyses of gender, see Byers.

10. This point is explicitly reinforced in the film through Gump's parodic commentary on the white bedsheets worn by members of the Klan. As the figure of white skin, the bedsheets can be cast off by Klan descendants, which means that the materialization of privilege symbolized by and invested in white skin has itself no necessary historical lineage. My thanks to Eva Cherniavsky for suggesting this reading of white skin.

11. More needs to be said about the evacuation of the black male from the scene of the bus stop. Why this denial of his participation as audience for Gump's national tale? Why the spectacular use of the black male as the protagonist's twin, buddy double—Bubba—who seems destined to die? On the one hand, the film's failure to imagine the black male as a witness to Gump's tale demonstrates the function of black male embodiment as the signifying means for constructing white liberal morality. Bubba's death offers to Gump the rationale for white retribution, a debt that can be paid. On the other hand, the film's positioning of Bubba symbolically feminizes blackness, as he comes to occupy the place of Jenny in the second scene of exclusion and outsider bonding on the school bus. It is Jenny, after all, who allows Gump a place to sit on the bus in the earliest scene when all the white boys have denied him room; when this racialized site is plumbed a second time, Bubba occupies the narrative space initially held by Jenny, and both of them by the end of the film die (Jenny from an illness implicitly framed as AIDS and Bubba in the Vietnam War). These deaths, as the deaths of the feminine and of the black male buddy, are crucial to Gump's simultaneous claim to and transcendence of injury, because they mark specific bodies as the bearers of national trauma—Jenny, we see, travels through the antiwar and drug cultures of the 1960s and 1970s, whereas Bubba becomes the fallen emblem of the war—and they do so within a context that disaffiliates white masculinity from the historical power and privilege of its social and economic position.

12. On the broader contexts of the remasculinization of the white Vietnam veteran, see Jeffords.

13. Gump wears other kinds of shoes in the film, but the meditation on shoes that opens the film—and subsequent meditations on his mobility—revolve around the Nike running shoes. Even the advertisements for the film, both in theaters and on video, feature Gump in his Nike running shoes.

14. Gump's run, although denied an explanation in the film, begins the day after July 4—the day after Jenny has "run off" without explanation. In the final moves of the narrative, we will find out that it was their encounter on the fourth of July that created "Little Forrest," thereby reinforcing the relation between paternity and the futurity of the nation.

15. I owe two notes of thanks here. One is to Eva Cherniavsky, who offered me an understanding of the material investment in whiteness as a relation of inexhaustibility to the commodity. The other is to Patricia McKee, who discussed with me the way that whiteness needs to be thought as a process of simultaneous materialization and dematerialization.

16. See Scott on the differences between Roediger and Allen.

17. As Roediger explains, "Complexity arises when we cease to regard racial and ethnic identities as categories into which individuals simply are 'slotted.' . . . James Baldwin's point that Europeans arrived in the United States and became white—'by deciding they were white' powerfully directs our attention to the fact that white ethnics . . . by and large chose whiteness, and even struggled to be recognized as white" (*Abolition* 185).

18. One of the challenges of thinking about the antiracist subject in the contemporary period is precisely to imagine that subject's political practices within categories of racialization that confer privileges based on color of skin. The current critical interest in rendering the visible unintelligible as a realist determination of racial belonging and self-definition, as Michael Berube would argue, does not undo the force of the visible as this culture's reigning logic, even if it unearths its faulty epistemology. No matter how many exceptional cases of passing and of nonwhite whiteness we can cite, it is the desire to make these paradigmatic for the material histories of racialized bodies that must be examined.

19. "What is the distinctive element of the American experience?" Ignatiev writes. "It is the shock of being torn from a familiar place and hurled into a new environment, compelled to develop a way of life and culture from the materials at hand. And who more embodies that experience, is more the essential product of that experience, than the descendants of the people from Africa who visited these shores together with the first European explorers . . . and whose first settlers were landed here a year before the Mayflower?" (*Irish* 19).

20. In drawing attention to the discourse of injury, I do not mean to discount—and I feel like I need to say this in capital letters—the importance of analyzing the many ways that the white permanent and working poor are representationally "trashed" in U.S. popular culture. Nor do I mean to obviate the way that both Wray and Newitz remark in their introduction on the problem of a vulgar multiculturalism that attends to whiteness only as victim. But I do think that the introduction is contradictory enough that these caveats are not constitutively formulated within the project's theorization of the permanent poor; rather the very risks that the authors note seem to be the foundational effects of their discursive practices.

21. In his contribution to *White Trash*, Lockley focuses on non-slaveholding whites in antebellum period under a similar set of disturbing assumptions: "[W]hiteness per se was not a ticket to the life of leisure. Living in a society which was based on a system of human bondage, and having little or no part in that particular system, gave non-slaveholding whites a unique social status" (59).

Works Cited

Allen, Theodore. *The Invention of the White Race*. London: Verso, 1994.

Baker, David P. "Converted by Love, a Former Klansman Finds Ally at Black Church." *Washington Post* 27 July 1997: A3.

Berlant, Laura. *The Queen of America Goes to Washington City: Essays on Sex and Citizenship*. Durham, NC: Duke UP, 1997.

Bragg, Rick. "In a South Carolina Town, a Klan Museum Opens Old Wounds." *New York Times* 17 Nov. 1996: 1:16.

Byers, Thomas B. "History Re-membered: *Forrest Gump*, Postfeminist Masculinity, and the Burial of the Counterculture." *Modern Fiction Studies* 42.2 (Summer 1996): 420–44.

Daniels, Jessie. *White Lies: Race, Class, Gender and Sexuality in White Supremacist Discourse*. New York: Routledge, 1997.

Fine, Michelle, Lois Weis, Linda C. Powell, and L. Mun Wong, eds. *Off White: Readings on Race, Power, and Society*. New York: Routledge, 1997.

Frankenburg, Ruth. *White Women, Race Matters: The Social Construction of Whiteness*. Minneapolis: U of Minnesota P, 1993.

Harris, Cheryl. "Whiteness as Property." *Harvard Law Review* 106.8 (June 1993): 1710–91.

Hill, Mike, ed. *Whiteness: A Critical Reader*. New York: New York UP, 1997.

Ignatiev, Noel. *How the Irish Became White*. New York: Routledge, 1996.

Ignatiev, Noel, and John Garvey, eds. *Race Traitor*. New York: Routledge, 1996.

Jeffords, Susan. *The Remasculinization of America: Gender and the Vietnam War*. Bloomington: U of Indiana P, 1989.

Kelley, Robin D. G. *Race Rebels: Culture, Politics, and the Black Working Class*. New York: The Free Press, 1994.

Lipsitz, George. "The Possessive Investment in Whiteness: Racialized Social Democracy and the 'White' Problem in American Studies." *American Quarterly* 47.3 (Sept. 1995): 369–87.

Lockley, Timothy J. "Partners in Crime." *White Trash: Race and Class in America*. Eds. Matt Wray and Annalee Newitz. New York: Routledge, 1996: 57–72.

Lopez, Ian F. Hanny. *White By Law: The Legal Construction of Race*. New York: New York UP, 1996.

Lott, Eric. *Love and Theft: Blackface Minstrelsy and the American Working Class*. New York: Oxford UP, 1993.

Newitz, Annalee. "White Savagery and Humiliation, or a New Racial Consciousness in the Media." *White Trash: Race and Class in America*. Ed. Newitz and Matt Wray. New York: Routledge, 1996: 131–54.

Pfeil, Fred. *White Guys*. New York: Verso, 1997.

Roediger, David. *The Wages of Whiteness: Race and the Making of the American Working Class*. London: Verso, 1990.

———. *Towards the Abolition of Whiteness*. London: Verso, 1994.

Sanchez, George. "Reading Reginald Denny: The Politics of Whiteness in the Late Twentieth Century." *American Quarterly* 47.3 (Sept. 1995): 388–94.

Saxton, Alexander. *The Rise and Fall of the White Republic: Class Politics and Mass Culture in Nineteenth-Century America*. London: Verso, 1992.

Scott, Jonathan. "Inside the White Race Corral." *Minnesota Review* 47 (1997): 93–103.

Segrest, Meg. *Memoir of a Race Traitor*. Boston: South End Press, 1994.

Ware, Vron. *Beyond the Pale: White Women, Racism, and History*. London: Verso, 1992.

Warner, Michael. "The Mass Public and the Mass Subject." *Habermas and the Public Sphere*. Ed. Craig Calhoun. Cambridge: MIT Press, 1992: 377–401.

Wray, Matt, and Annalee Newitz eds. "Introduction." *White Trash: Race and Class in America*. New York: Routledge, 1996: 1–12.

Chapter Eleven

Interdisciplinarity

A Consideration from African American Studies[1]

Lindon Barrett

Proposing fundamental liaisons between interdisciplinarity and social justice is a fraught consideration, because interdisciplinarity, however finally defined, connotes the problems of taxonomy and administration, whereas social justice, alternately, connotes "the shift in the way that community is formulated as an idea-object," in the words of the cultural critic Hortense Spillers (Spillers 81). Still, as marked by a series of methodologic self-reflections in journals such as *Eighteenth-Century Studies* (McKeon; Fenves; Suskin), *Poetics Today* (1991, 2003), and *PMLA* (1996, 1997) in the 1990s, these two formations might coalesce with some regularity within the amorphous research program of cultural studies. The anthropologist Renato Rosaldo codifies cultural studies as beginning

> with Raymond Williams, E. P. Thompson, and Antonio Gramsci as representative cultural Marxist thinkers whose work retains an analysis of political economy and a concern with human emancipation alongside an understanding of culture, ideology, and human agency. In this context, culture is laced with power and power is shaped by culture. Subsequent links in this genealogy include the reconceptualizations required by the emergence of gender, race, and sexuality as analytic concepts deriving from social movements of feminists and their allies, members of historically subordinated racialized groups and their allies, and gays

and lesbians and their allies. Such a genealogy problematizes
previously taken-for-granted monolithic social unities. (525)

In "Whose Cultural Studies?" Rosaldo calls, first, for the broader
acknowledgement of anthropologic paradigms within the research program
of cultural studies, because anthropology is always already concerned with
the structures of culture. Furthermore, Rosaldo calls for the open recognition of the fraught relations between cultural studies and the agendas of
ethnic studies programs, initiated in the academy in earnest in the 1960s
and 1970s:

> If senior anthropologists feel that the discipline's crown jewel
> has been ripped off by cultural studies, faculty and students in
> ethnic studies programs often feel that cultural studies is an only
> slightly disguised effort to restore white male authority in areas
> where ethnic studies programs have a chance of speaking with
> some authority. If certain majority scholars distance themselves
> from cultural studies saying that it is nothing more than ethnic
> studies writ large, certain minority scholars counter that the
> covert agenda of cultural studies is to allow white authority to
> co-opt ethnic studies programs. (527)

In short, the tensions defined by Rosaldo highlight the boundaries that
mark disciplinary coherence or hegemony and, coincidently, the competition between academic discourses and social formations that either aim to
forward or thwart social protest as an epistemological dynamic. George
Yudice makes similar observations in the 1996 *PMLA* forum "Defining
Interdisciplinarity," noting that the "predicament [of ethnic studies programs]
is compounded by the availability of new forms of inter- and transdisci-
plinarity, such as multicultural and cultural studies. With the waning of
affirmative action and other Great Society programs, boards of trustees
and university administrations can more easily justify cutting ethnic studies
programs or folding them into cultural studies programs that presumably
address issues of race and gender while enjoying wide popularity and a
solid market share in journals, university press publications, and the media"
(Yudice 275). In other words, from the perspective of those proposing social
protest as an epistemological ground, that is, the measure of certainty by
which one forms, approaches, or recognizes knowledge and the terms of
reason, the new means of survival for ethnic studies might, ironically, more

readily thwart than forward these very premises of ethnic studies. In the 1997 *PMLA* forum "Interconnections," Purnima Bose draws up a compelling set of questions for cultural studies that retain the originary measure of certitude initiating ethic studies programs: "The task of criticism should be to uncover trauma—bodily injury caused by an external agent—in all its modalities in commodity culture by asking the following questions: What are the conditions that allow for the articulation of an image or a narrative at a particular moment? What kind of national ethos does the representation of a commodity evoke and to what extent does the representation acknowledge or occlude the struggles of those who are resisting the state's authority?" (282) Restated, forms of knowing, academic disciplines being among the most fully and openly regulated configurations of knowing, always already hold direct consequences for the social landscape through which all forms of knowledge must circulate and by which they are sponsored. As these observations on the changing configurations of academic knowledge production suggest, the sometimes profound tensions between the matters of interdisciplinarity and social justice, particularly as marking the emergent field of cultural studies, remain the issue of "whether historically laden disciplinary epistemologies and economies can be adapted to emergent social and political considerations" (Murray 280), in the words of Timothy Murray.

The reassessments in the 1990s of the academic fields that, at present, most forthrightly address the human and the civic, economic, historical, imaginative, and legal situations designated by the concept of racial blackness—African American Studies, African Studies, and their diasporic configuration as Africana Studies—also acknowledge these tensions. For instance, Victor Okafar, in "The Place of Africology in the University Curriculum," remarks on the dramatic reorganization of the academy following the social and epistemological struggles of the 1960s, noting that since the establishment of the first Black Studies department at San Francisco State in 1968, by 1995 and 1996, "the National Council for Black Studies (NCBS) lists three hundred institutions of higher education in the United States where Black Studies is obtainable in one form or another—that is, in the form of a certificate, minor or major, or a master's or doctoral degree" (695). Insofar as the originary move behind the dramatic formulation is a direct challenge to the rationaliz[ing] of the oppression of people of color" (693), the sanctioned intellectual landscape of official knowledge production is transformed in ways that leave the academy fractured in seemingly irresolvable ways. Iris Berger, in "Contested Boundaries: African Studies

Approaching the Millennium," her presidential address to the 1996 African Studies Association Annual Meeting, notes that a "primary rationale for areas studies [in the Cold War era] from the start was its interdisciplinary perspective," resulting in a tension between local and global knowledges attempting to manage the "constant and breathless motion as multi-directional flows of people, capital, technology, culture and ideas render local, national and regional borders meaningless" (5). This modernist and postmodernist assault on borders and their sedimented meaningfulness, both geopolitically and in the academy, receives the various, diffuse attentions of cultural studies and its detractors.

Insofar as African American Studies privileges objectively and methodologically perhaps the starkest symptomatic drives of the accumulating progresses of Western modernity, the insistent, mass violence by which Western modernity reiterates itself, the field demonstrates the ideological stakes of the intellectual reassessments of the 1990s. The intellectual terms of African American Studies are exemplary of the ideological impasse that the cultural critics noted above identify. The more explicitly social valence of the impasse might be understood as the ongoing crisis of the humanities and social sciences to which these critics implicitly speak, as they also trouble the tensions between interdisciplinarity and social justice insinuated in the widespread currency of cultural studies. The particular illustrative claim made here is that the purview of African American Studies excavates in a variety of ways the synchronic terms or problems of the social and cultural teleologies of Western modernity, which—as cultural studies insists—are paradigms of knowing.

Knowing the Violences of the Modern

To employ some of the principle paradigms of cultural studies, the concept of commodity fetishism provides a useful conceptual marker. In the article "Marxian Value Theory and the Problem of the Subject," the economists Jack Amariglio and Antonio Callari argue that the concept of commodity fetishism provides a succinct rendition of the Marxist codification of subjectivity. "Marx," they write, "has had a theory of the subject, the theory of commodity fetishism. To the extent that it attempts to conjoin the analysis of commodity production and circulation with a discussion of 'ideology,' commodity fetishism does discuss the peculiar subjectivity typical of capitalist social formations" (188). In particular, Amariglio and Callari point out that the Marxist understanding of "socially necessary labor time" as the essential value masked in commodity fetishism clarifies the subjectivizing force of the modern market, which is to say, the imperatives "naturalizing" the difference between the social conditions of the labor yielding the commodity and the failure of the commodity to resemble those conditions in the exchange. In this way, "the act of exchange is not simply the site of an economic process but also one of the key locations within capitalism where a symbolic order is particularly constituted and learned" (215). The concept of commodity fetishism describes the phantasmatic torque of rational exchanges so as to abrogate, in the words of Amariglio and Callari, the "unnecessary gulf [that] has come to exist between two important areas of theoretical work in contemporary Marxism, with the theory of value (the economics, if you will) on one side and the nature and role of subjectivity (an antieconomism) on the other" (186). The ideally infinite arena of ideally infinite exchange of the modern abstracted market forms the most efficient nexus of material and conceptual exchange. In the historical trajectory, the cultural trajectory, and the trajectories of subjection, commodity fetishism depends on and stands for the fantastic impossibility by means of which not only the possible seems coherent but, more importantly, the force of the actual seems coherent. This nexus is racial in character insofar as the phantasmatic, geopolitical, and economic coincidence yields the modern declensions of humanity and subhumanity.

In the signal study *Black Marxism: The Making of the Black Radical Tradition*, the political scientist Cedric Robinson emphasizes, in particular, the role of race in the entangled economic and subjectivizing trajectory of Western modernity: "The creation of the Negro was obviously at the cost of immense expenditures of psychic and intellectual energies in the West. The exercise was obligatory. It was an effort commensurate with the importance Black labor power possessed for the world economy sculpted and dominated by the ruling and mercantile classes of Western Europe" (4). Robinson employs the term "racial capitalism" to foreground analytically the brutalization of African-derived persons in the development of quintessentially modern systems of exchange, material and otherwise: "The development, organization and expansion of capitalist society pursued essentially racial directions; so too did social ideology. As a material force, then, it could be expected that racialism would inevitably permeate the social structures emergent from capitalism. I have used the term 'racial capitalism' to refer to this development and the subsequent structure as an historical agency" (3). The early modern fortunes of sugar as a commodity provide the fundamental illustration of the structural and historical imperatives designated by the concept "racial capitalism" as well as the psychic (dis)identifications paradigmatic for the social relations of "racial capitalism": "The invention of the Negro was proceeding apace with the growth of slave labor. Somewhat paradoxically, the more that Africans and their descendants assimilated cultural materials from colonial society, the less human they became in the minds of the colonists" (164).

The phantasmatic contours of modern subjectivity are insinuated in these effects. The historian David Eltis, in the article "Europeans and the Rise and Fall of African Slavery: An Interpretation," draws this compound economic and imaginative impress for disposing sub-Saharan Africans and their descendants in the European modernity. The historian David Northrup's *Africa's Discovery of Europe: 1450–1850* provides a cognate of Eltis's argument because of the longstanding cultural and commercial relations between European and African peoples that the Atlantic slave trade revises starkly. Nonetheless, rehearsing in particular the unpursued and potentially far greater economic promise of European enslavement in the Americas, Eltis queries "which groups are considered eligible for enslavement" (1400) in the mercantilist era and its aftermath. He proposes that the "crux of the matter is shipping costs, which comprised by far the greater part of the price of any form of imported bonded labor in the Americas" (1405). The scope of Eltis's argument is not bound by national jurisdictions but is international, demonstrating "that economic motivation should be assigned a subsidiary role in the rise and fall of the exclusively African-based bondage that Europeans carried across the Atlantic" (1401). The shorter voyage from Europe to the Americas, the less closely packed ships of these routes, the lower mortality and morbidity rates in the North compared with South Atlantic transportation, the accessibility to European convict labor given that major European population centers abut navigable waterways, Eltis argues, attest to the far from complete role of economics in the arraignment of mercantilist labor forces. Rather, Eltis states, "the most cursory examination of relative costs suggests that European slaves should have been preferred to either European indentured labor or African slaves" (1404).

The confluence of imagination, economics, and race is plain: "The most that can be said by way of comparison is that the spread of African slavery in the Americas coincided with the spread of forced labor in punishment systems within Europe (transportation in the English case). But no one was in any doubt about the distinctions between the two" (Eltis 1411). The ultimate point is that the "absence of European slaves, like the dog that did not bark, is perhaps the clue to understanding the slave trade and the system it supported" (1422). The more than simply economic question foregrounds the *imagination* of the European subject, as well as attendant political and material forces, the quandary being "that the peoples with the most advanced capitalist culture, the Dutch and the English, were also the Europeans least likely to subject their own citizens to enforced labor," circumstances disclosing that "the celebration of British liberties—more specifically, liberties for Englishmen—depended on African slavery" (Eltis 1423).[2] Drawing a circumference around the entire Atlantic circuit, Eltis's argument extrapolates in important ways from the thesis of the historian Edmund Morgan's *American Slavery, American Freedom*, broadening its ideas so as to encompass the psychic and political subjectivity of modernizing Europe generally. In sum, the thesis of Edmund Morgan's classic examination of colonial Virginia is "not . . . that a belief in republican ideology had to rest on slavery, but only that in Virginia (and probably in other southern colonies) it did" (381).

David Eltis's more general rendition of the principle bears noting: If, in the episode of mercantile capitalism, the "early modern Europeans shifted property rights in labor toward the individual and away from the community" (23), then, as clearly, these reorganizations shift property rights in labor (as well as in epistemological and cultural systems) across continental divisions: toward Europe and the Americas and away from the west coast of Africa. The Atlantic accessibility of the African continent provides the means for dismantling the long-standing systems of property rights, commercial trade, legal and penal systems, and intercultural contact of the self-governing jurisdictions arrayed along the broad continental swath in which, in the words of the economists Henry Gemery and Jan Hogendorn, "few—perhaps no—West African peoples appear to have been living on the very margin of subsistence during the eighteenth century . . . [for] research almost always seems to disclose some surplus output and some interregional trade even in the most isolated areas" (153). In short, the modern transfer of rights toward the European(ized) individual and away from the community has patent inverse effects on the eastern and western arcs of the Atlantic rim. To summarize, the fact that the modern "individual" and its revolutionary civic and political protocols *did not precede* the transfer of rights from the community to the individual, or from the eastern to the western arcs of the Atlantic, reveals plainly the powerful turns of the imagination that accrue along the western rim of the Atlantic in the modernizing centers of Europe and its outposts—fully in tandem with the vast economic values in question.

The modernity of *individual* psychic positions is forged from the same enterprise as the modernity of mercantilism agendas as well as their revised, dramatic, and exorbitant nationalisms. For these reasons, the conceit of racial blackness, which indiscriminately catalogues dark-skinned Africans and their descendants, can be understood as a powerful analog of the complex of commodity fetishism. That is, the extended quarantining of the African-derived population largely and effectively promotes key turns of the imagination that *naturalize* the gulf between the social conditions of the labor yielding the commodity for exchange and the failure of the commodity to resemble those conditions in the exchange—in other words, the dissemblance by which it is not as readily apparent that what passes as rational economic transactions always dispossesses some of the parties attendant to the exchange. In the most routine protocols of the Atlantic economies, the difference of phenotypes hyperbolically redacts the diacritical positions on either side of the commodity form, positions ideally opposed as *production* and *consumption*. The difference of phenotypes in these turns of mind *naturalizes* the co-implicated subjective and economic feints of commodity fetishism, that is, the misperception that "producers" and "consumers" contend equally within the interests of modern market relations. These turns of the imagination are racialized in key, stark manners for the modern West because of the radical modern dispositions of populations according to continental origin. These radical dispositions dichotomize Europe and Africa, consumption and production, supervision and subordination, reason and unreason as indices of race within the modern circumstances of unprecedented demographic proximities. On this point, the historian Robin Blackburn notes, importantly: "Although data on the immigration of free persons to the Americas are much less precise, it seems probable that enslaved African immigrants to the New World outnumbered Europeans by about four or five to one during the eighteenth century" (384).

Compared with the occurrences in Europe and the Americas, the personal securities of the populations of the various polities along the coast of West Africa "evaporated to facilitate a trade that was a constant threat to their existence" (Rodney 259). For instance, Senegambia, the northernmost coastal region disrupted in the vast triangulation of the Atlantic economies, includes the polities of the Bijangos, Mande, and Mandingas, among others, and although it is the region that supplies the least number of enslaved conscripts to the expansion of capital accumulation, it nonetheless registers fully the effects of the international violence. Beyond the widespread warfare that does not arise necessarily from—but necessarily inflames—regional political animosities, a variety of legal and extralegal threats reorganizes and frustrates quotidian life across the Senegambia: various systems of land tenure, based on land stewardship by the nobility or reciprocal labor, are compromised; penal systems are recalculated to broaden and expedite the possibilities of seizure for enslavement; the means of exploiting personal and class rivalries expand enormously; and the enticements to lawlessness, such as kidnapping, alter both personal and organized political calculations. Most importantly, drawing the region into even greater entanglements with the ideally infinite arena of Europe and the "New World" of ideally infinite exchange, the enveloping threat to travel and unfamiliar intercourse weakens the internal commercial relations of the Senegambia. The disruption of the political economies along the lower Guinea and west-central coasts, territories of the Angolans, Kongolese, Oyo, Yoruba, and others, is even more acute, providing "ample proof that the economic pull of the American market could force a fundamental change within Africa" (Lovejoy 57). The volume, rapidity, and high consequence of the overwhelming transfer of the African labor forces to the western rim of the Atlantic is noted by the historian Paul Lovejoy:

> The largest exporting region in the early seventeenth century is west-central Africa, which continued sending thousands of slaves a year to the Americas, thus consolidating a pattern that had began a century earlier. Senegambia and Benin maintained their relatively modest share of the trade as well, each providing about a thousand slaves a year. Slaves came from elsewhere too. The really dramatic expansion of the Atlantic trade began after 1650, and from then slave exports affected ever larger parts of Africa, not just the Kongo region. In the last fifty years of the seventeenth century, more slaves were sold to Europeans on the Atlantic coast than in the previous two hundred years combined. This phenomenal growth was a response to the spread of plantation slavery in the Americas. From the 1640s through the 1660s, sugar spread from Brazil to the lesser Antilles—Barbados, Martinique, Guadeloupe, St. Kitts, Antigua—and these new colonies acquired tens of thousands of slaves. The figure of the third quarter of the seventeenth century was double the previous twenty-five year period, averaging 17,700 per year, while in the last quarter, almost 30,000 slaves were exported annually. By now sugar plantations were being established on Jamaica and Saint

Domingue, which rapidly became the two largest producers of
sugar. As a result, the dramatic surge in slave exports continued
into the eighteenth century, reaching figures in the order of 61,00
slavers per year for the whole century. (46)

Moreover, it is important to understand that the violence of the
Atlantic conscription is neither random nor absolute. Lovejoy notes the
closely deliberative aspects of the undermining of the political jurisdictions
of the coast: "The introduction of new crops from the Americas increased
food production and thereby helped to maintain population levels despite
the export of slaves. Advances in commercial institutions including credit
facilities, currency, bulking, and regularized transportation, assisted in the
movement of slaves" (68). In short, whereas the intrusive transatlantic contact
"implies disorder in the social framework wherever the external trade was
important, the effective organization of slave supply required that political
violence be contained within boundaries that would permit the sale of slaves
abroad" (Lovejoy 66). On this point, Achille Mbembe's acknowledgment
of the relations between massacre, bureaucracy, and Western rationality is
trenchant. In the article "Necropolitics," Mbembe draws the concatenation
of the slave trade, plantation slavery, and the colony to define the fundamental insinuation of race with the abstract reason of Western modernity,
writing: "In fact, in most instances, the selection of races, the prohibition of
mixed marriages, forced sterilization, even the extermination of vanquished
peoples are to find their testing ground in the colonial world. Here we see
the first syntheses between massacre and bureaucracy, that incarnation of
Western rationality" (23).

The period of this reimagination is also the period of the annexation of
the Americas and the polices governing the opportunities to raise and traffic
enormous quantities of goods in the new arena of the Atlantic economies,
which transform the significance of the premodern axes of long-distance
trade. The economic values of the emergent Atlantic economies abruptly
eclipse those of the traffic of the Baltic Sea primarily in timber and fish,
the trade in primarily the luxury items of fabrics and spices (including
sugar) exchanged across the Mediterranean Sea, as well as the transfers of
silk, lacquerware, coral, pearls, horses, wool, linen, and aromatics moving
across the Indian Ocean as well as through the vast intercontinental arena
of the silk roads. The newly promoted European desires for sugar and
other tropical products that circulate in trans-Atlantic relays following the
fifteenth century formalize in the seventeenth and eighteenth centuries the

enormous trade circuit termed the triangular trade, fusing the formerly disparate economies of the Americas, western Europe, and the West African coast from Senegambia, Sierra Leone, the Windward and Gold Coasts, and the Bight of Benin, to Benguela beyond the Bight of Biafra, jurisdictions inhabited by Akans, Angolans, Ashante, Bambara, Igbo, Kongolese, Kru, Mandingas, Mende, Oyo, Vais, Yoruba, and others, who are hard-pressed by the demands of the European modernity. In the triangular circuit of the new Atlantic economies, European-manufactured objects are disposed on the African coast in trade for slaves, who are shipped across the Atlantic as the requisite labor force for the massive production of the cash crops that, in the final segment of the circuit, are traded under the nationally protectionist policies of the European metropoles to serve the rearticulated desires of mass populations. These are fundamental developments for Western modernity, yet their consideration, to borrow a statement from the literary critic David Shumway, is "rarely intended to contribute to [the interrogation rather than] assum[ption] that the lesson to be learned from the past is the superiority of the present" (218).

Claiming the Ideological Lack of the Subject

In this way, the question of desire is crucial because, finally, the question of desire is ideological. The question might be, in what ways is the para-digmatic rationalizing "the oppression of people of color" formative, then, of the subjectivity Western modernity seeks and reiterates? To what extent is this a paradigmatic reiteration of Western modern subjectivity? To what extent might forms of knowledge within and without the academy fortify or reconfigure the paradigm? In particular, if cultural studies can accom-modate this scoring of the progression of Western modernity inherited from the epistemological upheavals of the 1960s and 1970s, then to what extent must its disciplinary unruliness be seen not only as unruly but reformative in its questioning of desire, the archival, discursive, economic, libidinal, and subjective trajectories describing the teleological form of desire indicated as Western modernity? Under what circumstances and in what forms might the regulated knowledge production of late capital desire or allow the nomination and enumeration of African-derived peoples? To what extent might this patently ideological question of desire determine whether "cultural studies can represent itself as the locus of social critique" (Bowlby 277), in the words of Rachel Bowlby? African American Studies takes as its object of inquiry what must be perceived as an unruly methodological inquiry: Racial blackness, the primary enabling point of exclusion for the development of Western modernity, complicates the legibility of modern subjectivity, the form of civic animation sustained by the international markets and trade that, accordingly, by the end of the eighteenth century, remains the iconic referent of collective human presence. These diacritical positions expose the unruly dilemma, the bold modern contrivance, the (un)certain proposition that human animation fails the criteria of human being, the policy providing the pragmatic meaning of the mass introduction and presence of African-derived persons in Western Atlantic commerce and societies. The questionable proposition has inevitable psychic, scripted, and social fissures.

These fissures reveal, in the instance we are considering, that programs of taxonomy and administration and programs of social critique are attended to with radical differences in order to make claims on the ultimate epistemological ground, the systemic subject of Western modernity. On this point, the Lacanian critical theorist Slavoj Žižek, in *The Sublime Object of Ideology*, formulates the conflicted principles of modern agency and consciousness that coordinate, nonetheless, the stable appearance of Western social reality. He does so by explicating Lacanian psychoanalysis in order to complicate Althusserian notions of ideology. In the analysis, the conflicted principles generating social reality most readily describe not an individual figure, but a fundamentally discursive scheme: a four-part structure of subjection revealing, at once, the progressive, retrogressive, and synchronous operation by which the subject is, at once, psychic, articulate, social, and self-divided. The paradigmatic aspect of the scheme is the transversal of the subject by the signifier–signified relation, the Saussurian sign. The kinesis of desire, however, profoundly frustrates the proposition, confounding any certainty that the transversal of the signifier–signified relation fixes ideally. Still, the transversal of the signifier by the subject realizes the *point de capiton*, at which "*pure difference is perceived as Identity* exempted from the relational-differential interplay and guaranteeing its homogeneity" (Žižek 99; italics in original). The two components of the Sausserian sign, the signifier and the signified, appear fused through all attenuation or, in other words, the appearance is of "the signifier maintaining its identity through all variations of its signified" (100). The subject is split in a variety of ways in this fusion with the signifying chain, thus the action of the mirror stage, the ego's constitutive alienation in the imaginary other. That is, the subject is split into an image (imaginary identification) and a gaze (symbolic identification), the imaginary identification reconstituting, through the trace of desire, the inspection of the symbolic identification. "We could say that in imaginary identification," writes Žižek, "we imitate the other at the level of resemblance—we identify ourselves with the image of the other inasmuch as we are 'like him,' whereas in symbolic identification we identify ourselves with the other precisely at a point at which he is inimitable, at the point which eludes resemblance" (109). Imaginary identification approximates an image projected from the subject and symbolic identification approximates a gaze directed on the subject, the dynamic by which the sign holds its greatest force.

These points of identification reflect the production of the ego in conflict with the point de capiton. The subject is the subject perpetually split by its "own" desire yet seemingly coherent in deference to the *point de capiton*, so that retroactively the subject is already the subject seemingly before as well as after the transversal of the sign, always already submitted to an alien code determining but also, as strictly, beyond consciousness. The subject is the lack of itself announcing itself, the lack of meaning announcing meaning, the apparent resolution of meaning deferring the preemptive play of enjoyment excessive to, yet traced through, the transversal of the sign. In coming into being, the subject and desire are fractured so inexorably that the voicing of the subject is always already the residue of this nonequivalence of desire and demand. The subject disappears as it articulates itself, voice and voicing being the trace of the disappearance, because they are at the same time the trace of the signifying order annunciating the subject, as nonetheless the subject also seems to annunciate the subject. Voice and voicing render the subject as a sonic fracture, being the remnants, the residues, of the functional alienation, identifications, and aggregate force by which desire and human presence effectively are reduced to the relation between signifier and signified.

Moreover, the subject is not just the lack of itself but the lack of the signifying order. The subject is the lack of the signifying order reflecting the allowance for enjoyment beyond interpellation, because the installation of the subject in the signifying order signals an opening or gap that constitutively precedes the subject. The subject is the inexorable point of the realization of the signifying order, without which the signifying order could not signify. These cancellations describe the point at which the discursive figure becomes ideological, insofar as the figure of the individual retains its credibility only through effects of imagination that are, rather than individual, aggregate, paradoxically like the conceptual polar opposite of the individual, the community, the opposition disclosing precisely the ground of ideology, the effective tracing and retracing of desire from individual to aggregate positions and aggregate positions to the individual seamlessly at best. In brief, there is virtually no individual presence in the arrangement.

Hence the subject is the concomitant product of fantasy, absolute signification, and an epistemological promise; subjectivity is the articulation of desire pressed into being between the "Real"—sensitivity, intention, meaning steadfastly resisting symbolization—and the "Symbolic"—the pure sedimentation of meaning as effortless, steadfast correspondence. The problem in perpetuity remains, however, that to occlude the concomitantly phantasmatic and epistemological ground of the signifying order is the very operation of the figure of the subject, the ideological premise of the subject.

Nonetheless, social justice is also an ideology, an alternative concomitant and constitutive play of the phantasmatic and the epistemological, that might establish the circuitries of the individual and particularly the community as idea-object. For these reasons, social justice as an open, constitutive possibility presents the supervision of the official production of knowledge with the task of negotiating the fraught question of what degree African American Studies and cultural studies, for instance, can or cannot articulate revisionary desires that are recalcitrant to being mapped within the absolute significations of the disciplines they emerge from and largely supercede. In other words, one pressing question, both within and without the academy, is how to live in unsettling circumstances nonetheless demanding the pretense—according to official or sanctioned discourse—that they are not unsettling, a subjectivizing principle that directly challenges the epistemological certitude of social justice. In this way, from the vantage of the late twentieth century, with the revisionary potential of African American presence and culture in mind, Toni Morrison is keen, scrupulous, when she repeats, paradoxically, "This is not a story to pass on" (275).

Notes

1. Lindon Barrett was not able to complete revisions to this essay before his untimely death. We publish it here in the form in which he left it with minor copyediting changes. Portions of this essay also appear in "Mercantilism, Federalism, and the Market Within Reason: The "People" and the Conceptual Impossibility of Racial Blackness" in *Accelerating Possession: Global Futures of Persons and Property*, eds. Bill Mauer and Gabrielle Schwab (New York: Columbia University Press, 2006): 99–131.

2. The torque and quandary are reckonable, to follow the arguments of the historian William Pierson, as a type of aesthetic transaction in which "certain black and white designs can be made to contain two vastly different pictures, the observed pattern depending upon which color our mind perceives at a particular moment to be dominant. . . . What would happen if we shifted our normal perspective so as to make our nation's black legacy, a primary point of reference? Just as in the visual image, the patterns of American history would instantly seem to reverse themselves. Such a process would not change the history, but it would offer a flash of Afrocentric insight—how changed the world could be if only we thought differently about things, at least for a moment" (Pierson ix).

Works Cited

Amariglio, Jack, and Antonio Callari. "Marxian Value Theory and the Problem of the Subject: The Role of Commodity Fetishism." *Fetishism as Cultural Discourse*. Ed. Emily Apter and William Pietz. Ithaca: Cornell UP, 1993.

Berger, Iris. "Contested Boundaries: African Studies Approaching the Millenium: Presidential Address to the 1996 African Studies Association Annual Meeting." *African Studies Review* 40.2 (Sept. 1997): 1–14.

Blackburn, Robin. *The Making of New World Slavery: From the Baroque to the Modern 1492–1800*. London: Verso, 1997.

Bose, Purima. "Interconnections." Forum essay. *PMLA* 112.2 (1997): 282–83.

Bowlby, Rachel. "Interconnections." Forum essay. *PMLA* 112.2 (1997): 277.

Eltis, David. "Europeans and the Rise and Fall of African Slavery in the Americas: An Interpretation." *American Historical Review* (Dec. 1993): 1339–1423.

Fenves, Peter. "An Introduction to 'Aesthetics and the Disciplines.' " *Eighteenth-Century Studies* 35.3 (2002): 339–41.

Gemery, Henry A., and Jan S. Hogendorn. "The Economic Costs of West African Participation in the Atlantic Slave Trade: A Preliminary Sampling for the Eighteenth Century." *The Uncommon Market: Essays in the Economic History of the Atlantic Slave Trade*. Ed. Henry A. Gemery and Jan S. Hogendorn. New York: Academic Press, 1979. 143–61.

Lovejoy, Paul. *Transformations in Slavery: A History of Slavery in Africa*. Cambridge: Cambridge UP, 1979.

McKeon, M. "In Retrospect: The Disciplines Revisited: The Origins of Interdisciplinary Studies." *Eighteenth-Century Studies* 28.1 (1994): 17–28

Morgan, Edmund. *American Slavery, American Freedom: The Ordeal of Colonial Virginia*. New York: Norton, 1975.

Mbembe, Achille. "Necropolitics." *Public Culture* 15.1 (2003): 11–40.

Morrison, Toni. *Beloved*. New York: Plume, 1987.

Murray, Timothy. "Defining Interdisciplinarity." Forum essay. *PMLA* 111.2 (1996): 279–80.

Northrup, David. *Africa's Discovery of Europe: 1450–1850*. New York: Oxford UP, 2002.

Okafar, Victor. "The Place of Africology in the University Curriculum." *Journal of Black Studies* 26 (July 1996): 688–712.

Pierson, William D. *Black Legacy: America's Hidden Heritage*. Amherst: U of Massachusetts P, 1993.

Poetics Today 12.2 (1991). Special Issue: "Disciplinarity."

———. 24.2 (2003). Special Issue. "The Cognitive Turn? A Debate on Interdisciplinarity."

PMLA. 111.2 (1996). "Defining Interdisciplinarity." Forum essays. 271–311.

———. 112.2 (1997). "Interconnections." Forum essays. 275–86.

Rodney, Walter. *A History of the Upper Guinea Coast, 1585–1800*. Oxford: Clarendon Press, 1970.

Robinson, Cedric J. *Black Marxism: The Making of the Black Radical Tradition*. London: Zed Books, 1983.

Rosaldo, Renato. "Whose Cultural Studies?" *American Anthropologist* 96.3 (1994): 524–29.

Shumway, David R. and Ellen Messer-Davidow. "Disciplinarity: An Introduction." *Poetics Today* 12.2 (Summer 1991): 201–25.

Spillers, Hortense J. "The Crisis of the Negro Intellectual: A Post Date." *boundary 2*, 21.3 (1994): 65–116.

Suskin, Clifford. "On the Sublime: An Interdisciplinary Forum." *Eighteenth-Century Studies* 28.1 (1994): 37–93.

Yudice, George. "Defining Interdisciplinarity." Forum essay. *PMLA* 111.2 (1996): 275–76.

Žižek, Slavoj. *The Sublime Object of Ideology*. London: Verso, 1989.

Chapter Twelve

Imagined Immunities

Border Rhetorics and the Ethos
of *Sans Frontièrisme*

D. Robert DeChaine

A way of seeing is always a way of not seeing.

—Kenneth Burke, *Permanence and Change*

To invoke the logic of "the border" is to bespeak a worldview. At present, public debates rage in the United States regarding the proposed completion of a twenty-five-hundred-mile fence along the U.S.-Mexico border, with the imputed aim of "sealing" and "securing" it and thereby curbing entry of "illegal aliens" into an "American" territory. Meanwhile, Microsoft has recently launched a new advertising campaign in print and on the Internet in which it touts its visionary business acumen and proclaims its stake in a globalized, cyberactive financescape: "We see business without borders." Though hardly unique, the examples are instructive. The nationalist rhetoric of U.S. immigration reform highlights in microcosmic form the juridico-historical operations by which the abject, inassimilable other, the illegal alien, is imagined, classified, and regulated—in this case, both fenced out and whited out from a sacrosanct space of citizenship (Pettman 287). On the surface, Microsoft's imagining of a borderless space of commerce gestures toward a liberatory politics of flows. Such a gesture, however, elides the clench of its monopolistic grip on global business software markets. Moreover, the instantiation of Microsoft's "We" throws into sharp relief the line separat-

261

ing those with access to computer technology and those without (although nearly all live its effects). More than anything, each example illustrates the supple *rhetoricity* of bordering practices: the ease with which physical and psychic borders map onto and reinforce one another; the imputed virtues and agencies of border crossing, redrawing, effacing. Utterly unquestioned are the metaphors of space, movement, and control on which each invocation of the border is founded. And space, as Michel Foucault insists, "is fundamental in any exercise of power" (qtd. in Rabinow 252). In fact, both examples reveal a tenacious adherence to border rhetorics and their territorializing logic. Some implications of those rhetorics and the quality of their tenacity are the subject of what follows.

An increasingly prevalent claim in contemporary scholarship, especially in the burgeoning literature on border studies and border theory, is that in whatever form they may take, borders are foremost politically motivated social constructs. In this view, a border is a bounding, ordering apparatus whose function is to designate, produce, and/or police the space of difference, simultaneously shoring up insides and marking off outsides while establishing the terms of their relationality (Soguk). The contingency of a border's configuration is often masked by political and economic discourses that labor feverishly to maintain the semblance of its reality, its permanence, and its integrity. Recent work in the field of communication studies, particularly in the area of immigration discourse, aligns with such a view of the truth-function of the border, focusing attention on its rhetorical constructedness and the ambivalent identities of b/ordered subjects (Flores; Ono and Sloop). From this rhetorical perspective, the border is a symbolic inducement to action, used to warrant claims to both unity and division (Demo; Shah). It serves as a robust metaphor that performs an ideographic function (McGee), an organizing doxa in a group's collective vocabulary.

Such critical theorizations of the border have in fact become commonplace in scholarship spanning the humanities and the social sciences. What is not so apparent in the literature is the disciplinary history that informs the present border epistemology. Gaining momentum in the wake of the incursion of postmodernist theory in the 1960s and 1970s in fields such as anthropology and sociology, and especially pronounced in "the spatial turn" in geography, the legacy of this history has witnessed a rather surprising development. As recent understandings of space and spatiality have become ever more infused into the global vernacular, an epistemological shift has begun to take place—a shift from an understanding of borders as contingent sites of contestation to the notion of *borderlessness*. The postmodern refiguration of "the border," formerly viewed predominantly as a warrant for acts of territorialization (b/orderings) and as an exigency for various modalities of resistance (crossings, transgressions), now also serves as a warrant for supposed acts of *de*territorialization. Borders, according to this logic, are not simply porous, they are erasable. The claim to borderlessness is an increasingly apparent feature of new social movement rhetoric. More significantly, "without borders" is coming to function as a trope for community in a globalized world. To wit, a new imagining of community is supplanting the traditional nation-based model in the form of *sans frontièrisme*, or "without borderism." Fashioned by a confluence of disciplinary scholarship in the humanities and social sciences, fueled by media culture, catalyzed in a variety of incipient modes of humanitarian-based social and political activism, and readily subsumed into the discourse of capitalism, *sans frontièrisme* plays on a kind of irreproachable moral ethos—an ethos that is rhetorically crafted so as to serve as a warrant for any actions carried out in its name. Moreover, as will hopefully become clear, the ethos of *sans frontièrisme* remains fully vested in the logic of the border—the same logic it claims to deconstruct.

A formative agency of the contemporary ethos of *sans frontièrisme* is the medical humanitarian group *Médecins Sans Frontières* (MSF), or Doctors Without Borders in its English iteration. Founded in 1971 by Bernard Kouchner and Xavier Emmanuelli along with a handful of other French doctors working for the International Committee of the Red Cross, MSF proclaims a dual mandate to assist "populations in danger" during humanitarian crises and to engage in *témoignage*, or public witnessing against those who commit violations of human rights and international law with regard to those populations. Directing its missions into sovereign territories, sometimes against the expressed will of ruling powers, MSF claims complete political neutrality regarding its relief operations and *témoignage*, premising its borderless actions on a professed *droit d'ingérence* or "right of interference" in the name of imputed transcendent humanitarian values. Awarded the Nobel Prize in 1999, with sections in nineteen countries, and the object of numerous high-profile media productions, MSF has led the call to *sans frontièrisme*, garnering international acclaim and spurring a global movement, evidenced by the literally thousands of organizations currently donning the "without borders" moniker. In examining the discourse of borderlessness, this essay advances an argument about the instrumental role of border rhetorics in shaping public perceptions of social space, and by extension, the character of global humanitarian action. The affect-charged exhortation of MSF to challenge geographical, political, and sociocultural borders in the name of humanity illustrates both the symbolic force and

the fraught logic of *sans frontièrisme* in present times. Its claim to a transcendent humanitarian space for social action involves an articulation of
language, ideology, and affect that reveals itself to be far from politically
neutral. Gaining broad moral legitimacy from its adherence to the conception of humanity enshrined in the United Nations Universal Declaration
of Human Rights, and gaining intellectual legitimacy from the postmodern
vernacularization of spatial theory, MSF is able to mobilize popular support
for its deterritorialized action. However, as this analysis will demonstrate,
any moves to deterritorialize space—in the name of humanity or anything
else—necessarily entail concomitant *re*territorializations that have implications for those in whose name action without borders is undertaken. In
examining the disciplinary substrate of *sans frontièrisme*, and by analyzing
MSF's particular embodiment of its ethos, the essay means to problematize
the epistemological crosscurrents that fund borderlessness as a warrant for
humane collective action.

Rather more tacitly, this essay means to underscore the need for
increased attention to the doxastic, truth-making function of rhetoric. Recent
moves by proponents of global humanitarianism to recast the social-spatial
imaginary as a deterritorialized space without borders prompts a redoubled
scrutiny in the figure of the border and the rhetorical power that it wields.
In his 1935 book *Permanence and Change*, Kenneth Burke calls attention to
the sedimented powers of symbolic terminologies to both direct and reflect
the experiential reality of symbol users. "A way of seeing," he reminds, "is
always a way of not seeing" insofar as "a focus upon object A involves a
neglect of object B" (70). Arcing Burke into the present, in a globalized world
predicated on the material reality of national borders, it is not surprising
that the terministic, directive logic of the border figures so prominently in
the everyday language of human relations. What is now vitally at stake is
an understanding of the *reflective* function of border(less) rhetorics and the
ease with which they serve as an alibi for the reterritorializing of power.
Academics and activists wishing to advance an interdisciplinary project
grounded in a horizon of social justice are admonished to attend closely to
the mechanisms that work to refigure space in the name of humanity.

Antecedents of *Sans Frontièrisme*:
The Vernacularization of the Spatial

The emergent borderless rhetoric that funds *sans frontièrisme* has been significantly fashioned by the disciplinary history informing contemporary studies

of space and territory. The effects of this history are especially pronounced in the wake of the incursion of postmodern theory and, particularly, the advent of "the spatial turn" in the social sciences and humanities beginning in the 1970s. Although a comprehensive recounting of this shift is beyond the scope of this essay,[1] some of its key constituents bear mentioning. A formative site for this shift is evident in the fields of human and political geography, particularly in their movements away from positivistic approaches to space. Prior to the 1970s, geographers held a general view of space as a natural, given, and absolute phenomenon; according to this view, space functions according to a geometric logic, as a grid for the emplotment of objects and events (Curry 5). Beginning in the 1950s, the Enlightenment epistemology of positivism, with its strict adherence to the values of objectivity, causality, and the rigor of scientific method, became the predominant lens through which geographers analyzed spatial functions and relations. The study of space thus involved the scientific analysis of patterns of organization that were, at least in theory, finite and measurable. Similarly at the time, theorists in the field of political geography held to an absolute notion of space and territory. Geopolitical space, according to such a view, was conceived as territorially fixed and organized by the demarcation of boundaries, mainly understood in terms of political limits of states (Van Houtum 673–74). Gradually, in the 1960s, geographical understandings of space and territory as absolute and given became subject to critical scrutiny, particularly with regard to the positivistic view of space as an objective phenomenon set apart from individuals' perceptions and experiences. This critique precipitated the development of more human-centered theories of space and approaches to spatial analysis and ushered in the emergence of the subfields of behavioral and humanistic geography (Hubbard, Kitchin, Bartley, and Fuller 33).

Notwithstanding geography's burgeoning intradisciplinary critique of space as an essentialized and absolute phenomenon, it was not until the 1970s and 1980s, with the mushrooming of postmodernist scholarship across the disciplines, that traditional conceptions of territory and space began to be vigorously questioned and radically refigured. A renewed focus on historical materialism and the ongoing relevance of Marxist theory spurred engagements between sociology and various branches of geography, resulting in a multiformity of analyses of space as socially produced, lived, shaped, and consumed (cf. Harvey; Jameson; Lefebvre; Massey; Soja). The postmodern reconceptualization of space as a production of (late) capitalist practices and relations sought to account for an overlapping, dynamic play of physical, mental, and social space—the articulation, in the words of Edward Soja,

of a "spatialized ontology": a call for "a reawakening to the spatiality of
being, consciousness, and action, a growing awareness of the possibility of
spatial praxis, an increasingly recognized need to rethink social theory so
as to incorporate more centrally the fundamental spatiality of social life"
(137). For his part, Foucault undertook genealogical analyses of the micro-
physics of power that drew heavily on spatial metaphors in describing the
operations by which disciplinary apparatuses are applied, distributed, and
dispersed across the social body (cf. *Discipline, History of Sexuality*). In "Of
Other Spaces," an essay published in the 1980s based on a lecture he gave in
1967, Foucault offered an account of historically contingent "heterotopias,"
the heterogeneous sites that, he argued, are characteristic of modern social
life. Against a view of space as static and given, he stressed the lived quality of spatial relations: "[W]e do not live in a kind of void, inside of which
we could place individuals and things . . . we live inside a set of relations
that delineates sites which are irreducible to one another and absolutely not
superimposable on one another" (23). Foucault's explorations of the social
production of space, along with those of other critical social theorists of the
era, succeeded in reorienting the study of space away from predominantly
positivistic analyses of natural and given space toward a critical interrogation of spatial/ized practices, representations, and imaginings.

Gradually, from the critical milieu of postmodernity, a new, interdisciplinary discourse of spatiality has emerged, in which space is conceived
"not as a neutral category but as something that is culturally produced,
lived, and represented in various ways" (Moran 165). The new focus on
spatiality, along with interanimating analyses of place and time, has fueled
the interdisciplinary projects of cultural studies, communication studies,
literary studies, and performance studies and has invigorated scholarship
in and across the disciplines of anthropology, sociology, economics, history,
politics, philosophy, architecture, and geography, among others. Studies of
spatial practices often bring together (albeit not always comfortably) a variety
of theoretical discourses, reflecting an expanding range of inter/disciplin-
ary sites for analysis: urban and rural city space; cyberculture; diasporic
communities; urban guerrilla theatre; postcolonial fiction; raced, sexed,
and gendered spaces; sites of public commemoration; affect and embodied
experience; formations of the nation-state—the list goes on. A plethora
of books, journals, and edited collections on spatiality has appeared and
continues to grow, as have academic seminars and programs, conferences,
research centers, and other indicators of an incipient interdisciplinary field
of "space studies." Indeed, it would be hard to disagree with Crang and

Thrift in their assertion that space has become "the everywhere of modern thought" (1), implicating itself thoroughly in the language and life of the academic imagination.

Two strands of the new focus on spatiality became especially important beginning in the mid-1980s and have particular relevance for this essay. One strand has focused primarily on the construction of "border identities" and the experiences of b/ordered subjects. Proceeding from an anthropological emphasis on culture as an instrumental shaper of truth and knowledge, the border is conceived as profoundly polyvalent—both real and imagined, material and constructed, permanent and ephemeral, a fraught but necessary structure always positioned at the nexus of cultural and political power (Fox; Rosaldo). According to this view, the border is a marker, or alternately a site, for the designation and hierarchization of sameness and difference, unity and division. As such, it serves a hegemonic function in the formation and maintenance of national and ethnic identity. A number of "border studies" scholars who follow this strand place its theoretical and analytical origins at the U.S.-Mexico frontier (cf. Michaelsen and Johnson; Vila) and point to Chicano studies as its major purveyor.[2] Of these, Gloria Anzaldúa's theorization of "the borderland" is perhaps the most celebrated. In *Borderlands/La Frontera: The New Mestiza*, Anzaldúa describes the polymorphic, ambivalent power of the border/lands:

> The U.S.-Mexican border *es una herida abierta* where the Third World grates against the first and bleeds. And before a scab forms it hemorrhages again, the lifeblood of two worlds merging to form a third country—a border culture. Borders are set up to define the places that are safe and unsafe, to distinguish *us* from *them*. A border is a dividing line, a narrow strip along a steep edge. A borderland is a vague and undetermined place created by the emotional residue of an unnatural boundary. It is in a constant state of transition. The prohibited and forbidden are its inhabitants. (3, emphasis in original)

In her designation of borderlands as charged, liminal zones of contact and division, "the border" comes to signify that which must be (constantly) negotiated—crossed, transgressed, played with, inhabited.[3] Other border studies scholars have focused more generally on borders as complex sites of sociospatial practice. For political geographers, this has meant that the border "is now understood as a verb in the sense of bordering" (Van Houtum

672). For others, it has involved such varied investigations as the cultural politics of border crossings in and out of Western subjectivity, the shifting political identities precipitated by border crossings of migrant laborers and refugees, and the effects of Enlightenment discourses on the limits of the nation-state (cf. Minh-Ha; Soguk; Welchman). The proliferation of border studies in the 1980s and 1990s, as John Welchman states, "marked a new stage in the debates over postmodernism, cultural studies and postcolonialism" (xii), and its provocations continue to animate discussions about border constructions, negotiations, and habitations in the present.

Another vibrant strand of theoretical-analytical work on spatiality—in some ways a response to the first—has developed in the context of globalization, and in particular, the increasing globalization of capital. As with border studies, the scope of this scholarship is broad, straddling a number of disciplinary orientations in the humanities and social sciences. Usually not explicitly linked to border studies per se, this work places emphasis on various modes of organization, movement, and exchange and their effects on globalized subjects through means of travel, migration, hypermediation, time–space compression, displacement, and hybridization (cf. Bhabha; Castells; Harvey; Giddens; Said). Arjun Appadurai's argument regarding the "complex, overlapping, disjunctive order" of the "new global cultural economy" ("Disjuncture and Difference" 296) is illustrative. Departing from an anthropological tradition that implicitly and explicitly links specific (knowable, coherent, manageable) cultures to specific (knowable, coherent, manageable) territories, Appadurai undertakes a reconceptualization of spatiality in terms of what he describes as deterritorialized, disjunctive cultural flows or "scapes." Invoking conceptual language from Gilles Deleuze and Felix Guattari,[4] he asserts, "Deterritorialization, in general, is one of the central forces of the modern world" ("Disjuncture and Difference" 301), responsible for shaping the character of social relations, media markets, and global finance. For Appadurai, deterritorialization effectively renders the notion of borders obsolete, insofar as the traditional model of the nation-state with its more or less coherent "imagined community" (Anderson) gives way in a globalized world to an increasingly complex circulation of people, money, technologies, media, and ideologies. Although Appadurai is clearly concerned with the cultural politics of deterritorialization, the brunt of his analysis is given to the formulation of a fluid, borderless understanding of spatiality, an understanding that has proven particularly durable in contemporary scholarship.[5] Challenges such as Appadurai's to the linearity and coherence of space have contributed to a shift toward borderlessness in contemporary academic scholarship. Moreover, as Crang and Thrift note, disciplinary discourses of globalization have given rise to a number of spatial "metaphors of longing and belonging," which "tend to be 'open,' based on 'points of encounter,' 'contact zones,' 'borderlands,' and 'hybridity' " (19), metaphors that rally the formidable energies of affect and imagination in forging a new understanding of space, distance, subjectivity, the local, and the global. Such metaphoric knowledge has thoroughly worked its way into academic discourse—so much so that the notion "that distance and physical limitations have become irrelevant is becoming a doxa of the globalizing era" (Schirato and Webb 152).[6]

Together, these two strands of spatial theory and analysis have reoriented public knowledge about the character of borders, boundaries, and territories. They have attuned scholars and activists to a view of space as a construction, a multivariate complex of operations by which psychic territories and their attendant cultural-ideological investments become mapped onto physical territories and their geopolitical investments. Concomitantly, they have led to an understanding of the power dynamics of spatiality, the recognition that "the geography of the world is not a product of nature but a product of histories of struggle between competing authorities over the power to organize, occupy, and administer space" (Ó Tuathail 1). With the increased prevalence of this refigured knowledge, the language of deterritorialized, borderless space has become ever more infused into the nonacademic sphere. The example of Microsoft's "business without borders" that opened this essay is but one example. From popular media to business and finance, from lawyers to architects, from political campaigns to humanitarian nongovernmental organizations (NGOs), the world, it seems, is now a space without borders, or at least, in the words of Manuel Castells, a "space of flows" in which boundaries are porous, contestable, and effaceable.

The vernacularization of spatiality, along with the turn from borders to borderlessness, is fueling the contemporary global social imaginary in the form of a broad-based movement of *sans frontièrisme* (without borderism). The term *sans frontières* itself predates the advent of the spatial turn in the disciplines. As early as the 1970s, a number of mostly French humanitarian organizations working both autonomously and together began to form alongside and out of MSF—among them *SOS Enfants* (Children) *Sans Frontières*, *Libertés* (Liberties) *Sans Frontières*, *Reporters Sans Frontières*, *Pharmaciens* (Chemists) *Sans Frontières*, *Hôpital* (Hospitals) *Sans Frontières*, *Quartiers* (Neighborhoods) *Sans Frontières*, and *Orphelins* (Orphans) *Sans Frontières*. As the number and size of these groups grew, the notion of *sans frontièrisme* as a movement began to gain currency, first in France, then in Europe and North America, and eventually worldwide.[7] With the recognition of *sans frontièrisme* as a global phenomenon, *sans frontières* has since emerged as a key word in the vocabulary of global humanitarianism. As a way of seeing the world, *sans frontièrisme* represents an articulation of linguistic and ideological commitments, or better, a constellation of linguistically constituted, real and imagined assemblages of places and spaces (Hubbard, Kitchin, and Valentine 7). Moreover, a borderless social imaginary presents a challenge to the traditional model of the nation-state as the primary mode of communal experience; increasingly, as old conceptions of borders dissolve, as a global "we" gains prominence in political, economic, academic, and popular discussions of human collectivity, it is becoming clear that "without borders" ranks as a master signifier for the new border rhetoric, an ascendant trope for the new, imagined community.

The shift from speaking about borders and bordered subjects to a future-present where the very concept of the border becomes an object of contestation presents novel challenges for social theory, challenges that beckon deepened critical attention. Notions of borderedness and borderlessness would seem, on the surface, counterposed to one another, or at least, to constitute an ambivalent relation. In actuality, however, as the following example of MSF demonstrates, they both depend on the same logic of territorialization, a logic premised on the ability "to organize, occupy, and administer space." The idea of borderless space, increasingly popularized in a globalized world, is being deployed under the aegis of a depoliticized rhetoric of humanitarian action—a rhetoric that has implications for the individuals and spaces in whose name it claims to speak.

Médecins Sans Frontières and the Ethos of Sans Frontièrisme

The current pull of *sans frontièrisme* in the global social imaginary is aptly illustrated in the humanitarian-based group *Médecins Sans Frontières*, and in particular, its crafting of a transcendent humanitarian space for action. Bolstered by the discourse of universal human rights, a discourse that serves as a warrant for its proclaimed moral imperative to intervene in humanitarian emergencies, MSF attempts to balance a politically driven mandate of neutrality against a morally based commitment to bear witness against human rights abuses on behalf of those whose voices would otherwise remain silent and/or silenced. Through MSF's mediatization of its humanitarian interventions, an action deemed necessary in the competitive arena of humanitarian aid agencies, the group publicly lays claim to its right and duty to deterritorialize space in the name of humanity. Fully funded by the vernacularized discourse of spatiality, MSF constructs and exploits the ethos of *sans frontièrisme*, a powerful form of rhetorical appeal in a globalized world. The group's deterritorialized actions are, however, far from neutral. Its morally charged ethos effectively superimposes a universal conception of Humanity onto the space of cultural particularisms. Securing public legitimacy as a morally just agent of Humanity, MSF's universalizing construction allows it to reterritorialize the space it claims as borderless, a reterritorialization effected through the naming—the bringing into reality—of MSF heroes, villains, and victims. MSF's ethos of *sans frontièrisme* and its crafting of humanitarian space represents a significant reworking of spatiality in contemporary global politics. Equally important, MSF's actions demonstrate the continuing prevalence of border logics and their effects on human social life. The example of MSF's imagining of global humanitarian community illuminates the consequential relationship between rhetoric, space, and power.

To understand the basis for MSF's construction of humanitarian space, it is important to acknowledge the humanitarian impulse that underlies the group's actions. This impulse, a driving feature of its mandate, is founded on a professed commitment to the principle of human dignity, enshrined in the United Nations Universal Declaration of Human Rights (UDHR). The UDHR states that each individual, irrespective of origin, physical location, or material condition, is endowed with a fundamental human dignity, usually expressed as an inalienable right of self-determination, and that such dignity must be respected and protected as "the foundation of freedom, justice and peace in the world."[8] The claim to a universal conception of humanity founded in individual dignity is codified in MSF's proclaimed *droit d'ingérence* ("right of intervention"), the moral conviction that a breach of national sovereignty is justified when human dignity is threatened. Originally conceived by MSF founder Bernard Kouchner as a *devoir d'ingérence* ("duty of intervention"), the idea was borne of criticism shared by early MSF members that traditional aid agencies were ineffective in providing assistance to those in need as a result of political and bureaucratic impediments. In 1987, Kouchner co-authored a book titled *Le Devoir D'ingérance: Peut-on Les Laisser Mourir?* (*The Duty of Interference: Can We Leave Them to Die?*) in which he argued that humanitarian aid workers as well as states should have a legal as well as a moral right to intervene across national borders when questions of human rights are at issue. In 1988, a UN Resolution was passed granting legitimacy to humanitarian NGOs to breach national borders to provide aid to victims of humanitarian emergencies, which at the time included natural events such as hurricanes, earthquakes, disease epidemics, and famines. Since that time, MSF has considered its "right to interfere" as a legal and moral warrant for undertaking interventional modes of action in the name of an imputed universal humanity.

In tandem with MSF's first professed directive to provide medical assistance to "populations in distress," its second directive involves a moral obligation to engage in *témoignage*, which it describes as a practice undertaken in order "to bear witness publicly to the plight of the people it assists" ("What is"). The organization offers an explanation of its humanitarian mandate on its Web site:

> MSF unites direct medical care with a commitment to speaking out against the causes of suffering and the obstacles to providing effective assistance. MSF volunteers raise the concerns of their patients with governments, the United Nations, other international bodies, the general public, and the media. In a wide range of circumstances, MSF volunteers have spoken out against violations of international humanitarian law they have witnessed—from Chechnya to Sudan. ("About Us")

Témoignage, translated literally as "testimony" or "witnessing," is the term invoked by MSF members to refer to the practice of publicizing and/or denouncing perceived human injustices that its volunteers encounter in their aid missions. The practice of *témoignage* intends to call attention to the underlying "causes of suffering" and, in the words of MSF member Françoise Bouchet-Saulnier, "to provoke a social and political reaction that recognizes the rights and the needs of populations in danger" (qtd. in Marschner 19). MSF's *témoignage* assumes a variety of forms and is enacted using a number of means, such as the deployment of witnesses to a site, and on occasion, direct confrontation of responsible parties. Most often, *témoignage* is practiced indirectly, by means of publicizing information regarding human rights violators and their actions in interviews, at conferences, international symposia, and traveling exhibitions and during UN proceedings. MSF publishes its findings in reports, editorials, videos, and on Web sites, and mounts "public education projects" that intend to bring to light the affronts to human dignity its members encounter in the field. MSF's *témoignage* has materialized in the form of denunciations of NATO-led peacekeeping forces in Kosovo and the publicizing of a cadre of pharmaceutical companies in their legal efforts to prevent affordable access to essential drugs. More recently, MSF *témoigneurs* have been vocal in their condemnation of actions against refugees by government-backed militias in Sudan and in publicly denouncing warring parties in Afghanistan. MSF's impetus for the practice of its *témoignage* is explained as a way of counteracting the notion, propounded by the group, that silence equals neutrality. As MSF President James Orbinsky publicly stated in his 1999 Nobel Prize acceptance speech, "We don't know whether words save lives, but we know for sure that silence kills." The act of witnessing on behalf of victims in the name of human rights serves as a means for MSF to connect moral action to social justice. The articulation of morality and justice in turn provides grounding for the group's *droit d'ingérence*, a right and duty it claims as a legitimate agent of universal humanity.

MSF's efforts to bring attention to humanitarian crises and to publicize human rights violations are complicated by the realities of contemporary politics in a mass-mediated world. As David Rieff states, "In a media-drenched world where the public's attention span is measured in seconds, and in the atmosphere of fierce competition between NGOs, and, for that matter, between UN agencies, aid officials need to be *seen* as helping" (298, emphasis in original). As such, humanitarian NGOs depend on the globalizing reach of the media to register and keep them on the public's radar. To this end, MSF has from its beginning acknowledged and exploited the power of the media as a means of publicizing its actions. Along with MSF's *droit d'ingérence*, Kouchner has been outspoken in endorsing *la loi du tapage* ("the law of hype") as a means of mediatizing the group's aid missions. Along with logisticians, MSF regularly deploys press officers whose charge is to vie for media exposure as well as to dramatize the exigency of the crisis at hand. Relevant to this practice, Kouchner readily acknowledges the rhetorical utility of appealing to emotions, deemed necessary by him in order "to popularize misfortunes and make use of feelings of remorse" (qtd. in Benthall 1). MSF's reliance on the *loi du tapage* and the mediatizing of its missions is routinely criticized, both from within and outside the humanitarian aid arena, as a means of "commodifying tragedy" (Leyton 166–68) in the name of gaining an increased "market share" in humanitarian crises (Rieff 228). Regardless, mediatization has remained an integral strategy for the group as a mode of securing its legitimacy in the global public sphere.

In its aim to secure public legitimacy as a morally committed humanitarian NGO, MSF focuses considerable effort on the crafting of a key distinction between the nature of humanitarian and political action. In its charter, the group claims that it "observes neutrality and impartiality in the name of universal medical ethics and the right to humanitarian assistance," a claim that warrants its "full and unhindered freedom in the exercise of its functions." Further, the charter specifies that MSF members undertake "to maintain complete independence from all political, economic, or religious powers." Given the group's insistence on the nonpolitical designs of its mission, how are "independence," "neutrality and impartiality" to be understood? How, in other words, given MSF's professed *droit d'ingérence*, its highly publicized *témoignage*, and its mediatization of humanitarian crises, is political action to be differentiated or disentangled from humanitarian action? While this hovers as a contentious subject within and without the group,[9] it is important here to mark the tension signified in the claim to a mode of action whose calling, authorized by a "higher power," supersedes (indeed transcends) the social and cultural particularisms of the political. What it allows, indeed, what it makes possible, is a novel reworking of the space of humanitarianism itself. MSF espouses the belief that universal human rights, enjoined with its *droit d'ingérence* and inscribed within its definition of humanitarian action, transcend spatial configurations. As such, MSF does more than pit humanitarian action against political action; it also positions the supposed borderlessness of humanitarian space against the b/ordering particularisms of political space. In so doing, MSF endeavors to refigure humanitarian aid in its own image. In the name of a transcendent, universal humanitarian action, MSF professes political borderlessness. In its claim to the bracketing of cultural experience, MSF professes ideological borderlessness. By recognizing yet willfully traversing bounded spaces, MSF professes geographical borderlessness.

MSF has been enormously successful in mobilizing its principles and practices to shape public perceptions of its legitimacy, and in so doing, to recast the face of humanitarianism. It has effectively crafted a rhetorical vision, an ethos of *sans frontièrisme*, through its reworking of space in the name of humanitarian action. MSF's crafting of this ethos in fact signifies two related and entwined projects. The first involves an attempt to reconfigure perceived understandings of the nature of space to accommodate a transcendent notion of universal humanity (via the discourse of universal human rights). The second entails capitalizing on the spatial vernacular: the rhetoric of deterritorialization that increasingly shapes understandings of globalized community. The synergistic force of these two projects is nowhere more apparent than in MSF's conception of "humanitarian space"—an oblique, affective signifier engendering the group's vision of borderlessness. Three general features of humanitarian space emerge in MSF members' accounts. First, it denotes a space for the ethical and humane practice of humanitarian action (according to MSF's definition). Underwritten by the moral authority of universal human rights, humanitarian space is said to transcend difference; as MSF's Orbinsky states, "Our imperative is to create a strong humanitarian space that acknowledges the humanity of 'the other' " (qtd. in Paupst 55). A second feature endemic to humanitarian space is an unequivocal freedom to act. It requires an ability of humanitarian actors to access populations, assess their needs, and secure protections against victims as well as aid workers (Tanguy and Terry 32). Finally, humanitarian space entails responsibility, one that differs in quality and kind from moral responsibility as such. In her attempt to tease out the character of this distinction, Bouchet-Saulnier, echoing MSF's ethic of *témoignage* and its refusal "to accept that silence is a precondition for its operational freedom," argues that MSF's public statements should be seen not as moralizing rhetoric per se, but rather as characteristic of the responsibility endemic to humanitarian space itself: "[S]uch statements must focus on the quality of humanitarian space rather than respect for human rights. . . . They derive not from general moral or legal considerations, but from the knowledge that there is an operational responsibility that is specific to humanitarian organizations" ("Principles and Practices"). Bouchet-Saulnier's claim illustrates the profound tension between MSF's morally funded discourse, clearly evidenced in its evocation of a universal humanity and its practice of *témoignage* as well as a supposed amoral "operational responsibility" that simultaneously marks off humanitarian space as a space devoid of moral content.

Taking (Un)bordered Space Seriously

What, then, is to be made of MSF's construction of humanitarian space? What are the potential effects of deterritorialized humanitarian action on the persons and places toward whom that action is directed? Furthermore, what are the implications of *sans frontièrisme* for those committed to humane social action? And how best to gauge the influence of its ethos in the global social imaginary?

The notion of a transcendent, borderless humanitarian space such as that propounded by MSF is profoundly fraught on a number of counts. The remainder of this essay will very briefly consider three interrelated, precipitant tensions with the goal of spurring further critical discussion. To begin, the instantiation of a universal Humanity that trumps the particularities of cultural difference is problematic. It suggests, for example, that the meaning of human dignity" could somehow be abstracted and measured independently from its specific cultural-temporal location in a group's constellation of values and practices. How, given such an abstraction, should a specific practice be judged, and who, shorn of all cultural bias, rightfully stands in omniscient judgment? Furthermore, as many analysts have noted, the very conceptualization of universal human rights has from the beginning been derivative of Western cultural values—values that predominate within the designs of the UDHR, the formative document from which MSF's humanitarian charge issues (Korey). Universalizing discourses have long served as an alibi for the promulgation of Western hegemonic practices. Does the invocation of a *droit d'ingérence* in the name of universal Humanity vouchsafe the actions of a morally committed group such as MSF?[10] The question is by no means simply academic. What if, as Jonathan Benthall wonders, "Hitler had been able to claim the *droit d'ingérence* to 'liberate' the Sudeten Germans, operating perhaps through some off-shore NGO" (2)? The issue of universalism points emphatically to a formative ethical dilemma of humanitarianism in a globalized world: Who defines Humanity, how so, and by what authority?

Entangled with the tensions inherent in a universal notion of Humanity, the positioning of humanitarianism over and against politics is problematic. With regard to MSF, an initial question concerns the independence, neutrality, and impartiality it seeks to affirm. Does "independence" signify a refusal to take sides between warring governments? Does it mean refusing to accept any form of governmental support? MSF lauds itself for its financial as well as political independence, emphasizing the care it takes to "not confuse foreign policy with donations" (Di Giovanni). How do MSF's claims to independence square with the fact that ninety percent of MSF-Belgium's funding and 40 percent of MSF-France's funding comes from their respective governments (Leyton 182)? "Impartiality" is another vexing term in MSF's rhetorical lexicon. Some stress that the ethical imperative for MSF members, as humanitarian actors, is to treat all victims impartially, an ethic that obliges them to "care for any individual who is a victim and to close their eyes to the person's past" (Bouchet-Saulnier, "Humanitarian Law" 183). Does impartiality in this sense mean somehow stepping outside one's social-cultural-political attachments—acting, to coin John Rawls, behind a "veil of ignorance" with regard to the other? In addition to questions and tensions regarding independence and impartiality, how is a professed ethic of neutrality to be reconciled with practices such as MSF's *témoignage*, which entails the naming and public denouncing of perpetrators and human causes of suffering? Does its underwriting by Humanity somehow render group members *tout à court* immune from the cultural biases they bring to their witnessing? What does neutrality come to mean when humanitarian NGOs like MSF capitalize on human suffering as a means of mediatizing their missions? Questions such as these prompt serious scrutiny. In the case of MSF, the signifiers "independence," "impartiality," and in particular, "neutrality" appear to serve as an ethico-rhetorical warrant for the group's imputed nonpolitical action. Their invocation endows them with a fuzzy yet powerful mystique: In effect, they become nonsummative God-terms in MSF discourse, charged with ideological presence. The *ur*-figure of neutrality, encountered widely across MSF's public speeches, reports, and educational campaigns, serves as a marker of the group's purity and status within civil society—the antithesis of corruption.

A final set of tensions concerns the conceptualization of an apolitical humanitarian space for action. MSF's attempt to deterritorialize and humanitarianize space prompts a number of questions. What, exactly, is being deterritorialized in such a move? What effects—immediate and residual, latent and manifest—are entailed in a rhetoric of deterritorialization, both for actors and those acted upon? What happens when a conception of space that professes to transcend difference comes into contact with spaces and places endemically marked by difference? As has been argued, the imputation of an Humane and thus ideologically purified motive for medical assistance confers on MSF the moral high ground, a nearly irreproachable position from which to move across spaces. MSF's rhetorical production of a moral discourse contributes to a construction of heroes, villains, and victims as essentialized, categorical types. In its public discourse, MSF volunteers are described as saviors, champions of the voiceless who willfully face the morally unrighteous enemies of humanity (DeChaine 73–77). Abetted by the purity bestowed on the volunteer by way of the rhetoric of neutrality, the hero is counterpoised to the villain-perpetrator, the ideological nemesis of the (MSF) humanitarian, who becomes an easy target for condemnation. Between the hero and the villain languishes the victim, whose lack of agency is instrumental to the construction of an "international event" necessary to command the attention of a mediated public (Brauman, "The Médecins"). The construction of and play between the hero, the villain, the victim, and the event punctuates much of the published accounts of

MSF's *témoignage*. It is a play with deadly serious consequences: Through its mediatized movements, MSF demonstrates its power to render events ("crises" and "emergencies") as effectively worthy or unworthy of public attention. Thus, for example, the situation in Rwanda became associated with genocide only after it had been made into a globally commodified spectacle, which in turn was possible only after MSF "victims" and "volunteers" had been discursively placed. As François Debrix argues, "the key moment in the production of the 'victim' and in the visual commodification of humanitarianism is not when the media take over. . . . It is rather when international medical assistance specialists [such as MSF] intervene across and beyond borders to find new territorial arrangements, new lands and new subjects to place inside these territories" (843).

MSF does more than exemplify the new spirit of global *sans frontièrisme*—it demonstrates its force as an agency of control over social-spatial topography. Space, as unencumbered as it may be imagined, is always invested with power. As this brief analysis has argued, part of that power is an effect of rhetoric: If MSF can effectively persuade the global community that its humanitarian action is pragmatic and morally justified, and in so doing effectively define the very terms of its engagement (volunteer, victim, neutrality, humanitarian emergency, without borders), then those within the community become party to the reterritorializing relations that frame the action. Moreover, the rhetorical appeal to neutrality as a warrant for humanitarian action entails real risks and consequences for its actors and the populations in whose name they act. Efforts to transcend boundaries, as witnessed in a variety of contemporary social movements, can have deadly, serious consequences for their participants that far exceed theoretical limits or academic squabbles. Challenges to sovereignty often meet with resistance, whether in the form of new or heightened nationalisms, physical violence, or the redoubling of efforts to silence the challengers. As more and more humanitarian NGOs become identified (deliberately or not) with governmental and institutional powers, they become increasingly susceptible to the violence and abuses they condemn. Some of MSF's interventions, for example, have netted deadly results, including the widely publicized murder of five MSF aid workers in Northern Afghanistan in 2004. In October 2006, the group was forced to drastically reduce its aid activities in Darfur in the face of threats of violence and death against aid workers in areas of Sudanese governmental control.

Aid workers are not the only people whose lives are at risk. Sustaining the presence of humanitarian aid in conflict situations can unintentionally prolong conflict and the suffering of those toward whom aid is directed, a condition Fiona Terry terms "the paradox of humanitarian action" (Terry; Kennedy; Moore) The deadly consequences of this paradox were dramatically evident in the Rwandan refugee camps in Zaire in 1994, wherein leaders of the Rwandan genocide were able to reside with impunity alongside refugees, manipulating aid and using the camps as a base for their operations. Furthermore, the ethos of humanitarianism, or what the United Nations High Commissioner for Refugees has referred to as the "humanitarian alibi," is readily conscripted for political, economic, and military projects. This was demonstrably the case in Bosnia and Herzegovina between 1992 and 1995, during which time humanitarian aid, including that offered by MSF, "was swept up in the vortex of the war, diverted from its objectives, stripped of most of its content and purpose, and manipulated by all sides" (Brauman "Refugee Camps" 191). At the time of this writing, the U.S.-led invasion and subsequent occupation of Iraq continue to exact a bloody toll, claiming more than forty thousand Iraqi civilians' lives at recent count. The Bush administration, banking on the borderless rhetoric of global humanitarianism for its justification of the invasion and occupation, proclaims its action as necessary to alleviate the suffering of an unfree population at the hands of a (now-deposed) tyrant. In the process, humanitarian NGOs working in Iraq, often hamstrung by the dangers they face on the ground, have been effectively coopted to serve as moral backing for the ongoing military occupation of the nation by coalition forces. Such examples underscore the tension and ambivalence associated with the actions of those whose ethos authorizes power to organize, occupy, and administer space. Ultimately, as the analysis has meant to emphasize, claiming authority to a deterritorialized humanitarian space operates according to the same b/ordering logic that it purports to overcome. Indeed, MSF's project of deterritorialization represents nothing less than a rhetorical refiguration of social space. As such, it serves as an alibi, whether intended or unintentional, a mechanism of immunity for those who undertake action in the name of a universal Humanity.

What, finally, is the meaning of the borderless humanitarian space that MSF so fervently extols? Whatever else it may be, its fuzzy invocation is shot through with moral values and attitudes. Imagined by MSF as the space of Humanity itself, inviolable and antithetical to the sociocultural particularities of ideology and politics, its moralistic and moralizing ethos serves as a warrant for acts of deterritorialization—a spatial movement imagined not in terms of border crossing, but rather as border *effacing*. The rhetoric of *sans frontièrisme* and its humanitarian ethos dovetails with arguments about globalization and its discontents and attendant calls for an understanding of community transcending that of the hegemonic nation-state model. The transcendent ethos of *sans frontièrisme* provides a propitious, hypermedia-friendly response, entirely hospitable to the commercial designs of capitalism. Scholars, activists, and anyone committed to a progressive politics of social justice should be wary of the rhetoric of deterritorialization that now informs popular understandings of space. *Sans frontièrisme* is in fact the new b/ordering logic, reterritorializing space as it moves through the global social imaginary.

This essay has mounted an argument premised on a view that problematizes borders and boundaries as both fostering and inhibiting freedom, as both protecting and violating life (Connolly 163). Its conclusions, however tentative, admonish scholars and activists to consider carefully the ethical and rhetorical implications of borderlessness as a claim to political immunity. Given the currency of *sans frontièrisme* as a spatial vernacular in contemporary society, and MSF's stature as a barometer for its broad implications, it may be tempting to ask: Is it possible to do without the notion of the border? This is the wrong question. Taking borders seriously in a globalized world now requires considering an alternative set of questions, such as those suggested by Henk van Houtum:

> If indeed we accept the view that borders are human made, it would be needed to not only ask the question why humans are producing and reproducing borders, but also what moral consequences do the (re)produced borders have, are they justified and are there socio-spatial alternatives that could be produced? In what way does the maintenance of borders help or not help to create a more equal world? What reality are we making when b/ordering ourselves and others? And at what price? (678)

Along with these questions, the globally expanding ethos of *sans frontièrisme* demands the addition of another vital inquiry: What reality are we making when *unbordering* ourselves and others, and at what price? The issue now confronts us; we ignore it at our collective peril.

Notes

1. For an historical and theoretical overview of the spatial turn in the social sciences and humanities, see Hubbard, Kitchin, and Valentine.

2. As Michaelsen and Johnson argue, "Chicano studies—more than ethnic studies or postcolonial studies or U.S.-Mexico border studies—has made the idea of the border available, indeed necessary, to the larger discourses of American literary studies, U.S. history, and cultural studies in general" (22).

3. Anzaldúa, along with other borderland scholars, has been criticized for her valorization of the border as a privileged marker of cultural identity, a marker that itself is based on an essentialist logic of exclusion (cf. Castillo and Tabuenca Córdoba 15; Fox 46).

4. The term "deterritorialization" was coined by Deleuze and Guattari in their book *Anti-Oedipus* to refer to "the unchaining of both material production and desire from socially restricting forces" (Best and Kellner 88). In Appadurai's reformulation, deterritorialization signifies the transnational movement to transcend not just territorial boundaries but also fixed notions of identity. In his words, deterritorialization "affects the loyalties of groups (especially in the context of complex diasporas), their transnational manipulation of currencies and other forms of wealth and investment, and the strategies of states. . . . The loosening of the bonds between people, wealth and territories fundamentally alters the basis of cultural reproduction" ("Global Ethnoscapes" 192–93).

5. Appadurai's notion of "scapes" and his arguments regarding the cultural politics of deterritorialization have also been the object of criticism. See, for example, Hyndman (33–34).

6. Much more could be said regarding the theoretical scope of perspectives on spatiality within this strand of research. My reliance on Appadurai as an exemplar is influenced by the degree to which his arguments have been incorporated into a number of interdisciplinary projects, and in the interest of demonstrating the relevance of a particular globalizing doxa.

7. For an autobiographical account of the emergence and development of *sans frontièrisme*, see Kouchner.

8. For discussions of the UDHR and its implications for humanitarian NGO politics, see Donnelly and Korey.

9. This is an issue that continues to vex the group and embroil analysts in debates that venture beyond the scope of this discussion. For an extended consideration of MSF's attempts to distinguish humanitarianism and politics, see DeChaine.

10. Some from within MSF's ranks have been critical of its invocation of the *droit d'ingérence*; see, for example, Rieff (289–90).

Works Cited

Anzaldúa, Gloria. *Borderlands/La Frontera: The New Mestiza.* San Francisco: Aunt Lute, 1987.

Anderson, Benedict. *Imagined Communities: Reflections on the Origins and Spread of Nationalism.* London: Verso, 1983.

Appadurai, Arjun. "Disjuncture and Difference in the Global Cultural Economy." *Theory, Culture and Society* 7 (1990): 295–310.

————. "Global Ethnoscapes: Notes and Queries for a Transnational Anthropology." *Recapturing Anthropology: Working in the Present.* Ed. Richard G. Fox. Santa Fe: School of American Research, 1991. 191–210.

Benthall, Jonathan. "Le Sans-frontièrisme." *Anthropology Today* 7 (1991): 1–3.

Best, Steven, and Douglas Kellner. *Postmodern Theory: Critical Interrogations.* New York: Guilford Press, 1991.

Bhabha, Homi K. *The Location of Culture.* New York and London: Routledge, 1994.

Bouchet-Saulnier, Françoise. "Humanitarian Law: All Bark But No Bite." *Populations in Danger 1995: A Médecins Sans Frontières Report.* Ed. François Jean. London: Médecins Sans Frontières UK, 1995. 97–104.

————. "The Principles and Practices of 'Rebellious Humanitarianism.' " Médecins Sans Frontières International 13 Mar. 2001 <http://www.msf.org/msfinternational/invoke.cfm?objectid=6589C8A5-DC2C-11D4-B2010060084A6370&component=toolkit.article&method=full_html>.

Brauman, Rony. "Refugee Camps, Population Transfers, and NGOs." *Hard Choices: Moral Dilemmas in Humanitarian Intervention.* Ed. Jonathan Moore. Lanham, MD: Rowman & Littlefield, 1998. 177–93.

————. "The Médecins Sans Frontières Experience." *A Framework for Survival: Health, Human Rights, and Humanitarian Assistance in Conflicts and Disasters.* Ed. Kevin M. Cahill. New York: Council on Foreign Relations, 1993. 202–20.

Burke, Kenneth. *Permanence and Change: An Anatomy of Purpose.* New York: New Republic, 1935.

Castells, Manual. *The Rise of the Network Society.* Cambridge, MA: Blackwell, 1996.

Castillo, Debra A., and María S. Tabuenca Córdoba. *Border Women: Writing from La Frontera.* Minneapolis and London: U of Minnesota P, 2002.

Connolly, William E. *The Ethos of Pluralization.* Minneapolis and London: U of Minnesota P, 1995.

Crang, Mike, and Nigel Thrift, eds. *Thinking Space.* London and New York: Routledge, 2000.

Curry, Michael. "On Space and Spatial Practice in Contemporary Geography." *Concepts in Human Geography.* Eds. Carville Earle, Kent Mathewson, and Martin Kenzer. Lanham, MD: Rowman and Littlefield, 1995. 3–32.

Debrix, François. "Deterritorialized Territories, Borderless Borders: The New Geography of International Medical Assistance." *Third World Quarterly* 19 (1998): 827–46.

DeChaine, D. Robert. *Global Humanitarianism: NGOs and the Crafting of Community.* Lanham, MD: Lexington, 2005.

Demo, Anne. "Sovereignty Discourse and Contemporary Immigration Politics." *Quarterly Journal of Speech* 91 (2005): 291–311.

Di Giovanni, Janine. "Angels in Combats." *London Times* 9 Dec. 2000.

Donnelly, Jack. *Universal Human Rights in Theory and Practice.* Ithaca, NY: Cornell UP, 1989.

Flores, Lisa A. "Constructing Rhetorical Borders: Peons, Illegal Aliens, and Competing Narratives of Immigration." *Critical Studies in Media Communication* 20 (2003): 362–87.

Foucault, Michel. *Discipline and Punish: The Birth of the Prison.* London: Allen Lane, 1976.

———. *The History of Sexuality.* Trans. Robert Hurley. New York: Pantheon, 1978.

———. "Of Other Spaces." Trans. Jay Miskowiec. *Diacritics* 16 (1986): 22–27.

Fox, Claire F. *The Fence and the River: Culture and Politics at the U.S.-Mexico Border.* Minneapolis and London: U of Minnesota P, 1999.

Giddens, Anthony. *Runaway World: How Globalization Is Reshaping Our Lives.* New York: Routledge, 2000.

Harvey, David. *The Condition of Postmodernity.* Oxford: Blackwell, 1989.

Hubbard, Phil, Rob Kitchin, Brendan Bartley, and Duncan Fuller. *Thinking Geographically: Space, Theory and Contemporary Human Geography.* London and New York: Continuum, 2002.

Hubbard, Phil, Rob Kitchin, and Gill Valentine, eds. *Key Thinkers on Space and Place.* London, Thousand Oaks, and New Delhi: SAGE, 2004.

Hyndman, Jennifer. *Managing Displacement: Refugees and the Politics of Humanitarianism.* Minneapolis and London: U of Minnesota P, 2000.

Jameson, Frederic. "Postmodernism, Or, the Cultural Logic of Late Capitalism." *New Left Review* 146 (1984): 59–92.

Kennedy, David. *The Dark Side of Virtue: Reassessing International Humanitarianism.* Princeton and Oxford: Princeton UP, 2004.

Korey, William. *NGOs and the Universal Declaration of Human Rights: A Curious Grapevine.* New York: St. Martin's Press, 1998.

Lefebvre, Henri. *The Production of Space.* Oxford: Blackwell, 1991. (Originally published in 1974.)

Leyton, Elliott. *Touched By Fire: Doctors Without Borders in a Third World Crisis.* Toronto: McClelland and Stewart, 1998.

Marschner, Alison. "A Scientific Approach to Témoignage." *Médecins Sans Frontières Activity Report: July 1998-June 1999.* Ed. Médecins Sans Frontières. New York: Médecins Sans Frontières International, 1999. 19.

Massey, Doreen. *Spatial Divisions of Labor: Social Structures and the Geography of Production.* London: Macmillan, 1984.

McGee, Michael C. "The 'Ideograph': A Link between Rhetoric and Ideology." *Quarterly Journal of Speech* 66 (1980): 1–16.

Médecins Sans Frontières/Doctors Without Borders USA. "The MSF Charter." *Doctors Without Borders USA* 24 Jan. 2007 <http://doctorswithoutborders. org/aboutus/charter.cfm>.

———. "What is Doctors Without Borders/Médecins Sans Frontières?" *Doctors Without Borders USA* 24 Jan. 2007 <http://www.doctorswithoutborders. org/about/>.

Michaelsen, Scott, and David E. Johnson, eds. *Border Theory: The Limits of Cultural Politics.* Minneapolis and London: U of Minnesota P, 1997.

Microsoft. "We See." *Microsoft* 20 Dec. 2006 <http://www.microsoft.com/emea/ content/about/ads/ad4.aspx>.

Minh-ha, Trinh T. "An Acoustic Journey." *Rethinking Borders.* Ed. John C. Welchman. Minneapolis: U of Minnesota P, 1997. 1–17.

Moore, Jonathan, ed. *Hard Choices: Moral Dilemmas in Humanitarian Intervention.* Lanham, MD: Rowman & Littlefield, 1998.

Moran, Joe. *Interdisciplinarity.* London and New York: Routledge, 2002.

Ono, Kent A., and John M. Sloop. *Shifting Borders: Rhetoric, Immigration, and California's Proposition 187.* Philadelphia: Temple UP, 2002.

Orbinsky, James. "1999 Nobel Peace Prize Acceptance Speech." *Doctors Without Borders USA* 15 Mar. 2001 <http://www.doctorswithoutborders.org/publications/speeches/1999/nobel.shtml>.

Ó Tuathail, Gearóid. *Critical Geopolitics: The Politics of Writing Global Space.* Minneapolis: U of Minnesota P, 1996.

Paupst, James. "A Meditation on Evil." *Maclean's* 1 July 2000.

Pettman, Jan J. "Border Crossings/Shifting Identities: Minorities, Gender, and the State in International Perspective." *Challenging Boundaries: Global Flows, Territorial Identities.* Eds. Michael J. Shapiro and Hayward R. Alker. Minneapolis and London: U of Minnesota P, 1996. 261–83.

Rabinow, Paul, ed. *The Foucault Reader.* New York: Pantheon, 1984.

Rieff, David. *A Bed for the Night: Humanitarianism in Crisis.* New York: Simon and Schuster, 2002.

Rosaldo, Renato. *Culture and Truth: The remaking of Social Analysis.* Boston: Beacon, 1989.

Said, Edward. "Invention, Memory, and Place." *Critical Inquiry* 26 (2000): 175–92.

Schirato, Tony, and Jenn Webb. *Understanding Globalization.* London, Thousand Oaks, and New Delhi: SAGE, 2003.

Shah, Hemant. "Race, Nation, and Citizenship: Asian Indians and the Idea of Whiteness in the U.S. Press, 1906–1923." *Howard Journal of Communications* 10 (1999): 249–67.

Soguk, Nevzat. "Transnational/Transborder Bodies: Resistance, Accommodation, and Exile in Refugee and Migration Movements on the U.S.-Mexican Border." *Challenging Boundaries: Global Flows, Territorial Identities.* Ed.

Michael J. Shapiro and Hayward R. Alker. Minneapolis and London: U of Minnesota P, 1996. 285–325.

Soja, Edward W. *Postmodern Geographies: The Reassertion of Space in Critical Social Theory.* London and New York: Verso, 1989.

Tanguy, Joelle, and Fiona Terry. "Humanitarian Responsibility and Committed Action." *Ethics and International Affairs* 13 (1999): 29–34.

Terry, Fiona. *Condemned to Repeat? The Paradox of Humanitarian Action.* Ithaca and London: Cornell UP, 2002.

United Nations General Assembly. *Universal Declaration of Human Rights.* UN General Assembly Resolution 217 A (III), 1948.

Van Houtum, Henk. "The Geopolitics of Borders and Boundaries." *Geopolitics* 10 (2005): 672–79.

Vila, Pablo. *Crossing Borders, Reinforcing Borders: Social Categories, Metaphors, and Narrative Identities on the U.S.-Mexico Frontier.* Austin: U of Texas P, 2000.

Welchman, John C., ed. *Rethinking Borders.* Minneapolis: U of Minnesota P, 1996.

Chapter Thirteen

Toward Collaborative Coalitions

From Internationalism to Interdisciplinarity

Leila Neti

This paper examines the black internationalist movement, and W. E. B. Du Bois's contribution to it in the first half of the twentieth century, to contemplate how contemporary academic formulations of interdisciplinarity and multiculturalism can be productively revised based on practical strategies learned from African American involvement in global anticolonial movements. What I suggest is that internationalism, by stringently attending to difference, departs from other global movements, such as cosmopolitanism, in that it anticipates and avoids some of the fault lines inherent in projects that attempt to traverse epistemological terrains. The ability to accommodate and include diverse sites of knowledge production within a coherent analytic structure is, I think, one of the central challenges confronting interdisciplinary studies in terms of creating viable points of contact while also allowing for necessary spaces of difference. In the course of my discussion, I suggest that interdisciplinarity turns on many of the same issues facing any attempt to theorize the relationship between universalism and particularism. Namely, through drawing an analogy between internationalist discourses and interdisciplinary studies, I will deal with the complexity of boundary crossing as it pertains to both disciplinary and global strategies for creating a place for dialogue within difference.

In considering what I am reading as Du Bois's model of intervening in national formations by means of internationalist collectives, I will begin by briefly outlining the political goals of the black internationalist movement. Du Bois's project of enabling international coalitions to effect changes to domestic structures of race and citizenship was mirrored in the larger movement of African American involvement in world politics. One of the primary grounds for linking antiracist and anticolonial projects was the black nationalist and internationalist model that posited African Americans as a colonized people within the American state, comprising, in effect, a "nation within a nation."[1] Du Bois and other internationalists extended the model of black nationalism outward to further concretize it by aligning it with anticolonialism, where the authority of the state was literally being disputed. In her excellent study of black internationalism, *Race Against Empire: Black Americans and Anticolonialism, 1937–1957*, Penny Von Eschen provides a sense of the far-ranging scope and magnitude of the internationalist movement. From W. E. B. Du Bois to Paul Robeson to Ralph Ellison to George Padmore and scores of others, the "African American anticolonial activists of the 1940s forcefully argued that their struggles against Jim Crow were inextricably bound to the struggles of African and Asian peoples for independence" (2). Von Eschen further writes, "Those black Americans who constructed diaspora identities did not posit themselves as members or potential members of a nation or advocate a return to Africa in the sense of a back-to-Africa movement. Yet the politics they fashioned did constitute a re-turning toward Africa and an identity defined in relation to Africa" (3). What was at stake was not simply a nation abroad, but also a means of drawing on a global movement to effect a corresponding change within the racial politics of the United States. In short, the larger movements of black nationalism and internationalism formulated their agendas in such a way as to pass through international encounters to return differently to problems confronting the American nation. In 1955, twenty-nine African and Asian countries mobilized an international conference on race in Bandung, Indonesia, where strategies were developed for producing concrete interracial and international solidarities. More recently, echoes of Bandung were present in the Third United Nations World Conference Against Racism, Racial Discrimination, Xenophobia and Related Intolerance held in Durban, South Africa, in 2001. Among other alliances, a dialogue emerged articulating struggles against caste oppression in India along with those against racism in the United States.[2]

The means by which the internationalist agenda may be mapped onto interdisciplinary practices would be through the borrowing of theory and methodology across disciplinary boundaries in order to effect changes within set disciplinary structures. Those of us engaged in working across disciplines must simultaneously contend with the existence of distinct disciplines even while attempting to strategically blur theses divisions, bringing, for example, the discussion of postcolonial feminism to bear on the studies of history *and* literature. The question that arises with regard to both interdisciplinarity and internationalism, however, is to what extent are we invested in preserving stable categories of discipline and nation, and to what extent would we like to subvert such categorization?

As much important work in the field of women's studies on the internal rifts between first- and third-world feminism testifies, interdisciplinarity that is motivated by universalism often runs the risk of reinscribing precisely those power dynamics of center and periphery that it ostensibly seeks to displace.[3] Interdisciplinarity is at the heart of the issue insofar as the problem of power, for example, in third-world feminist critiques, can only be broached through working at the intersection of gender studies and ethnic studies. At the same time, without some degree of autonomy, these very disciplines, themselves already fairly marginal within the larger politics of the academy, lose their capacity to challenge and intervene in the authority granted both to each other and to other, more firmly established disciplines. What is at stake, then, is not so much a removal of disciplinary autonomy as a redistribution of disciplinary power. Once again, larger global movements provide a useful architecture with which to conceptualize the problem. What I hope to suggest, by comparing two modes of thinking globally, is that strategies for dealing with difference are at the crux of the debate on how to best implement interdisciplinarity, and indeed, of how to think about what interdisciplinarity in fact signifies.[4]

Lisa Lattuca, in her work *Creating Inderdisciplinarity*, notes that interdisciplinarity at the current moment has shifted from its "largely instrumental" origins to become more "revolutionary," whereby "faculty in the humanities and social sciences pursue interdisciplinary work with the intent of deconstructing disciplinary knowledge and boundaries" (3). What is at stake in this new form of interdisciplinarity, Lattuca suggests, are the very modes by which knowledge is structured and contained within constantly dissolving parameters. As was the case in the relationship between internationalism and the nation, it becomes necessary to examine the function of disciplinary categories within an interdisciplinary structure. One of the goals of interdisciplinarity is a more politicized understanding of knowledge production as occurring within a dynamic interplay between various sites. This involves radically rethinking the manners in which departments and disciplines have historically solidified around certain epistemological premises.

Yet, as Lauren Berlant cautions, such deterritorialization of disciplines exacts a heavy cost from faculty and departments already committed to politically engaged academic work. Writing of the tension in the practice of interdisciplinarity between the goals of intellectual exchange and the real politics of resource allocation (both financial and pedagogical) in an article titled "Feminism and the Institutions of Intimacy," Berlant addresses the problem of competing demands on time and resources made of politically engaged faculty:

> [T]his rivalry for resources has intellectually and politically debilitating effects on the ways aspirations for social change are imagined and worked through. For one thing, the incitement to interdisciplinarity and increasingly comparative work requires us constantly to be developing unfamiliar knowledge and working outside of our areas of training and expertise. This is a good effect (keeping professors closer to experiencing in public the vulnerability of not knowing), but interdisciplinarity is not something that can be achieved by will, with the new knowledge a merely additive supplement to traditional disciplinary training. (157)

Under conditions of increasing academic corporatization, the "rivalry for resources" to which Berlant points often produces the effect of furthering competition rather than cooperation. As marginalized departments compete for funding and faculty allocations, disciplinary boundaries are at times reaffirmed as a means of gaining institutional recognition. Moreover, in addition to placing strains on faculty to learn across disciplinary boundaries, there is the counter pull to compete for resources while working within those disciplines. As is the case within debates on internationalism, the crux of the problem is locating a space for alliances within competing strategies of difference and universalism. Again, I would emphasize the need for the production of alliances across spaces of difference, rather than the dissolution of those differences themselves.

Among contemporary theorists, the collectivity imagined by internationalists has largely taken a backseat to critiques of global expansionism under the recognition that first-world capital has proven to be a far more effective means of uniting people than third-world solidarity. Yet one of the most prominent current attempts to think in terms of a certain global community is cosmopolitanism, among whose proponents are Kwame Anthony Appiah and Bruce Robbins. Unlike the internationalism of the early twentieth century, which was based in a solidarity of race and therefore had its own strategic principles of exclusion, cosmopolitanism, in an arguably more conservative move, tries to imagine a world where difference is made almost immaterial. A curious formulation within cosmopolitanism, however, is Appiah's notion of "cosmopolitan patriotism." In pairing the universal and the particular, the nation and the world, in terms of an ideal of common feeling, Appiah seems to invoke some of the same issues at work in Du Bois's project of internationalism. Moreover, Appiah, in relation to theories of cosmopolitanism, at least implicitly seems to be working against the universalizing tendencies that are all but inherent in imagining a world without borders.

A careful balance in treading the line between universalism and particularism is a central aspect of Appiah's cosmopolitanism and Du Bois's internationalism, both of which rely on a political model based in subjects' asserting bonds with one another across national boundaries. Cosmopolitanism departs from black internationalism, with Du Bois as one of its most prominent advocates, in its treatment of such bonds. Cosmopolitanism, I think, tends to approach the individual via a collective unity flattened of difference.

In outlining a justification for the project of *Cosmopolitics*, Robbins situates the text in relation to contemporary politics of American multiculturalism:

> There are of course local reasons for the existence of a book on cosmopolitanism here and now. One reason is the state of the debate over U.S. multiculturalism, which has been misperceived (and, to a lesser extent, has misperceived itself) as merely particularistic, a celebration of difference for its own sake. Our elaboration of the term *cosmopolitics* represents one effort to describe, from within multiculturalism, a name for the genuine striving toward common norms and mutual translatability that is also part of multiculturalism. (12–13)

Robbins implies here that cosmopolitanism, if it is to be politically engaged, must move beyond a "celebration of difference for its own sake" so as to position itself as enabling viable intergroup solidarities. The cosmopolitan project envisions itself not as bracketing off difference as an abstract category, but as participating within a larger goal of creating dialogues between various communities. But in his ready dismissal of "difference for its own sake," Robbins does in fact abstract difference from its concrete and rooted presence as a lived condition. One can only critique "difference for its own sake" if one conceives of difference as something that can be unmoored from its material context. If difference becomes nothing more than an abstract category that can be summarily acknowledged and then parceled off in the interest of "common norms," the recognition of difference paradoxically becomes little more than a universalizing gesture. Perhaps even more suspect in this formulation, however, is the appeal itself to "common norms and mutual translatability." The terms "common" and "mutual" create an aura of equality, as though dynamics of power have somehow been dissipated. What this aura conceals is that these terms are linked within the very project of cosmopolitanism to "norms" and "translatability," and these are terms that are shot through with inequalities of power. It is both curious and telling that the moment of working toward such goals as "norms" and "translatability" is also the moment that sidelines self-interested difference.[5] I would suggest that it is precisely when collective solidarities are being posited that difference must be rigorously addressed. Failing to do so merely reifies dominant power structures, because only a position of dominance would benefit from labeling difference as self-interested and then proceed to marginalize it. Robbins seems to argue that once the human is theorized beyond the level of the local, a transcendent humanity can be articulated as unharnessed from real relations of power. In aspiring to a universal humanism, albeit a humanism that is self-aware of the problems of such a project, Robbins disengages his discussion of the subject from the structures of power that construct that subject's lived experience. The question then remains: How do we translate, or cross borders, between languages and nations and disciplines without doing away with difference and the boundaries it gives rise to altogether?

Returning, then, to what is at stake in Appiah's positing of a "cosmopolitan patriotism," I would offer the preliminary answer that what he seems to be searching for is a space for preserving difference. In Appiah's framework, in subtle distinction from Robbins's, "the cosmopolitan patriot can entertain the possibility of a world in which *everyone* is a rooted cosmopolitan, attached to a home of his or her own, with its own cultural particularities, but taking pleasure from the presence of other, different, places that are home to other, different, people" (91). The subordination of people to places in Appiah's formulation is not incidental. Rather, it is all but inevitable when relations of difference are only posited in terms of the pleasure they may yield. If places come to stand in for material bodies, then differences that evoke pleasure can be enjoyed without memory or attention to differences structured in pain and dominance. It is my contention that difference must be kept in the foreground not only in moments of pleasure, but also in moments that demand for example, responsibility, redress, and reparation. Patriotism, attached as it is to pleasure located within a national ethos, seems an inadequate model with which to conceive of working across differences to moments of productive collaboration.

Later, working explicitly against the flattening tendencies of liberal humanism, Appiah writes that "[t]he humanist requires us to put our differences aside; the cosmopolitan insists that sometimes it is the differences we bring to the table that make it rewarding to interact at all" (111). For Appiah, one of the primary sites of grounding difference in such a way that it can be broached is through recourse to the patriotism that grows out of a shared national culture that is not necessarily defined by the state-apparatus to which it is ostensibly linked. Appiah seems to be attempting to define a space in which differences are pronounced enough that a dialogue across multiple positionalities can take place, while also emphasizing a shared positionality such that meaningful solidarities can be created. Admittedly, this is a difficult task, but Appiah, like Robbins, seems insufficiently attentive to the fact that differential relations of power impact the ways in which patriotism is, and can be, deployed. Appiah's insertion of the concept of patriotism seems to pose a challenge to the tendency within cosmopolitanism to imagine an undifferentiated global unity of experience, but it does little to enable specific moments of alliance.

In a departure from the lingering emphasis on the transcendent humanism of cosmopolitanism that all but sidelines race, Du Bois's vision for a global solidarity situates itself firmly and unequivocally within a politics of racial empowerment. Writing in 1906 for *Collier's Weekly* in an article titled "The Color Line Belts the World," Du Bois argued presciently, in a critique that could be aptly lodged against cosmopolitan multiculturalism, that

> most Americans are simply tired and impatient over our most sinister social problem, the Negro. They do not want to solve it, they do not want to understand it, they want to simply be done with it and hear the last of it. Of all possible attitudes this is the most dangerous, because it fails to realize the most significant fact of the opening century, viz.: The Negro problem in America is but a local phase of a world problem. "The problem of the twentieth century is the problem of the Color Line." (42)

Reiterating his famous pronouncement from *The Souls of Black Folk*, Du Bois here extends his analysis of America's race problems outward in order to foreground race as the most predominant *global* concern. In addition to drawing attention to race as the basis for shared histories of oppression, Du Bois also highlights the centrality of race in the resistance to such oppression.

In articulating what he looks forward to as the inevitable rise of the "darker races," Du Bois is mindful of the adversarial nature that has characterized relations between whites and non-whites:

> The awakening of the yellow races is certain. That the awakening of the brown and black races will follow in time, no unprejudiced student of history can doubt. Shall the awakening of these sleepy millions be in accordance with, and aided by, the great ideals of white civilization, or in spite of them and against them? This is the problem of the Color Line. Force and Fear have hitherto marked the white attitude toward darker races; shall this continue or be replaced by Freedom and Friendship? (43)

For Du Bois, the encounter between whites and the darker races is not rooted in pleasure, but rather is posited with a tense wariness. The presumed enmity between whites and people of color is counterbalanced with an implied solidarity of the goals, if not organized actions, of the yellow, brown, and black races. Du Bois's title "The Color Line Belts the World" draws attention to the ways in which, for him, the colored world is both jointly oppressed by the problems created in the name of the color line and also held together in unity because of the existence of the color line. The form of solidarity that Du Bois envisions, then, has much in common with the ostensible goals of cosmopolitanism in terms of human unity, but it works from the margins against the authority of the center with the recognition that unity does not presuppose equality. The question with which he ends posits the possibility of cooperation between races but is adamant that racial struggle is not dependent on the sanction of the power that has historically attached itself to whiteness. In this sense, Du Bois's formulation, perhaps partly because of his historical location, can serve as a corrective against the cosmopolitan shunting off of questions of violence, power, and race.

Where internationalism intervenes in the politics of the nation, particularly at the height of anticolonial independence movements, is through a strategic collaboration with other burgeoning state models. Because these state formations were at their foundation structured in opposition to colonial and racist hegemonic structures of power, internationalism sought to emphasize ideological solidarities between global peoples of color in order to bring the United States into alignment with larger struggles for racial justice and empowerment. Yet in articulating solidarities, there is also a need for asserting differences so as not to replicate the universalizing tendencies I discussed earlier with regard to cosmopolitanism. To borrow Gayatri Spivak's words, "both separations and false continuity are therefore part of the problem" (258).

Indeed, Spivak's discussion in "Scattered Speculations on the Question of Culture Studies" of revision strategies for decentering the canon in literature departments is perhaps an appropriate way to refract the discussion of internationalism onto that of interdisciplinarity. Tackling the power dynamics associated with literary canonicity head-on, Spivak proposes a series of significant changes to English and comparative literature departments. What must go, she insists, are single-author courses for English majors. They centralize the power of the canon, and the canon in turn is "a political matter" with the task of "securing authority" (276). What must also be removed, Spivak argues, is the emphasis on Anglophone postcolonial literature as a **kind** of new canon by which to challenge the old. Working across disciplinary boundaries, Spivak calls for "yoking" the study of world literature across different departments. "In my thinking," she writes, "this study [that of world literature] should yoke itself with other disciplines, including the social sciences, so that we have degrees in English *and* History. English *and* Asian Studies, English *and* Anthropology, English *and* African Studies, where the English half of it will allow the student to read critically the production of knowledge in the other discipline, as well as her own all-too-easy conclusions. *Mutatis mutandis*, metropolitan national literature departments can also serve as bases" (277). In positing this compound emphasis and a corresponding compound degree, Spivak is in effect arguing for the disciplinary limitations of English, both as a language and literature of study, and as a critical apparatus, in adequately addressing the study of world literature. What is at stake, again, is a question of difference, a difference that can be broached, for Spivak, only through active translation by the student, rather than **by** passive reception of previously translated texts. Placing a heavy emphasis on area studies, Spivak writes, "On the level of the English major, especially if we keep the single-author courses, a survey course is an insult to world literature. I would propose a one-semester senior seminar, shared with the terminal M.A., using the resources of the Asian, Latin American, Pacific, and African studies, in conjunction with the creative writing programs, **in which** the student is made to share the difficulties and triumphs of translation. There is nothing that would fill out an English major better than a sense of the limits of this exquisite and supple language" (276). For Spivak, a crucial aspect of the process of translation is the effect of being othered by the text, where the reader's position is one of marginality in relation to a language that cannot reinforce the centrality of one's own subjectivity. The act of translation, situated as it is in the moment of working across difference, serves as an apt framework for thinking through projects of internationalism as well as **of** interdisciplinarity.

In many ways, Spivak's model is very similar to Du Bois's internationalism, insofar as both attend to spaces of difference by borrowing from other sources to effect changes in the structure of the model within which they are working—disciplinarity for Spivak and nationalism for Du Bois. The ways in which one goes about placing the "inter" in both of these projects is related. To this end, it is no coincidence that the list of departments Spivak lists as a source of resources (Asian, Latin American, Pacific, and African studies) reads like a list of internationalist solidarities. The goal is to translate across difference without normativizing, for **which** internationalism offers a productive model.

What emerges through internationalism, as Brent Hayes Edwards points out, is a mode of "translation" wherein unity is structured by comparison, not identity. Returning to Bruce Robbins's initial configuration of the goals of cosmopolitanism as centered around "the genuine striving toward common norms and mutual translatability," it becomes clear that both cosmopolitanism and internationalism are deeply invested in negotiating spaces of translation but differ, again, in their approach to making room for difference. In Edwards's model, internationalism functions as a means toward situating the practice of translation within a meaningful agenda of social change. Returning once again to the question of interdisciplinarity and internationalism, it is clear that in both of these practices, the space of difference must be accounted for both in the act of reaching out toward translation and in the moment of translation itself. Drawing on Stuart Hall's essay "Race, Articulation, and Societies Structured in Dominance," Edwards suggests that for Hall, "Articulation here functions as a concept-metaphor that allows us to consider relations of 'difference within unity,' non-naturalizable patterns of linkage between disparate societal elements" such that unity does not presuppose identity (11).

What can be regarded as another model of translation is one of Du Bois's most compelling and oft-cited formulations is what he describes in *The Souls of Black Folk* as the "peculiar sensation, this double-conscious-ness, this sense of always looking at one's self through the eyes of others, of measuring one's soul by the tape of a world that looks on in amused contempt and pity" that characterizes the African American experience of race. Du Bois goes on to say, "One ever feels his two-ness—an American, a Negro; two souls; two thoughts; two unreconciled strivings; two warring ideals in one dark body, whose dogged strength alone keeps it from being torn asunder" (5). What I locate in internationalism is Du Bois's attempt to fracture the binds of double-consciousness by turning toward a third space—a way of seeing from without, in order to come to within, a place beyond the veil. What I would call for in the university is a parallel ges-ture, a working both across and within spaces of difference to challenge boundaries and enable productive, viable *interdisciplinary* solidarities.

Notes

1. As Alys Weinbaum notes, the model of African Americans constituting a nation within a nation was announced at the Sixth Party Congress meeting of the Comintern (Communist Party International) in 1928, the same year that *Dark Princess* was published (34). As a program for racial and class justice, black inter-nationalism was heavily invested in world communist politics.

2. For a detailed discussion of the history of Afro-Asian cultural politics, and the solidarities that have emerged within a global discourse of antiracism, see Prashad. Reddy provides a nuanced discussion of contemporary Afro-Asian collec-tives in the wake of Durban in her article "The Ethnicity of Caste."

3. Chandra Mohanty's "Under Western Eyes" addresses precisely this issue. From a more theoretical position, Gayatri Spivak's foundational essay "Can the Subaltern Speak?" also raises a similar set of issues.

4. Here I am thinking about the various typologies of interdisciplinarity, including "informed interdisciplinarity," "synthetic interdisciplinarity," "transdisci-plinarity," and "conceptual interdisciplinarity" put forth by Raymond Miller, Lisa Lattuca, and others. For treatment of the definitional aspects of interdisciplinarity, see Lattuca and Klein.

5. A similar dynamic arose with regard to questions of subjectivity, which have been debated since post-structuralism's pronouncement of the death of the author. Roland Barthes and Michel Foucault famously strip the author of a claim to subjective agency, rendering him/her instead a product of discourse (Barthes, Foucault). Some postcolonial critics, however, have responded with the critique that the death of the author, although useful in some contexts, comes at precisely the

moment when minority and third-world writers are beginning to assert themselves
as subjects and authors (Spivak, "Can the Subaltern Speak?").

Works Cited

Appiah, Kwame Anthony. "Cosmopolitan Patriots." *Cosmopolitics: Thinking and
Feeling Beyond the Nation*. Minneapolis: U of Minnesota P, 1998. 91–114.

Barthes, Roland. "The Death of the Author." *Image/Music/Text*. Ed. and trans.
Stephen Heath. New York: Hill, 1977. 142–48.

Berlant, Lauren. "Feminism and the Institutions of Intimacy." *The Politics of
Research*. Ed. E. Ann Kaplan and George Levine. New Brunswick, NJ:
Rutgers UP, 1997.

Du Bois, William Edward Burghardt. "The Color Line Belts the World." *W. E.
B. Du Bois: A Reader*. Ed. David Levering Lewis. New York: Henry Holt,
1994. 42.

Edwards, Brent Hayes. *The Practice Of Diaspora: Literature, Translation, and the
Rise of Black Internationalism*. Cambridge: Harvard UP, 2003.

Foucault, Michel. "What Is an Author?" *Language, Counter-Memory, Practice*. Ed.
Donald F. Bouchard. Trans. Donald Bouchard and Sherry Simon. Ithaca:
Cornell UP, 1977. 113–38.

Klein, Julie Thompson. *Interdisciplinarity: History, Theory, and Practice*. Detroit:
Wayne State University, 1990.

Lattuca, Lisa R. *Creating Interdisciplinarity: Interdisciplinary Research and Teaching
Among College and University*. Nashville: Vanderbilt UP, 2001.

Miller, Raymond C. "Varieties of Interdisciplinary Approaches in the Social Sciences." *Issues in Integrative Studies* 1 (1982): 1–37.

Mohanty, Chandra. "Under Western Eyes: Feminist Scholarship and Colonial
Discourses." *Third World Women and the Politics of Feminism*. Ed. Chandra
Talpade Mohanty et al. Bloomington: Indiana UP, 1991. 51–80.

Prashad, Vijay. "Bruce Lee and the Anti-imperialism of Kung Fu: A Polycultural
Adventure." *Positions: east asia cultures critique* 11.1 (2003): 51–90.

Reddy, Deepa S. "The Ethnicity of Caste." *Anthropological Quarterly* 78.3 (2005):
543–84.

Robbins, Bruce. "Actually Existing Cosmopolitanism." *Cosmopolitics: Thinking and
Feeling Beyond the Nation*. Minneapolis: U of Minnesota P, 1998. 1–19.

Spivak, Gayatri Chakravorty. "Can the Subaltern Speak?" *Marxism and the Interpretation of Culture*. Ed. C. Nelson and L. Grossberg. Basingstoke, England:
Macmillan Education, 1988. 271–313.

———. "Scattered Speculations on the Question of Culture Studies." *Outside in
the Teaching Machine*. New York: Routledge, 1993.

Von Eschen, Penny M. *Race Against Empire: Black Americans and Anticolonialism, 1937–1957.* Ithaca, NY: Cornell UP, 1997.

Weinbaum, Alys Eve. "Reproducing Racial Globality: W. E. B. Du Bois and the Sexual Politics of Black Internationalism." *Social Text* 67 (Summer 2001): 15–41.

Chapter Fourteen

Interdisciplinary Investigations and Cross-Sector Interventions

Ellen Messer-Davidow

Although the astonishing growth of the "new studies"—feminist, ethnic, cultural, and gay, lesbian, bisexual, and transgender (GLBT)—and their achievements in paradigm shifting popularized interdisciplinarity in humanities and social-science circles during the 1980s, these fields did not innovate the synthesizing techniques and structures that make it possible to produce hybridized knowledges. Since the early twentieth century, scientists and scholars have launched hybrid fields across the boundaries separating not only their disciplines from one another but also academe from nonacademic sectors. In *Crossing Boundaries: Knowledge, Disciplinarities, and Interdisciplinarities*, Julie Thompson Klein traces interdisciplinary and cross-sector knowledge to the late-nineteenth-century project of land-grant universities and the U.S. Department of Agriculture, which together set up stations in farming states to conduct research on agricultural problems and educate farmers about practical matters (175). It is no accident that Klein chose, as a pioneering example, a field that combined science and technology, research and application, for most interdisciplinary fields from about 1900 to the present have hybridized sciences and/or technologies—for instance, astrophysics, artificial intelligence, biochemistry, biomedical engineering, cybernetics, environmental studies, immunopharmacology, interfacial engineering, molecular biology, plate tectonics, radio astronomy, and solid-state physics.

Although all interdisciplinary fields form in historically, materially, and intellectually specific ways, we can identify some conditions of possibility: They are fueled by human and financial resources, stabilized through institutionalization, and shaped by both academic and nonacademic forces—government, business, private foundations, and social movements. Sociology, for instance, emerged in the United States from the interstices of traditional humanistic social thought, European structuralism, social reform projects, and the already established disciplines of political science and economics to carve out its niche as the scientific study of "the social." At the University of Chicago and a few other universities, the departmentalization of sociology was fueled by federal and state grants awarded to researchers and their students who produced knowledges useful to government—from large-scale surveys in the early part of the century to research on group behavior, organizational dynamics, and social deviance after World War II (Bottomore and Nisbet; Halliday and Janowitz). Since the mid-twentieth century, American sociology has maintained relatively permeable boundaries that allowed practitioners to diversify the intellectual core with quantitative and qualitative methods, proliferate the subfields, and form specialisms with other disciplines such as social psychology and political sociology. By contrast, physics, which had been an academic science since the late-nineteenth-century rise of U.S. research universities, was transformed into "physics-as-big-science" during and after World War II, when the military-industrial complex enfolded it and funded large basic research and weapons laboratories (Pickering). Again by contrast, American studies originated in an early-twentieth-century project to establish the legitimacy of American literature alongside British literature in English departments and went through several transformations under pressure from extramural forces. First institutionalized through literature-plus-history courses and graduate programs in American civilization, it became disciplinarily diversified and ideologically tilted with the infusion of government funding during the Cold War and then more ideologically sensitive when it incorporated the critical-analytical orientation of the 1960s and 1970s movements (Shumway, *Creating* 212–18, 299–344; Shumway, "Nationalist"; Heller). Today, American Studies exists in the familiar disciplinary form with its own departments and programs, professional association, and publications, but on some campuses its multidisciplinary scope is quite large. At the University of Minnesota, for instance, core and affiliate faculty hail from anthropology, economics, geography, history, law, literary studies, medicine, policy studies, political science, and public health as well as from feminist, GLBT, cultural, and ethnic studies. In the past two decades, the field also became more transnational as universities abroad established American studies centers and panels at the annual conference of the American Studies Association focused on linkages through immigration, international policies, and globalization.

As these historical snapshots suggest, interdisciplinary activity comes in many forms that depend upon a project's purpose, stage of development, and problem-solving span. The activity could be a research project and take the form of a transitory discussion group at a university or, thanks to the Internet and other conferencing technologies, among geographically distant scholars. It could be an emerging field, as the "new knowledge studies" was during the early 1990s, that depends upon loose networks of scholars, occasional large conferences, and publication in venues devoted to other disciplines or interdisciplines (like *American Sociological Review*, *Poetics Today*, and *History of Science*). It could be an older specialism like interfacial engineering, which tends to be located in engineering colleges and associations, or it could be an emerging specialism like neuroeconomics, which is housed in a few research centers of its own rather than in departments of neuroscience or economics. The activity could be an established interdiscipline, like biochemistry, that has its own infrastructure of university departments, professional associations, and publications, or, like feminist studies, that has both freestanding and incursive infrastructures. Within ten years of its emergence, that field was institutionalized in university-based women's studies programs and feminist subfields within mainstream departments, in its own national associations (e.g., the National Association of Women's Studies, the National Council for Research on Women) and research divisions within the disciplinary associations, and in feminist journals/presses and feminist scholarship published by mainstream journals/presses.

Often overlooked by academic scholars, interdisciplinary activity has always been located at nonacademic sites. One example is the matrix structure, a program that cuts across the compartmentalized structure of a business organization (Klein, *Crossing* 23): An automobile company, for instance, integrates personnel from the design, engineering, production, testing, marketing, and legal divisions to develop and launch a new product. Another example is the task force, which the Bush administration used to respond to the disasters of our post-9/11 era, such as the turf wars and other failures of the intelligence agencies, the lack of coordination in dealing with the Hurricane Katrina disaster, and the assessment of the war in Iraq. Long used at the local level, the temporary team is set up to solve a problem or conduct a planning process: For instance, a committee of architects, engineers, doctors, nurses, patients, neighbors, city council members, and health department officials is assembled to work out the design of a new community hospital. Yet another example is the multisectoral event, such as the annual economic summit held in Davos, Switzerland, and attended by leaders from government, business, academe, and the media. And finally, we must not forget that interdisciplinary knowledge production is institutionalized through a multitude of nonacademic organizations—government laboratories and bureaus, corporate research divisions, think tanks, and international agencies like the United Nations and the Organization for Economic Cooperation and Development (OECD) that address both specialized and expansive problems. In fact, crediting the OECD as an early catalyst of interdisciplinarity, Klein recounts that starting in the late 1960s it conducted surveys on interdisciplinary research and teaching, sponsored international seminars and conferences, and published several books that defined and disseminated the language we use about disciplinary, interdisciplinary, and multidisciplinary activities and structures (*Interdisciplinarity* 28, 36–38, 40–41, 58, 63).

In what follows, I want to provide a brief demonstration of my own interdisciplinary and cross-sector work, an analysis of the conservative bloc's policy initiatives that targeted higher education between 1995 and 2006. First I will sketch the economic trends that made academic institutions vulnerable to conservative initiatives, and then I will review some of the initiatives in the areas of student access, education programs, and research. The review will foreground an infrastructural innovation: Conservatives welded their social movement organizations to the machinery of government in a seamless policy-making process through which they were attempting to appropriate chunks of the higher-education system in order to advance their larger economic, political, and social agendas.[1]

Crunching Academic Institutions

After World War II, higher education experienced nearly three decades of unprecedented growth fueled by federal and state appropriations for research, education, student aid, and building construction. Small colleges ballooned into universities and universities into mutiversities with thirty thousand or more students, city-sized campuses, and such enterprises as medical centers, technology parks, and nuclear laboratories. But then starting with the 1973 oil crisis, these institutions found themselves caught in a financial crunch perpetuated on one side of the ledger by the soaring costs of building construction and maintenance, energy, employee benefits, library acquisitions, new technology, and regulatory compliance and on the other side by sluggish revenues from federal, state, and private sources. In addition, the burgeoning student enrollments that had once enriched college coffers turned into a liability because as government student-aid appropriations stagnated and the purchasing power of scholarships declined, tuition revenues subsidized a smaller portion of the student education and service costs, which at the same time were rising (Graham and Diamond; St. John and Parsons; Ehrenberg; Smallwood; Hebel, "Private"; Hebel, "Unequal").

To deal with the new fiscal complexities, institutions hired financial officers who imposed standards of productivity and cost-effectiveness on academic and nonacademic units. The pain of balancing the budget may have been less acute for well-endowed private colleges than for public universities trying to staunch the fiscal hemorrhaging of high-overhead medical centers and science laboratories, but all institutions resorted to similar measures. To increase income they raised tuitions, ramped up grant applications, formed corporate partnerships, and launched fundraising drives with goals for major universities rising from $200 million in the mid-1980s to more than $1 billion by the late 1990s. To cut costs, they deferred building maintenance, trimmed nonacademic staff and services, reduced library budgets, eliminated academic programs, and converted full-time faculty lines to part-time instructorships.

Focused on solving budget problems, administrators did not anticipate what would happen when conservatives ascended to power in 1980. Rather, they simply reacted to developments on an as-come basis, experiencing inflated hopes when Reaganomics folded federal funding into block grants to the states; keen disappointment when their share of state money declined relative to the rising appropriations for criminal justice, health care, and welfare; and renewed hope when the Clintonian boom revved up government spending, investment income, and thus college revenues. Then at the end of 2001 they were hit by a double whammy: After the stock market tanked and the Bush administration launched its costly war on terrorism, academic institutions found themselves scrambling to cope with plunging income from investments, deficit-burdened states, and federal sources. When the states slashed their appropriations by 5 percent to more than 20 percent, the chronically underfunded community colleges were the hardest hit, but universities lost millions, and even private colleges receiving minimal state support were pinched (Selingo). In short, the financial crunch turned into a full-blown crisis that made academic institutions even more exquisitely vulnerable to conservative initiatives.

Restricting Student Access

After World War II, Congress demonstrated its commitment to educational access through new forms of student assistance: the GI Bill of 1944 made portable scholarships available to veterans, the Higher Education Act of 1965 (HEA) created the TRIO programs to increase the college readiness of disadvantaged high school students, and the 1972 HEA reauthorization established the Pell Grants for low- and middle-income students. Also using its purse power, Congress passed the sweeping Civil Rights Act of 1964 that prohibited discrimination based on race, national origin, and later sex by all programs receiving federal funding. To implement the act's mandates, a raft of federal agencies circulated guidelines on nondiscrimination and affirmative action, investigated complaints, negotiated with noncompliant programs, and in some instances threatened to terminate their federal funding. Between 1970 and 1974, many academic institutions implemented affirmative action, particularly in student admissions.

Almost immediately, rejected white male applicants sued, claiming that affirmative action violated the Constitution's equal protection clause and Title VI's nondiscrimination mandate by discriminating against them on the basis of race. In *DeFunis v. Odegaard* (1974) and *Regents of the University of California v. Bakke* (1978), the plaintiffs and conservative organizations siding with them in *amicus* briefs described affirmative action as a system of reverse discrimination that gave unmerited preferences to less qualified racial-minority applicants and a quota that restricted the access of more qualified white ones. The Supreme Court opinion in *Bakke* was not a clear-cut endorsement or repudiation of affirmative action because the justices split into two four-person camps, leaving Justice Powell to navigate between them. He agreed with one camp that the affirmative-action procedures used by the University of California, Davis, medical school were unlawful, and to palliate the other camp he declared that the achievement of campus diversity was a sufficiently compelling governmental interest to justify the use of race as one of several factors in student admissions.

During the next five years, conservatives generated lawsuits geared to dismantling affirmative action in education, employment, and government contracting. Whereas the earlier cases were crafted by law centers that litigated on diverse issues, such as the Washington Legal Foundation and the Pacific Legal Foundation, a shift to specialization occurred during the 1990s with the founding of four organizations that specifically targeted higher education. Both the National Association of Scholars (NAS), which mobilized conservative academics, and the Center for Equal Opportunity (CEO), which churned out "research studies," mounted public relations campaigns and filed complaints with federal agencies; the Center for Individual Rights (CIR) handled litigation; and the American Civil Rights Institute (ACRI) orchestrated voter referendums. Together, they won bans on affirmative action in California, Washington, Texas, Louisiana, Florida, Georgia, and Michigan, and shortly thereafter the indefatigable ACRI announced that it would organize 2008 referendums in Arizona, Colorado, Missouri, Nebraska, and Oklahoma (Schmidt).

In July 2003 the Supreme Court issued long-awaited rulings on *Gratz v. Bollinger* and *Grutter v. Bollinger*, crafted by the CIR for Jennifer Gratz and Barbara Grutter, respectively denied admission to the University of Michigan undergraduate program and law school (in choosing these plaintiffs, the CIR cleverly pitted white women, a population that has benefited from affirmative action, against racial minorities). Although the Court upheld the law school admissions process because it relied on individualized reviews of many applicant factors and did not use numerical racial goals, it found the undergraduate admissions to be unlawful by these same standards. Of course, any leeway for affirmative action that might have been possible under the *Grutter* ruling was eliminated a few years later when a slim majority of Michiganders voted for the ACRI's ban on affirmative action in education, employment, and government contracting. The consequences for racial-minority students in Michigan remain to be seen, but we know what they are in other states where affirmative action was banned. California, Texas, and Florida instituted "percent plans" that guaranteed state university admission to the top X percent of each high school graduating class, but the university systems swiftly experienced a trend to resegregation. Applications and admissions of African Americans, Hispanic Americans, and Native Americans declined at flagship institutions, these groups cascaded to second-tier universities and to community colleges, and their dropout rates rose, a result that empirical studies attribute to insufficient financial aid, heavy family and work responsibilities, and chilly campus climates (Office for Civil Rights Staff; Horn and Flores; Marin and Lee; Tienda and Niu).

Whereas the affirmative-action initiatives show how conservatives use their organizations to push change through the channels of the courts, executive agencies, and electorate, my next examples show that they also fused their organizations to government in a seamless policy-making process. After George W. Bush assumed the presidency in 2001 and Republicans regained control of the Senate in 2002, conservatives once again moved against welfare recipients. Their think tanks and advocacy organizations had long depicted welfare recipients as lazy, promiscuous individuals who were draining the public coffers, but now this message was amplified by Bush administration officials and conservatives who were invited to give testimony as Congress prepared to reauthorize the Personal Responsibility and Work Opportunity Reconciliation Act of 1996. Despite abundant research showing that this so-called welfare reform act, rather than fostering financial self-sufficiency, had plunged most families into deeper poverty, Republicans (and some Democrats) enacted a more punitive version in 2003 that increased the recipients' workload from thirty to forty hours a week, left support services underfunded, and decreed that no postsecondary education except for minimal vocational training could count as work hours. The recipients—90 percent are single mothers and 70 percent are women of color—have little or no education, job training, health care, transportation, and child care, yet are expected to work forty hours a week at low-wage jobs that often evaporate within a year (Mink and Solinger; Hays; Polakow et al). Under these conditions, how many women can find the time and money to attend community college and earn a medical technician degree that would position them to earn a steady living wage—*if* they could find employment in this era of downsizing, outsourcing, and offshoring?

Instead of examining the barriers to higher education erected by welfare policy and employment trends, Congressional conservatives blamed academic institutions for creating a "college affordability crisis" by raising tuition. What drove tuition increases, as I explained earlier, was the convergence of declining government support and rising business costs that in turn decreased the purchasing power of the Pell Grants and other scholarships. In 1975, the maximum Pell Grant covered 84 percent of the total cost of attending a public university, but in 2001 it covered 39 percent of tuition only (Office for Civil Rights Staff 106). Although well aware that insufficient financial aid prevented many students from attending even relatively cheap community and state colleges, Congressional conservatives voted to increase the maximum grant of $4,000 by a mere $50, where it remained for five years, and declined to raise the cap on wages that grant recipients could earn. Fortunately, their proposal to tighten the Pell Grant needs-analysis formula failed when the Department of Education estimated that 84,000 students would lose their grant eligibility, but by then the damage was done because economic factors had prevented 250,000 eligible students, disproportionately minority students, from attending college in 2003–2004 alone (Fleming; Brainard, "Senate Passes"; Field, "Senate"; Burd, "Too Much"; Arnone, "Two Hundred"). Six months earlier, the American Association of Community Colleges and the American Association of State Colleges and Universities had warned that economic factors would be " 'the silent killer' " of minority enrollments, particularly because "half of the nation's 2.95 million black and Hispanic college students" attend the chronically underfunded community colleges bearing the brunt of state cuts (Evelyn). Only after regaining control of Congress in 2006 did Democrats reenter the fray, proposing to raise the maximum Pell Grant to about $4,600. While the House and Senate worked on reconciling their bills, President Bush announced that he would veto a bill containing any increase (Field, "Senate").

Meanwhile, the USA Patriot Act also took a toll on student access and campus diversity. As implemented, government agencies interview, fingerprint, vet, monitor, detain, and evict foreign students and faculty, activities that are supposed to be facilitated by a compendious and glitch-ridden databank called Sevis (Student and Exchange Visitor Information System). While civil liberties groups and education associations were criticizing these measures, the Justice Department was busy drafting a more draconian Patriot Act II. Although some Democrats objected to enlarging the government's powers, they did not brief the media and the public on the damage already done. Beginning with the 2002–2003 academic year, foreign student applications and enrollments at both the undergraduate and graduate/professional levels dropped precipitously. Between 2003 and 2004, applications for post-baccalaureate study beginning in the fall term plunged by 32 percent overall, with a drop of 76 percent by Chinese students, a 31 percent drop by Middle Eastern students, and a 30 percent drop by Western European students. Although academic institutions reported modest enrollment gains for 2008-08, they could not relieve foreign students and their governments of the impression that the U.S. government had made it difficult and dangerous to seek an education here (Arnone, "New Survey"; Bollag; Jacobson, "Foreign-Student").

What are the consequences of conservative access initiatives? Policies that restrict the access of racial-minority students will turn back the clock on the century-long struggle to desegregate higher education. Policies that keep student aid at inadequate levels will grow the underclass population at a time when this country's economy, politics, and world stature depend upon having a highly educated populace. Policies that deter foreign students will not only intensify the international resentment of the United States already enflamed by the Bush administration's actions but, together with the restrictions on visiting foreign scholars and on information flows to and from abroad, may well isolate the U.S. intellectually, culturally, and economically.

Regulating Education and Research

To justify imposing unprecedented regulations on higher education, conservatives trumpeted the allegation that academic institutions were not accountable to government and hence to taxpayers. At March 2003 hearings sponsored by the Department of Education (DOE), conservative education experts testified that the government should require colleges to provide data on student progress, including retention, transfer, and graduation; learning as ascertained by national competency tests and student-parent-alumni satisfaction surveys; job placements and salaries; and graduate and professional school performance (Burd, "Education Department"). At a time when many citizens were deeply disturbed by the increased government surveillance at home and abroad, national education officials chose to take a narrow legalistic approach, warning that government agency access to such data would violate the Family Educational Rights and Privacy Act of 1974 (FERPA). House education leaders appeared to backpedal but apparently found a way around FERPA because in 2005 the Department of Defense (DOD) announced that it would assemble a database on high school and college students, which was legal under a FERPA amendment. When education officials expressed concern that other government agencies would access the data under the DOD's "loosey-goosey rules" and in any case that the cost of providing data would strain college budgets (Lipka), a DOE official remarked, with astonishing hypocrisy, " 'The color of change is not always green' " (Burd, "Bush's").

Green, however, was what Congressional conservatives manipulated to secure the changes they wanted to make in research and education. In 2003, Congressional pork for academic institutions topped $2 billion, with $223 million going to projects on terrorism and security and the Department of Homeland Security (DOHS) alone allocating some $90 million to centers conducting research on security issues (Brainard and Borrego; Borrego, "Homeland"). For 2004 and 2005, the DOHS budgeted $70 million annually for university-based projects, with $45 million earmarked for Homeland Security Centers of Excellent at the University of California, Texas A&M, and the University of Minnesota (Field, "U.S. House"). For 2005, the Republican-controlled Congress approved a mind-boggling total appropriation to the DOD of $416.2 billion, with $6.4 billion for defense research in legislators' districts (Field, "Congress Passes"). Having fueled military and security research, they now needed to control its circulation. In 2003 the DOD proposed that academic scientists conducting this research would have to obtain clearance to publish their findings. When an outcry caused the DOD to backpedal, President Bush instituted broader controls, authorizing a half-dozen federal agencies—Defense, State, CIA, EPA, Agriculture, Health and Human Services—to label research as classified or sensitive and to restrict its circulation (AAUP Special Committee).

As the president's own rhetoric indicated, military and religious imperialism are wedded in Christian Right doctrine, so it was no surprise that conservatives used the movement and government's meshed machinery to secure government funding for faith-based ventures, a Christian Right cause ever since *Bob Jones University v. United States* (1983). The Supreme Court's ruling that the IRS could deny tax-exempt status to the university on grounds that it was practicing racial discrimination intensified the Christian Right's resentment of not only the church–state separation doctrine but also the diversity requirements of college accrediting associations that, when not met, made colleges ineligible for federal funding. While continuing to file lawsuits on behalf of religious organizations denied government funding for their educational and social service programs, the Christian Right worked its cause through the legislative and executive branches. In October 2002, the American Council of Trustees and Alumni (ACTA), cofounded by Lynne V. Cheney, denounced the accrediting associations and recommended eliminating accreditation as a funding requirement. Shortly thereafter, Rep. Thomas E. Petri introduced HR 5501 to eliminate this requirement, and the DOE listed the elimination of statutory and regulatory barriers to faith-based education as one of its objectives during the reauthorization of the Higher Education Act (Morgan, "Group Criticizes"; Morgan, "Lawmakers"; U.S. Department of Education). The ACTA-Petri proposal failed to pass the Senate, but federal agencies nevertheless funded faith-based education programs. In early 2005 the Center for Public Integrity announced that Mercyhurst College, located in the hometown of former DOHS Secretary Tom Ridge, had received a $90,000 no-bid contract to train DOHS analysts, and the Freedom from Religion Foundation filed a lawsuit against the

DOE for granting more than $1 million to Alaska Christian College, an unaccredited institution with thirty-seven students (Field, "Small College"; Field, "U.S. Education"). The faith-based maneuvers only confirm what the media finally began to circulate in the long run-up to the 2008 presidential election: namely, that politicians who won their offices through the efforts of Christian Right activists return the favor by appointing them to government positions and allocating government funds to their organizations.

Just as conservatives used the movement and government's meshed machinery to fund their projects, they also used it in attempts to defund research and education that offended them. The model was provided by Lynne V. Cheney, who chaired the National Endowment for the Humanities (NEH) from 1984 to 1994. Cheney not only used her position as a bully pulpit to denounce scholarship on gender, race, class, and theory, but also packed the national council, staff, and peer-review panels with conservatives who marked this work down in grant competitions (Messer-Davidow, "Dollars"). Subsequent defunding efforts were less covert. In November 2003 a House committee heard conservative criticisms of the National Institutes of Health (NIH) for sponsoring studies of sexual behavior and ordered the agency to review 190 studies on a list that, it turned out, had been compiled by the right-wing Traditional Values Coalition. The defunding threat was defused when the NIH reported on the significance of these studies for public health (Brainard, "NIH Begins"; Brainard, "NIH Director"), but another threat was under way. After conservatives testified at a House subcommittee hearing that area studies programs purveyed anti-American criticism of U.S. foreign policy, Congressional Republicans passed a bill that established an advisory board charged with evaluating the programs for federal grants. By specifying that three members would be appointed by the Secretary of Education and one each by the majority and minority leaders of the Senate and House, they locked up a 5–2 conservative majority (Jacobson, "The Clash"). Although I agree with educators who worried that the board will defund area studies programs that offend partisan views, I don't think they realize the scope of the danger. If the board chooses to flex its muscles, it will be able to reach beyond area studies programs to other academic units, such as languages, history, anthropology, geography, and political science, where area-studies courses are based.

Another defunding initiative was revealed in January 2004 when the *Chronicle of Higher Education* published a front-page article on the resumption of "flagging" at the NEH. Agency officials, the story claimed, "[i]dentify specific grant applications—often, these days, projects dealing with sexuality, race, or gender—for extra review. In some cases, flagged proposals that receive high marks from peer-review panels are rejected, while those with low marks receive funds" (Borrego, "Humanities"). Soon after the article appeared, the NEH inspector general began investigating not the flagging but the whistle-blowers and threatened a former NEH official with civil and criminal action. When anonymous parties complained about the retaliation, the General Accounting Office (GAO) ordered the inspector general to investigate the flagging and retaliation allegations, telling a *Chronicle* reporter that the GAO responds to those complaints it believes to have merit (Field, "Humanities" and "Congressional").

Not to be deterred, conservatives exercised their negative purse power by cleverly hog-tying the Fund for the Improvement of Postsecondary Education (FIPSE), a DOE program established in 1972 to support innovation in higher education through grant competitions. In January 2005 the DOE announced that it was terminating the grant competitions because Congress had earmarked 89 percent of the total FIPSE appropriation for pet projects in legislators' districts. Those who wonder why FIPSE earmarks have soared from $4.5 million in 1998 to an astonishing $146.2 million in 2005 may wish to ponder two opposing views. Rep. Ralph Regula, who chaired the House subcommittee that budged FIPSE, opined that Congress was "more in tune with the needs of colleges and universities in their districts than the fund's program managers," but critics retorted that many of the earmarked projects did not advance educational innovation or even education, such as the new $5 million Strom Thurmond Fitness Center at the University of South Carolina in Columbia (Field, "Pork").

Meanwhile, the science community was mounting widely publicized counteroffensives against conservative attempts to undermine mainstream scientific research on stem cells, evolution, climate change, energy, sexuality, obesity, tobacco use, and workplace injury. Working together, conservative organizations, the Bush administration, and Congressional Republicans used such tactics as denying the validity of mainstream scientific findings, promulgating junk science, packing federal science-advisory panels with members who supported the conservative pro-business policy agenda, weakening federal agency peer-review processes, defunding mainstream science projects, restricting publication, and denying visas to foreign scientists who were invited to speak or teach in the United States. Some of these tactics were disclosed in *Scientific Integrity in Policymaking: An Investigation into the Bush Administration's Misuse of Science*, a report issued by the Union of Concerned Scientists and signed by sixty top scientists, including twenty Nobel laureates. Many more machinations have been exposed by the American Civil Liberties Union's *Science Under Siege: The Bush Administration's Assault on Academic Freedom and Scientific Inquiry*, journalist Chris Mooney's *The Republican War on Science*, and the Union of Concerned Scientists' Web site.[2]

What are the consequences of conservative research and education initiatives? The fiscal crunch I described at the start of this essay makes academic institutions (and individual faculty members) exquisitely vulnerable to political intrusions: Although resenting them, they will undoubtedly prefer to win government rewards than suffer government penalties. Conservative initiatives, however, go beyond incentivization; they erode academic freedom, which, contrary to popular opinion, is not simply the faculty member's power to make decisions about her research and teaching, nor is it simply the institution's power to govern itself. Rather, the exercise of these powers is the effect of structuration—namely, the organization of academic activities by a network of policies inscribed in university handbooks, the American Association of University Professors (AAUP) documents, and other higher-education texts. Any stability that academic freedom has derives from the academy's success in justifying its prerogative of self-governance to the forces that impact it—government, business, movements, religion, media, and diverse publics. According to the traditional justification, American higher education must be administered by those who have the requisite expertise to manage its advanced and specialized activities in research, teaching, and service. Until the conservative onslaught, Congress and the courts often deferred to academic expertise, but they did not hesitate to override it when they thought that academic practices violated the dictates of statutory and constitutional law. In the domain of the law, territorial encroachments that are prevented by strong doctrines, such as the separation of powers and the public–private division, are not prevented by the weaker principle of academic freedom. In sum, the initiatives I have described eviscerate the rationale of scholarly expertise at the heart of academic freedom, transfer to politicized government chunks of academic decision making on student admissions, research, and education, and suppress the critical analyses that drive intellectual and pedagogical innovation.

To conclude, I want to return to hybrid formations—social structures and problems, interdisciplinary and cross-sector knowledges. Conservatives are the first to acknowledge that the Civil Rights movement was their paradigm for infrastructure building. Starting in the mid-1960s, the Old Right (sometimes called The Remnant) reached out to young people and

faith-based groups (mainly evangelicals and Catholics); using such existing forms of organization as conservative periodicals, campus groups, and
churches, this network began to establish think tanks, advocacy groups,
training institutes, mass-membership organizations, and media. Conservative
organizations were quick to realize the potential of new technologies that
could be used for fundraising, issue framing, recruitment, and mobilization. Richard Vigurie, who had worked on the 1964 Goldwater campaign,
provided direct-mail consultations and services. From Washington, D.C., the
Free Congress Foundation launched National Empowerment Television, a
cable network used to promote conservative causes and train activists out in
the states, and the Heritage Foundation set up Town Hall, a Web operation
that linked individuals with one another and with organizations. Heritage
and other large organizations adopted business management techniques,
including the outsourcing and insourcing of professional public relations,
to sell issues (Messer-Davidow, "Manufacturing"). They used this infrastructure to capture the Republican Party, win elections, and gain control
of the federal government and many state governments. With the election
of George W. Bush in 2000 and the congressional gains mentioned earlier,
the infrastructural form morphed: Welding movement organizations to
government, they used the hybridized machinery to make structural changes
in the economic, political, social, and cultural spheres.

On one hand, conservatives' control of this cross-sector formation was
an innovation which flew in the face of the leftist doctrine that a movement's
cooperation with the establishment and particularly the government would
result in its cooptation. On the other hand, their attempt to accession
higher education's power of producing knowledges and subjects seemed
to confirm the leftist critique that this system served the interests of the
corporate-liberal state. Conservatives, however, wanted to reorient higher
education so that it served as an instrument for realizing the theocratic,
free-market state they envisioned (which is why, to put it trivially, they
complain that conservatives are underrepresented in college faculties and
administrations). The conservative agenda for American higher education
takes on a more critical significance when viewed in the larger context of
global capitalism. If the transition to this new formation merely unsettled
the mid- to late-twentieth century world order, its increased concretization
in the twenty-first century has made supra-hybridization all too apparent.
Through new communication technologies, infrastructures and ideologies
are fused in more potent combinations--for instance, the resource power
of neoliberal states and multinational businesses, the geopolitical fluidity

of fundamentalist movements and safe-harbor regions, and the rhetorical force of free markets and faith.

But even before the emergence of these hybrid formations, every important problem facing this nation and the world was always a cross-sector conjuncture that required (and did not consistently receive) interdisciplinary and multisectoral analysis—for instance, imperialism, racism, poverty, environmental degradation, and now the deep recession following the 2009 economic meltdown. Confronted with these real-world complexities, what does a practitioner of interdisciplinarity do? She doesn't layer a few quotes from J. L. Austin's speech-act theory into her analysis of political campaign rhetoric. Nor does she present a simplified definition of chaos theory and hunt for themes of chaos in postmodern novels. Neither does she expound on globalization by overshadowing a skimpy assortment of empirical data from economics, politics, and culture with abstract theory talk. The negatives I mention—layering, thematizing, theory-talking—are examples of borrowing without operationalization. To be interdisciplinary, practitioners have to *operationalize* the data, methods, concepts and/or theories borrowed from other fields in their analysis of . . . whatever they are analyzing (Pahre). For example, the research on copyright was not interdisciplinary when literary studies scholars were looking at developments in eighteenth-century British authorship and publication, but it became an interdisciplinary project as it attracted other scholars who applied the data, methods, and models of history, economics, politics, law, policy studies, and the new media and technologies.

This point leads to my last one. Just as social formations are historically and culturally specific conjunctures, so too are knowledge formations that probe and represent them. Our knowledges are not formulated by generic knowers, situated in intellectual outer space and gazing down upon the dynamics they purport to explain, a point made by Marx when he satirized the young Hegelians in *The German Ideology*. But if material and social forces shape us as knowers who, together with these forces, shape the social problems we investigate, how can we step outside of this sociointellectual order? We can't. The best we can do is oscillate among diverse data sets, methods, and social formations (including disciplines and interdisciplines), using each one as a lens for illuminating and modifying the other.

Notes

1. The material used in this analysis (and updated for it) comes from my article "Why Democracy Will Be Hard To Do."

2. For the Union of Concerned Scientists' report and information on its ambitious project of monitoring government policies and practices, circulating information, and formulating a plan to restore scientific integrity to policy making, see Web site <www.ucsusa.org/scientific_integrity>.

Works Cited

AAUP Special Committee on Academic Freedom and National Security in a Time of Crisis. *Academic Freedom and National Security in a Time of Crisis*. Washington DC: AAUP. 2003 <www.aaup.org/statements/REPORTS/911report.htm>.

American Civil Liberties Union. *Science Under Siege: The Bush Administration's Assault on Academic Freedom and Scientific Integrity*. New York: ACLU, 2004.

Arnone, Michael. "New Survey Confirms Sharp Drop in Applications to U.S. Colleges From Foreign Graduate Students." *Chronicle of Higher Education* 4 Mar. 2004. Web. 25 Apr. 2004. <www.chronicle.com/daily/2004/03/2004030403n. htm>.

———. "Two Hundred Fifty Thousand Eligible Students Shut Out of College, Group Says." *Chronicle of Higher Education* 30 Jan. 2004: A21.

Bollag, Burton. "Graduate-School Applications From Overseas Decline Again, Survey Finds." *Chronicle of Higher Education* 10 Mar. 2005. Web. 22 Mar. 2005. <www.chronicle.com/daily/2005/03/2005031006n.htm>.

Borrego, Anne Marie. "Homeland Security Department Seeks Proposals to Create University Centers." *Chronicle of Higher Education* 24 July 2003. Web. 9 Aug. 2003. <www.chronicle.com/daily/2003/07/2003072401n.htm>.

———. "Humanities Endowment Returns to 'Flagging' Nontraditional Projects." *Chronicle of Higher Education* 16 Jan. 2004: A20–A21.

Bottomore, Tom, and Robert Nisbet, eds. *A History of Sociological Analysis*. New York: Basic Books, 1978.

Brainard, Jeffrey. "NIH Begins Review of Studies That Were Questioned at a Congressional Hearing." *Chronicle of Higher Education* 7 Nov. 2003: A24.

———. "NIH Director Upholds Scientific Merit of Controversial Sexuality Grants." *Chronicle of Higher Education* 13 Jan. 2004. Web. 13 Feb. 2004. <www. chronicle.com/daily/2004/01/2004011301n.htm>.

———. "Senate Passes Bill Financing NIH, Pell." *Chronicle of Higher Education* 11 Nov. 2005 <www.chronicle.com/weekly/v52/i12/12a02803.htm>.

Brainard, Jeffrey, and Anne Marie Borrego. "Academic Pork Barrel Tops $2-Billion for First Time." *Chronicle of Higher Education* 26 Sep. 2003: A18–A22.

Burd, Stephen. "Bush's Next Target?" *Chronicle of Higher Education* 11 July 2003: A18–A20.

———. "Education Department Hears Appeals to Make Colleges More Accountable for Student Performance." *Chronicle of Higher Education* 10 Mar. 2003.Web. 15 Mar. 2003. <www.chronicle.com/daily/2003/03/2003031002n.htm>.

————. "Too Much Work?" *Chronicle of Higher Education* 8 Aug. 2003: A18–A19, A21.

Ehrenberg, Ronald G. *Tuition Rising: Why College Costs So Much.* Cambridge: Harvard UP, 2002.

Evelyn, Jamilah. "The 'Silent Killer' of Minority Enrollments." *Chronicle of Higher Education* 20 June 2003: A17.

Field, Kelly. "Congress Passes Defense-Spending Bill for 2005 with Large Increases for Research." *Chronicle of Higher Education* 26 July 2004. Web. 28 Aug. 2004. <www.chronicle.com/daily/2004/07/2004072601n.htm>.

————. "Congressional Agency Seeks Investigation of Humanities Endowment." *Chronicle of Higher Education* 3 Sep. 2004. Web. 31 Aug. 2004. <www. chronicle.com/weekly/v51/i02/02a02601.htm>.

————. "Humanities Endowment Opens Inquiry into Alleged Leak to a Reporter." *Chronicle of Higher Education* 28 May 2004. Web. 31 Aug. 2004. <www. chronicle.com/weekly/v50/i38/38a02201.htm>.

————. "Pork Crowds Out the Competition" *Chronicle of Higher Education* 7 Jan. 2005: A33.

————. "Senate Passes $600-Billion Spending Bill for Health and Education." *Chronicle of Higher Education* 2 Nov. 2007. Web. 4 Dec. 2007. <www. chronicle.com/weekly/v54/i10/10a01601.htm>.

————. "Small College Wins No-Bid Contract from Homeland Security Department, Prompting Cries of Favoritism." *Chronicle of Higher Education* 18 Mar. 2005. Web. 22 Mar. 2005. <www.chronicle.com/daily/2005/03/2005031803n. htm>.

————. "U.S. Education Department Is Sued over $1 Million in Earmarks for Tiny Christian College in Alaska." *Chronicle of Higher Education* 28 Apr. 2005. Web. 28 Apr. 2005. <www.chronicle/com/daily/2005/04/2005042802n.htm>.

————. "U.S. House Approves Homeland-Security Bill with Money for Colleges; Similar Measure Advances to Senate." *Chronicle of Higher Education* 21 June 2004. Web. 28 Aug. 2004. <www.chronicle.com/daily/2004/06/2004062105n. htm>.

Fleming, Brendon. "House Panel Approves 2005 Spending Plan." *Chronicle of Higher Education* 6 Aug. 2004 <www.chronicle.com/weekly/v50/i48/48a02303. htm>.

Graham, Hugh Davis, and Nancy Diamond. *The Rise of American Research Universities: Elites and Challengers in the Postwar Era.* Baltimore: Johns Hopkins UP, 1997.

Halliday, Terence C., and Morris Janowitz, eds. *Sociology and Its Publics: The Forms and Fates of Disciplinary Organization.* Chicago: U of Chicago P, 1992.

Hays, Sharon. *Flat Broke with Children: Women in the Age of Welfare Reform.* New York: Oxford UP, 2003.

Hebel, Sara. "Private Colleges Face Cuts in Public Dollars." *Chronicle of Higher Education* 1 Aug. 2003: A19–A20.

———. "Unequal Impact: Community Colleges Face Disproportionate Cuts in State Budgets." *Chronicle of Higher Education* 30 May 2003: A21–A22.

Heller, Lee E. "Made in the U.S.A.: The Construction of Academic Knowledge and the Limits of National Culture." *Poetics Today* 19.3 (Fall 1998): 335–56.

Horn, Catherine L., and Stella M. Flores. *Percent Plans in College Admissions: A Comparative Analysis of Three States' Experiences*. Cambridge: Harvard Civil Rights Project, February 2003.

Jacobson, Jennifer. "Foreign-Student Enrollment Stagnates." *Chronicle of Higher Education* 7 Nov. 2003. Web. 3 Nov. 2003. <www.chronicle.com/weekly/v50/i11/11a00101.htm>.

———. "The Clash Over Middle East Studies." *Chronicle of Higher Education* 6 Feb. 2004: A8–A10.

Klein, Julie Thomson. *Crossing Boundaries: Knowledge, Disciplinarities, and Interdisciplinarities*. Charlottesville: UP of Virginia, 1996.

———. *Interdisciplinarity: History, Theory, and Practice*. Detroit: Wayne State UP, 1990.

Lipka, Sara. "Pentagon Plan to Gather Student Data for Recruiters Raises Privacy Concerns." *Chronicle of Higher Education* 24 June 2005. Web. 27 June 2005. <www.chronicle.com/daily/2005/06/2005062401n.htm>.

Marin, Patricia, and Edgar K. Lee. *Appearance and Reality in the Sunshine State: The Talented Twenty Program in Florida*. Cambridge: Harvard Civil Rights Project, February 2003.

Messer-Davidow, Ellen. "Dollars for Scholars: The Real Politics of Humanities Research and Education." *The Politics of Research*. Ed. E. Ann Kaplan and George Levine. New Brunswick, NJ: Rutgers UP, 1997. 103–33.

———. "Manufacturing the Attack on Liberalized Higher Education." *Social Text* 36 (Fall 1993): 40–80.

———. "Why Democracy Will Be Hard To Do." *Social Text* 24 (Spring 2006): 1–35.

Mink, Gwendolyn and Rickie Solinger, eds. *Welfare: A Documentary History of U.S. Policy and Politics*. New York: New York UP, 2003.

Mooney, Chris. *The Republican War on Science*. New York: Basic Books, 2005.

Morgan, Richard. "Group Criticizes Link between Accreditation and Federal Student Aid." *Chronicle of Higher Education* 1 Oct. 2002. Web. 3 Oct. 2002. <www.chronicle.com/daily/2002/10/2002100101n.htm>.

———. "Lawmakers at Hearing on College-Accreditation System Call for More Acountability." *Chronicle of Higher Education* 2 Oct. 2002. Web. 3 Oct. 2002. <www.chronicle.com/2002/10/2002100200.htm>.

Office for Civil Rights Staff. *Beyond Percentage Plans: The Challenge of Equal Opportunity in Higher Education*. Washington D.C.: U.S. Commission on Civil Rights, Nov. 2002.

Pahre, Robert. "Mathematical Discourse and Crossdisciplinary Communities: The Case of Political Economy." *Social Epistemology* 10 (1996): 55–73.

Pickering, Andrew. "Anti-Discipline or Narratives of Illusion." *Knowledges: Historical and Critical Studies in Disciplinarity*. Ed. Ellen Messer-Davidow, David R. Shumway, and David J. Sylvan. Charlottesville: UP of Virginia, 1993. 103–22.

Polakow, Valerie, Sandra S. Butler, Luisa Stormer Deprez, and Peggy Kahn, eds. *Shut Out: Low Income Mothers and Higher Education in Post-Welfare America*. Albany: SUNY P, 2004.

Schmidt, Peter. "5 More States May Curtail Affirmative Action." *Chronicle of Higher Education* 19 Oct. 2007: A1, A19–A20.

Selingo, Jeffrey. "The Disappearing State in Public Higher Education." *Chronicle of Higher Education* 28 Feb. 2003: A22–A24.

Shumway, David R. *Creating American Civilization: A Genealogy of American Literature as an Academic Discipline*. Minneapolis: U of Minnesota P, 1994.

———. "Nationalist Knowledges: The Humanities and Nationality." *Poetics Today* 19.3 (Fall 1998): 357–73.

St. John, Edward P., and Michael D. Parsons, eds. *Public Funding of Higher Education: Changing Contexts and New Rationales*. Baltimore: Johns Hopkins UP, 2004.

Smallwood, Scott. "The Crumbling Intellectual Foundation." *Chronicle of Higher Education* 20 Sep. 2002: A10–A12.

Tienda, Marta, and Sunny Niu. "Texas Percent Plan: The Truth behind the Numbers." *Chronicle of Higher Education* 23 Jan. 2004: A10–A12.

Union of Concerned Scientists. *Scientific Integrity in Policymaking: An Investigation into the Bush Administration's Misuse of Science*. Cambridge MA: Union of Concerned Scientists, 2005.

U.S. Department of Education. "Reauthorization of the Higher Education Act of 1965." 2005 <www.ed.gov/print/policy/highered/leg/reauthorization.html>.

Chapter Fifteen

Accounting for Interdisciplinarity

Miranda Joseph

Preface

This essay has been written during my service as chair of the University
of Arizona Strategic Planning and Budget Advisory Committee (SPBAC).[1]
The writing has been an effort to bring the critical tools available to me
as a scholar to bear on the practices in which I am engaged, with which I
am complicit. By doing so, in this public forum, I hope not only to work
out a personal strategy for this participation, but also to provoke a larger
discussion and mobilize the broader engagement that might provide bal-
last for those of us who, in these roles, find our power as individuals to
be severely limited. I focus here on two overlapping issues: the changing
meaning and role of *interdisciplinarity* and the complex and dynamic demands
for accounting and accountability.

SPBAC, the membership of which is broadly representative, including
vice presidents, deans, staff, academic professionals, and students as well
as faculty (a majority of voting members), is responsible for participating
in institutional governance, primarily through the annual crafting of the
five-year Strategic Plan, although also by providing budget advice, which
generally means advice on how to handle relentless budget cuts. And I
am completing this essay as the university is deciding how to manage the
most drastic cuts in state funding in its history. Identifying performance
measures for both internal and external accountability is a routine part of
the strategic planning process; in relation to these budget cuts, the stakes
go up as I participate in selecting performance measures by which to make
consequential decisions about which programs and departments should be
cut more or even eliminated entirely. For me, the questions raised here

(and only partially answered) are pressing—I need to know what to say in the meeting I will walk into tomorrow.

The Business of Interdisciplinarity

> The university of the future will be inclusive of broad swaths of the population, actively engaged in the issues that concern them, relatively open to commercial influence, and fundamentally interdisciplinary in its approach to both teaching and research.
>
> —"The University of the Future," *Nature*

"In science, interdisciplinarity is the way business is done." Mike Cusanovich, former University of Arizona vice president for research, former interim provost, and then director of Arizona Research Labs, made this statement several years ago at an informal meeting called to discuss a possible conference on interdisciplinarity. What he meant most explicitly is that interdisciplinarity is the norm; as he recently explained, "[A]s a consequence of technology and the complexities of the problems scientists face, no one individual can have the necessary expertise to address the important questions" (personal communication). This view is affirmed by the article in *Nature* quoted in the epigraph, which also asserts, "Many argue that in a host of areas—ranging from computational biology and materials science to pharmacology and climate science—much of the most important research is now interdisciplinary." I will argue that one might also read his statement as having a second meaning: that interdisciplinarity is the way *business* is done. In the wake of the Bayh-Dole Act of 1980, which allowed universities to patent and become owners of intellectual property produced in the course of research funded by federal grants, and in the context of financial constraints that have led universities to eagerly seek new revenue sources,[2] including those research grants, direct industry sponsorship of research, and income from the licensing of that intellectual property, interdisciplinarity has become an official priority at many research universities. But what is meant by interdisciplinarity in the context of university administrative discourse?

First, as Cusanovich suggests, interdisciplinarity means "collaboration" among scholars with different disciplinary training and expertise. But in administrative discourse, it also means cross-sectoral collaboration between nonprofit universities and for-profit corporations. So, in the course of working on the University of Arizona Strategic Plan, I learned that local business and political leaders are explicitly enthusiastic about interdisciplinarity on the model of our BIO5 Institute. The mission of BIO5, as it appears on its Web site:

> BIO5 brings together scientists from five disciplines—agriculture, medicine, pharmacy, basic science and engineering—to treat disease, feed humanity and preserve livable environments. BIO5 creates science, industry and education partnerships to engage in leading-edge research, translate innovations to the market and to inspire and train the next generation of scientists. (BIO5 Institute, *Home*)

What begins to emerge in the BIO5 mission statement is that interdisciplinarity does not only mean collaboration but also has a special relationship with "applied" research, in which application is understood to occur through commodification: "BIO5 teams with the University of Arizona Office of Technology Transfer to facilitate connections between researchers and industry that translate university research to the marketplace where it can directly and more quickly impact people" (BIO5 Institute, *About*). The strategic plans of several major public research universities similarly suggest that interdisciplinarity is a priority, that interdisciplinarity involves collaboration across fields but also across institutional sites and economic sectors, and that its purpose is to produce knowledge that can be commodified, often framed in terms of application to societal problems or challenges, not always quite so explicitly as translation to the market. For instance, one of four main sections of the University of Minnesota, Twin Cities, "Strategic Positioning Report to the Board of Regents: Transforming the U for the 21st Century," called "Exceptional Innovation," is focused on interdisciplinarity. A side bar in this section (35) features a graphic that shows "disciplines" leading to "new knowledge," intersected by "institutes" with an arrow leading to "real world issues":

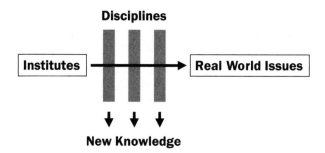

Likewise, Purdue's new strategic plan, entitled "New Synergies," features interdisciplinarity as part of its overall vision statement:

> Purdue University will set the pace for new interdisciplinary synergies that serve citizens world-wide with profound scientific, technological, social, and humanitarian impact on advancing societal prosperity and quality of life. (5)

Although the issue of revenue is sometimes downplayed in the prose, it becomes clear in the performance measures associated with these strategic plans. For instance, the University of North Carolina, Chapel Hill, Academic Plan has six major "Priorities," the second of which is: "Further integrate interdisciplinary research, education and public service" (21). Among the measures related to this goal are: "Funding generated by centrally supported interdisciplinary initiatives.

As a cultural studies, women's studies, and queer studies scholar, my own fantasy of interdisciplinarity—far from being "the way business is done"—has always been that it meant "no business as usual" or even that "interdisciplinarity is the way capitalism is critiqued." And the ongoing downsizing and financial impoverishment of the humanities in general and, to some extent, of our interdisciplinary fields (though the funding dynamics for women's studies and ethnic studies are not the same as those for the traditional humanities disciplines) makes it easy to believe that our work takes place at some distance from the market, a belief affirmed in the groundbreaking research of Sheila Slaughter, Larry Leslie, and Gary Rhoades in two books, both called *Academic Capitalism*, that trace the shifts since the 1980s in resources (human and financial) across fields and institutional units according to proximity to the market (the spatial metaphor is theirs).

(No doubt you are already irritated by my use of "we" and "our." I chose these terms deliberately, though I am uncertain of the referent—and I will discuss differences among "us" shortly. I do so in order to invoke the sense of us and them that structures our relations with our science colleagues, a sense of us and them that I would suggest needs to be broken down.)

Where, according to the strategic plans I have mentioned, practical application is identical with commodification, by contrast, it is precisely in the moment of claiming practical application that Stuart Hall, describing the imaginary of early cultural studies at Birmingham, notes—with what? regret? pride?—distance from the market:

We tried, in our extremely marginal way up there on the eighth floor in the Arts Faculty Building, to think of ourselves as a tiny piece of a hegemonic struggle. Just one tiny bit. We didn't have the illusion we were where the game really was. But we knew that the questions we were asking were of central relevance to the questions through which hegemony is either established or contested. (Hall, "Emergence" 18)

The fantasy that cultural studies is distant from the market has been most famously challenged by Bill Readings. In *The University in Ruins*, published in 1996, he identifies "Excellence," a management discourse that circulated widely in the academy in the 1990s and early 2000s, as a rationale of bureaucratic accounting that is indifferent to particular cultural content, concerned only with performance indicators that abstract from and make equivalent (commensurable) any particular content. He argues that where the university once functioned to create a national culture, it now supports globalization through this empty discourse of Excellence. And he argues that the institutionalization of cultural studies, a field that he defines as coherent insofar as it exists to contest the centering of high national cultures, has been made possible by Excellence—the loss of any cultural center to contest—and in effect subtends that discourse.

Whereas Readings clearly means for us to be scandalized by the resemblance between and participation of cultural studies and/in globalization, Ira Livingston, in his book *Between Science and Literature*, offers us a different possible response. Noting that new theories of nature developed in biology and physics—theories of autopoeisis, of complex self-organizing systems—are often presented in metaphors borrowed from globalizing capitalism (see 138–40), he suggests that rather than reading these resemblances as scandal—and going beyond the constructionist notion that the socioeconomic dynamics of this historical moment are determining scientific thinking—we should understand that both science and capitalism participate in what they represent, which, in the case of autopoeisis and global capital, is the logic of self-organization: "We come to recognize self-organization because we as a global species have attained it to some critical degree" (140). Livingston's claim itself resembles Marx's argument in the Introduction to the *Grundrisse*, where Marx seeks to explain the ability of Adam Smith to conceive of "labor in general": "As a rule, the most general abstractions arise only in the midst of the richest possible concrete development, where one thing appears as common to many, to all. . . . On the other side, this abstraction of labour . . . corresponds to a form of society in which individuals can with ease transfer from one labour to another, and where the specific kind is a matter of chance for them, hence of indifference" (*Grundrisse* 104).[3]

One might, and Livingston does, point out that the resemblance among contemporary conceptualizations of economic, biological, and physical phenomena as complex, open, self-organizing systems extends to the concepts produced by interdisciplinary humanities scholarship, which has "increasingly recognized the interdependence of identities . . . and [] begun to treat them as emergent and internally heterogeneous constellations in ongoing ecologies" (110). Livingston's argument suggests that we are "where the game really is" to a much greater extent than Hall thought (or most of us feel—but I will want to make a distinction between being "distant" from the market and being *in* a failing business). Rather than get hung up on this "complicity," I would suggest that we extend his nonscandalized reaction to the recognition that interdisciplinarity is after all business as usual and forge ahead with our critical analysis and intervention. Livingston argues that being in the game is not the same as changing it: "The interrelationality and plurality of all formations are good places to start and ongoing axioms in an argument, not the payoffs of one" (110). He argues that those payoffs "had better be sought in the creative and counterhegemonic possibilities of their pluralities and contradictions" (Livingston 110).

Likewise, Marx does not merely accept the notion of labor in general as a natural empirical category—this is precisely the flaw in bourgeois political economy; nor does he reject the notion of "abstract labor" because it has been enabled by capitalism itself. As is already clear from his assertion that the notion of abstract labor participates in a reality in which labor has been generalized and that this is an historically specific emergence, Marx rejects the version of abstraction that involves stripping away history and specificity to identify a common core. Likewise, he rejects a version of empiricism that conceives of the concrete as "given [and] observable" in favor of a notion of "complex" or "differentiated" "unities," which are a "rich totality of many determinations and relations" (Hall, "Marx's Notes" 129). As Hall says, Marx argues, "In order to 'think' this real concrete historical complexity, we must reconstruct in the mind the determinations which constitute it." The task then becomes a different kind of abstraction, the grasping of the "abstract determinations [that] lead towards a reproduction of the concrete by way of thought" (Hall, "Marx's Notes" 129). Here, abstraction is not generalization but rather selection, the pulling of one thread at a time. Ultimately, however, the threads must be rewoven;

"thought must rise from the abstract to the concrete." It strikes me that this, in fact quite familiar, methodology—one that enables the identification of contradictions—rather than interdisciplinarity (or challenging national cultures) per se, is the distinctive meaningful feature of cultural studies as a critical enterprise. I mean to both use this approach here and advocate for it as a strategy for both understanding and intervening in the ways we do business and the ways we account for ourselves. But I am getting a bit ahead of myself. . . .

The university strategic plans, like the mission statement of BIO5, consistently claim that interdisciplinarity is meant to solve, as the Purdue plan says, "societal grand challenges." That bringing the knowledge to market as private property is often presented as the only path by which knowledge can be "applied" in the "real world" is obviously a cause for concern (especially given that much of the research behind this intellectual property is paid for by the federal government, and thus what is happening is the privatization of public goods), as is the faith, apparent in some of these projects and programs, that technology is, by itself, sufficient to solve these great problems. It is also worth noting, though, the proliferation of programs related to the environment, sustainability and climate change that explicitly bring together physical, biological and social sciences, emphasizing the importance of "ecological, economic, and sociocultural factors" to, for instance, "the complex problems of sustainability of arid lands" (Graduate Interdisciplinary Program in Arid Lands Resource Sciences, *Home*).

The claim that this work will feed the hungry, preserve the environment, improve health care, and so on, suggests that our interdisciplinary science colleagues share some of the concerns of the scholars in interdisciplinary humanities and social science fields. That is, we too like to think that our work addresses "real world issues" and great social problems, although we tend to articulate those problems in terms of what we might see as underlying systems of meaning and power (gender, race, etc.) rather than the particular material manifestations of those power dynamics—poverty, illness, environmental degradation. On the other hand, at least one side of a debate within our fields values "translating" (or immediately producing) our knowledge for use in practices and policies to address precisely those material manifestations. It strikes me that we may not have adequately explored potentials for alliance and collaboration. And although I acknowledge that it is hard to imagine (and, for some of us, to desire) "selling" our work for practical use, I note that the project of "translation" is not always obvious even in technoscience fields: The University of Arizona is holding a symposium on Translational Environmental Research (TER), titled "Making the Connection," that aims to "build capacity" through, for instance, a session called "Paired Researcher and Stakeholder Point-Counterpoint: How Does TER Really Work?"

However, it has not been so much in attempts at translation or application as by virtue of our interdisciplinarity itself that some of us have imagined we might change the game, wanting to believe that our scholarly practice is itself a political practice insofar as transforming the structure of knowledge contributes to transforming the social hierarchies sustained by knowledge production. One of our central projects has been to show how social hierarchies are created and sustained through the interplay of economic, political and social/cultural processes, describing, among other things, how the separation of those domains (and the division of knowledge production about them into distinct disciplines) worked to naturalize those hierarchies.

Hall casts the project of cultural studies as, originally, an attempt "to address the manifest break-up of traditional culture, especially traditional class cultures . . . the fluidity and the undermining impact of the mass media" (Hall, "Emergence" 12). He casts this set of concerns as directly opposed to the then-dominant perspective in the humanities: "[T]he humanities . . . were conducted in the light, or in the wake, of the Arnoldian project. What they were handling in literary work and history were the histories and touchstones of the National culture, transmitted to a select number of people" ("Emergence" 13). So, according to Hall, the initial project had to include the demystification of the disciplines, to show "the regulative nature and role the humanities were playing in relation to the national culture" (15). But then in developing a positive agenda—the study of the "concept of culture," "contemporary cultural forms," "the political questions, the relationships, complex as they are, between culture and politics"—the cultural studies project involved not "a coalition of colleagues from different departments" (16) but "a series of raids on other disciplinary terrains. Fending off what sociologists regarded sociology to be, we raided sociology. Fending off the defenders of the humanities tradition, we raided the humanities. We appropriated bits of anthropology while insisting that we were not in the humanistic anthropological project and so on" (16).

I do not, by the way, mean to suggest that interdisciplinarity in the sciences is, by contrast with "us," merely "a coalition of colleagues from different departments" or that the scientific disciplines have not themselves been transformed. A quick review of the Web sites of various interdisciplinary scientific endeavors here at the University of Arizona suggests that they, too, entail politically significant transformations of the structure of knowledge and, implicitly, the social categories upheld by those knowledge structures.[4] Meanwhile, although the notion that interdisciplinarity implies the transformation of disciplines and not merely collaboration between disciplines is central to some of "us," "we" are riven by differences including, but by no means limited to, the extent to which we are invested in a critique and transformation of the disciplines (not to mention the identities and social hierarchies that some of us think are upheld by the disciplines). It is no accident that I have, so far, located my argument in the work of Stuart Hall. Although I might, of course, have found scholars of women's studies or ethnic studies or queer studies to cite on behalf of my fantasy of interdisciplinarity, I would have felt truly presumptuous (or rather, simply incorrect) making broad epistemological claims for women's studies or ethnic studies.

>   *During our last bout of downsizing and reorganization, called Focused Excellence, the president and provost, for the most part, took it upon themselves to discern where to cut or invest; however, in four areas they put faculty committees to work to sort out what to do. Of the four, only the one I co-chaired, the Cultural, Ethnic, Gender and Area Studies Study Team, was outside the sciences. (The CEGA team, as we called it, included representatives from Mexican American Studies, Latin American Studies, American Indian Studies, Middle East Studies, Africana Studies, and in my body, both Women's Studies and LGBT Studies, plus a few others whose representational role was less clear.) And while the other three teams were meant to develop new interdisciplinary initiatives (and one did lay some of the ground for the BIO5 Institute discussed above), ours was, I have always assumed, meant to negotiate/neutralize politically difficult waters in the hope that we might voluntarily come forward with some sort of money-saving proposal for combining units—not unlike what we are being asked to do now.*
>
>   *Initially, I took the formation of the team to be an extraordinary opportunity. In my experience, the units represented on the team engaged in notably little collaboration; the fact that we were going to have to work together seemed to open the possibility for moving beyond political and historical divides, such as that between area studies, rooted in Cold War government funding and still international*

in orientation, and U.S. ethnic studies rooted in political struggles oriented to the nation-state, and—underwriting as well as cross-cutting the others—the fundamental political and epistemological differences between those of us oriented toward applied social science and those with some combination of roots in the humanities, post-structuralism, and left/progressive political commitments. Although we were able to support each other in practical ways, putting the whole team behind the requests of particular units for lines and other resources and engaging in crucial information sharing and strategizing vis-à-vis policies that would affect us all (though there were holdouts to the last), we failed to bridge or even create spaces for bridging the historical, political, and epistemological fault lines among the units.

We produced a principled thirty-page report full of specific proposals for simultaneously respecting the autonomy of and strength-ening the individual units while building structures for collaboration such as interdisciplinary programs and centers. We tried to make audience-based arguments, articulating our proposals in terms of "excellence," which we interpreted to mean being on the cutting edge intellectually, being nationally or internationally recognized (and we especially emphasized our responsibilities as an Association of American Universities (AAU) institution), and of course, being fundable by foundations, government agencies, and private donors. (It is important to note that our interpretation attempted to shift the meaning of Excellence away from the meaning Readings had identi-fied and back toward traditional qualitative professional standards.) With a price tag of a mere $2 million (one-twentieth of the size of the proposals made by the science teams), ours was received as a doable modest proposal. . . . until, nearly simultaneously with our receiving a very encouraging official response from the provost, the next round of budget cuts was announced. Adding insult to injury, at least from my perspective, while telling us that our proposals would have to be deferred to some future in which the budget would be better (i.e., never), the provost invited the CEGA team to write itself into the margins of a health sciences funding request by adding some language about ethnic and gender health disparities and the cultural competencies needed by health professionals.

The CEGA team responded to this situation in several ways. First, we took up the invitation to supplement the health sciences funding request. Given that several of the units involved could benefit substantially if the request were to be funded due to their own emphases on applied social science of health, there was no way to say no.

At the same time, we responded by making an array of astoundingly conservative arguments for the humanities (and I played a particularly central role in crafting this particular memo). We argued that money should not be allowed to be the mission of the university, that we have an ethical responsibility to pursue an educational and scholarly mission and to find the money to do it; and we suggested that our mission could be articulated in terms of the national security concerns that were a hot issue both at the state-level in the form of an anti-immigrant voter initiative and at the national level in the form of a reckoning with the "intelligence" failures that had enabled 9/11—I quoted Porter Goss, then-nominee to head the CIA, regarding the necessity of training in languages and cultures. (Was it inevitable that, in arguing for what I called in this context "humanities and humanistic social sciences," I would simultaneously invoke nationalist arguments?) But at the same time, we tried to learn, really learn, that what is valued is money: We rebudgeted our proposals at $20 million. And we got a commitment from the president that he would bring (some revised politically palatable version of) our proposal forward as a state budget request. This went nowhere, as such requests depend on support from the governor (a Democrat dealing with a Republican legislature), and she was unwilling to take even a politically sanitized version of our proposal to the Arizona legislature.

Our flailing around for arguments on behalf of our proposals (and the fact that we ultimately found that we were subject to a political arena) raises a larger issue. To whom are we accountable, and on what terms?

Accounting for Interdisciplinarity

There are three modes of accountability that are relevant to those of us in interdisciplinary fields such as women's studies, ethnic studies, and cultural studies. First, professional accountability: the formal peer review processes that determine publication, tenure and promotion, honors and awards but also, more informally, the respect of colleagues, our reputation, and the impact of our scholarship on others in the field. Second, political accountability: To various degrees, we hold ourselves accountable for the extent to which we are contributing to a political movement, creating knowledge that is useful for policy, will change lives, and change the perspectives of our students or a larger public. And third, as I have already suggested, institutional and public accountability with regard to money and productivity that takes the form of an array of performance and financial measures that shape the institutional conditions within which we seek professional and political achievement. From an institutional, state, and public perspective, this third mode—a component of what has been called "The New Public Management," a neoliberal governance technology that pushes state agencies to operate like private businesses, in fact privatizes government functions and manages through outcomes measurement rather than substantive direction—has completely eclipsed the first two.

The tensions between the first two modes of accountability—professional and political—have garnered substantial attention within women's studies and cultural studies. And it is this tension that seems to be one of the prime motivations for this volume. Among the key issues for the editors—as expressed in the book proposal, titled "Interdisciplinarity and Social Justice: Revisioning Academic Accountability," which they shared when inviting me to contribute—is that although interdisciplinary programs (explicitly: gender and ethnic studies, with the more recent additions of lesbian/gay/ queer, environmental, cultural, postcolonial, and critical legal studies) were originally *accountable* to social justice movements and to "disenfranchised people," "perhaps they can no longer be said to be tethered to their political origins." That is, they pose the problem that Robyn Wiegman has taken up at length in various essays on women's studies.

Wiegman responds to an array of "laments," issued within the field of women's studies, that bemoan the very success of women's studies in gaining institutional space and legitimacy, which they see as leading to greater emphasis on professionalization as against feminist activism.[5] Describing these works as calling for accountability to real women, a call often staged against *Theory*, engagement with which is cast as professional cooptation, Wiegman argues that such accountability produces an array of epistemological constraints, temporal and spatial—more ball and chain than mere tether. Building on Jane Newman's "The Present in Our Past: Presentism in the Genealogy of Feminism," Wiegman argues that the imperative to be accountable to the feminist movement requires that the measure of all knowledge be its present usefulness ("Academic Feminism" 21). This "presentism," she argues, is enacted "in the figure of the live, suffering woman for whom academic feminism bears its guilty obligation of justice; in the rhetorical gesture toward the priority of discerning the materiality of the everyday; in the live encounter between researcher and researched" ("On Location" 13–14), which in turn has disciplinary implications, pushing us towards "humanistic and interpretative [but also, I would add, *quantitative*] social scientific inquiry" ("Academic Feminism" 29). And this in turn actually aligns our work with the "university's own instrumentalization of identity," which supports the efforts of the United States to "extend its imperial mission into a seemingly ethical globalizing human rights agenda (and with it various forms of economic 'development'. . . .)" ("Academic Feminism" 22). Likewise, she argues, "Women's Studies own self-defined justification as the academic arm of the women's movement can function as a territorial one, foreclosing in the present the interdisciplinary extension of feminist knowledge into domains that will have no obvious connection to the field's self-narration (such as the sciences)" ("On Location" 5).

My own argument pursues Wiegman's implicit directive to focus not on the tension between professionalization and political engagement but rather on the implications of what I have called the third mode, the institutional and public demands for accountability through accounting. Wiegman's analysis leads her to make the case that women's studies should pursue "a non-instrumentalized relation to knowledge production" ("Academic Feminism" 33), that is, an argument for what we might call "basic science." Such an argument is difficult to make even in the sciences these days.[6] And despite the fact that I completely endorse the effort to pry open a space for "basic science," I am—to the limited extent that I am able—undertaking an instrumental, present, and political project here.[7] In doing so, I suggest a definition and temporality for *the political* that contrasts with the one Wiegman describes: rather than accountability to a (nostalgically remembered) political movement imagined to be by definition representational, one that would tie us to social scientific study of the live suffering woman now, this notion of the political is about ongoing struggle, requiring us and holding us accountable to bring to bear an analysis on the conditions in which we find ourselves in order to shape effective intervention; our strategies—representational, methodological, disciplinary—would be contingent on our informed assessment of those conditions.[8]

Although Wiegman is entirely correct in her brief description of the emphases and impacts of "the broader institutional demands about

accountability and 'excellence' " ("Academic Feminism" 19), I want to begin
to explore the demands for accountability in somewhat more detail, to pry
them apart enough that we might start to plot a critical intervention in the
accounting of our work.

What does this third mode look like in practice? First, it is crucial to
recognize the enormous number and diversity of particular sets of metrics
through which any given university is accounted: Data about the University of Arizona are collected by the federal government (the Integrated
Postsecondary Education Data System established by the National Center
for Education Statistics);[9] the College Board (The Common Data Set);[10]
the state governor's office; the Arizona Board of Regents; and accrediting
bodies for the university as a whole and for individual programs. And
then, of course, there are the various purveyors of university rankings: the
most notorious is the *US News and World Report* ranking system, always
criticized for being largely based on reputation; others, thought to be more
legitimate because based on quantifiable data, have gained currency: Thus
the National Research Council (NRC) is in the process of producing a new
set of rankings of doctoral programs based on quantifiable data,[11] and the
Center for Measuring University Performance produces a ranking of "The
Top American Research Universities" based on nine factors (informally
referred to as the "Lombardi Measures"):

> Total Research Expenditures
> Federal Research Expenditures
> Endowment Assets
> Annual Giving
> National Academy Members
> Faculty Awards in the Arts, Humanities, Science, Engineering,
>   and Health
> Doctorates Awarded
> Postdoctoral Appointees
> SAT Scores

In response to the threat of a federally mandated regime of accountability
that seemed a clear and present danger in the context of the Department
of Education as led by George W. Bush's Secretary of Education Margaret
Spellings[12] (i.e., something that would go beyond the existing data collection to a more public, comparative, and potentially consequential collection, analysis and presentation of data, including, most importantly, some

standardized mode of "learning outcomes assessment"), the organizations of universities have begun to generate their own voluntary rubrics, such as the "Voluntary System of Accountability,"[13] which requires use of one or another of the recently developed and more or less palatable measures of the quality of undergraduate education such as the Collegiate Learning Assessment (a test of critical reading and writing) and the National Survey of Student Engagement (not a test but rather a survey that asks students the extent to which their experience has included certain activities and practices that are educational "best practices").[14]

The values that are embodied in these various sets of measures differ from each other; and, in fact, one can discern a tension that parallels the tension between professional and political accountability for individual faculty members. In this context, political accountability is not an individually generated sense of obligation as a direct imposition. Federal and state governments and the governing boards have articulated the mission of higher education principally in terms of national economic competitiveness and economic development. So "key indicators" in the Arizona Board of Regents "2020 Vision" system-wide strategic plan, which first and most importantly seeks to elaborate our previous governor's pledge to double the number of bachelor's degrees produced by the state's universities annually by 2020,[15] include: number of degrees awarded (bachelor's, master's, and doctoral, with the explicit rationale that those with degrees have higher lifetime earnings and are potentially attractive to high-tech employers), "degrees awarded in high demand fields" (which generally means Science, Technology, Engineering and Math [STEM] or health care, though this measure is not yet defined), technology transfer (measured by "invention disclosures transacted"), "research expenditures," "impact of community engagement activities" (yet to be defined), and "total income and expenditures related to service and engagement activities." These last three all assume that the expenditures employ people and buy things and thus multiply as they trickle out into the local economy; although it is not one of Arizona's "key indicators," the value of research is often measured in terms of "return on investment," meaning either this multiplier effect or, more specifically, the extent to which dollars invested by the state leverage federal or industry dollars. Accessibility, affordability, and efficiency are central in this context; thus this plan measures community college transfers and degrees awarded to community college transfers, because it is cheaper to let the community colleges provide the first two years of credits towards the bachelor's degree; number of bachelor's degrees awarded per hundred full-time equivalent

(FTE) students, a time-to-degree measure, because faster is cheaper; total educational expenditures per degree awarded (is it better to spend more or less?); cost of attendance as a percentage of Arizona median family income; and comprehensive financial index, a measure of an institution's "financial health," calculated from four financial ratios based on the university's audited financial statements: primary reserve ratio; viability ratio; return on net assets ratio; and net operating revenues ratio.

Meanwhile, university administrators, like faculty, are concerned with their standing among peers and thus with rankings and the measures that contribute to the rankings they value. For instance, when discussing what measures should be included in our strategic plan, our president inevitably suggests starting with the Lombardi measures, which, it is important to note, place very high value on funded research and faculty accomplishments in contrast with the measures related to undergraduate education that are the focus for the various governments and governing boards. In this context, National Science Foundation rankings of universities by research expenditures often trump all other measures. The conflict between the values of administrators and those of political actors was evident during the last year, as I observed the monumental battle waged by our administration to have "research" or, more accurately, "research expenditures"[16] included in a meaningful way in the Arizona Board of Regents' system-wide strategic plan. Their efforts were motivated by the assumption that these measures would be integrated into a funding formula and thus have financial implications.

But really, what is the impact of all this accounting and on our inter-disciplinary fields in particular? At least until recently, didn't we faculty just go on about our business, trying to get our research done and our classes taught, leaving it to our department heads to deal with bureaucratic reporting requirements and negotiations with deans for money and lines?[17] As Michael Power has argued in *The Audit Society*, auditing can fail in two opposite ways: It can distort the substantive activity of an organization (and it might depend on one's political perspective whether changes to the substantive activity constitute distortion or improvement), or the accounting can take place in a kind of administrative shell at the surface of the organizing that actually shields the daily work of most participants. Shore and Wright, in a Foucauldian argument drawing on Power's work, emphasize the shift from one to the other, the subjectification of the institution as a whole, as it creates new procedures—record keeping and control systems—to make itself an "auditable commodity" (72), and the individuals within it, as they respond to the new panoptic technologies by "freely" regulating their own conduct to meet the measured goals (62).

When I started as a member of the University of Arizona Strategic Planning and Budget Advisory Committee two years ago, I immediately joined the "measures committee" and was struck by the disconnect between the regimes of accountability that I was familiar with as a faculty member—annual performance reviews, tenure and promotion reviews, student course evaluations—and the measures that we were discussing as the possible ways to measure the university as a whole. That is, none of the information that we all submitted in the form of CVs and narratives about our accomplishments served as useable data to be assessed cumulatively for the university as a whole—we simply had no mechanism for doing so; faculty CVs did not get dumped into a database for sorting and counting in any way. In some ways I was appalled and in others relieved to find that the regime of accountability was unable to see the real work of the faculty, that it was to a large extent irrational and ineffectual—we would measure those things for which we had data, for which we could show progress—not the things that mattered in relation to our stated mission and goals. Whether I am more appalled or more relieved in a given moment depends on whom is to be held accountable: I want meaningful measures to hold the whole institution accountable for making progress on diversifying the faculty; and I want resource allocation to be made on some basis other than cronyism or mistaken prejudices about productivity and financial return on investment (for instance, good financial accounting can sometimes counteract the assumption that big science indirect cost recovery subsidizes the rest of the university and show instead that big science is subsidized by other revenue sources such as state funding). As a friend recently commented, decisions based on data are an improvement over the "faith-based" decision making of the Bush II administration.

As chair of SPBAC, I find myself trying to close the gaps between what faculty actually do and what is measured, between what we as an institution say we intend to do and what is measured. At the request of our new provost, SPBAC recently undertook a project that aimed to select a "robust" set of measures, such that we could measure every single goal in the strategic plan and reframe the goal as

a numerical target. (Although even the provost understood, as I had
come to understand, that measuring can be an enormously expensive
undertaking, primarily in personnel time, and that the value of each
new metric had to be weighed against the cost.) Frustrated again
and again by the lack of data to support measures of the things we
claimed to value, and even though I knew better, I proposed that
faculty submit at least portions of their annual performance reviews
online such that the information could be dumped into a database that
could then be drawn on to find out, for instance, how much "public
service" our faculty do (we are a land-grant institution, after all) or,
as an indicator of "interdisciplinarity," how many joint and affiliate
appointments our faculty have or how many are participating in grants
with co–principal investigators from different departments. On the
theory that what is counted is what counts, I found myself advocating
for certain problematic measures simply as placeholders, a stake in
the ground for the significance of the object imperfectly measured:
So, desperate for some measure of teaching quality, against the bet-
ter judgment of faculty colleagues, and ultimately unsuccessfully, I
proposed that we use teacher/course evaluation data. And specifically
in order to preserve some of the professional power of faculty against
the power of administrative management, in selecting measures, I
advocated for a publications and citations measure because it refers
back to peer evaluation, even though the most established publications
and citations database uses only selected journals (not books) as their
raw data and so undercounts in "book" fields while missing entirely
the output of our colleagues in fine arts.[18] No doubt, the commonly
used measures stack things in favor of certain fields. . . .

My sense that the institutional and state-mandated measures fail to
see us, or at least fail to see us as we see ourselves, fail to value what we
value, registers the discrepancy between that regime of accountability and
the (themselves potentially contradictory) professional and political modes
of accountability that are still more primary for most of *us*. The disjuncture
can make these newer measures feel impactful when deployed inside the
institution, potentially shifting resources and thus gaining our attention,
forcing us to seek ways to defend ourselves in their terms. Sheer quantities
of research dollars, student credit hours, or degrees produced can become
local-level measures used to rate the productivity or "cost efficiency"[19] of
departments or degree programs against each other. At the University of

Arizona, the data collected for the new NRC rankings of doctoral programs are being deployed (in conjunction with narrative self-evaluation and justification) for a review of all of our graduate programs with an eye toward the potential elimination of programs that fair poorly in this assessment (a similar consequential assessment recently took place at Ohio State University). And the emphasis on financial accountability likewise rolls down—many universities now use some form of what is called "responsibility-centered management" or "responsibility-based budgeting," which, despite its name (suggesting that money would be distributed based on "responsibility," i.e., role in fulfilling the mission), starts with an accounting of who is bringing in money and only then taxes this income so as to redistribute resources to subsidize units perceived to be important but not adequately revenue generating (think of your university library as a "welfare queen").[20]

As I have already illustrated in the CEGA Study Team story, this regime of accounting (or I should say this complex interplay between potentially contradictory regimes of accounting and accountability), exacerbates existing differences—between "us" and the "sciences" and among us, between those whose work is visible in the accounting scheme and those who appear unproductive by those measures, or between those who produce research expenditures or commodifiable knowledge products and those who produce student credit hours and degrees (most often not the same scholars or academic units, though there is the occasional "double threat," such as the Psychology Department at the University of Arizona, which brings in very substantial research dollars and provides vast quantities of undergraduate instruction). What now seems obvious to me is that the only way we might have made a case for anything beyond fundable applied social science of health research (that is, those aspects of cultural, ethnic, gender, and area studies that register in terms of research expenditures) would have been to claim that we would be increasing the efficiency and quantity of undergraduate degree production, and even then it would have been a weak claim because we neither offer degrees in STEM fields nor train health care providers. Our knowledge production quite literally does not count.

How should we respond to this situation?

As many have noted, the most common impulse of humanities (or, more broadly, qualitative or interpretive) scholars in response to quantitative accounting is to refuse—to claim that qualities cannot or should not be counted (see, e.g., Scobey). Readings argues, against the counting of "credit hours," that "the complex time of thought is not exhaustively accountable"

(127–28). Poovey proposes that the humanities should refuse commodification by refusing quantification, laying claim to goods that, she claims, are not quantifiable: "the goods of living culture, which embody and preserve human creativity" (11–12). In this response, they rely on a long history of critique of quantitative accounting as a social scientific methodology, for the ways it reduces diverse particulars to commensurable and exchangeable units, for the ways it inevitably seems to redeploy preexisting social categories and thus reaffirms existing social hierarchies, and for the ways it is used to constitute social problems requiring intervention (and thus is a central component of governmentality). Against counting, they tend to place a great deal of political optimism on qualitative or narrative accounts of the "singular" ("Singularity . . . recognizes the radical heterogeneity of individuals" (Readings 115). In discussing the evaluation of teaching quality, for instance, Readings suggests that in place of the usual student course evaluations that ask students to rate various aspects of a course on a numerical scale, students should "be required to write evaluative essays that can themselves be read and that require further interpretation" (133). Readings offers this approach as a way of accepting the imperative to evaluation—"Those in the University are called upon to judge, and the administration will do it for them if they do not respond to the call" (130)—while "refus[ing] to equate accountability with accounting" (131).[21]

I find that I no longer feel comfortable with the claims that "quality can't be counted," or that "what we do can't be measured." No doubt, my discomfort with these answers finds one of its sources in the immediate personal discomfort I feel when counting and measuring are demanded and what I want to do is show that we measure up. That is, the refusal of accounting puts us in a rhetorically untenable situation, dismissible as the arrogant sour grapes of those who don't measure up. Describing the closely related difficulty of defending scholarship that does not produce immediately applicable knowledge (knowledge that measures up by the appointed measures), Poovey says, "It is impossible to defend reviving the values that associate learning with curiosity and knowledge with freedom by any means that don't seem self-serving or nostalgic" (420). More importantly, the notion that qualities can't be counted, quantified, and commodified is simply wrong; commodification is a process by which qualitatively distinct products are made commensurable by being considered abstractly, as products of human labor according to Marx or as marginally useful (i.e., objects of demand) in neoclassical economic theory and thus exchangeable (e.g., human labor is made commensurable with money). And we know this insofar as we know that professional accountability through qualitative peer review, which relies on notions of the singular, has provided little resistance to managerial accountability as the number of publications or grant dollars expected for each step up the ladder has relentlessly accelerated.

Isn't it the case that our problem is not so much that our products have been commodified as that they have failed as commodities? We invest in producing, but the product does not sell—the market for our knowledge is relatively small—one might even say that, in this historical context, it has little socially recognized use value; without use value, no exchange occurs, and the product does not become commensurable with other valuable commodities, with money.[22] While we may want to resist commodification, it seems to me that the crucial aspect of commodification to resist is exploitation in the production process, not the marketing efforts that would teach our constituencies (dare I say *customers?*) the potential uses of the particular qualities of the goods we create.[23] This marketing effort might very well involve abstraction and quantification: We will want to engage in the Marxist version of abstraction—analysis of determinations—as a kind of market research, but then abstraction as reductive generalization and quantification will probably be crucial to the rhetoric of the marketing efforts themselves.

Gayatri Spivak offers one of the most savage critiques of empiricist knowledge production: In the context of a critique of international "development" efforts aimed at women, she argues that the production of "the generalized name of 'woman,' " which involves the suppression of "singularity in order to establish a 'fact,' works to "ensure predictability in the field of women" and to create a "common currency" that enables entities such as the United Nations and the World Bank to "operate in the field of gender" (*Death* 44–45). She states baldly that "positivist empiricism" is "the justifying foundation of advanced capitalist neo-colonialism." But Spivak also encourages us to make use of this critique with some cautiousness: "A just world must entail normalization; the promise of justice must attend . . . to the anguish that knowledge must suppress difference as well as differance, that a fully just world is impossible, forever deferred and different from our projections, the undecidable in the face of which we must risk the decision that we can hear the other" (*Critique* 199). Spivak learns from Derrida that "responsible action" requires accounting, requires deploying the "calculus" of "accountable reason," even while we keep "always in view" that "if responsible action is fully formulated or justified within the system of the calculus, it cannot retain its accountability to the trace of the other (*Critique* 427–28). That is, instead of *replacing* accounting with accountability, we might *supplement* accounting with accountability, push accounting to its limits as we also stake a claim to goals, to values, not currently articulated within the regime of accounting to which we are subject.

When I say push accounting to its limits, I mean two different things. On one hand, let's refuse to say that anything is beyond measurement until we have done our best to measure it. And I would argue that we are nowhere near doing our best. As I've already suggested, good financial accounting can counteract our assumptions about who among us is really responsible for various costs and revenues. Also, a recent national study of higher education finance has revealed that in contrast with the presumptions underlying the public outcry over the rising costs of higher education, in fact, costs have remained remarkably stable (especially at public institutions)—tuition has gone up because states have shifted the burden of those costs onto individual students (Wellman). On another front, although we employ extraordinarily sophisticated quantitative researchers in our institutional research office, we generally don't ask them or allow them to do anything beyond simple counting—they are kept too busy assembling data to actually analyze it. So when it was proposed that we measure interdisciplinarity through a social network analysis (think of a Facebook friend wheel but more so), this was ultimately shot down as just too daunting—this is too bad, as I suspect that we would do very well in such a measure. And I wonder if similar quantitative techniques might not be useful in making the impact of our work in relation to "real world issues" visible in new ways. Although I reach the limits of my own disciplinary knowledge too quickly to be very specific here, I suspect that serious engagement in the details of what is measured and how might provide authoritative ways to participate in the battles over priorities and policies both internally and publicly.

One the other hand (this is the second way in which I suggest we "push the limits" of accounting), we must intervene in the accounting of our work by reshaping the common denominators by which our work is measured and compared, by which it is enabled to circulate as valuable. But before we can do this, we should probably begin with the analysis of determinations and thus, potentially, contradictions in the currently dominant regimes of accounting.

While the higher education mission and the forms of accountability demanded by state actors are often articulated in terms of expanding the availability of affordable education, in *Unmaking the Public University*, Christopher Newfield argues that, in fact, the driver has been an attempt to control the democratizing force of the expansion of higher education that took place between the end of World War II and the early 1970s. He argues that "culture wars" attacks on universities of the 1970s to the 1990s, which focused on so-called "political correctness," affirmative action, and the introduction of "multicultural" content in both curriculum and research, worked in tandem with the discourse of market fundamentalism that gained dominance during the same period to delegitimize the whole notion of racial and economic equality, narrow the mission of universities to economic rather than general social and human development (thus specifically devaluing cultural as opposed to technical knowledge), and undermine the credibility of higher education (that is, the professional authority of the faculty), which enabled funding cuts—real reductions in the resources for the middle class as the cost of education was shifted from the state to individual consumers of education in the form of tuition—and, I would add, opened the way for the relentless performance and financial auditing to which we are now subject (per Power and Shore and Wright, audit performs and extends mistrust [Shore and Wright 77]). That is, Newfield suggests that the three forms of accountability I identified earlier—professional, political, and managerial—have been played off against each other, with political attacks, deployed to undermine professional credibility (and thus confidence in the existing systems of accountability that depended substantially on qualitative peer evaluation), legitimating new modes of managerial and financial accountability that are a Trojan horse for a political project of privatization and exclusion. Historicizing the current regime of accountability in this way, as the outcome of particular battles, suggests that we too might intervene, manipulate the modes of accountability and galvanize the interests of various players, to reshape what counts and who gets to count.

What would this look like? I do not have *the* answer, but the trajectory of this essay does suggest some avenues we might explore. I noted earlier that "we," interdisciplinary scholars in cultural, gender, and ethnic studies, might not have adequately explored potential collaboration and alliance with our science colleagues on the "societal grand challenges." The intellectual value of such collaborations is probably substantial, but such collaboration might also create opportunities for a reconstruction of our image and status as experts.[24] Meanwhile, I wonder if we could reappropriate the demands for affordable accessible higher education and for economic development? Rather than reject accounting per se, retreat to professional accountability, or hold ourselves accountable to an originary moment of identity-based social movement, we might engage in a broader contestation over the scope and goals of higher education. We might affirm the democratizing and developmental goals our states and governing boards have articulated but hold them accountable to those goals in ways they did not necessarily intend or envision.

> *Trying to think through how to deal internally and externally with the impending budget cuts, a colleague proposed that in order to really galvanize ourselves to fight, we might need to abandon "craven" economic development arguments for more heartfelt arguments for the value of knowledge itself, noting that economic development is not really what moves us and that if all we are about is workforce development, that really could be done more cheaply. But he recognized the inevitable problems—we would come across as elitist, pompous, arrogant, and in true academic form would wind up wanting to surround our affirmation of knowledge with caveats about its link to power. In response, I wrote the following:*

> > *I don't think that an argument for the value of knowledge per se will get us anywhere in the present political moment. However, we might ask some questions/make some arguments about the definition and scope of "economic development":*

> > *If, for a moment, we accept the notion that economic development refers only to for-profit business development, we might still ask if technoscience knowledge is sufficient in itself to drive economic development. What range of knowledge, skills and personal attributes are necessary to invent a new product or service, one that will actually meet the needs and desires of humans in their cultural, social, psychological complexity and diversity, believe you can build a business around it, sell the idea to investors, gather, organize and manage the people needed to produce your great new thing, communicate what it is, how it works and why it is desirable to consumers. . . .*

> > *And, is "economic development" a means or an end? If it is a means, providing the material basis for something more than itself (let's say relationships with—pick your favorite—other people, the god of your choice, nature, arts, the wondrous new gadgets developed by other people who are doing "economic development," etc), then those other areas might need some attention from educational institutions as well.*

Who is meant to benefit from "economic development"? Is this about a few entrepreneurs making fortunes, while everyone else is a low-paid cog in the machine? At the national level, we've been hearing a lot about access and affordability regarding higher ed. Shouldn't we be holding our elected officials accountable on this front (the rhetoric has been about holding the universities accountable, but the politicians must be held to account as well).

And, I would ask the question deferred above: are for-profit corporations the only kind of activity/organization needed for economic development or might we need expertise in public policy, social service provision, education itself? That is, might economic development mean more than business development?

While our legislative leaders don't care about any of this—they seem quite explicitly committed to reducing access to education (and the political and economic power that comes with it), preferring to incarcerate those that, if educated, might threaten them—a broader public might actually care.

Notes

This essay was written during the 2008–2009 academic year.

1. We also have a faculty senate, which is responsible for academic governance (matters related to curriculum, faculty, etc).

2. The trajectory of university funding has been detailed by a number of scholars. Poovey provides a good quick summary in "The Twenty-First-Century University and the Market" (especially 3–5). See also Wellman et al. "The Growing Imbalance," especially 19–22.

3. As will become clear, my attention was directed to the "Introduction" to the *Grundrisse* as an important methodological contribution by Stuart Hall's essay "Marx's Notes on Method: A 'Reading' of the '1857 Introduction.'" Although the publication date for this essay is 2003, a prefatory note suggests that earlier versions were presented in "a series of Centre seminars" and Hall's "Cultural Studies: Two Paradigms" of 1980, includes a brief version of the same reading of the "1857 Introduction."

4. So, for instance, from the Web site for the Department of Biochemistry and Molecular Biophysics: "Biochemistry is, by definition, the study of the molecular basis of life processes. . . . [Students of today must be well prepared in . . . : chemistry,

physics, mathematics and biology.] With recent developments in microanalytical chemical techniques, including DNA chip technology and related methods, mass spectrometry of biological molecules, and other nanoscale bioanalytical methods, coupled with the developing genome databases and computational methods to interrogate the databases, the future promises to be even more exciting than the past" (Department of Biochemistry and Molecular Biophysics Current Situation). And "Cognitive Science is the interdisciplinary study of the mind, encompassing the study of intelligent behavior as well as the brain mechanisms and computations underlying that behavior. The field is at the intersection of several other disciplines, including philosophy (knowledge representation, logic), psychology (basic human cognition, perception, and performance), computer science (computational theory, artificial intelligence, and robotics), linguistics (theories of language structure), and cognitive neuroscience (brain mechanisms for intelligent behavior). Typical research areas include judgment and decision making, language comprehension and production, language acquisition, visual recognition of objects and events, goal-directed movement in complex environments, and consciousness" (Cognitive Science Program Home).

5. In "Academic Feminism Against Itself," Wiegman cites Gubar's "What Ails Feminist Criticism," Messer-Davidow's *Disciplining Feminism: From Social Activism to Academic Discourse*, the special issue of *differences: Women's Studies on the Edge*, edited by Joan Wallach Scott, and a number of the individual essays in that volume.

6. Scanning today's issue of *Inside Higher Ed*, as I feel obliged to do every morning when I open my e-mail, I noticed an article, "Outmoded Engineers?" reporting that, following similar moves at other universities, Cornell has merged the Department of Theoretical and Applied Mechanics into another engineering department (a step toward phasing out that field altogether). The reasons: This department brings in only $2 million per year in grants (the lowest of the engineering departments) and pursues "curiosity-driven" rather than laboratory-based experimental (implicitly more "applied") research.

7. It strikes me that any binary opposition between instrumental and noninstrumental is unworkable. The deconstructive question: What is at stake in the distinction, in the categorization of some ends as the ones that "instrumental" knowledge production would promote?

8. I am deeply grateful to Elizabeth Lapovsky Kennedy and Adam Geary for suggesting that I clarify this point and to Kennedy for articulating this vision of *the political*.

9. As described on the Web site of the U.S. Department of Education National Center for Education Statistics page listing "Surveys and Programs": "The Integrated Postsecondary Education Data System (IPEDS), established as the core postsecondary education data collection program for NCES, is a system of surveys

designed to collect data from all primary providers of postsecondary education. IPEDS is a single, comprehensive system designed to encompass all institutions and educational organizations whose primary purpose is to provide postsecondary education. The IPEDS system is built around a series of interrelated surveys to collect institution-level data in such areas as enrollments, program completions, faculty, staff, finances, and academic libraries."

10. As described on the Web site of the University of Arizona Office of Institutional Research and Planning Support: "The Common Data Set provides information on the following topics:

A. General Information about the University of Arizona
B. Enrollment and Persistence
C. First-Time, First-Year (Freshman) Admission
D. Transfer Admission
E. Academic Offerings and Policies
F. Student Life
G. Annual Expenses—tuition, fees, room, and board
H. Financial Aid
I. Instructional Faculty and Class Size, Student to Faculty ratio
J. Undergraduate Degrees Conferred—by area of study

11. Variables that will go into NRC rankings:

Percent of faculty that is female
Percent minority faculty
Average number of annual Ph.D. graduates 2001–2006
Median time to degree for FT and PT Ph.D. students
Percent female Ph.D. students in 2005
Percent of minority Ph.D. students in 2005
6-Year completion rate for male students (8-Year for Humanities)
6-Year completion rate for female students (8-Year for Humanities)
Percent of students with individual work space
Percent of FT first-year students with full support
Percent of first-year students with external fellowship
Percent of first-year students with external traineeship
Citations for faculty publications
Faculty awards and honors
Placement of graduate students
Percent of faculty who are principal investigators on grants
Faculty size

12. The Spellings "threat" was made fairly explicit in the so-called Spellings Commission Report, the official title of which is "A Test of Leadership: Charting the Future of U.S. Higher Education" (U.S. Department of Education).

13. According to its Web site, "The VSA is a voluntary initiative for 4-year public colleges and universities. Developed through a partnership between the American Association of State Colleges and Universities (AASCU) and the National Association of State Universities and Land-Grant Colleges (NASULGC), the VSA is designed to help institutions meet the following objectives:

Demonstrate accountability and stewardship to public
Measure educational outcomes to identify effective educational practices
Assemble information that is accessible, understandable, and comparable

14. The political battles between the Department of Education (and its Secretary, Margaret Spellings, who is also responsible for "No Child Left Behind"), the Higher Ed accrediting agencies, the higher ed institutions, and Congress regarding the question of learning assessment (which is really a question of who gets to control assessment) have been tracked extensively in *Inside Higher Ed* and *The Chronicle of Higher Education* during the last several years (see, for instance, the article in *Inside Higher Ed* today, "A Call for Assessment—of the Right Kind," regarding a new statement on the subject issued by the Association of American Colleges and Universities). In fact, this debate has generated so much ink that I cannot even begin to engage it here.

15. Now that Democratic Governor Janet Napolitano has been replaced by Republican Jan Brewer, the prioritization of education may be replaced as well. We will see.

16. I pushed for including a "publications and citations" measure, and it was there for a while. I'm not sure when or why it vanished, but its disappearance affirms that what is relevant about research is that it is in itself and promotes (through tech transfer) economic activity, not that it produces new knowledge.

17. Liz Kennedy has quite correctly pointed out that for women's studies faculty, leaving the battles for resources to our department heads is a privilege of the second and third generation that was not available to the founders. The founding of women's studies required all hands on deck. Kennedy reads my argument here as suggesting that this may be another "all hands on deck" moment.

18. It is obvious but maybe still worth emphasizing that accountability is nothing new in the academy. Hoskin and Macve argue that accountability—by which they mean the deployment in large corporations of integrated financial and performance measurement that ultimately makes humans calculable—got its start in medieval universities, where new techniques for "gridding" information "plus the use of the formal examination" were developed and then took another leap in nineteenth-century universities with "the introduction of written examinations

and mathematical marking systems" (37). They credit the development of accountability systems in the United States largely to regimes implemented at West Point Military Academy (regimes modeled on the École Polytechnique), which not only included extensive marking and grading (sorting into a hierarchy) of the students' performance (and personal finances [see footnote 12) (45–49) but also that of the instructors (59). However, we are most certainly experiencing a change in the mode of accountability: What is measured, by what techniques, for what purposes and audiences are all in flux and thus demand analysis and struggle.

19. A faculty committee on which I participated developed a "cost efficiency ratio" that calculated the relation of state dollars invested to research expenditures and student credits hours (each as a portion of the university total).

20. Although RCB [Responsibility Centered Budgeting] is of great relevance to the question of accounting and accountability, I have largely bracketed it here, as it would quickly overtake the entire essay. There is a growing literature on the topic; for brief introductions see Hearn et al. and Fuller et al. Newfield offers a critique in his chapter on "The Costs of Accounting."

21. In fact, in the world of student outcomes assessment, portfolios of student work including self-reflexive essays are something of gold standard.

22. Marx argued that commodities are composed of use value and value—use value being the concrete object with particular qualities for which uses have been developed in a given historical context and value being the quantity of abstract socially necessary labor that produced the object. For capital (a form of value) to circulate, it must be embodied in particular useful products (though in the twenty-first century, those products may be far less "concrete" or object-like than Marx imagined).

23. Newfield argues that literary studies (and other humanities fields) have partially accepted "the 'market' as the arbitrator of the shape of the profession" (147) insofar as they have accepted as *facts* reduced demand for their products (primarily publications, especially books, and Ph.D.s, which is to say professors). However, he points out that they have failed to learn the other half of "the lesson of business," which is "how to manage markets—how to discover hidden demands, how to create demand for products one thinks are important, how to adapt the market to one's output, how to subordinate markets to the needs of one's 'customers,' not to mention the wider society" (148–49).

24. Paquette makes a similar argument: "Scholars in the social sciences, arts and humanities should consider seriously how the often underestimated value of their teaching and research could be further justified to the wider public through substantive contributions to today's most pressing policy questions." Building on a report from the British Academy, "Punching Our Weight," Paquette specifically argues for collaboration between government and university researchers (while acknowledging the potential dangers of such collaboration to distort knowledge production or place it in service of problematic political ends).

Works Cited

Arizona Board of Regents. "2020 Vision: The Arizona University System Long-term Strategic Plan 2008–2020 (Draft)." 28 Dec. 2008 <www.abor.asu.edu/1_the_regents/meetings/board_book/2008-08-Aug/item-15-App-2008-08.pdf>.

"A Call for Assessment—of the Right Kind." *Inside Higher Ed* 8 Jan. 2009. 8 Jan. 2009 <http://www.insidehighered.com/news/2009/01/08/aacu>.

BIO5 Institute. *Home.* The University of Arizona. 8 Jan. 2009 <http://bio5.arizona.edu/index.php>.

BIO5 Institute. *About.* The University of Arizona. 8 Jan. 2009 <http://bio5.arizona.edu/about/about_home.php>.

British Academy. "Punching our weight: the humanities and social sciences in public policy making." A British Academy Report. 17 Sept. 2008. 22 Jan. 2009 <http://www.britac.ac.uk/reports/wilson/index.cfm>.

Cognitive Science Program. *Home.* The University of Arizona. 26 Dec. 2008 <http://cogsci.web.arizona.edu/>.

Department of Biochemistry and Molecular Biophysics. *Current Situation.* The University of Arizona. 14 Sep. 2008 <http://www.biochem.arizona.edu/dept/overview.html>.

Fuller, Rex, D. Patrick Morton, and Ann Korschgen. "Incentive-Based Budgeting: Lessons From Public Higher Education." *On Becoming A Productive University: Strategies for Reducing Cost and Increasing Quality in Higher Education.* Ed. James E. Groccia and Judith E. Miller. San Francisco: Jossey-Bass, 2005. 34–43.

Graduate Interdisciplinary Program in Arid Lands Resource Science. *Home.* The University of Arizona. 12 Dec. 2008 <http://www.alrsgidp.arizona.edu/>.

Gubar, Susan. "What Ails Feminist Criticism." *Critical Inquiry* 24 (Summer 1998): 878–902.

Hall, Stuart. "Cultural Studies: Two Paradigms." *Media, Culture and Society* 2 (1980): 57–72.

———. "The Emergence of Cultural Studies and The Crisis of the Humanities." *October* (1990): 11–23.

———. "Marx's Notes on Method: A "Reading" of the '1857 Introduction.'" *Cultural Studies* 17.2 (2003): 113–49.

Hearn, James C., Darrell R. Lewis, Lincoln Kallsen, Janet M. Holdsworth, and Lisa M. Jones. " 'Incentives for Managed Growth': A Case Study of Incentives-Based Planning and Budgeting in a Large Public Research University." *The Journal of Higher Education* 77.2 (March/April 2006): 286–316.

Hoskin, Keith W., and Richard H. Macve. "The Genesis of Accountability: The West Point Connections." *Accounting, Organizations and Society* 13.1 (1988): 37–73.

Livingston, Ira. *Between Science and Literature: An Introduction to Autopoetics.* Urbana: U of Illinois P, 2006.

Marx, Karl. *Grundrisse*. Trans. Martin Nicolaus. New York: Random House, 1973.

Messer-Davidow, Ellen. *Disciplining Feminism: From Social Activism to Academic Discourse*. Durham, NC: Duke UP, 2002.

Newfield, Christopher. *Unmaking the Public University: The Forty-Year Assault on the Middle Class*. Cambridge: Harvard UP, 2008.

Newman, Jane. "The Present in Our Past: Presentism in the Genealogy of Feminism" in *Women's Studies on Its Own*. Ed. Robyn Wiegman. Durham, NC: Duke UP, 2002 141–73.

Office of Institutional Research and Planning Support. *Common Data Set*. The University of Arizona. 27 Dec. 2008 <http://oirps.arizona.edu/Common-DataSet.asp>.

"Outmoded Engineers" *Inside Higher Ed* 8 Jan. 2009. 8 Jan. 2009 <http://www.insidehighered.com/news/2009/01/08/cornell>.

Paquette, Gabriel. "The Relevance of the Humanities." *Inside Higher Ed* 22 Jan. 2009. 2 Feb. 2009 <http://insidehighered.com/views/2009/01/22/paquette>.

Poovey, Mary. "For Everything Else, there's . . ." *Social Research* 68.2 (2001): 397–426.

———. "The Twenty-First-Century University and the Market: What Price Economic Viability?" *differences* 12.1 (2001): 1–16.

Power, Michael. *The Audit Society: Rituals of Verification*. New York: Oxford UP, 1997.

Purdue University. "New Synergies: Strategic Plan: 2008–2013 (Draft 4/21/08)." West Lafayette, Indiana.

Readings, Bill. *The University in Ruins*. Cambridge: Harvard UP, 1997.

Scobey, David. "Meanings and Metrics," *Inside Higher Ed* 19 Mar. 2009. 19 Mar. 2009 <http://www.insidehighered.com/views/2009/03/19/scobey>.

Scott, Joan Wallach, ed. "Women's Studies on the Edge." Special issue of *differences* 9.3 (1997).

Shore, Cris, and Susan Wright. "Coercive Accountability: The Rise of Audit Culture in Higher Education." *Audit Cultures: Anthropological Studies in Accountability, Ethics, and the Academy*. Ed. Marilyn Strathern. London: Routledge, 2000. 57–89.

———. "Whose Accountability? Governmentality and the Auditing of Universities." *Parallax* 10.2 (2004): 100–16.

Slaughter, Sheila, and Larry L. Leslie. *Academic Capitalism : Politics, Policies, and the Entrepreneurial University*. Baltimore: Johns Hopkins UP, 1997.

Slaughter, Sheila, and Gary Rhoades. *Academic Capitalism and the New Economy: Markets, State, and Higher Education*. Baltimore: Johns Hopkins UP, 2004.

Spivak, Gayatri. *Death of A Discipline*. New York: Columbia UP, 2003.

———. *A Critique of Postcolonial Reason: Toward a History of the Vanishing Present*. Cambridge: Harvard University Press, 1994.

Strathern, Marilyn, ed. *Audit Cultures: Anthropological Studies in Accountability, Ethics, and the Academy.* London: Routledge, 2000.

The University of North Carolina at Chapel Hill. "Academic Plan." July 2003.

University of Minnesota. "Transforming the U for the 21st Century: Strategic Positioning Report to the Board of Regents." September 2007.

U.S. Department of Education. *A Test of Leadership: Charting the Future of U.S. Higher Education.* Washington, D.C., 2006.

U.S. Department of Education National Center for Education Statistics. *Surveys and Programs.* 27 Dec. 2008 <http://nces.ed.gov/surveys/SurveyGroups. asp?Group=2>.

Voluntary System of Accountability. *Home.* 28 Dec. 2008 <http://www.voluntary-system.org/index.cfm?page=homePage>.

Wellman, Jane V., Donna M. Desrochers, and Colleen M. Lenihan. "The Growing Imbalance: Recent Trends in U.S. Postsecondary Education Finance." Washington D.C.: Delta Cost Project, 2008.

Wiegman, Robyn. "Introduction: On Location." *Women's Studies On Its Own.* Ed. Robyn Wiegman. Durham: Duke UP, 2002. 1–44.

———. "Academic Feminism Against Itself." *NWSA Journal* 14.2 (2002): 18–37.

Afterword

Justice without Truth?

Ranu Samantrai

Is a certain conceptual distance between scholarship and activism not only inevitable but desirable?[1] Of course, we know that the categorical distinction between intellectual and political work is false. We are all political animals, in that what we do as scholars is not without consequence in the wider world. Moreover, many of us are actively involved in pressing for social change. Indeed, as the rationale for this volume and many of the essays herein suggest, the impulse toward interdisciplinarity often arises from suspicion of the knowledge protocols that undergird or naturalize unsavory norms, be they the tethers of racial or gender identity challenged by ethnic and women's studies or the distribution of resources queried by postcolonial and environmental studies.

That is certainly the case with my field, cultural studies, which, as it emerges from the Birmingham Centre, is rooted in the desire to serve the cause of justice.[2] Cultural studies is about the economic stratification of the national culture, with analyses undertaken in order to address the symbolic and material effects of that stratification. Of the founding figures—among whom I count Richard Hoggart, E. P. Thompson, Raymond Williams, and Stuart Hall—at least three came from outside the English intellectual class. Two (Hoggart and Williams) had working-class origins; two (Hall and Williams) were migrants; and all refused the distinction between politics and scholarship that is supposed to signal the credibility of the latter. Between them they were involved in the launch of *The New Left Review* (Hall; Thompson; Williams) but also in the Campaign for Nuclear Disarmament (Hall; Thompson). They taught the children of the elite in universities, but also working-class men and women in extramural settings (Hall; Hoggart; Williams).

353

This first generation succeeded in widening the scope and changing the object of intellectual inquiry. They insisted, for instance, that members of the working class are not dumb victims of the institutions of mass cultural production or only approachable as the oppressed, the marginalized—in other words, those less fortunate than ourselves in need of our rescuing attention. If, instead, members of the working class are creative individuals whose own expressive and lived cultures are complex accomplishments with public implications, then the example of the founding generation suggests that solidarity, rather than service, should characterize the relation between intellectual and political work. The two are joined in their aims, as well as in the person of the investigator/activist.

With this amendment of the relation of the observer to the observed, we shift from the intellectual vanguard to the organic intellectual.[3] For the vanguard occupies a position of well-intentioned superiority vis à vis the needy masses. The organic intellectual attempts to break from this essentially bourgeois philanthropic position with the radical suggestion that perhaps the intellectual need not be a member of the bourgeoisie. Arising from the people, the organic intellectual speaks for and to the people; hence the emphasis within cultural studies on participant observation and explicitly interested work. Of course, the model of the organic intellectual still relies on class analysis—that is, on knowing who the people are (by virtue of their location in a class structure) and what their interests are (objectively derived from that location). That becomes decreasingly viable as cultural studies moves from its originary moment and addresses, for instance, the social movements that, although they have a class component, are not reducible to class.

So now we have questions regarding the proper objects of knowledge and questions regarding the status of the knower. Together the two lead to what I believe is the fundamental distinguishing characteristic of cultural studies: a critique of the disciplinary production of knowledge. As I understand it, cultural studies is not multidisciplinary; its task is not to assemble enough disciplinary tools so that we can finally see the object of inquiry whole. Quite the contrary: the effect of the juxtaposition of disciplines is that each one exposes the limits of the truth producing mechanisms of others. What is an appropriate object of study? What are appropriate methods of study? What counts as evidence? And, finally, what counts as knowledge? The disciplines give dramatically different answers to these questions. Far from the happy meeting ground where disciplines complement each other in the humanistic dream of perfect knowledge, cultural studies renders truth claims provincial in a decidedly antihumanist gesture. Using the tools of one discipline to lever open the closed world of another, it exposes not the open view of the universe but only the partiality and interestedness of our elaborately constructed knowledge-producing apparatuses. And this is entirely in keeping with its political commitments, for what better start to changing the status quo than turning a critical eye on its truth? There is no escaping the imbrication of power and knowledge.

Hence we dispense with the first term of my title, "truth," which is never what it claims to be. We are left extraordinarily self-conscious in the position of perpetual critique. Onward to "justice": what are the implications of epistemological uncertainty for the project of social justice? Let me think through this question using the example of the events around the attempted premier of *Behzti (Dishonour)*, a play by Gurpreet Kaur Bhatti. On December 18, 2004, about four hundred demonstrators attempted to storm the Birmingham Repertory Theatre in England (BBC, "Theatre"). They smashed windows, destroyed backstage equipment, and clashed with eighty-five police officers, thirty of whom were in riot gear (Branigan; Branigan and Dodd). They were protesting the production of *Behzti (Dishonour)*. Set in a gurdwara (Sikh temple), the play includes scenes of rape and murder, as well as revelations regarding homosexual relationships between putatively respectable Sikh men. Protestors succeeded in stopping the production: fearing for the safety of its audience, cast, and workers, theater management opted to evacuate some eight hundred people (*Guardian*, "Playing").[4] In the days that followed, unable to secure assurances from Sikh religious leaders that the violence would not be repeated, the sold-out run of the play was cancelled altogether as Bhatti and her family, inundated with death threats and hate mail, went into hiding (BBC, "Author"; Branigan and Dodd).[5]

When interviewed by the BBC, Sewa Singh Mandha, the chairman of the council of Sikh Gurdwaras in Birmingham, declared, "In a Sikh temple sexual abuse does not take place; kissing and dancing don't take place; rape doesn't take place; homosexual activity doesn't take place; murders do not take place" (Left). Mohan Singh, from the Guru Nanak Gurdwara of Birmingham, told *The Guardian*, "Free speech can go so far. Maybe 5,000 people would have seen this play over the run. Are you going to upset 600,000 Sikhs in Britain and maybe 20 million outside the UK for that? Religion is a very sensitive issue and you should be extremely careful" (Left).

But Hanne Stinson, Executive Director of the British Humanist Association and one of more than seven hundred signatories of an open letter supporting Bhatti, suggests a very different scenario than that of a community rising to defend its insulted religious honor:

A Sikh woman writes a play popular with young Sikh women, perhaps because the issues it raises are important for them. Other Sikhs, nearly all male, protest violently outside the theatre, claiming the play is offensive. [. . .]

Were these violent protests about an insult to strongly held religious beliefs? Or were they about suppressing dissident voices, especially women's voices, within the Sikh community? Stinson's view is clear:

It is all too easy to assume that faith communities are homogeneous and to forget that religious and community leaders, mostly male, may not be speaking for the whole community. We, and indeed the Government, need to make sure that we also hear the voices of the more integrated and progressive elements within ethnic and religious minorities, including the voices of women. (Stinson)

Is there any truth to Stinson's claim that the response to *Behzti (Dishonour)* exposes a constituency fissured along the lines of gender? A few days following the play's cancellation, *The Guardian* gave five "experts" a challenge: what would they do faced with this and other controversial works? In addition to *Behzti (Dishonour)*, the works in question included three that address religion in some way—Salman Rushdie's novel, *Satanic Verses*; Jim Allen's play, *Perdition*; and James Kirkup's poem, "The Love that Dares to Speak Its Name"—and two that contain no reference to religion—homophobic dancehall lyrics by Jamaican musicians and misogynistic lyrics by Eminem (*Guardian*, "Censorship").[6]

Among the invited commentators was Dr. Kanwaljit Kaur Singh, chair of the British Sikh Education Council. Whenever the controversy in question was about religion, Dr. Singh recommended censoring the offending work. Hence she recommended banning *Satanic Verses* on the grounds of offense to Islam and *Perdition* if it caused offense to Jews. But she took pains to distinguish religious insult from general offense, for instance in the case of "The love that dares to speak its name," and did not advocate censoring the latter. Hence, regarding Eminem's misogynist lyrics, she said, "This does not provide children with good role models. I would not want my children to hear it. I'm not sure I would ban it, the lyrics are ridiculous. I would advise people not to listen to it."

Oddly, the restraint that she demonstrates in this case is not exercised in the case of homophobic dance hall lyrics, the only other nonreligious example. These are censorable, although they do not insult religion. Wherein lies the difference between misogynous and homophobic lyrics? There is little, if any, difference in content, given the violence of the misogyny and homophobia spewed in Eminem's lyrics. The most obvious difference has to with their targets: women, in the case of Eminem, and gay men in the case of the dance-hall lyrics. In a surprisingly progressive move, Dr. Singh appears to believe that gay men deserve the same protection as straight men. Fearing that "abuse of gay people" could incite violence, she is willing to violate her own principle that only religious insult, and not general offense, necessitates legal intervention. Apparently both the bodies and the sensibilities, religious and otherwise, of men require state protection.

By contrast, for Dr. Singh, women do not need that protection. Are women's bodies and sensibilities so much tougher than those of men? Or is it perhaps that their relationship to the state should differ from that of men? Interestingly, the case of Eminem is also the only instance when Dr. Singh's perspective shifts from general to specific targets that may be damaged. We move suddenly from the harm that may come to hypothetical people to a domestic scene where harm may be done to her own children. In this context, she sees no need for state intervention. What happens to her children and perhaps by extension to others in the domestic realm is a decision that remains within the family. The reach of the state stops at the door to the home.

Why don't women require the protection of the state? Dr. Singh's perhaps inadvertent linkage of women (targets of misogyny) and children (audience of lyrics), and her withdrawal of both from the reach of the state, provide the answer: women do not require state protection because, along with children, they are properly protected within the intimate sphere of the family. The state must differentiate between men and women. Symbolically occupying the public sphere, men encounter the state as public actors and thereby as the appropriate representatives of the private sphere. As the latter, too, they mediate the relationship between women, children, and the state. By contrast, what happens to women is an internal family matter. Consider, then, the enormity of the violation when one of them—the women who are supposed to remain in the intimate sphere—steps out to speak publicly, and to outsiders, about private matters.

Thus far Stinson's analysis appears accurate. But before we join in recommending that laggers should integrate into a "progressive" gender system, let us consider the implications of the desire to change a community so that it no longer segregates the sexes, however symbolically, into public and private spheres, with women contained in the latter and with an attendant differentiation in protections accorded by the state. To advocate such change would be to impose the gender norms and family structure of the dominant majority on an already beleaguered minority. It would be to insist on an assimilation so complete that no small zone of privacy is left for a dissenting minority, for the state would regulate even its most intimate relationships, changing the nature and finally the self-understanding of the minority subject until whatever alterity that subject might once have possessed disappears. It would be to complete, finally, the unfinished mission of colonization and turn this resistant subject into a modern European individual, bearer of rights and encased in individuality.

Which side would you be on: gender equity or cultural equity? We live in a world of incommensurate truths. Justice for one will be injustice for another.[7] There is no reconciliation possible here, no way that everyone can win. We have to choose: protect the minority or the minority within the minority. We have no way of knowing which is the right choice, no way of knowing which community representatives to believe, no teleology or predictive mechanism that will assure the right outcome. And we are in the uncomfortable position of invoking the power of the state to back our choice, to reward and punish according to our wishes.

The model of the organic intellectual would have us act in solidarity with the people. But who here are the people? The traditional disciplines might proceed by discovering the terms of legitimacy for community representatives, investigating how, in a plural society, majority and minority groups interact, how social resources are distributed along those fissures, and so forth. In cultural studies we are more likely to ask, from our antidisciplinary perspective of uncertainty, how has minoritization occurred? That is, how is this society organized by and enfranchisement within it governed by the idea of culture? How have people come to believe themselves to be enculturated subjects? And what interests are served by enculturation, even by those whose enculturation is injurious? One way to think about the difference between the two kinds of questions, from the perspective of the activist, is that the former asks for justice for extant cultural minorities, while the latter opts for destabilization of present majority–minority configurations in favor of an uncertain but perhaps better future.[8] Or the former might opt for strengthening the position of the disenfranchised, while the latter asks them to desire their own obsolescence.

Coincident with the events surrounding the Birmingham Repertory's attempted production of *Behzti (Dishonour)* was the introduction into Parliament of the then–Blair government's latest antiterrorism bill, called the Serious Organised Crime and Police Bill, the legislation that used the fear of terrorism as a cover to justify a vast, U.S.-style expansion of state power. There had been anticipation that in that parliamentary session the Blair government would move to repeal Britain's statute against blasphemy (BBC, "Anger"). Because it only protects the Church of England, that statute has long been criticized as a discriminatory tool that relegates non-Anglicans to second-class status. Instead, tucked into the antiterrorism bill was a proposal to make incitement to religious hatred a new category of criminal offense.[9] The measure was a sop to the targets of the proposed expansion of antiterrorism powers, Muslim leaders, in the hope that they would accept that, in the words of Liberal Democratic member of Parliament Evan Harris, "the law the government is bringing in will give them equality with Christianity" (BBC, "Anger"). Local religious leaders, of course, would have to identify when such incitement has occurred.

In other words, in exchange for its vastly expanded powers, the state offered to recognize minority constituencies as little fiefdoms in which locally dominant actors could exercise borrowed sovereignty over their dissenters.[10] That is a kind of equality. From another angle, such a settlement is tantamount to accepting current majority or minority status and seeking to maintain the stability of that social arrangement into the future. The more dangerous option for the both majority and minority constituencies would be to refuse the recognition of the state, and hence to leave themselves open to unpredictable change. From the point of view of a critique of the norms that defer homogeneity from the nation to its problematic cultures, this is the better option. But it asks people to see themselves as effects of the conditions of their production. If they wish to change the conditions, they must invite their own obsolescence.

My stance would not make me an organic intellectual, but I reject the demand of speaking from and for and to. To begin with, I don't know who the people are. My stance would put me on the side of Bhatti, but not necessarily because she has a program of gender equity (that has its own analysis). She is searching for an exit from the status quo. But if I were asked if this change will be good, I would have to say that I don't know. It must be tested in its effects, a task for activists. All I know is that in order to shake the norms that make us, we must be willing to be other than we are.[11]

You see the problem: "Resist who you are" is not a very compelling rallying cry. It does not translate easily into an agenda for action. So at last I come to the meeting point of justice and truth, activism and scholarship. If the models of the traditional, the vanguardist, and the organic intellectual are not available to me, what remains? Perpetual critique, based on uncertainty—in other words, the position of the dissenter. The activist needs the doubt of the scholar, just as the scholar needs the test of the activist.

Perhaps there is an irreconcilable tension between activism and scholarship. It may be a difference of emphasis and degree rather than kind, but difference there is, even though the two be combined in one person. And that is as it should be. In fact, in the quest for solidarity, a critical distance between the two may be advisable. Without the test of effects in action, the dissenter could easily slip into the smug satisfaction of the vanguard. Without the questioning of foundations, the activist's certainty would make for an equally smug self-congratulation. Perhaps the best way we can help each other is by keeping a suspicious eye on each other.

Notes

1. My thanks to Joe Parker for his thoughtful reading.

2. The Centre for Contemporary Cultural Studies was founded by Richard Hoggart at the University of Birmingham in 1964. Stuart Hall, who worked with Hoggart as the centre's deputy director, became its director in 1968. The Centre was closed in 2002. For the Centre's early history, see Turner.

3. This parsing of the ideological affiliations of intellectuals is Gramsci's.

4. The number of people evacuated includes those attending a Christmas show in the main auditorium of the theater.

5. For some background and context for these events as well as a brief excerpt of a scene that depicts rape and references homosexuality, see Dodd.

6. Despite protests by some Muslims against what they considered to be blasphemy in *Satanic Verses*, the novel was not banned in Britain, where blasphemy laws protect only established churches. The Royal Court abandoned its 1987 production of *Perdition* when some Jews objected to its depiction of some Zionists during the Holocaust. "The Love that Dares to Speak its Name" portrays a Roman centurion having sex with the corpse of Christ. It was banned in 1977 under Britain's blasphemy laws following a private prosecution by Mary Whitehouse against *The Gay News*, which had published the poem on June 3, 1976. *The Guardian* report

does not specify which dance hall lyrics its experts were asked to judge. It notes only that "The Metropolitan police are investigating the lyrics of a number of Jamaican dance hall artists over claims their songs incite fans to kill gay people" (*Guardian*, "Censorship"). Likewise, rather than specifying any particular lyrics by Eminem, the article claims simply that, "The influential US rapper has caused outrage with misogynistic lyrics."

7. I am borrowing Lyotard's description of the relation between the *petits récits* that replace metanarratives in postmodernity.

8. I have explored this question in much greater detail and with respect to both race and gender in *AlterNatives*. See especially chapter 2, "States of Belonging" (29–58).

9. The government cut the provision from the bill following widespread objections so that the bill would pass into law before the 2005 dissolution of Parliament and general election. The provision finally became law in 2006 as the Racial and Religious Hatred Act.

10. In the subsequent months as it prepared to fight an election campaign, the Blair government proposed drastic curbs on immigration and the entry of refugee and asylum seekers (the latter two in contravention of the 1951 United Nations Declaration on Refugees, of which Britain is a signatory) and restrictions on the rights of all foreign nationals, including the right of family unity (in contravention of the European Union). It also contemplated the elimination of the adversarial system of justice in trials involving terrorism (in favor of the inquisitorial system, and again in contravention of a thousand years of British legal precedent).

11. My thoughts on these questions, as on so many matters, are indebted to Foucault. See, for instance, his comments on the government of individualization ("The Subject and Power"), on the intellectual ("Concern for Truth"), and on transformation (*Remarks on Marx*) of the status quo ("What is Enlightenment?").

Works Cited

Bhatti, Gurpreet Kaur. *Behzti (Dishonour)*. London: Oberon Books, 2005.

Branigan, Tania. "Tale of Rape at the Temple Sparks Riot at Theatre." *The Guardian* 20 Dec. 2004. 21 Dec. 2004 <http://www.guardian.co.uk/uk/2004/dec/20/arts.religion>.

Branigan, Tania, and Vikram Dodd. "Writer in Hiding as Violence Closes Sikh Play." *The Guardian* 21 Dec. 2004. 22 Dec. 2004 <http://www.guardian.co.uk/2004/dec/21/religion.arts>.

British Broadcasting Company (BBC). "Anger at No Repeal on Blasphemy." *BBC News* 27 Nov. 2004. 28 Nov. 2004 <http://news.bbc.co.uk/1/hi/uk_politics/4047425.stm>.

———. "Author Defends Sikh Protest Play." *BBC News* 13 Jan. 2005. 14 Jan. 2005 <http://news.bbc.co.uk/1/hi/entertainment/arts/4170297.stm>.

———. "Theatre Stormed in Sikh Protest." *BBC News* 19 Dec. 2004. 20 Dec. 2004 <http://news.bbc.co.uk/1/hi/england/west_midlands/4107437.stm>.

Dodd, Vikram. "Why A Play Prompted Violent Protest." *The Guardian* 21 December 2004. 22 Dec. 2004 <http://www.guardian.co.uk/uk/2004/dec/21/religion.arts1>.

Foucault, Michel. "Concern for Truth." Trans. Alan Sheridan. *Politics, Philosophy, Culture: Interviews and Other Writings, 1977–1984.* Ed. Lawrence D. Kritzman. New York: Routledge, 1988. 255–70.

———. *Remarks on Marx: Conversations with Duccio Trombadori.* Trans. R. James Goldstein and James Cascaito. New York: Semiotext(e), 1991.

———. "The Subject and Power." *Art After Modernism: Rethinking Representation.* Ed. Brian Wallis. New York: Museum of Contemporary Art, 1984. 417–32.

———. "What is Enlightenment?" Trans. Catherine Porter. *The Foucault Reader.* Ed. Paul Rabinow. New York: Pantheon, 1984. 239–56.

Gramsci, Antonio. *Prison Notebooks: Selections.* Trans. Quintin Hoare and Geoffrey N. Smith. New York: International Publishers, 1971.

The Guardian. "Can Censorship Ever Be Justified?" 22 Dec. 2004. 23 Dec. 2004 <http://www.guardian.co.uk/stage/2004/dec/22/theatre.religion>.

———. "Playing with Fire." *The Guardian* 21 Dec. 2004. 22 Dec. 2004 <http://www.guardian.co.uk/world/2004/dec/21/religion.arts>.

Left, Sarah. "Play Axed After Sikh Protests." *The Guardian* 20 Dec. 2004. 21 Dec. 2004 <http://www.guardian.co.uk/uk/2004/dec/20/arts.religion1>.

Lyotard, Jean-François. *The Postmodern Condition: A Report on Knowledge.* Trans. Geoff Bennington and Brian Massumi. Minneapolis: U of Minnesota P, 1984 (1979).

Samantrai, Ranu. *AlterNatives: Black Feminism in the Postimperial Nation.* Stanford: Stanford UP, 2002.

Stinson, Hanne. Letter. *The Independent* 23 Dec. 2004. 13 Jan. 2005 <http://www.independent.co.uk/opinion/letters/making-cancer-not-look-so-bad-insult-to-sikhs-and-others-699631.html>.

Turner, Graeme. *British Cultural Studies: An Introduction.* London: Unwin Hyman, 1990.

List of Contributors

Lindon Barrett, professor, Department of English, University of California, Riverside, and former professor, Comparative Literature, and former director of the Program in African American Studies, University of California, Irvine.

Patrick Brantlinger, Rudy Professor Emeritus, English Department, and co-founder, Cultural Studies Graduate Program, Indiana University, Bloomington.

Mrinalini Chakravorty, assistant professor, Department of English, University of Virginia.

D. Robert DeChaine, associate professor, Departments of Liberal Studies and Communication Studies, California State University, Los Angeles.

Miranda Joseph, associate professor, Women's Studies, University of Arizona.

Alexandra Juhasz, professor, Media Studies, Pitzer College.

Lisa Lowe, professor, Department of Literature, with affiliations in the Department of Ethnic Studies and the Program in Critical Gender Studies, University of California, San Diego.

Ellen Messer-Davidow, professor, Departments of English, Cultural Studies, American Studies, and Women's Studies, and Scholar of the College at the University of Minnesota, Twin Cities.

Raquel Montoya-Lewis, associate professor, Fairhaven College, Western Washington University.

Leila Neti, assistant professor, Department of English and Comparative Literary Studies, Occidental College.

Joe Parker, associate professor, International and Intercultural Studies, Pitzer College.

Mary Romero, professor and Carnegie Scholar, School of Justice & Social Inquiry, Arizona State University.

Ranu Samantrai, associate professor, Department of English, University of Indiana, Bloomington.

Michael Soldatenko, department chair, Chicano Studies, California State University, Los Angeles.

Robyn Wiegman, professor, Programs in literature and women's studies, and former director, Women's Studies, Duke University.

Index